PROLOGUE

In 1996, Peter Wesley, recently retired from the Ordnance Survey of Great Britain, was asked by the then Director General, Professor David Rhind, to undertake a task that would encapsulate a pivotal moment in both the history of the organisation and the nation's relationship with its land.

Founded in 1791, Ordnance Survey had long been the custodian of Britain's geographic knowledge. Its maps were trusted tools for everything from military strategy to civil planning. Yet as the world entered the digital age, those cherished paper maps, meticulously created and carefully stored, were facing an uncertain future. The solution? A massive project to convert the entire archive of 230,000 paper maps into digital form. This undertaking was to be the catalyst for not only technological innovation but also social transformation, as Ordnance Survey's staff, many of whom had spent decades working in traditional ways, were thrust into the complexities of a rapidly changing world.

Involving meticulous research and containing personal anecdotes, Peter's report is a story of the challenges faced, and of an institution grappling with the available technology (almost always behind the curve) which Ordnance Survey itself developed and adapted ingeniously. It is a story of perseverance, at times in the face of very real doubt and criticism, and of a radical shift in the way people would engage with the landscape of Great Britain.

However, when Peter completed the report two years later, the winds of change had shifted at Ordnance Survey. A new management team, perhaps uneasy with the candid portrayal of the organisation's struggles, decided not to publish the work despite the monumental effort it represented. In 1999, a small ceremony was held to acknowledge Peter's contribution, with a handful of typographically enhanced hard copies and a PDF version presented to him as a token of recognition. And there it remained, a quiet record of an extraordinary time in the organisation's history.

Fast forward to March 2021. Concerned that this vital piece of history could be lost to time, Peter reached out once more to Ordnance Survey but it seemed that the organisation was still not ready to embrace this part of its past. Undeterred, he turned to me, a friend and former work colleague, asking for help in preserving this important narrative for future generations. Over the next three years, conversations with senior managers at Ordnance Survey, archivists at The National Archives, and ultimately The Charles Close Society (CCS), led to a breakthrough. Just two days before Christmas 2024, the report was officially deposited in the CCS Archives at Cambridge University's Map Library, ensuring that this fascinating account of technological innovation, cultural transformation, and organisational change would be safeguarded for scholars and historians alike.

Yet, while the report is now available, it remains a challenge for most of us to access. This book serves as a tribute to Peter Wesley's unwavering commitment to preserving the story of Ordnance Survey's digital transformation. It is an invitation to those who may not have the means to visit the Map Library, and a call to others who are passionate about the intersection of technology and history, to engage with the remarkable journey contained within these pages.

As Peter himself wrote in his letter to Ordnance Survey's Chief Executive: "*I have never sought reward for my efforts but simply wanted to preserve the information and pay due credit to the organisation of yesteryear, of which I have remained very proud.*" This book stands as a testament to his dedication and a reminder of the silent, largely unrecognised, work that underpins the very maps that guide us through the land we call home.

Peter Staniczenko   **January 2025**

AN UNEASY TRANSFORMATION

Delivering Ordnance Survey's Digital Mapping of Great Britain 1962–95

A personal account by Peter Wesley

This work refers to the period when Ordnance Survey transitioned to digital mapping and is a former employee's account. Although events described in this work concern the operation of Ordnance Survey, this is not an authorised or official Ordnance Survey record. As such Ordnance Survey disclaims all liability whatsoever and howsoever arising in relation to the contents of this work.

Please note, this work is created solely by Peter Wesley in a personal capacity. Consequently, the views expressed herein are his own and not those of Ordnance Survey.

Contents

Foreword to the account of Ordnance Survey's project to convert Great Britain's large-scale national mapping to a digital form

Peter Wesley
1997–99

This is an in-depth account of a major technical development in the field of Great Britain's national mapping. It seeks to document the history of a development that was to become a major project that required substantial and sustained investment by HM Government. The project was eventually scaled and resourced to convert into a computer-compatible form the national large-scale base mapping of Great Britain. In all, nearly a quarter of a million different maps made up Ordnance Survey's large-scale map archive of Great Britain. These maps or plans had traditionally been published by lithography on chart-paper, supported by stable-based working documents for the surveyors in the field who were engaged on revision, as change occurred in the landscape of Great Britain. The digitising project's origins lay in the 1960s and represented an enormous act of faith by a small group of individual senior managers who demonstrated great vision at Ordnance Survey, the British Government's national mapping organisation.

Ordnance Survey initiated and made progress with the project at a time when existing and available technology poorly supported such an ambitious project. Its eventual completion was to prove to be a world first and, as a result, Ordnance Survey has been well placed to face the many challenges of the twenty-first century. The digitising project spanned an incredible revolution in the technology employed and was finally completed in the mid-1990s, following almost three decades of quite rapid technological change and innovation. The cost of the project, however calculated, certainly exceeded one hundred million pounds in total commitment. In the early years of the project the funding was achieved by reallocation of existing resources. Later on additional funds had to be sought to secure progress with the project. This ambitious project, running for such a long timescale, with so little direct or immediate return, is almost unthinkable in the contemporary commercial context of the short investment horizons so frequently demanding rapid payback in business.

Enthusiasm for the digitising project itself was stimulated by the prospects for improved production and reduced costs of reconstructing up-to-date national mapping, itself a major commitment tasked by an external review of Ordnance Survey just before World War Two. This latter project was scheduled to span almost all of the post-war years up to and including 1980. The results of the digitising project, upon completion, have served to provide the fundamental basis of Ordnance Survey's business from the year 2000 onwards. Beside that, the fruits of this lengthy project have contributed materially to the foundation of a modern industry that serves to supply, to manipulate and to present geographic or spatial information.

From the maintained geographic database that had been created a wealth of products and services have emerged, which are used routinely for the conduct and management of business across Government, both national and local, and in a broad spectrum of private-sector business and commercial activity. Already at this time, the spectrum of use of spatially-based data is diverse and profound. The digitising project has proved fundamental to Ordnance Survey's vital remodelling of its business at the start of the twenty-first century. As the project to convert the mapping to a computer-compatible form neared completion, Ordnance Survey was able to commence the development of a wide portfolio of products derived from it. These included customised graphics (Superplan®) and data outputs, road and highway subsets (OSCAR), a national address product (ADDRESS-POINT®) among many others. After a two-hundred-year history, Ordnance Survey was finally freed by this innovative project from the constraints and strictures imposed by sheet-based lithographic maps and their subsequent revisions. More importantly, so were their customers.

This account is intended to record and to acknowledge the persistence and dedication, at times in the face of very real doubt and criticism, of the many staff deployed on this project at Ordnance Survey over this long period. Staff at all levels served this project either with some or all of vision, sheer endurance, skills of innovation and development as well as in the more mundane but long hard grind of production outputs, both to create and maintain the map database. The sometimes critical but generally unwavering support by and cooperation with a relatively small number of 'champions' of this project outside Ordnance Survey, who shared the 'vision', is also sincerely and gratefully acknowledged by this account.

The writer of this account served as a professional land surveyor at Ordnance Survey in a variety of roles. He was initially employed during the 1960s on the very earliest of experiments and developments in computer mapping. He later served in a more formalised Research and Development Unit, with responsibility for many of the contemporary research and development topics seeking to progress the digitising project and later still served as Head of Topographic Surveys, managing Ordnance Survey's field operations, where the concept and operation of digital-based map revision was initiated and brought to a successful roll-out across Great Britain. He finally served as Director of Marketing, tasked with all market and product development and especially those associated with the digitising project.

This record of the digitising project is set out as a narrative account with a more or less consecutive timeline followed by several key thematic elements that will serve to expand and to inform the narrative account. The work is based on personal observations and privileged contemporary witness by the author. The author's recall of events is firmly underpinned by very thorough literature research of contemporary documents, correspondence and official files, by courtesy of the Ordnance Survey management, during the closing years of the twentieth century. My sincere thanks are due to all concerned for this privileged access.

Chapter 1
The impact of Ordnance Survey and its culture on the project to digitise the large-scale maps of Great Britain

To understand the origins and the evolution of the digitising project, which eventually led Ordnance Survey, some thirty years later, to complete the digital database containing the large-scale maps of England, Wales and Scotland, it is important to explore Ordnance Survey's history. To develop an insight into the cause and effect of what was a world-first project, the contemporary nature of Ordnance Survey, its prevailing culture and the impact of its social fabric needs to be considered. The background of any organisation or business, particularly if as long and somewhat chequered as that of Ordnance Survey itself, inevitably conditions its values, its attitudes and outlook and the very nature of any response to opportunities that occur. The modern term for all these is described as an organisation's corporate culture. The map digitising project, which had its origins in the 1960s, was clearly influenced and affected by the prevailing nature and the attitudes of the organisation that conceived and eventually nurtured it.

Most unusually for Ordnance Survey at the time, the map-digitising project was based, on what, by any standards, were leading-edge technical innovations associated with developments in computing and graphics. These were already taking place with ever-increasing rapidity in the world outside Ordnance Survey. This eventual and positive response to external developments was somewhat out of character for an organisation that had frequently eschewed – or at least delayed – the introduction of technical development and equipment innovation during its lengthy history.

Ordnance Survey had usually been inclined to base its domestic technical operations on relatively 'low tech' methods, most of which had been tried and tested with great rigour in-house before use and almost all of which best suited its unusual employee and social fabric, which had in turn derived from its long-term military structure and organisation. In the early years of the digitising project its eventual impact on Ordnance Survey itself could not realistically have been foreseen. During the project's lengthy lifecycle the digital project itself increasingly proved influential and indeed formative on Ordnance Survey's own economic and social development. Indeed, the creation and exploitation of digital map data soon became a fundamental core activity, which increasingly helped to drive the business forward. In turn, it brought about profound internal social changes within and quite different external relationships, with a new and demanding body of customers, some traditional but many new. However, when digitising began, the prevailing and deep-seated internal culture had a significant impact upon the nature of the project and its subsequent evolution.

It is certainly difficult, when looking back over three or more decades, in the light of all that has happened since to Ordnance Survey, to maintain an objective and balanced judgement about the nature of the organisation and the impact of this on the project. It is neither particularly helpful nor fair to judge Ordnance Survey as it was when digitising began in the 1960s, in the light of all that has happened since, nor by reference to values or criteria that have actually been adopted or have become fashionable in more recent times. Inevitably, so many influences came to bear on a project spanning some three decades. To develop the context, however, it is necessary to make judgements about the effect of these, but hopefully within the context of the values extant at the time. As Ordnance Survey developed and changed so dramatically in the late 1970s and 1980s, as the digitising project continued-to run its course, it is also important to understand the impact of the more important changes within Ordnance Survey on the eventual outcome of the project.

The predominant characteristics of Ordnance Survey when the digitising project was first conceived and the many influences that came to bear upon it subsequently, before its completion, influenced the degree of progress achieved and, indeed, the nature of the project's eventual outcome. Ordnance Survey in the 1960s was very much the product of its long and difficult history, and the conditions then prevailing in terms of the functions it was expected to fulfil and in its own sense of direction. It is necessary to isolate and then to consider the effect of these organisational characteristics which had an impact on the digitising project, particularly in the early and formative years. Such understanding helps to explain the initial burst of enthusiasm and the lost momentum during the project's first 10 to 12 years before 1978. Later, as the digitising project grew in scale and gathered momentum, particularly in the level of demand that it made on the overall resources and production capacity of Ordnance Survey, it became increasingly subject to the many pressures and influences that also came to bear on the organisation itself.

The radical changes to the role and nature of Ordnance Survey, which have taken place since 1965, some volunteered from within and others imposed from without, have been profound in both their scope and impact. These changes, some radical indeed, have been of a political, social and business nature. This chapter seeks to examine the impact on the digitising project itself of what is now termed corporate culture or the interaction, behaviour and response of the people who served at Ordnance Survey. The profound changes to Ordnance Survey's business and political goals and to its corporate culture greatly influenced the path and progress of the project, particularly in later years.

These many changes go some considerable way to explain the wavering progress of the project for much of its life, the often-qualified commitment to its completion by several members of Ordnance Survey's senior management teams and the eventual climate almost of surprise within that the digitising might eventually be fully and successfully completed. What is certain is that the digitising project proved vital and strategic for the success and commercial well-being of Great Britain's national mapping agency as it approached the turn from the twentieth to the twenty-first century.

The digital map data that has been collected and stored underpins a very large percentage of the business activity of Ordnance Survey. Not only that but the data and its derivatives today play a key role in Great Britain within a very broad spectrum of commercial and social activity, ranging from the multifaceted business of central and local government and that of the utility industries through to a very wide range of business and commercial enterprises that it fuels and serves; all of which could not even exist without Ordnance Survey's map database.

In order to understand and appreciate the attitudes and the collective corporate behaviour of Ordnance Survey in the 1960s, when the digitising project began, it is important to remember that all central government departments went about their business largely unchallenged in a society radically different from that of today. Even departments of government that were generally expected to deliver services to the nation largely remained untroubled by any serious concern about the modern concept of customers, their demands and expectations. Government departments in the 1960s were rather remote from the society they were expected to serve and still very secretive.

Credible attempts at critical and public evaluation of the performance and outputs of government departments were rarely made. The value for money they gave in return for their parliamentary vote and the quality and fitness for purpose of the services they delivered were rarely questioned or examined. Most departments of central government were simply left to tackle their particular remit as they saw fit. Simply put, government departments tended to dictate what they believed was required and got on with performing their respective functions, largely without challenge. This inertia within Great Britain's Government was really only finally addressed during the reforming years of the 1980s and, in truth, was by then long overdue.

As did most other departments of government, Ordnance Survey in the 1960s issued two formal external communications annually. An official but quite secretive annual budgetary estimate was made to Parliament through the parent but often changing government ministry, which held responsibility for the affairs of the department. This estimate of budget requirement normally achieved a further renewal of resources for the stated task. There was indeed a black art required of civil servants, in achieving what could reasonably be expected. Secondly, an annual report was published and rendered to stakeholders on a much wider basis. This report indicated very broadly, in technical terms, the activities undertaken in the previous year on which resources allocated by government to Ordnance Survey had been expended.

Ordnance Survey's Annual Reports to its Minister of State, at the time when the digitising project began, were very stiff in style and quite formal. Successive Annual Reports in reality offered the stakeholders no real prospect at all of any effective interaction with Ordnance Survey to influence its goals. The Annual Reports each year tended to dwell at great length on technical and production matters rather than on users and customers and how their current or latent needs could best be met. The reports described the very lengthy remapping and reconstructive programmes. Successive Reports singularly failed to look into the longer-term future. They tended to be rather mundane and somewhat tedious reads.

The prevailing attitude at Ordnance Survey throughout the 1960s and the 1970s was paternalistic to its staff and users and somewhat patronising. The presumption was that Ordnance Survey knew best and could be relied upon, as it had for much of its history, to determine and to supply what its many stakeholders were judged to require. Ordnance Survey certainly operated throughout the 1960s very much along these stereotypical lines as successive contemporary Annual Reports clearly demonstrate. In point of fact, the military origins of Ordnance Survey and its continuing military senior management tended to make Ordnance Survey even less communicative than most truly civilian departments of government. This particular attitude prevailed and was the subject of considerable comment and some serious criticism when eventually the external Review of Ordnance Survey sat and finally delivered its judgements on the Department in 1979.

There were serious dangers in such an outlook and responses. The highly innovative project to digitise the basic-scale maps of Great Britain was, of course, handled no differently. The digital mapping project was initiated by Ordnance Survey at the outset within a complete vacuum, devoid almost of any input at all from customers. In fairness, the initial view was that such a project would, at best, be most beneficial to internal mapping programmes associated with an almost religious zeal, hoping to lead to eventual completion in the year 1980. In point of fact, only a handful of staff were engaged on the development of early computer-based digital techniques. Traditionally, external comment on the contemporary ways and means of Ordnance Survey and any public criticisms at all were normally dealt with in a climate of suspicion and hostility. Ordnance Survey remained remote from its stakeholders by tradition and determined intention.

Having been given a revitalised sense of purpose and direction in post-war Great Britain by the resurvey activities arising from the pre-war Davidson Committee's recommendations, in most respects, Ordnance Survey was managed carefully and prudently on a domestic basis. The primary goal for the Department's management was to achieve increasing levels of output of new and reconstructed mapping. This in itself was a daunting programme of work. This new-found sense of purpose was mainly focused on achieving higher levels of output at less cost. This was the prevailing climate inside Ordnance Survey throughout the 1950s and the 1960s which gave rise to the first experiments with digitising. The aim either of increasing levels of production or reducing costs had become a major and enduring goal for the Department, with much less attention being paid to what was actually being produced.

Planning and management for the completion of the 1980 plan to reconstruct and to revise Great Britain's large-scale national mapping became the driving theme for Ordnance Survey throughout the 1960s and 1970s. As the remapping project increased in momentum over the many years that it took, and with resource levels for the task generally sustained by annual parliamentary vote, Ordnance Survey developed something of an arrogance about the worthiness of its approach to the task in hand. This prevailing attitude soon became apparent with the digitising task too. As a department of government of the time, Ordnance Survey had failed to develop any real skill at self-critical review.

This fundamental weakness soon applied also to the digital mapping project, which, once the pilot project had been initiated, began to develop a momentum of its own, which charitably might be termed an act of faith by the Department. The much more recent concepts of value for money and fitness for purpose of deliverables did not loom very large within the functions of government at this time and certainly received very limited consideration at Ordnance Survey in the 1960s and for much of the 1970s. The externally focused and somewhat ceremonial reviews of Ordnance Survey by the Janes Committee and later the Ordnance Survey Review Committee led by Sir David Serpell, initiated and completed in the 1970s, were the first truly critical external reviews that provided any real focus for Ordnance Survey on markets, customers and the fitness for purpose and the cost of the services that it provided to the nation.

Aspects and matters of structure and organisation, departmental values and the type of response that the Department made to any given circumstances, which together today are termed corporate culture and behaviour, were based on previous custom and practice, which had become long established. The culture within Ordnance Survey, which existed when the digital mapping project began, had evolved in sympathy with the prevailing conditions of Great Britain's society post-war and especially because of the unusual manner in which Ordnance Survey was staffed and managed by the military management. Certainly Ordnance Survey really was a most unusual organisation at the time when the digitising project began.

By the early 1960s Ordnance Survey was an organisation with a lengthy and largely distinguished history, originally founded in science but more latterly based on its role as steward and provider of Great Britain's national mapping. Inevitably, Ordnance Survey was the product of all the many influences that had come to bear upon it. The Department had continued to struggle to recover from the damaging, resource-depleted 1930s interlude, which in turn had led to declining standards and unreliable mapping, and also from its truly military wartime role. Fortunately, the damaging pre-war interlude had helped to create and nurture post-war a stubborn corporate resolve, bolstered in turn by the conclusions drawn by the pre-war Davidson Committee, that it should never again have its role and functions so jeopardised.

Significantly, by comparison with what had gone before, Ordnance Survey post-war enjoyed a very clear but somewhat narrow remit. Despite several depressed economic cycles nationally in the 1950s and 1960s, the goals and the cost of Ordnance Survey's post-war remapping programme were never seriously challenged by government paymasters. This demanding and protracted programme was supported with adequate resources by successive governments, and the general and undisputed wisdom of Davidson's recommendations were never really even debated. The highly planned remapping project – dubbed the 1980 plan – was scheduled to be completed in the year of its title. This extended mapping programme was planned eventually to provide modern large-scale map cover for all areas of Great Britain, which would then be kept up to date by a process of continuous revision. The mapping comprised 1:1250 scale maps for larger urban areas, 1:2500 scale maps for all agricultural areas and other towns and 1:10000 scale maps for remoter areas of mountain and moorland.

Ordnance Survey had become an organisation with deep-seated and enduring traditions. Because of its history and the sheer size of its task and the timescales involved, it was already well used to embarking on and completing lengthy programmes of work, themselves spanning several decades. As the post-war remapping task gathered increasing momentum, Ordnance Survey was structured by its military management as a highly and carefully planned industrial unit, with its several major individual production functions, such as surveying, drawing, reprographics and printing, carefully integrated and totally interdependent for workflows. Such function and organisation quickly induced an unquestioning and almost soporific climate, where little change or innovation was ever seriously contemplated, at least 'until the 1980 Plan is completed'.

By the late 1960s, when the writer was experiencing life at Ordnance Survey for the first time, with a fresh and open mind, the analogy of Ordnance Survey with a seagoing supertanker, low in the water and slow to change course quickly sprang to mind. It soon became apparent, given increasing familiarity with the Department and its operations, that it would be very difficult to alter either its speed or direction. The ship was cumbersome and unresponsive to the helm. The resulting single-minded and unquestioning culture had become almost all pervasive. The organisational structure and the control of the workforce was tailored to suit the task by training and design, with all employees given carefully defined but very limited roles. This approach to the use of the staff led, in Bookturn, to operations that were highly regulated and completely controlled by complex instruction manuals, where almost any eventuality was, at least, theoretically anticipated in their contents.

Corporate culture normally develops out of custom and practice and the sum of the nature of all the employees it is meant to influence. The Department by the late 1960s, had already developed a most unusual social fabric between its very distinct groups of employees. The workforce, both military and civilian, were left with a culture that was largely unquestioning, very limited in terms of innovation by lack of practice and certainly incapable of critical self-review. Taken together, these characteristics served to create a rather stultifying atmosphere at the end of the 1960s.

Ordnance Survey had become set in its ways with its management generally quite resistant to or fearful of change and innovation, even when the need for fresh thought and a change of approach to a particular task had become quite apparent. Burdened by its long-term tasking, it had become risk averse. Ordnance Survey had largely managed to get away with this attitude simply because it didn't need to be otherwise. It had fulfilled the main requirements of annual estimates followed by annualised reporting to its paymaster. Not surprisingly, all these fundamental characteristics, which had arisen from Ordnance Survey's response to the lengthy post-war task, soon became weaknesses, when new approaches were eventually attempted or demanded.

Ordnance Survey's lengthy but more recent and troubled history before World War Two, the general stability of its technology whereby staff mastered generally low-tech processes for an epoch, the necessarily long-term nature of its production programmes and associated manufacturing flowlines, its itinerant military management and the very nature of government itself during this period, all conspired to make Ordnance Survey extremely conservative in outlook and approach. It had become an organisation generally resistant to change and usually very inward looking. That said, Ordnance Survey also demonstrated the important virtues of great industry and single-mindedness, given that its long-term goals had largely been set externally.

The 1980 Plan, as it had become known in the early 1960s, served to create a severe corporate version of tunnel vision in connection with its assumed task. Along with its more positive virtues and more worthy traditions, Ordnance Survey, by 1960, had already accumulated a good deal of historic baggage. The debilitating side-effects of this historic baggage were poorly understood outside Ordnance Survey by its government paymaster and in general by the map-user community at large. Generally, in technical terms, the more damaging aspects of its previous history were not really faced up to within the Department itself.

Senior management positions at Ordnance Survey had traditionally been filled by serving military officers from the Corps of the Royal Engineers. Despite considerable individual and personal commitment and dedication to the task that confronted them during their service, this arrangement to provide the organisation's senior and middle management generally served to create something of a transient outlook in much of Ordnance Survey's senior personnel. New brooms among the many military officers who served there usually came and went back to military duty frequently frustrated by their inability to achieve meaningful changes at Ordnance Survey.

Even among senior military personnel, most radical or innovative ideas concerning the task at Ordnance Survey were dealt with negatively and, at times, quite harshly. The project to digitise the basic-scale mapping was supported initially only because it was sold very strongly by its pioneers as a major cost-reduction procedure in the overall and long-term production task. These claims eventually proved unsustainable, but by then the project had developed a momentum of its own and only further on still did the project eventually come to be recognised as an end in itself, most particularly when real customers for digital map data began to appear in the marketplace.

Longer-term issues, such as the variable and at times indifferent (below specification) quality of some of the mapping produced in the period between the two world wars, continued to bedevil Ordnance Survey. Despite what was said in public, the problem of substandard work was not simply confined to overhauled mapping in rural areas. A significant number of urban 1:1250 scale diagrams suffered from flawed accuracy because of unsatisfactory ground-control propagation methods, which Ordnance Survey had adopted when surveying by traversing methods were first introduced. This type of problem, the scale and extent of which was never really reliably determined, was simply not addressed. These problems were a major element of concern by users and the opportunity to correct previous bad work coincident with digital capture was never seriously contemplated by Ordnance Survey's senior management.

Staff in areas of weakness came to understand their local difficulties and continued to work round the problems. The almost ceremonial accuracy tests conducted by Ordnance Survey did very little to help by way of true quality assurance. Remedial action, where it was taken, was driven almost entirely by customer complaints. These complaints increasingly came from more rigorous use of the mapping or ground control by some external customers. These 'too difficult' types of problem, which demanded expensive and longer-term solutions, were simply deferred to some time in the future and were not addressed at the time.

Part of the reason for this was the enduring and comfortable culture of 'handing on of the baton' from one group of military management to the next, with their overlapping successions. The enduring problems of map accuracy and reliability, the need for a more suitable specification and contents for the modern and future eras, the lack of height information or the third dimension and the lack of a credible approach to systematic map revision were all, in turn, to have a profound effect on the eventual outcome of the digital mapping project, which for almost all of its life simply represented the mapping it took up, but via a very different medium. On the particular issue of map quality and accuracy, only limited and local action was taken.

No significant remedial action was taken in a systematic manner to address the problems, even when available or emerging technologies and methodologies, such as modern instrumental photogrammetry, became universally available in the 1960s and 1970s. A change of approach then could have offered significant improvement without the need to make a complete fresh start, something that the sheer size of the programme precluded. In the mid-1960s the bulk of the 1:2500 scale remapping task still remained to be tackled. The benefits from a change of approach would have been substantial and enduring, not least for the digitising project.

The product of the project could have been greatly improved and new methods of data capture would, almost certainly, have become available. Because of the prevailing tunnel vision at Ordnance Survey, the opportunity to improve on the approximate 'Cotswolding' techniques for restructuring the 1:2500 scale rural mapping was never taken at any time. It proved easier for Ordnance Survey in the 1960s and beyond to continue with its routine outputs from the highly planned task of the 1980 Plan, carried out fully to its planned conclusion. The unfortunate consequences of this particular missed opportunity continued to bedevil Ordnance Survey and its many customers for some time.

Over the years there had been some individual military officers of exceptional calibre who, during their service at Ordnance Survey, were capable of thinking fundamentally about certain aspects of the national mapping task. These exceptional characters had been able to demonstrate their ability to judge the likely impact of emerging technologies on current operations of Ordnance Survey. In past epochs this benefit had been bestowed particularly on matters of geodesy and control networks. This proved to be the case again with the advent of the digital computer and the ability, potentially at least, to process and store large volumes of map data.

This account will record a very significant innovation that managed to gain support, albeit slowly but most often with strong and sustained opposition to it from within. It was such vision and an appreciation of the potential impact of an emerging technology that, still quite early in the modern computer era, led to the concept and birth of the large-scale map digitising project. This type of innovative approach was very much the exception rather than the rule at Ordnance Survey. Given the initial innovation, largely by one or two individuals, the overpowering contemporary climate and culture at Ordnance Survey were eventually to determine the particular nature of the digitising project during its first 10 years.

It was to require a further external review, which uniquely empowered customers and commentators in the affairs of Ordnance Survey, by a Review Committee led by Sir David Serpell in 1978. It was left to this external Review Committee to direct the thinking of Ordnance Survey at a strategic level with regard to the digital mapping project. By the time the Review Committee sat, the digitising project had very much 'run out of steam', had become badly stalled, without any real sense of urgency or direction applied from within Ordnance Survey.

Personal experience of the writer at the end of the 1960s serves to characterise Ordnance Survey as a negative and inflexible organisation, but with proud traditions and a very great wealth of experience and authority. Key issues came up afresh in a cyclical fashion every few years, largely because of the itinerant military management. At this particular time Ordnance Survey was very much in 'head down' mode of psychology and operation in pursuit of its declared objectives, with carefully planned goals and targets. It remained very inward looking in attitude.

Apart from its published small-scale map series, such as the 'one inch to one mile', neither Ordnance Survey itself nor the sheer complexity and volume of the basic-scale mapping task were at all well understood, either by its government paymaster or by the wider population of Great Britain. In the 1960s Ordnance Survey, besides being very inward looking, was typically very remote from the government of the day and generally from society at large. It is certainly quite difficult some thirty years on to look back even-handedly and objectively to this particular epoch, especially with full knowledge of all that has happened since; but descriptive terms, such as 'conservative', 'inflexible', 'secretive' and 'defensive', all contribute to a description of Ordnance Survey when this account must necessarily begin.

The 1979 Report of the Review Committee, looking at Ordnance Survey, serves as a more formal and unbiased contemporary reference concerning the inherent nature of the Department when the Review took place. The sociological order of Ordnance Survey's workforce and the prevailing culture of the Department that existed in contemporary UK society, toward the end of the 1960s, and the manner in which both developed, reflected its lengthy history and its peculiar organisational structure. These were both unusual even when judged against the wider standards that existed elsewhere in the 1960s.

It is necessary, when interpreting all that happened, to have a good understanding of the organisation's structure and 'social culture'. A good understanding of Ordnance Survey's strengths and weaknesses helps to explain many of the events that were critical to the technical and business changes that the emerging technological revolution were to bring about. Some of the predominant characteristics of Ordnance Survey and its staff were commented upon somewhat critically by the Review Committee when it reported in 1979.

These views of the Review Committee also best summarise the environment at Ordnance Survey when the seeds of the digitising project were first sown. On the nature of Ordnance Survey itself, the Report of the Review Committee remarked 'Through concentration on the resurvey task, Ordnance Survey had not, in our view, given enough attention to maintaining close contact or collaboration with other organisations, to modifying its products and methods in response to user needs and to assessing critically its approach to the other main Davidson Committee strategy of maintenance of the survey up to date'. The Report also described Ordnance Survey as 'having a tendency to inertia in the mainstream of surveying and cartographic activity'.

In truth, such public criticism could well have been stronger and harsher but the findings of most such ceremonial reviews are generally subject to much modification by iteration and negotiation with the subject body. This was certainly the case with the Serpell Committee Report when it did eventually surface.

By the late 1960s Ordnance Survey had developed a remarkable but rigid and enduring layered structure for its employees. The system was based on the carefully planned and limited interrelation of distinct groups or classes of staff. The arrangements had become the accepted norm for the known and predictable task and remained largely unchallenged. Each group within this structure clearly had great strengths, but put together, the social fabric at Ordnance Survey had debilitating weaknesses, particularly for the future health of the Department, when changes of direction and changes of emphasis and priority were clearly called for by changing circumstances. When looking at cause and effect in connection with the early years of the digitising project, the deeply rooted and unusual staffing arrangement at Ordnance Survey demand examination and evaluation.

Without any doubt, the unusual social fabric of Ordnance Survey led to a most unusual internal environment generally lacking in innovation and challenge, which in turn limited the Department's competence at conducting external relationships. These aspects proved critical in the early and formative years of digital mapping.

At the top of this structure within Ordnance Survey was the military management. Almost all the senior and middle management posts at Ordnance Survey, with the exception of a very small number occupied by civil servants from the administrative cadre, were filed by serving officers from the Corps of Royal Engineers who had been recruited and trained for the generality of contemporary military survey requirements. Almost all had received relevant 'postgraduate' level training at the School of Military Survey, which was located for much of the post-war era at Hermitage near Newbury. Generally, the military management, many of whom returned for tours of duty at Ordnance Survey as their military careers progressed, managed to sustain a high level of loyalty and commitment to Ordnance Survey and its long-term, highly planned task.

Some, however, came simply to see duty at Ordnance Survey as part of a much wider and enduring military role. Only occasionally did this unusual supply line for the Department's management produce innovative and challenging intellects for sustained periods of time. This, in turn, inevitably meant that many of the more fundamental, enduring and inherited problems and weaknesses accruing from Ordnance Survey's history were simply either avoided or not addressed properly. Military officers served at Ordnance Survey generally for all-too-short three- or at most four-year tours of duty. Some officers, who were found to be compatible with service and management at Ordnance Survey, returned at different times and in different roles as their military careers progressed.

In the 1960s, the highest rank of Major General realistically achievable for surveying and mapping oriented officers of the Corps of Royal Engineers coincided with Ordnance Survey's most senior position, that of its Director General. The 1979 Report of the Ordnance Survey Review Committee succinctly described the situation as follows: 'The military are necessarily transient. Their career interest lies elsewhere than in Ordnance Survey.' Inevitably, there was a division if not a conflict of loyalty and commitment between Military Survey and Ordnance Survey. Among the many military officers who served at Ordnance Survey, there were some who developed a clear preference for a more civilian, 'out of uniform' lifestyle while working at Ordnance Survey.

These officers immersed themselves with considerable commitment in the management of Ordnance Survey and, in several cases, in seeking to address some of the more profound technical problems associated with its task. However, for most officers, with the route to more senior military rank based on varied service at Military Survey head office in the UK and from duty on other postings, many of the military who served at Ordnance Survey failed to get to grips with either the technical detail or the complex issues that confronted them during their tours of duty. The tendency, if one can generalise in these cases, was simply one of delegation of control of the day-to-day operations to the cadre of civilian technician or 'non-commissioned officers' who traditionally served below them at Ordnance Survey.

Ordnance Survey by 1970 had already developed an unusual demographic pattern. In the years between 1965 and 1970 there was an annual average of 24 serving military officers employed within the organisation. During this same period there was an average of only four civilian professional staff, some 3,744 technical or technician staff from all the various disciplines employed and an annual average of some 385 administrative and clerical staff.

Although the military management cadre was very small in number, in reality the task of the Department was fairly constant and predictable. Most officers who served at Ordnance Survey as an interlude in their military career tended, if one can fairly generalise, to manage and administer what they found there on arrival without challenging and questioning either objectives or methods. Some officers failed to get to grips with the essentials of what really needed to be done. They leant heavily on the civilian technician supervisors and junior management below them. Most, after an initial burst of enthusiasm, concluded that the Ordnance Survey production 'engine' was simply too powerful and the task too predetermined in what was a highly planned, thirty-year remapping programme.

A proportion of military officers who served at Ordnance Survey quickly sensed the very real danger that if they questioned or interfered with its operations, without the full and detailed knowledge and experience to do this safely, they risked slowing or even stalling the large production engine, with consequential damage to their own reputations and career prospects. The momentum and energy of the enormous 'flywheel' of Ordnance Survey's 'production engine' could generally be relied upon to see their relatively short tour of duty out. Initial acquaintance with Ordnance Survey's production machine and the sheer volume and continuity of the carefully planned and integrated remapping task was most certainly a very daunting and humbling experience.

One soon became aware that any material changes to the 1980 plan very quickly created severe imbalances in various parts of the complex production flowlines, some of which extended over periods of years rather than months. Not only that, but with the very rigid and inflexible staffing and structure, severe imbalance in either work or resources quickly occurred and the lumbering nature of the organisation simply wasn't able to adjust for these in a short timescale. The nature of the Department's staff served to create enormous inflexibility and major constraints, even within the 1980 Plan.

The most significant consequences of the unusual staff structure at Ordnance Survey at the end of the 1960s meant that it was difficult for those successive senior management teams to really acquire a thorough grasp and full understanding of the Department, its roles and its procedures. In many cases, even at more senior levels, the military officers who came and went at Ordnance Survey were neither capable of effecting changes of a fundamental nature at the strategic level nor of achieving any real longer-term accountability for plans laid or for action taken. It was quite common for military personnel, who had almost complete responsibility for the management of production functions, simply to delegate to their supporting civilian technical supervisors and junior management who were normally well equipped with intimate knowledge and experience of their own very limited production procedures.

This situation contributed greatly to an inertia whereby any significant change or serious innovation was unlikely. Not surprisingly, given their relatively short stay and the daunting size and complexity of the production 'engine', it proved easier for many of the military officers simply to supervise and to 'lubricate' the 'flywheel' of the engine that had been created years before. Few were either capable or willing to innovate or indeed to seriously question the status quo by seeking or devising alternative approaches. The oppressive climate thus created over many years served to stifle innovation but had the virtue that it ensured that a programme, once embarked upon, would be driven through to completion with great discipline. The traditional culture of Ordnance Survey demanded that even quite minor changes to map specifications, production techniques and methods as well as the materials employed in production were evaluated almost to death by large departmental committees following extended trials, before even modest changes could be introduced. Such an approach was always defended internally in the cause of maintaining the national specifications while preventing any serious disruption to the system. It was common for military officers who served at Ordnance Survey simply to elect to manage the status quo for a further period, for the duration of their 'civilian' tour of duty.

The Report of the Review Committee in 1979 reflected in its conclusions on the subject of staffing and management at Ordnance Survey, the unsurprising military point of view that 'Ordnance Survey had received a better quality of officer than it would otherwise expect to attract, particularly in the scientific and military field, where Ordnance Survey benefits from Military Survey contacts with military research and developments, notably in the USA'.

However, to the knowledge of the writer, Military Survey head office at Feltham became aware of and actually deployed technologies for their own purposes that had been obtained on the secret USA/UK military network. Because of American embargoes on such secrets, during the ongoing cold war, these technological 'breakthroughs' could neither be divulged nor deployed at Ordnance Survey to assist the digitising project. If it is possible at all to make a broad generalisation about the military officers who served at Ordnance Survey in the 1960s and 1970s, it is that they fell into two broad types. There were firstly those of the type described above who simply supervised and exercised stewardship of what they found there on arrival. There were also some who, from time to time, were well equipped with exceptional intellects and who had come from advanced training in certain subjects cognate to the technologies that might be employed at Ordnance Survey and with previous exposure to modern developments within the surveying and map production industry.

The regular passage of military personnel, some with graduate and postgraduate qualifications, through Ordnance Survey meant that, from time to time, an exceptional talent became available. In general terms, officers of this type enthused and flourished at Ordnance Survey. They found a stimulating challenge in grappling with the Department's many problems but, quite amazingly, in the light of modern management, they were precluded by their transient nature from real ownership of the problems and accountability for their decisions and actions. At differing times in its history Ordnance Survey was fortunate to have individuals of exceptional talent from the military serving there, who were willing and able to grapple with emerging technologies and the profound 'step changes' that they typically brought with them.

Fortunately, this was the case with one individual who was equipped with a mathematical and engineering background. He had already become involved with the use and application of computer technology and he recognised the potential this technology offered for a variety of purposes, including the use of automation in cartographic production. Although a few individuals at Ordnance Survey had already managed to stimulate sufficient interest in the potential of automating some of the tedious and time-consuming cartographic production processes to the extent that initial experiments and investigations had been initiated, it was the eventual arrival of a pioneering military officer at the Southampton headquarters that really stimulated progress.

The individual concerned was Colonel Robin C Gardiner-Hill RE, who was quite unlike the 'run of the mill' officer who typically served with Ordnance Survey. His posting by the Director General to a key new post at Ordnance Survey with responsibility for 'planning and development' was indeed timely. Traditionally, there had been no effective research and development function as it is generally understood in the national survey. Innovative thought had largely been confined to working production test groups charged with evaluating new methods or materials. The arrival of Gardiner-Hill rapidly led to the initiation of investigations associated with using computer technology to improve Ordnance Survey's map production, all riding on the back of the deployment of mainframe computers in government to facilitate accounting, asset management and planning.

It was for this purpose that the digital mapping project was formally initiated. There was a good deal of opposition to this initiative and resentment from Gardiner-Hill's senior colleagues. This didn't trouble the Colonel whose sharper perceptions gave him considerable faith in what he was doing and that his lesser mortal colleagues couldn't really see or comprehend. When he arrived, he found the prevailing social fabric at Ordnance Survey most irritating and in a climate of suspicion as to his motives he soon began to work across conventional management lines to achieve a small but central development unit largely involved in investigations associated with automated cartography.

To staff this small unit he obtained a handful of the new civilian graduates who were coming to Ordnance Survey under cross posting machinery for the first time from the Joint Survey Service, and he also added a technician middle manager to introduce domestic experience to the new mix of skills and backgrounds. The resources of this small unit were complemented on a very novel and informal basis by Gardiner-Hill's skill at enlisting resources held elsewhere within the Department's very formal management structure.

In the late 1960s the next staff group after the military officer corps was the technician workforce. This was by far the most numerous and this group included those who had risen into supervisory and junior management posts. The technicians were, in almost every case, 'home grown', 'career for life', civilian Ordnance Survey staff. However, many of the older staff had served in the Royal Engineers Ordnance Survey Battalion in wartime and post-war service. Their supervisors, within a tightly regulated system of training and production, were simply those technicians who had demonstrated an ability to supervise and eventually to manage their own craft skill in ever larger units of production, as their careers progressed, but almost always below the lowest rank at which military officers were employed at Ordnance Survey.

Age and competence at 'coexistence' with the military were important qualities for the few technicians who progressed to middle management, usually of larger numbers of specialists engaged in their own original craft skill. Cross-postings between disciplines only came with the advent of more enlightened management at Ordnance Survey later in the 1970s. No real concerted attempt was made by the military before 1970 to develop technician workers beyond their one craft skill. They were kept confined within their original craft skill. The ceiling on their progress into management was self-evident and was then only being questioned, really for the first time, by domestic trade unions. Technicians who progressed into line management were simply not adequately equipped, through no fault of their own, to address high level strategy or to tackle the more complex and enduring problems or indeed any fresh opportunities that confronted Ordnance Survey.

Their limited experience, although extensive in a narrow field, and their lack of wider developmental training, left them poorly equipped to address strategic or quantum changes associated with the broader aspects of national mapping at the end of the 1960s. The sheer futility and waste associated with the military and civilian technician silo system of human resource management was quickly demonstrated, following the eventual removal of the military entirely from Ordnance Survey. Under an increasingly enlightened civilian management, following the departure of the military, it soon became apparent that there was a considerable depth and breadth of talent with considerable potential. The undeniable strength of the itinerant military officer supported by long serving and very knowledgeable senior technicians managing the workforce was the proven ability of this blend to manage the highly planned status quo at Ordnance Survey associated with 1980 remapping programme. As the 1960s gave way to the 1970s the right of the military to hold all technical directing posts, those at middle and senior management and, indeed, the post of the Director General himself was starting to be questioned, both inside by newly arrived graduates and the trade unions and outside the Department.

The structure described above within Ordnance Survey in the 1960s and the 1970s reflected that very broadly of the contemporary British military structure. The small cadre of military management that ran the Department typically tended to be very remote by plan and practice from the far more numerous technician workforce. The extent of the ambition allowed to the civilian technician cadre was realistically limited to a range of junior and middle management posts and to the supervisory posts associated with the highly regulated production work within the several disciplines then deployed. The supervisory staff were confined in a very rigid cell-like structure of production staff and ran the day-to-day, carefully planned operation.

These arrangements, which replicated the organisation of the army itself, meant that an overwhelmingly large proportion of the workforce played absolutely no part at all in developing either the overall direction of the Department or the means whereby it could move towards the future. The vast bulk of the considerable workforce was engaged wholly on technical and routine production operations, which, by design, were simply repetitive. The workforce was effectively disconnected from its senior management to what the writer, in the late 1960s, when experiencing it for the first time, found a most remarkable and dangerous degree. With the military officers generally inclined simply to manage the status quo and the technicians, through no fault of their own, ill equipped by lack of development to see the wider issues, radical change could realistically only come from outside the Department.

The very limited and local innovation that did come from workers and supervisors engaged in production was confined to local methods and the materials and equipment used. As in all matters, these prevailing organisational arrangements inhibited genuine innovation and further development once the digitising project had been devised and initiated. Ultimately, these same forces led to stagnation and lack of sequential development as the project struggled to establish its worth in the search for lower costs and increased outputs. As time passed and as the rigid structure continued to endure, it was most unlikely that Ordnance Survey, from its own resources alone, could possibly take any radical changes of direction of a quantum nature.

Ordnance Survey had, at best, become an organisation that moved by slow and carefully worked out incremental changes. It was the mix of all these characteristics that in the early 1970s left Ordnance Survey unable to change radically its strategic direction or approach as demands placed upon it began to change. As the first customers began to emerge for digital map information, Ordnance Survey had firmly committed to a response which was locked into the production of published maps from the data so tediously created.

The prevailing social fabric within Ordnance Survey, with its domestic culture and a commitment to an externally commissioned remapping task, generally left Ordnance Survey typically unwilling to look outwards and outside. There were a few exceptions and it was largely fortuitous, and because of their strength of character that a few individuals with more open minds, who continued to nurture the germ of an idea that would eventually preoccupy Ordnance Survey and its customers for almost three decades, were in fact permitted to apply themselves to the embryonic digitising task.

In an extremely risk-averse organisation wrestling long term with the most effective use of the resources allocated to national mapping, the digitising project was increasingly seen as a venture to improve productivity. Interestingly, the continuing inability of those concerned with the project for much of the 1970s to demonstrate in successive assessments that the computer-based methods were either faster or cheaper was a cause of some considerable satisfaction within the conventional production areas at Southampton throughout this period.

The conclusions of the external Review Committee in 1979, which reviewed the digital mapping project, provided the first sustained and neutral support for the initiative by providing a fresh rationale for the future of digital mapping and substantial evidence of current and latent customer needs. Prior to that it was only the enthusiasm of the few staff engaged on the project that had managed to keep the project going in the face of mounting evidence that the digital techniques could not compete in the simple challenge of cost comparison in the production and publication of large-scale mapping. By the time the Government reacted, without any real urgency at all, to the recommendations of the Review Committee there was a widening appreciation within Ordnance Survey of the eventual impact and the external consequences of building a map information database, at least of parts of Great Britain.

With the overall day-to-day management and performance of the conventional production task in the hands of by far the largest group of employees, the technician staff, this group provided the energy which drove the 'flywheel' of the map production 'engine'. Most of the senior technicians who had worked their way up through a series of promotions into junior management posts really only understood certain aspects of the overall production task. Most had intimate knowledge of the processes and procedures associated with their own craft skill but very few were able to gain sufficient breadth of knowledge and understanding to judge the value of departmental strategies and programmes. It simply wasn't possible for even the most experienced of employees from this group to initiate alternative and innovative approaches on a wider basis.

Even in the early 1970s the clear divisions between the few officers and the many production workers caused no real concern or embarrassment to the officers for that was the status quo and the regular normality within their military careers. Opportunities for progression into the ranks of senior management simply didn't exist for technicians. The traditional military 'occupation' at Ordnance Survey served to enhance military careers but did nothing for the vast majority of the Department's staff. The prevailing 'apartheid' or separate development meant that often talented staff at Ordnance Survey remained underemployed and frustrated.

The very small number of posts at divisional officer level which remained the pinnacle of the technician's realistic career ambitions, did little to ameliorate this frustration at the lack of development opportunities. In the case of the digitising project, as in all other matters, there was only low-level input by technicians during the early years of the project's life. However, Gardiner-Hill did enlist ideas from right across the social divides, more than had ever been accomplished before him. The groups of staff at Ordnance Survey kept very much to themselves and tended to preserve their own cultures and prospects. When the digitising project was initiated, there was almost no cross-fertilisation between the groups of staff. This was to prove to be very debilitating until the situation began to be corrected in the early 1980s.

The third main group of staff who served at Ordnance Survey in the 1960s and 1970s held power and authority in the Department quite disproportionate to their numbers and possibly their abilities. These were the staff from the clerical and administrative cadre of the Civil Service. Their relative power and authority stemmed from two main causes. The first arose from their relative permanence at Ordnance Survey. Only rarely were individuals from the wider Civil Service posted in, usually to fill only the most senior positions that their 'tribe' customarily held. Hence the administrative staff generally served at Ordnance Survey for the totality of their careers and, not surprisingly, they acquired extensive experience of the management of the Department.

The most senior rank of this group was at director level; however, very few sought or acquired any real understanding of the more demanding strategic and technical aspects of the Department's operations. The second cause of their disproportionate authority was the simple fact that they controlled the key business levers of finance and the full range of 'establishment' matters, which included personnel management (recruitment, training, promotion and so on). The military management at Ordnance Survey almost always deferred in all these matters to the administrative staff, with the result that their authority and control over the transient military officers continued to grow. The military management of Ordnance Survey generally neither sought nor maintained much understanding of matters pertaining to the important aspects of finance and the complexities of the management of all civilian staff within the Department.

The authority and power of this small group of administrators and their support staff was further enhanced by their responsibility as guardians of the important external links with government, principally HM Treasury, the Civil Service Department and Ordnance Survey's own parent department within government (The Ministry of Agriculture later followed by The Department of the Environment). Again continuity provided the rationale for the retention and management of these important external connections. Most military officers who served at Ordnance Survey had to rely on the relay of essential information from the senior administrative group. This was often relayed selectively and with care to ensure that their power base was not eroded such that the military could never wrest any real authority from the administrators. These rivalries did nothing at all to improve internal communications or efficiency and effectiveness.

Worse still, because of early non-technical initiatives, the administrative cadre populated and managed the evolving and increasingly vital 'computer unit', which was regulated in time-honoured fashion by a large committee which purported to represent all those work areas with an interest in it. The capacity of the Department's mainframe computer was controlled and managed by this committee. Exceptionally, within this area, there were at least a few staff from the technician cadre. Although contemporary computer practice demanded separate systems analysis and programming functions, a few staff with a technical background had been employed there and a small group of these were eventually to play a significant role in the development of the digital mapping techniques.

As a result of these divisions, the business side of the Department became increasingly disconnected and remote from production operations. Also, as the need to engage more with customers emerged, almost all such contact was placed firmly in the hands of the administrative staff, with the result that professional and technical staff were excluded, undoubtedly to the detriment of the Department's external relations. In the 1970s Ordnance Survey continued to be managed in a two-sided manner, with serious suspicion and mistrust ever present between the sides on a whole range of issues, such as funding, strategic direction, staff training, personnel development, career paths and longer-term prospects.

All posts were individually designated as reserved for individuals from one of the staff groups and appointments and promotions were universally watched with jealously and great suspicion as to motive by all staff, and more particularly by the separate staff trade unions.

The most recent stimulus to change in the traditional 'social fabric' at Ordnance Survey arrived with the creation of a fourth group of staff, very small in number initially but destined to grow. This fourth group of staff arrived following the creation by government of the graduate professional Joint Survey Service in 1969. This new service aimed to offer cross-postings for qualified civilian graduates with professional qualifications between the Directorate of Overseas Surveys, Military Survey and Ordnance Survey. The creation of this new cadre of civilian graduate and professional staff came about several years after the eighth Report of the Estimates Committee of the House of Commons in 1962–63.

The Joint Survey Service initially provided a very small number of staff from quite different backgrounds for Ordnance Survey. Tours of duty were initially planned to be even shorter than those of the military. The result of the blatant divisions and trade union sensitivities that continued to flourish at Ordnance Survey initially meant that early arrivals were kept out of line management or, indeed, executive positions. However, when it became apparent that Ordnance Survey would move, albeit slowly, toward eventual full civilianisation, longer-term career prospects for civilian graduate professional staff at last started to emerge. The graduates, of whom the writer was one of the first to be posted to Ordnance Survey, with few exceptions lacked, at the outset, as had their predecessors the military, any profound knowledge of Ordnance Survey and its diverse operations.

Consequentially, they were themselves free of historical 'baggage' or prejudice about Ordnance Survey. They arrived with open minds, and although they made mistakes and errors of judgement in the very early years, they were able to challenge the conservatism of 'conventional wisdom' and 'the hundred and one reasons why this or that might not work'. Their learning curve, soon after arrival at Ordnance Survey, was steep indeed. In the early years they were able to ask naive and searching questions of those above. To placate the far more numerous technician staff, most graduates, in the early years, were confined to gainful employment away from the traditional production areas.

This initial period for the graduates at Ordnance Survey fortunately coincided with the initiation of the 'Planning and Development Unit' mentioned above. This largely fast-moving development environment, completely project-based, was easily able to accommodate the short tours of duty that graduates initially faced at Ordnance Survey. This new unit was led by Colonel Gardiner-Hill and it was this unit that picked up the early digital mapping experiments and eventually established and supervised the pilot production trial. Gradually, those graduates who had developed an interest in and an affinity with the challenge contained within Ordnance Survey's task later began to return for further and longer tours of duty within the wider management structure.

In the early years a succession of graduates were assigned to the many development projects associated with digital mapping. It was particularly useful at a time of need for intensive development of new techniques that a succession of fresh minds could be deployed on problem solving. It was particularly beneficial that people from quite different backgrounds, with diverse postgraduate backgrounds and training, were involved with the early stages of different production techniques. As the 1970s passed graduates also began to replace the more junior military officers on a much wider basis. The military had planned to delay the entry of civilians into the more senior posts but, in offering junior posts for civilian replacement at the outset, this soon led to the supply of officers for the more senior appointments drying up. Hence, eventually, full civilianisation at Ordnance Survey was accomplished.

The civilian graduates who arrived initially at Ordnance Survey didn't fit very easily into the 'apartheid' culture at the organisation. The traditional system's fundamental weaknesses were instantly apparent to graduates coming in from outside. The technician group, not surprisingly perhaps, feared that the graduates would simply replace the military officers and thereby continue to frustrate their own collective ambitions and prospects. With the prospect of subsequent tours of duty at Ordnance Survey and the real possibility of longer-term careers within Great Britain's national mapping department, most of the civilian graduates immersed themselves with enthusiasm in Ordnance Survey's task, its 'society' and its many issues and problems.

They generally sought to understand and to get to grips with the challenge that Ordnance Survey presented. On arrival the first graduates were assigned to a plethora of investigations into automated cartography and digital mapping at the beginning of the 1970s. This early development work was seen by most people in the mainstream of the Department's work as an aberration and a dangerous distraction 'by a few clever folk' who tended not to understand the Department and its true task. The view of many of those in the military still in authority who had developed at least an understanding of the progress achieved in automation was that the remapping programme, as then understood and planned using conventional technology and methods, should first be brought to a successful conclusion.

Most felt, quite sincerely, that no significant level of resources should be diverted to computer-based mapping activities, which were widely described at the time as a mere 'distraction'. The digital mapping initiative represented a challenge on several planes. It soon came to be regarded as a divisive issue between traditional elements within Ordnance Survey, who sought mere replication of conventional maps, and those for whom the complete development sensibly demanded major changes in map style and presentation; the better to employ the advantages of some of the new techniques, particularly if costs were to be sensibly reduced.

The former view tended to prevail at some considerable cost to progress and to the overall budget of the embryonic digitising project. It was this deeply ingrained and 'single strand' philosophy of completing one programme before starting another that inhibited the digital mapping work and prevented the initiation of a credible programme for revision and maintenance of the post Davidson mapping. These were the main strands of criticism of Ordnance Survey that appeared in the Review Committee Report in 1979 and which have already been remarked upon.

Following this early development work, it soon became apparent that the graduate civilian staff had a major contribution to make to the work of Ordnance Survey and they generally and very quickly developed a deep sense of loyalty and commitment to the Department. In many cases they did also soon win the acceptance and cooperation of the technician cadre, particularly those with whom they worked. Previous social barriers associated with the era of military management also soon started to be broken down through sporting and leisure links. With increasing authority arising from a series of more senior civilian graduate appointments at Ordnance Survey, the career prospects for technicians were also gradually improved, as the old divisions were increasingly challenged and overcome.

The Serpell Review Committee Report in 1979, when considering the social fabric at Ordnance Survey, concluded that 'The Army, the Joint Survey Service and the technician cadre segregation is not conducive to the creation of a corporate management purpose at Ordnance Survey'. This Report itself, even before the Government's belated response to it was known, was to prove to be a major catalyst for very rapid social change at Ordnance Survey. The civilian management team soon began to tackle many of the inherent weaknesses arising from the previous social order. The full potential of all staff came increasingly to be realised with much more training and the development opportunities available to them. The beneficial effects of this, particularly in connection with the new approach in digital mapping and its exploitation, brought rapid progress and eventual success.

The distinct and competing groups of staff and the prevailing culture at Ordnance Survey before the watershed of the Review Committee Report in 1979 was very traditional and military, rooted firmly as it was in the Department's history. Technician workers were typically confined to one narrow craft skill for their entire career. These craft skills were only updated in slow time by internal training programmes as changes in methods and materials were introduced. Fortuitously for Ordnance Survey in more recent times, and because of the educational standards demanded for recruitment and entry into the Civil Service, and because of the small percentage of young people progressing to tertiary education in Britain after the Second World War, many of Ordnance Survey's employees had talents and potential which invariably had not been realised and had not been exploited.

Also, because of the type of person who was attracted to the work of Ordnance Survey and because of the poor remuneration of staff within government, particularly on this type of work, many Ordnance Survey staff only fulfilled their potential after hours, outside the Department. Ordnance Survey in the 1960s was alive and vibrant with a great variety of talent and energy expended on a bewildering variety of activities and enterprises, but sadly not to the advantage of the Department itself. The

Department consistently failed to use or exploit this talent and energy among its technician workforce. To the newcomer such as the writer, this was a clear symptom of the wasteful failure of structure which had prevailed for so long. This very large and talented workforce generally lay dormant, awaiting some future and radical social change within the Department with regard to innovation and flexibility of the workforce in totality.

The structure had developed and had endured successfully throughout the 1960s, with the workforce deployed on the remapping project of the 1980 plan. This work was planned with almost eccentric precision to 0.1 of a worker and to decimal parts of a single map, with work and outputs managed in a 'Stalinist' style of a 'command economy'. The vast majority of the workforce were technicians either 'on the bench' or in supervisory or junior management roles. The military management sent down orders and instructions within this command economy through a series of ranked relays to the most senior of the technicians, and via them on downwards.

At the same time there was very little feedback upwards in the system. Orders were seldom, if ever, questioned – at least formally or openly. The military management tended to simply drive on with the task planned in annualised segments, to which it had been committed so many years before. It would have been remarkable in such a hierarchical and autocratic environment if the workforce and their supervisors were either willing or able to question fundamentals or to be able to recognise and grasp any emerging opportunities external to Ordnance Survey.

In summary, Ordnance Survey's long enduring social fabric led inevitably to an environment, at the start of the 1970s, which was resistant to change. There was no real climate of innovation with regard to strategy or approach or indeed to customers. The very nature of Ordnance Survey and its principal remapping task tended to underpin the climate of stability and endurance that was constructed round the technical operations demanded by the lengthy production programme. The concept of the customer and service to users of its services and products simply hadn't really been developed at all.

The Ordnance Survey Review Committee concluded in 1979 by summarising its findings as follows: 'The question now must be how can the technical excellence and traditional pride of Ordnance Survey be harnessed with its stated willingness to change, so as to produce a role for Ordnance Survey which allows Ordnance Survey to identify and adapt to changing public needs consistent with an acceptable financial performance'. Such profound change demanded urgent and radical changes to the Department's social fabric. The key ingredients of innovation such as leadership, of fresh vision communicated clearly, of challenged staff at all levels, of changing technology or the development of a fresh business strategy, were perhaps, not surprisingly, slow to build within what was such a conservative environment.

In essence these universal needs also encapsulated what really needed to be done to revitalise the digital mapping project in the wake of the Review Committee's findings and conclusions. These critical change-enabling factors did start to become more evident within Ordnance Survey as the digitising project itself soon began to gather momentum once more. Changes of a more profound or strategic nature in connection with Ordnance Survey and its role had traditionally come from outside the Department, typically from public and ceremonial reviews of its performance, its role and the public's expectations of it. Indeed the Review Committee of 1978 was to be the 20th such review conducted in 150 years of Departmental history.

The internal social order that had existed within Ordnance Survey through the 1960s and the 1970s really did mean that the Department was quite unable to reinvent itself, an essential skill that it has since come to understand. Even changes of a tactical nature (normally in terms of methods employed and of materials used) had always come about in a very slow and deliberate fashion, following exhaustive and protracted trials and assessments and following lengthy internal committee deliberations. Because of attitudes inside Ordnance Survey and also because of the lack of challenge generally abroad in British society in the 1960s, particularly to government departments, there was only very limited cross-fertilisation of ideas from outside Ordnance Survey.

Users were simply told (and even then, not in every case) what was to be produced. A further facet of contemporary Ordnance Survey attitude that had tended to prevail was that, with a virtual monopoly of talent in most cognate fields available to them through the system of military postings, Ordnance Survey usually claimed that it knew best and wasn't slow to say so or to show by its actions that it did. This attitude had prevailed through the 1960s to the 1970s with the occasional external critic or challenger that hove into view, usually 'seen off' quite comprehensively at the few professional gatherings or conferences that were available then, or perhaps more often by waspish correspondence. Ordnance Survey had developed a profound suspicion of anyone outside who perhaps sought more information than was customarily dispensed or who advocated fresh approaches to its routine tasks. Against this cultural background, which sets the scene, it is now necessary to relate the key stages and influences on the digital mapping project.

Chapter 2
From the very beginning, external influences and surprising vision

The very first discernible steps that were eventually to lead to the national digitising project came, perhaps not surprisingly, from outside Ordnance Survey. The Director General of the day, Major General Henley Dowson, received an exploratory circular letter from the Government's Department of Scientific and Industrial Research at the end of 1962. There was mounting concern in contemporary government that Great Britain should not lose out in 'the white heat of the technological revolution' that was foreseen by the central Government of the day. The letter solicited any interest in potential support for and perhaps a commentary on a proposal by Dobbie McInnes (Electronics) Ltd of Glasgow. This electronics company had worked, thus far, with The Oxford University Press® on the concept of and the eventual development of an automated cartography system, using computer technology.

Ordnance Survey was already struggling to meet the demands of a project, described by Davidson before the outbreak of war in 1939 and eventually scheduled for 35 years from 1945 onwards, to modernise and bring to a common standard the national mapping of Great Britain. Perhaps surprisingly, having received a generally lukewarm reception from his director colleagues at Ordnance Survey, when the proposal was circulated to them, the considered but extremely far-sighted vision sent as a response from Major General Dowson himself, on behalf of Ordnance Survey, read:

'As regards possible applications to Ordnance Survey, I think I can conceive of our putting on to tape (magnetic) the topographical information from field sheets of our basic large scale surveys

41

at 50 inches, 25 inches and 6 inches to the mile and subsequently mechanically fair drawing the information for basic scale maps and plans, provided the machine can work to the accuracy we need and still maintain economical results compared with manual drawing.'

With remarkable insight Major General Dowson continued:

'If it were possible also to incorporate subsequent field revision on the tapes and thus produce new editions by much the same process, it would be a great advantage.'

The Ordnance Survey response continued:

'We might also be able to use basic topographic data for the production of smaller-scale maps, including their revision. Though much of our work since World War Two is nearing completion, there would still be some scope for the future, especially at the 25 inch scale and the revision of both this and the 50 inch scale.'

The response finally ended:

'My own feeling is that this development may very well lead to more economical mapping and probably an acceptable accuracy but with some less elegant results. Even so, there would be a clear gain, so I recommend proceeding with the development at least to a point where its future application can be assessed.'

Albeit with no commitment, but coming when it did in 1962, at a time when Ordnance Survey's effort was still totally dominated by the Davidson Committee-inspired post-war charter, this judgement of the importance of emerging technology was breathtaking, both in its prophetic nature and in coverage of Ordnance Survey's modern operations that, in their entirety, have only recently been fully met. Clearly, with little guidance, Dowson could neither have any real idea of the enormity of the task he had attempted to describe nor the level of resources and equipment that it might ultimately consume.

Beyond Ordnance Survey's response, the approach to Great Britain's mapping and charting community by The Department of Scientific and Industrial Research eventually stimulated sufficient supportive responses from commercial companies and other departments of government such that in due course it approved funding for a project to develop a prototype of what had become known as the Bickmore-Boyle system. Dr Ray Boyle was, at the time, the Managing Director of Dobbie McInnes Ltd and Mr David Bickmore was Head of the Cartography Department at the Oxford University Press. HM Government, through the Department of Scientific and Industrial Research, agreed to fund two thirds of the estimated £58,000 budget required to produce a system prototype for evaluation.

The 'mission' for this development project was described as 'enabling cartography to keep pace with other sciences in which automated data processing is already being used'. Given the funding, Dobbie McInness, or Dmac Ltd as this pioneering company soon became known, duly delivered the prototype called 'The Oxford System of Cartography' in June 1965. Typically for new technology at this time it took almost six more months to achieve any sort of operational status. Perhaps not surprisingly, components proved unreliable, and as in all developments at this time, interfaces between sub-units were an ever present 'Achilles heel'.

It is perhaps worth noting what the system offered in the light of Ordnance Survey's initial response to the proposal. The system included a 'pencil follower' device, which enabled a trained operator to scale, trace, encode and transfer selected data from a map onto computer-compatible magnetic tape. This pioneering digitising device, which was the world's first free cursor digitising table, offered a facility which was said to be 10 times faster than conventional manual drawing. The second element of the system was a playback drawing device or 'plotter' that could be driven by the computer to create a plot from data collected by the digitiser.

This facility also enabled the power of the computer to effect scale changes and line character changes and so on from the data. The third element of the system, perhaps reflecting more the Oxford University Press' own particular atlas cartography needs, was designed to provide semi-automatic name placement facilities. Place names were to be held as character data in the computer and, after editing, could be located directly on to a graphic, thus avoiding a very labour-intensive manual task. This development project was an interesting example of technology responding to a rather specific industrial need, in which Ordnance Survey had at least played some part by describing so clearly its vision for the future.

It was also at about this time that literature searches and international conferences heralded or actually reported developments for automated cartography along similar lines, mainly within various units of the American Department of Defense. Because of its military status, Military Survey at Feltham and Ordnance Survey, still something of a military surrogate, did – despite an obsession with security matters – manage to receive 'security sanitised' versions of publications reporting such developments. This information, together with the British prototype system, served as a glimpse at least of 'enabling' technology for those in the cartographic and survey business, who were disposed to think about the future and the potential that the computer age perhaps held for their crafts.

The next significant step in the story of 'automated cartography', as it was then becoming known in Great Britain, was the preparation and forwarding of a report by the same David Bickmore to what had, in the interim, become the National Environmental Research Council (NERC) in November 1966. This report made a case for suitable funding and support for a cartographic 'laboratory'. This formal approach presented a persuasive argument in drawing attention to three emerging issues or problems. These issues were the apparent potential of cartography to create useful but very large amounts of data, the new speeds of information handling available with the capacity associated with large computers and their storage devices, and finally the potential of new display and presentation techniques.

By this time other British electronic engineering companies, for example, Ferranti Ltd®, in Edinburgh, were already developing equipment to address these particular needs and opportunities. It was, in fact, this particular company that was eventually to play such an important role in equipment development and supply, during the early stages of Ordnance Survey's quest to automate its cartographic processes. Also at this time, a variety of companies overseas were similarly developing solutions to these problems from differing directions and perspectives.

The observable 'tensions' that were soon to surface and develop and which eventually were to pervade relations between David Bickmore and his team at the Experimental Cartography Unit (ECU), as it became known, on the one hand and Ordnance Survey on the other, had their origins in the mission statement for the experimental unit. This document stated that 'the Unit, if it came into being, would undertake multi-science thinking but an early theme would be data transfer and communications with a clear recognition that cartography should be improved in terms both of its cost and flexibility.'

This approach was soon to create growing unease within Ordnance Survey itself, in view of its traditional culture that it generally knew best and that it alone should rule in such domestic matters. When the proposal was passed to Ordnance Survey, during a consultative phase, it was interpreted as implying criticism at a time when the organisation was already deeply embroiled on its long-term mapping task, very much in 'head-down' mode. Despite clear attempts by Ordnance Survey to devalue the idea, the decision was taken by NERC to meet and to satisfy Bickmore's personal ambitions. One of Bickmore's strongest suits was his apparent dominating self-confidence, his connections in academic and scientific circles nationally and his considerable skill as a self-publicist.

This all at a time when Ordnance Survey's senior personnel were transient and typically publicity shy. To support Ordnance Survey's somewhat jaundiced view, all the early releases from his newly established unit indicated a very broad desire to tackle almost anything that cropped up. Early proposals for projects ranged from deploying all surveyed data (and not just that of a topographical nature), through the creation and management of databanks to manage the burgeoning data possibilities, to a somewhat vague prospect of a great variety of sciences and disciplines having 'conversations' with maps, by virtue of these emerging technologies. These statements merely served to confirm Ordnance Survey's suspicions and worst fears that what it saw as its own agenda might, to some extent, be hijacked by the newcomer on the block. Contemporary comment from within the meticulously planned Ordnance Survey on such wide-ranging and vague proposals ranged from modest and limited token support, through growing mistrust and cynicism, to outspoken internal allegations of 'pseudo-science' on the part of Bickmore. There is no doubt that what some saw as implied criticism of Ordnance Survey and the other mapping and charting arms of government stimulated at least a few low-key initiatives.

Developments within Ordnance Survey itself at this time illustrate a clear divergence of opinion about any role for or possible participation in the affairs of the ECU project. Perhaps the initial and wisest internal response was the formation of a small and fairly low-key working party in 1966, led by Major Frank Fortescue RE, who had secured a permanent civilian appointment on the reprographic side of Ordnance Survey operations as its 'Investigations Officer'. This working party attempted initially to evaluate and to assess the possible impact of the new technology described in the ECU approach on the main elements of the Ordnance Survey task. Despite the early and visionary response by Henley Dowson, the Director General, some four years before, the working party's conclusions very much reflected the thinking of the lower and middle echelons of a task and production-oriented organisation.

Most people contacted within Ordnance Survey by the working party felt that the organisation really couldn't afford any distractions from its all-consuming national mapping task. Contemporary papers and records indicate that, in its earliest deliberations, the working party received no top down or strategic guidance from the upper echelons of the Department. However, quite quickly and by the time of the working party's third meeting, a further external influence had begun to bear on Ordnance Survey, with respect to the prospects of automation of some, at least, of its processes.

The departments of HM Government with mapping and charting responsibilities had, for some years, all participated actively in a body called the Joint Advisory Survey Board (JASB). This Board had been created to facilitate liaison, at head of department level, consultation and sharing of experience. Below the heads of department JASB operated through a series of subcommittees covering common interests or technologies within the realm of mapping and charting. The Hydrographic Department of the Navy, Military Survey, from which appointees to Ordnance Survey's more senior posts had traditionally come; the Directorate of Overseas Surveys and Ordnance Survey itself were all represented on JASB. Chairmanship of the Board rotated round the constituent departments.

Following the initial contact with them all, and again stimulated, in some measure at least, by the emergence of and publicity about Bickmore's new unit, the JASB agreed also in 1966 to establish an interdepartmental automated cartography working party. The working party's terms of reference were to investigate and document present and future cartographic activities within government departments and to determine those processes which automated methods might benefit most. Thus an internal and an external dimension had been created for the enquiries. Having done this through a series of meetings and internal departmental questionnaires, the JASB working party tasked itself with devising specifications, in general terms, for automated systems to perform those processes felt to be most responsive to automation in each organisation.

The objective of these specifications, which were to be in sufficient detail, was to enable electronic and mechanical engineers to understand the cartographer's problems such that they could take their technical solutions through to preliminary design stage. Thus Ordnance Survey participated, admittedly still at quite a low level, in a shared role in identifying and stimulating technological developments from the private sector. Thus it was that the JASB working party on automation met for the first time in August 1966 under the Chairmanship of Ordnance Survey's Colonel EPJ Williams. The previous appointment of a rather low-key Ordnance Survey working party enabled collaboration with JASB colleagues and was soon tasked with marshalling the organisation's considered response.

Interestingly, the Ordnance Survey internal working party drew its membership from the disciplines of cartography and photogrammetry, as well as the 'one man band' of 'Internal Investigations'. With nothing really equivalent to modern research and development in house, Major Fortescue, within his role of investigating materials and methods for domestic use, almost at once became the focus for the early automation studies. The thinking of the Ordnance Survey working party, at this time, can really only be described as limited in its vision, based as it was on initial internal responses, focused almost entirely on the possible benefits to be gained from the automation of data plotting. The need, even for this, was initially assessed in submissions by production managers as low key and likely to be confined to plotting grids and graticules and control information, for which tasks mechanical coordinator graph equipment already existed.

The more significant workload associated with the plotting of optical tachometric field surveys was also identified as a possibility for automation. Having just decentralised this task to field offices, at some considerable expense, little benefit was judged to accrue from any new technological support, almost certainly centralised, for this routine task possibly because of the passage of time, the transient nature of senior military appointments and the very real 'disconnection' between senior and more junior staff, the remarkable vision, four years earlier, expressed so well by Major General Dowson failed to persuade or guide the working party at its early meetings that the digital capture of large-scale mapping itself, might one day prove worthwhile by automated methods.

The JASB interdepartmental working group was eventually to endure for a good many years despite its changing personnel. It was, in terms of its mutual support, cross-fertilisation and general catalytic effect in what was a very conservative community in these early days that one would assess as the group's most significant and beneficial contribution. The group enabled opinions about equipment and service delivery by equipment manufacturers to be correlated, with suitable pressure brought to bear. Colonel EPJ Williams from the outset chaired the working group from Ordnance Survey, and Major Fortescue acted additionally as the group's secretary. At this early but formative stage Major J Coulson represented Military Survey while Mr Godfrey Murt and Mr J Howison represented the Hydrographic Department and the Directorate of Overseas Surveys respectively.

The mix of departments on the working party represented something of a challenge in itself, with their diversity of goals, technologies and methods all with products of quite different natures and purposes. Nevertheless, in those early days of its existence the working party served to fuse differing ideas and thinking into a reasonably coherent theme, such that by early 1967 the working group had developed three separate specifications for systems that, potentially at least, could offer some prospect of meeting some of the needs of the participating mapping and charting organisations. The first specification devised sought to describe an automated line following device to encode and supply digital data of lines and points taken from a conventional map or chart graphic, with a computer-based facility for their individual identification. The second specification described a plotting system to produce final negatives or positives from an edited compilation using digital data created by the first device. The third specification described a device that would permit the display and examination of digital data in live mode and, where necessary, its correction. In modern parlance, this specification described an automated map editing system, for which the cartographic industry had in fact to wait a further 10 years at least.

In seeking to evaluate the impact of each, it is important at this stage to take forward together the twin themes of external stimuli and internal activity. As Ordnance Survey's input to the JASB working group was being blended into the three equipment specifications, Mr David

Bickmore had come to Ordnance Survey seeking support for his unit to perform investigatory projects, associated with the use of the Boyle-Bickmore technology described above. This particular approach was not well put together and typically was far too vague and speculative for Ordnance Survey. It contained very little detail or specific project proposals and their likely cost-benefit, which perhaps reflected in part the lack of any cooperation at all in its development. This approach to an organisation, such as Ordnance Survey, that customarily went into anything with great thoroughness and attention to detail was doomed to failure.

Externally, the Ordnance Survey response from Brigadier A Walmsley-White was extremely cool, stating that Ordnance Survey needed time to reflect on this very complex and far-reaching prospect. This rather unenthusiastic response was lightened slightly by closing with the statement that any effort expended on forecasting data volumes from Ordnance Survey mapping would assist, as would work on data capture and output to acceptable standards. It is clear that these initial contacts between Ordnance Survey and the ECU, as it became known, had got off to a poor start. Lack of real progress on its own account inside Ordnance Survey, Bickmore's rather flamboyant style and the inward-looking culture of Ordnance Survey and its staff all conspired to heighten mistrust right from the start, when Ordnance Survey opinion was sought on the need for, and the benefits to be derived from, Bickmore's initiative with NERC. This early mistrust is encapsulated in the report back to the Director General's Committee by the director responsible for map production: 'I find the whole project tends to be clouded by vested interest and anxieties. One would wish that such work was in the hands of someone who did not have a private commercial axe to grind at the same time he is engaged in a public project.' This engenders undertones of mistrust somewhat discrediting the team and its work, although these sentiments were not expressed in public.'

The strength of feeling that stemmed from the initial contact seeking Ordnance Survey's views on the need for an experimental body elsewhere, other than at Ordnance Survey itself, had served to dominate the early relationship between the two. Somewhat later, this antipathy can be distilled from the record of the highest executive committee (Director General's Committee) within Ordnance Survey two years after in November 1969. Here it was concluded that Bickmore's ECU 'should not be regarded or named as a national research centre for cartographic science but at most should be regarded more simply as a research unit for automation in cartography'. Specifically, it was decided that the Unit must not be allowed to represent itself as a national mapping research unit.

It was also decided that this potential threat to Ordnance Survey's 'kudos' and eventually 'perhaps' also to its funding, should be raised at JASB, thereby seeking to create a consensus view aimed first and foremost at containing Bickmore's ambitions. In seeking to avoid a terminal rift and the harmful consequences to Ordnance Survey that might flow from such a negative response, it was concluded that Ordnance Survey should limit any research done for it by the ECU to such peripheral subjects as new area measuring techniques, the use of symbols and the testing of new equipment.

The view that the unit might 'be killed by kindness' was discussed. The Ordnance Survey high-level decision, at this point in time, precluded the external unit doing any production work at all, but the 'engagement' with Bickmore certainly persuaded Ordnance Survey to equip itself with some equipment that would help it to evaluate the feasibility of a map information databank and to study the economy of automating some processes. In then normal fashion, Captain M Irwin from Ordnance Survey was booked to deliver a lecture at the Royal Institution of Chartered Surveyors to place these decisions on the public record. Perhaps this view in 1969 represented an accumulation of sentiment about Bickmore and his new unit, but there was real mistrust and suspicion about his motives almost from the outset.

The initial approach from Bickmore seeking support for his ideas had, without any doubt, caught Ordnance Survey unprepared. By the summer of 1967 the JASB specification documents had done the rounds and had been completed to each participating department's satisfaction. It wasn't long, however, before knowledge of the existence of these specifications soon spread and this quickly brought representatives of several interested manufacturing companies knocking on Ordnance Survey's own doors. It was perceived that the largest public task (not subject to the Military's Official Secrets Act) and therefore the largest potential demand for equipment would be found at Ordnance Survey. For a response to the approach by Bickmore; the Director General tasked staff with preparing the peripheral research objectives while stimulating thought about the wider aspects of automation that Ordnance Survey should consider.

Despite Ordnance Survey's initial and 'lukewarm' reception, Bickmore had managed to generate sufficient support for his proposed unit.

In February 1968, with this momentum achieved, Bickmore, recognising the strength of Ordnance Survey's influence on and dominance of opinion in British cartography at large, sought and won a meeting between the small team he had initially assembled and a broad cross section of Ordnance Survey's senior management. The ECU, in its opening presentation, divulged details of its quarter-million pound equipment portfolio and its initial programmes for software development and the data projects it planned to tackle. Ordnance Survey responded with its then current thoughts on automation, and these are interesting.

In the brief interim, it had concluded that digitising its large-scale plans was not worthwhile and that the capture and maintenance of 1:10000 scale mapping and smaller scales would be most beneficial. The need for contour and boundary information was also seen as important. Discussion followed on the feasibility and role for databanks. Following this meeting, which was conducted in a civil manner, despite the mistrust and antipathy on the Ordnance Survey side, it is worth noting that action was taken to upgrade the level of representation on the in-house working party on automation. This was followed by the creation of a small study team, adequately resourced, to identify the totality of the elements of the basic-scale map specifications.

Each element was to be listed and its origin identified whether as surveyed or generalised or shown by means of a symbol. Further, record was to be made whether it was to be carried forward to any other Ordnance Survey produced scales of mapping. A fresh approach was made to all directorates with the task of reviewing afresh the potential of automation in their work. Other questions posed inside Ordnance Survey concerned the scale of any databank, in which coordinate system would any data be held and what further identification of elements of data would be required.

Following the original meeting between the ECU and Ordnance Survey, fairly routine contact was maintained with the ECU, at least by individuals. During this period the Director General tasked his senior staff with considering the question whether basic large-scale mapping should in fact be digitised, thus fairly quickly challenging a major conclusion that Ordnance Survey had previously relayed for the JASB report. It was during this period that serious thought was at last given to this far-reaching topic. Conclusions reached at this time were to have a major impact throughout the life of the digital data capture project, which was in turn to come to dominate life and business inside Ordnance Survey.

Considerable resource and effort were put into the project to document the nature of basic-scale map information. Definitions of 'surveyed' (detail on documents accurate in ground position), 'as surveyed' (drawn by draughtsmen with correction of field errors by squaring and smoothing), 'centreline in surveyed position and displaced' were all agreed and published. Such definitions were to be vital in the long march toward a future digital databank. This work soon made clear that Ordnance Survey's initial and stated belief that digitising was best accomplished at 1:10000 scale for a databank was unsound as very little information could be taken forward from the underlying map without displacement or generalisation. Even the more reactive elements in Ordnance Survey were coming round to the concept of capturing and holding map data at basic scales, although it seemed an insurmountable but unquantified task. The catalytic effects of JASB and the ECU had, in early 1969, brought Ordnance Survey to the 'starting line', with the concept of a major project to digitise the basic-scale mapping of Great Britain beginning to take shape, at least in some of the sharper minds within.

Chapter 3
Gathering momentum but still no clear mission

Following the important meeting with the team from the ECU led by David Bickmore, in February 1968, there was, at least, a sense of raised interest among some of those who were present representing Ordnance Survey. The apparent zeal for the new technologies demonstrated at this meeting by the visitors; clear evidence of a strong commitment to cartography by another and possibly rival organisation with a portfolio of new equipment which had cost a quarter of a million pounds; and the assembly of diverse skills and talents, some of which were new to the cartographic industry and its traditional problems, all contributed to an increased interest by Ordnance Survey. As a result of this meeting, the Director General demanded that a suitable research programme be devised and initiated, that the internal working party considering these matters should have its status raised, with more senior members of staff to be involved, and that a project to identify and catalogue all the elements of map information of the large-scale map series should be begun. Increasing interest in and concern for these matters is reflected from this time onwards, intermittently in the contemporary records of the weekly meetings between the Director General and his directors at Ordnance Survey.

What had become increasingly apparent was that previous conclusions and decisions, made after limited consideration at much too low a level inside Ordnance Survey and without any overarching strategic vision or guidance, should, of necessity, be revisited. The first conclusion by Ordnance Survey had dismissed the basic large-scale mapping from the potential benefits of automation. The second conclusion directed attention more to securing data at the first scale of national map coverage – that is at the scale of 1:10000, from which, optimistically, it was felt other series of mapping (as in the conventional mapping sense) might also perhaps be derived. Contemporary records illustrate the major conflict of opinion about what was seen as the best way forward for Ordnance Survey with the prospects of automation. The debate that followed, inevitably, focused on two major issues. The first centred on the inherent distortions in field documents, which stored the basic-scale mapping between periodic and printed new edition publications. These were habitually driven by a dual formula based on age since the last new edition and the amount of change which had actually occurred on the ground.

The second issue concerned the lack of knowledge about the volumes of data that any automated activity might generate and the generally poor understanding with regard to the problems of data security and integrity associated with long-term storage on computer systems. Following substantial and prolonged internal debate, the Director General's Committee agreed to task the ECU with a project to digitise basic-scale point and line map detail. This was seen internally as demonstrating a desire not to be seen to wish to break with Bickmore's ECU. In tandem with this external tasking, the newly revitalised internal committee set out through internal consultation 'to examine and make recommendations on likely applications for automated cartography in all aspects of the broad task of Ordnance Survey'.

By the conclusion of the eighth in a series of meetings over several months of the internal Ordnance Survey working party, some fairly fundamental decisions were taken which were to have a far reaching and an enduring impact on what was to become Ordnance Survey's map digitising programme. It is interesting to note that these decisions were developed by the working party, 'off line', as it were, from mainstream departmental activity. These conclusions and the embryonic plans were not evaluated with anything like the sheer caution and deep deliberation that normally prevailed for almost any other aspects of technical activity within Ordnance Survey. Minor changes to the large-scale specification or to materials and methods used in their production were, by prescription, always evaluated, scrutinised and tested carefully under the oversight of the committee of managers before eventual implementation, where found to be beneficial. There is no contemporary record of any substantial debate at the top of the organisation, inside Ordnance Survey, before the following fundamental 'principles' were established for a future digitising project.

These principles were to endure for the duration of the project that eventually got under way and which was only finally completed in 1996. This was interesting as such a project was not widely believed to be possible or desirable, and it most certainly had not been evaluated properly in terms of its likely impact on the organisation and all its other activities. The internal committee certainly moved these matters forward quite quickly by declaring the fundamental principles that any map data captured should be held in the National Grid coordinate system; that digitising of detail as separate features was a necessity, that there was a clear need to produce topographic data, that the block size for digital data should be a 1:2500 scale sheet size (that is a one kilometre square); that there should be an identifying code for each feature (a small working group was then tasked with creating such a system); and that the cartographic databank, which would eventually be created, would be held in a form that 'outsiders' could also use. This terminology is somewhat symptomatic of contemporary thought inside Ordnance Survey during this era. It was clearly much too early to identify any specific external users of any digital data collected, but this decisive recognition of, at least, a latent requirement, at a time when the drive inside Ordnance Survey was centred on domestic production methods is interesting.

It was at this time that Major F Fortescue returned to his original discipline of reprographics. Throughout these early months and years he had represented a focal point for almost all involvements, both internal and external, in connection with developments in automation of cartography, from the time the Director General's attention had first been drawn to the possibilities arising from new technologies. Whilst also taking these decisions which would serve to shape future internal digitising activity the internal committee tasked with making progress with automation sought and obtained approval, at the highest level, to submit to the ECU team a test designed to evaluate the feasibility and cost of digitising adjacent 1:2500 scale map sheets. This first phase of the trial was to be followed by an attempt to use the centrelines of linear features to make a derived 1:10000 scale map, rather than, as was customary, by means of simple photographic reduction.

This twin goal project illustrates the enduring belief within the upper and middle reaches of Ordnance Survey thinking that automation's future role, if indeed it was to have one, must lie with the derived mapping sector of national mapping activity. The view was still widely held inside Ordnance Survey that if automated cartography was to bring any benefits it would most certainly be that 1:25000 scale mapping might be 'squeezed' from 1:10000 scale map data rather than from benefits within the basic large-scale sector of activity.

This relative flurry of activity in connection with the need to identify and, hopefully, to realise the potential of automated methods, heralded a much more focused study, following high-level consideration of these issues at the Director General's Committee. This Committee represented the highest executive level of authority within Ordnance Survey. It can be seen from contemporary records that there was less a growing interest in such matters but more a concern that Ordnance Survey was making insufficient progress, which could potentially lead to public embarrassment.

In October 1968 a young graduate military officer, Captain Mike Irwin RE was transferred from his post in Ordnance Survey's Air Survey Unit to conduct a study of the potential of automation, with the following terms of reference: 'To study the application of automated methods to all stages of production of Ordnance Survey mapping, from initial collection of data by field and air survey for the basic survey and revision through to production of the final negative of the map. The study should include derived mapping.' Captain Irwin was tasked with producing a report by January 1969 that would at least outline the systems that might be adopted by Ordnance Survey and the immediate steps that might be taken using equipment, then currently available.

He was further tasked by mid-1969 with developing estimates of the sorts of levels of equipment and staff required to make progress with automation and with illustrating the likely levels of saving from the use of staff otherwise employed but without the support of automation. In reality this was to be a cost/benefit study, and it is interesting that the terms of reference set were also to introduce what proved to be the distracting influence of attempts to automate data capture from photogrammetric machines. Such an outcome in fact took many more years to achieve.

Up to this point in time, the view persisted that any automated methods should afford 'faster' and 'cheaper' production with fewer staff deployed for the same head of work. The base line for judgement was set to mean more for less. Using available equipment, this was by no means certain and validity could only really be established within very carefully controlled trial conditions. Coincident with the tasking of Captain Irwin, an Ordnance Survey delegation once again met with the ECU team. Besides announcing progress made, Ordnance Survey agreed to loan an experienced cartographer to the ECU joint project, with a view to 'demystifying' Ordnance Survey in-house conventions and working practices for the ECU.

Ordnance Survey also agreed to supply to the joint ECU project its catalogue of all point and line detail found on the basic-scales mapping that had already been prepared a short while before. All this was designed to help the ECU to produce an estimate of the likely data volumes associated with basic-scale map coverage which could be prepared and supplied to Ordnance Survey. However, doubts about the will and the sustained level of commitment by ECU toward Ordnance Survey obligations that were eventually to assume 'rift' proportions between the two bodies, were already, at this time, beginning to emerge and to intensify within Ordnance Survey. Closer and continuing contact with the ECU already embarked on tackling a rather vague self-imposed remit with very wide and diverse goals, and its enormous range of potential customers – established at the outset by David Bickmore – all appeared to confirm the impression, emerging within Ordnance Survey, that the ECU, on closer acquaintance with some of the challenging problems, was perhaps less interested in the task of collecting and processing topographic map data.

Project work on which the unit embarked and the background of several ECU staffers appeared to suggest a very real bias toward the mapping and use of statistical data. These somewhat destructive impressions of the ECU arose partly because of Ordnance Survey's almost innate suspicion of anyone who attempted 'to play on their pitch' but also from ECU's apparent lack of 'staying power' to achieve objectives and deadlines, a real lack of longer-term goals, their changing multi-goal ambitions and the lack of evidence of real focus, as Ordnance Survey had traditionally understood it. Mounting concern was becoming evident within Ordnance Survey at this time that an eventual and serious breach in relations with the ECU might have wider and potentially damaging repercussions because of the unit's publishing and political skills.

In July 1968 the record of the Director General's Committee, which was still the highest executive authority within Ordnance Survey, contained the following conclusion: ' Ordnance Survey's interest in the application of automated techniques to the drawing and revision of maps at all scales and especially at the largest scales was very strong. In view of potential savings we could afford relatively high expenditure on development work and we must think seriously about the possibility of initiating development work ourselves.'

This important directive was given following a review by Ordnance Survey's senior management of the rather fitful internal progress that had been achieved to date and in preparing a response to the JASB initiative. Because of the remoteness of senior management and the absence of effective internal communications within Ordnance Survey and the very restricted access to the record of the Director General's Committee, this strategic statement largely failed to galvanise the organisation into action in a way that it perhaps should have. It did possibly help to sustain the interest of those concerned in finding a suitable tasking for the ECU.

The type of activity sought or commissioned by Ordnance Survey in 1968 of the ECU was planned and designed with only very limited forethought by the small number of personnel involved. The overall objective was to establish both the technical feasibility and the cost-effectiveness of applying the new computer-based technologies to the Ordnance Survey task, at a time when equipment associated with the new technology appeared, to those involved, to be both expensive and extremely unreliable. The three goals set for the ECU work were to establish that individual map features could be digitised reliably and consistently; that the computer could be programmed to correct distortions (inherent in some mapping, or otherwise felt to be induced by the act of digitising itself); and to evaluate whether a programme could be written and tested to make necessary joins at sheet edges, thus making the computer-produced mapping continuous and 'seamless'. In effect these goals developed further the fundamental principles that Ordnance Survey had established for digital mapping, which have already been referred to above. This latter conceptual requirement was in fact to bedevil Ordnance Survey philosophy and practice for many more years to come, and it is interesting at least that it surfaced so early in the piece.

The ECU used two separate equipment systems to produce results for evaluation of the Ordnance Survey commission. The Geameter digitising table, which provided map data to be plotted on the Geagraph plotter, and the Dmac digitiser outputting data to the Geagraph plotter. Ordnance Survey's internal Automated Cartography Committee members, when viewing the results of the ECU's efforts, concluded that outputs were not generally acceptable, tending to reinforce wider and more sceptical views

that the 1:2500 scale overhaul map production task, planned in any case for completion in 1980, was too far advanced for any major efficiencies or significant cost reductions arising from automation to come in time.

It was also concluded that such systems, because of quality of output, would be unlikely to materially assist in the continuing derived mapping production task where the compilation of a small-scales databank would be too complex and time consuming. However, it was decided to submit such a proposition to further trials. This evaluation by those responsible inside Ordnance Survey, almost all at middle management level, illustrates very clearly the prevailing attitude at Ordnance Survey that map production by tried and tested methods was still largely seen as the key activity and the overarching importance of the 1980 commitment could not be put at risk by any new approaches to the task.

The conclusion that automated techniques had no real part to play in the production of the basic-scale 1:2500 mapping did, however, lead to some further consideration of other in-house activities that might possibly be supported by automation. As a consequence, a new assignment was put to the ECU whereby it was tasked with capturing a total of 100 square kilometres of line and point detail from the parent mapping. The data was to be captured at 1:6250 scale from input documents reduced from their original 1:2500 scale masters. The task design called for internal constituent map edges to be adjusted and also called for the inclusion of contours (a subject which was itself to prove something of a distraction for a period of time in the future, before it became a reality).

Contemporary in-house activity in connection with automation saw the timely release of an interim report on Captain M Irwin's tasking in February 1969. His very painstaking and detailed assessment had looked at how the current and overall Ordnance Survey task could perhaps be better executed with the aid of automated techniques. He concluded that all experimental automated work to date was beset by technical problems and equipment failures, but more important, perhaps, that to date all trials had involved very small areas and volumes of data. Conclusions from such trials were often, therefore, largely theoretical rather than based on rigorous production trials of any significant extent.

He concluded somewhat strategically that there might well be a place for maps in digital form and clearly recognised a future possible benefit from automation in speeding up the processes of basic-scale map revision, where production delays between survey and the availability of revision information to end-users was typically of the order of two years, via costly new editions. He also concluded rather boldly that automating the residual 1980 tasking would add some £3.5 million to the cost with only a very modest saving (digitising versus scribing) in labour of 65 man-years of effort in total, in the 12 remaining years to 1980. He further concluded that typical field documents could not easily be digitised using state-of-the-art equipment. Other conclusions reached were:

- In view of the shortcomings in hardware, Ordnance Survey should not purchase any automated equipment other than some shaft encoders for a photogrammetric plotting machine (either Thompson Watts Mk 11 or Wild A8) to permit trials to be conducted' of the automated capture of contours. This was to prove to be a major and wasteful distraction from the mainstream of automated cartography.

- A study should be made of all automated equipment currently available on the market and a register or file should be maintained up to date, as further development and improvements occurred.

- Computer programs for generalisation (the cartographer's eternal 'dream') should be kept in view. This necessitated continuing literature searches.

- More investigative work should be performed to investigate both the content and nature of medium-scales mapping.

- Further work should be done on classifying and coding detail at the basic scales of mapping.

His final conclusion was that studies should be conducted on the development of display screens which might permit real-time interaction with map data (visionary considering the poor state of the art), computer needs for automation and automated names placement for mapping.

The broad result of Captain Irwin's work, although for some, being seen to confirm their perception of old concerns and prejudices that they considered already existed among Ordnance Survey's management that there was little benefit in this new technology for the basic-scales task, did importantly lead to a further round of investigative work. Trial operations within the broad area of computerised support for traditional tasks were planned. And so, while seeking to work with various commercial organisations (but always on Ordnance Survey terms) that professed to have suitable equipment available, trials were initiated aimed at the automation of Ordnance Survey's boundary making and recording task, at the continuous revision task and with 'generalisation' facilities required for the derived mapping task. In addition, the analysis and definition of the basic-scales map content project continued to receive support, which is again surprising, bearing in mind the tendency to forsake this very considerable sector of Ordnance Survey effort in his major recommendations.

This ambiguous and uncertain approach by Ordnance Survey illustrates, perhaps, the lack of a top down or strategic direction in the organisation for the concept of automation. This was at a time when such a few individuals were aware of what was happening with automation, when internal communications and cross-fertilisation were so inhibited by the military-based management pyramid in a highly compartmentalised organisation, and which had not, up to this time, produced or developed a champion for automation and the future within the senior management team. It was also at this time that the Dmac digitiser, which had been purchased by Ordnance Survey and found wanting, was modified and improved by lowering the coil on the digitising head closer to the plotting table, such that it would be more sensitive and responsive to pen movements initiated by the operative.

During this period of considerable doubt and scepticism within Ordnance Survey about the potential and the reliability of these technologies generally and their ability to deliver adequate results from trials, regular external contact was still maintained with the ECU, both at St Giles in Oxford and with their new production unit, which had been established in Exhibition Road, London SW7. There was also an increasing awareness, thanks to the discipline of literature searches, among a few professional staff inside Ordnance Survey of work in connection with automation that was going on elsewhere in the world. However, the required catalyst for the use by Ordnance Survey of computer-based technology eventually came in the form of what transpired to be a most beneficial and productive senior military appointment to Ordnance Survey.

This appointment from the military was devised initially and primarily to shake up and to improve the machinery of centralised production planning. Ordnance Survey had, by this point in time, 'evolved' rather than designed very complex and cumbersome production planning for the '1980 task', which typically produced factors as detailed as 0.01 of a map as a work unit and for 0.1 of a production operative. Colonel Robin Gardiner-Hill RE duly arrived at Ordnance Survey head office in September 1969. He proved to be a most unconventional, challenging and somewhat irreverent military officer, with a style very much his own. He was extremely intelligent with a lively mind, somewhat academic in approach and quite different to the 'run of the mill' type of military officer who had traditionally served at Ordnance Survey before him.

With his academic background in engineering and mathematics he had already acquired a very good grasp of computer science, modelling and computer technology, which in truth was not very common in this era when computers were largely driven and their needs serviced by technician men 'in white coats'. The professions and technologists in society at large had generally, at this time, to explain their technical and scientific needs from computers to these 'broker/operators' who had responsibility for systems analysis and programming. Colonel Gardiner-Hill mistrusted and positively disliked formal structures within the organisation and its management structure, particularly those that, by tradition and past practice, prevented him from seeking precious resources held elsewhere or from approaching the holder of a solution to a problem directly rather up and down through both respective chains of management.

His frequent fact- or solution-finding 'walkabouts' within Ordnance Survey were tracked with considerable apprehension and suspicion by fellow colonels and brigadiers, and there were occasions when staff in other 'commands' were briefed not to talk either to him or 'his folk', particularly if he appeared likely to challenge their existing resource base allocation. Gardiner-Hill had all the skills of a modern 'mover and shaker'. He challenged the defensive and the traditional and had a great dislike of 'vested interest'. Because of his undoubted intellect and unconventional approach, he was able to exert substantial pressure on weaker officers above himself in the management pyramid and on several important occasions persuaded the high command of Ordnance Survey to almost see 'the emperor's new clothes' in these early days of digital mapping.

His arrival coincided beneficially with the arrival of the first graduates via the good offices of the Joint Survey Service, which had been established in 1968. The formation of this interdepartmental staff group is dealt with in more depth in subsequent passages. They too were not strong in structure and formality, having largely served overseas with the

Directorate of Overseas Surveys and who generally were not inhibited by traditions and past practices of Ordnance Survey which were usually trotted out as some of the '101 reasons' why an initiative wouldn't work. The author of this piece was indeed one of the first such folk to arrive at Ordnance Survey and, after a short stay managing basic-scale cartography to gain experience, was then deployed on the various automation studies.

Coincidentally and almost exactly at this time, a further external influence came to bear on Ordnance Survey in the shape of a potential customer for any fruits of the developments in automation. Birmingham City Council, with which Ordnance Survey was destined to have a long and productive relationship, had become aware of the work that had been done to date and their in-house mapping and computer experts initially sought a cooperative approach in a contact through their regional Ordnance Survey office, which was quickly relayed to head office. Soon after this initiative, in July 1970, the somewhat unlikely Civil Service Department of HM Government launched an initiative to disseminate information on the potential of computer-based mapping.

Both Ordnance Survey's and the ECU's efforts to date were described to a gathering of potential users and suppliers that Ordnance Survey had called into being. Ordnance Survey explained that 'selected features of component large-scale maps had been digitised by manual line following and then output to a reel of magnetic tape, whereby a stream of x and y coordinates, suitably encoded to represent point and line detail of the source maps, had been retained. The tape had been processed by computer to transform the coordinates from their arbitrary origin to National Grid values and the tape could then be databanked. Using an automated draughting system, it is also then possible to draw this and other maps. The meeting served to identify a still rather vague but emerging demand in central government, nationalised industries (mainly utility providers), local authorities and in a few commercial companies (the computer company ICL® [International Computers Ltd] was already apparently embarked on an information system project for London Electricity®, which, potentially at least, required mapping for its successful operation).

The apparent and expressed potential of this demand clearly surprised the Ordnance Survey representatives at this gathering. The meeting witnessed, really for the first time, the opening up of a second and important dimension to what had, up to this point, largely been seen as an alternative domestic production technique. Contemporary records of Ordnance Survey illustrate a very broad-based and strong scepticism inside Ordnance Survey about whether these latent and somewhat vague needs could ever be translated into a market for what was still a very variable product of a tedious and unreliable methodology. The potential for distraction from the task to which Ordnance Survey was already deeply committed was seen as the most unacceptable spin-off of these developments.

Meanwhile, at the same time and with Ordnance Survey's blessing, the ECU had taken the smaller scale (six inches to the mile), input documents of the Bideford area of Devon and commenced the digital capture of roads, railways, coastline and water features (largely represented by curvilinear lines). Their efforts were constantly beset by stubborn and frequent equipment failures and 'system' shortcomings. It should be said that this work was conducted in a 'seat of the pants', research environment (and therefore quite undisciplined in Ordnance Survey's contemporary judgement) but, by June 1970, a variety of ECU project staff had managed to complete phase two of data capture, following several missed deadlines (again seen as a serious and damning weakness to Ordnance Survey's traditional but disciplined eyes). It soon became evident following a detailed evaluation by Ordnance Survey, however, that results were only just satisfactory for eventual output at 1:25000 scale (and certainly not suitable for plotting at the input scale of six inches to the mile). The data collected could not meet the accuracy standards of the six-inch map series.

This worrying conclusion certainly led to a push both by the ECU and Ordnance Survey to evaluate and test new and emerging equipment, both on the digitising and plotting fronts. In February 1970 Ferranti Ltd from Edinburgh approached Ordnance Survey seeking their input to the specification requirements for a digitising system based on the Bendix Freescan solid state digitising tablet, which was developed, manufactured and already marketed in the United States of America. In parallel, Ordnance Survey upgraded their electro-mechanical digitising system, which, temporarily at least, had been diverted from the basic-scale automated cartography drive. The fitting of Rank shaft encoders to the lead screws of an A8 photogrammetric plotting machine to collect contour output via the Dmac data collection system was to be the subject of a distracting trial.

The Ordnance Survey Central Computer Unit (consisting of one or more mainframe computers and ancillary equipment), which was in being to address traditional technical survey and business system tasks (for example, ranging from triangulation computation and adjustment through to stores accounting) was tasked with producing some software designed to facilitate the necessary processes required of automated cartography. Gardiner-Hill had also secured agreement, in the face of Captain Irwin's imminent departure back to military duty, for a replacement post within his 'command' to continue in the same broad area of enquiry. After the normal internal machinations of this era aimed at securing a further military appointment, a civilian post was eventually created at a similar level from the newly created civilian Joint Survey Service.

The Joint Survey Service, previously mentioned, implemented with effect from January 1969, was designed to manage a cadre of professional surveyors either recruited anew or drawn from the professional staff of the Directorate of Overseas Survey. This new civilian service was created following a review of the staffing of Ordnance Survey and a consequential decision to break the military stranglehold on most management appointments there. To further the aims of cross posting between the three consistent organisations (the Directorate of Overseas Survey, the Mapping and Charting Establishment of Military Survey and Ordnance Survey), the writer was sent for postgraduate training at Glasgow University® prior to taking up such an appointment for the first time at Ordnance Survey.

The software that Ordnance Survey Computer Unit produced in response to Gardiner-Hill's commission converted a Dmac digitising output tape to an ICL (mainframe computer) format. Duly corrected set-up errors indicated by the operator transformed coordinates to the National Grid and corrected for document distortion or digitising table aberrations. Data was put through a routine to place the data into basic grid square units. Where it could, it also corrected for coding errors and generated a sequential serial number for each feature. The software next generated a plot tape for a 24-vector 633 Calcomp drum plotter with a 770 tape unit, which had been acquired following Gardiner-Hill's arrival at Ordnance Survey. Although not a precision plotter, it was reasonably fast and accurate, but was justified when purchased for the planned graphical outputs from management information.

The principal architect and producer of this software was another somewhat unusual character who had previously worked for Ordnance Survey for many years on the surveying side. Clearly with an interest in and an affinity for the emerging potential of the technology of electronic computing, Mr Syd Hull, who had moved into the Computer Unit soon after its formation on the technical side, duly proved to be one of the key figures in the development of automated cartography at Ordnance Survey and sustained this role over a considerable number of years. Officially classified as a technician – albeit a very gifted practitioner, knowledgeable indeed about products and the task – he was to remain involved with the automation programme for nearly two decades. During this time he saw the rotation of a good number of military and civilian professional managers of varying abilities, and despite his critical and somewhat cynical outlook, he was a considerable and sustaining source of ideas and usually clever problem-solving software.

Although without formal qualification, he was the intellectual equal of Gardiner-Hill, who was able to stimulate and channel his interests and abilities very productively through a very early form of 'empowerment', quite beyond the formal management structure typically found at Ordnance Survey. Gardiner-Hill never had line management responsibility for Mr Syd Hull but tasked him during his frequent 'walkabouts' and through long brainstorming sessions in Gardiner-Hill's cigar-smoke-filled office. The writer was present at almost all of these meetings, which frequently ran late into the evening and following almost ritual intellectual 'point scoring' between Gardiner-Hill and Syd Hull, the stimulating business of the automated future was invariably tackled with shared enthusiasm.

The following months saw progress on two fronts. In-house, Ordnance Survey made progress with several experiments whilst externally there was increasing evidence, albeit of a still very vague but persistent expectation and requirement for the products of automated cartography. On the experimental side, a 300-metre square block from the 1:1250 scale sheet SJ31841E was digitised at scale on the Dmac digitiser at Ordnance Survey. After processing it was plotted on the Hydrographic Department's Kongsberg Kingmatic precision plotting table (courtesy of the JASB contacts) using two codes only, for solid and pecked lines following at least one edit loop. The accuracy was assessed as 0.4 mm or 0.5 m on the ground. This sample of computer-based mapping was used to demonstrate the potential of the technology at several external meetings with potential customers.

In November 1970 a further experiment was initiated with the aim of determining more clearly the economics of digitising 1:1250 scale mapping. The four quadrants of the 1:1250 scale sheet TQ3381SW located in central London, enlarged to 1:500 scale with a 50-m grid overlaid, were digitised in a more disciplined and controlled trial. Following processing through the newly developed suite of programs, the data was plotted on the Calcomp drum plotter with maximum error of 0.2 mm achieved. Coincident with this project and because of a growing realisation that higher-accuracy plotting output would be required if Ordnance Survey was to continue to make progress in-house, a study was launched to evaluate the precision draughting machines available on the market at this time. The performance of four machines in all were reviewed. These were the Coragraph by Contraves®; the master plotter by Ferranti; the Kingmatic of Kongsberg, as already tested briefly at the Hydrographic Department; and the Gealux by AEG®.

Almost all of the external contact with potential or interested customers during this period had come about through the running that they themselves had made with Ordnance Survey. There was, however, still an overriding conviction amongst those involved with these developments inside Ordnance Survey in 1970, that any benefit accruing from automation would come from improving production techniques for the 1980 task. Through continuing contact with Calcomp, which had supplied Ordnance Survey with their drum plotter, British Oxygen sought digital data of Great Britain from Ordnance Survey, which included coastline, roads and railways and major towns and cities. It was this initiative that led in December 1970 to Ordnance Survey digitising the two-sheet Route Planning Map, published annually at 1:625000 scale. It was also at this time that the Civil Service Department of HM Treasury hosted the gathering of those organisations with a potential interest in large-scale map data already referred to. Lateral discussions with Ordnance Survey were also initiated by London Electricity Board, which were, with ICL, seeking to develop a business-wide information system that included map-based plant records.

Chapter 4

Continuing experimentation with digital cartography at Ordnance Survey

Throughout 1970 and during most of 1971 sustained efforts were made by the six or seven people at most, who under Gardiner-Hill's enthusiastic leadership had become involved with the developments in automation of cartography at Ordnance Survey. Besides the two members of staff committed full-time to this work within the embryonic Research and Development Unit, led as part of Gardiner-Hill's responsibilities together with a centralised Planning Unit, there was a systems analyst, two programmers in the Computer Unit and a person in Computer Operations whose duties included managing the quirky initiatives and developments in this new field of activity. This 'cross command' and multidisciplinary approach to problem solving was indeed a rather radical innovation at Ordnance Survey, which had traditionally operated on rigid directorate lines, chiefly dictated by its military traditions. This reflected Gardiner-Hill's more liberal approach to tackling issues.

It is difficult, if not almost impossible when looking back from the vantage point of almost three decades beyond, equipped as we are today with all the benefits and advantages that have come from intense and sustained developments in computer and graphics technologies, to comprehend the tediousness of software development in the batch processing environment associated with contemporary mainframe computer operations. Recompilation of programmes to effect even modest technical changes or to remove 'bugs' could take a day or two depending on conflicting priorities. The mandatory (for almost all UK government departments) ICL mainframe computer at Ordnance Survey had, until 1971, only been justified on the basis of a workload associated with sundry administrative tasks and scientific work associated with geodesy and the horizontal and vertical control networks of Great Britain.

The tedious development of software for automated cartography, written in Fortran and machine language for optimised running on the mainframe machine and a series of experiments associated with its use, slowly, and with considerable denial from other user areas, began to establish a place at least in the priorities for the limited mainframe computing capacity at Ordnance Survey head office.

Another vital group of activities of the Development Unit staff assigned to the automation study was a continuing appraisal of the equipment market and subsequent liaison with manufacturers and with other government departments represented on the JASB network and with the ECU. The former activity involved visits to inspect equipment and the management and conduct of 'benchmark' trials using Ordnance Survey's own map material. This was certainly a time when the work itself proved a hearty and stimulating mix. The atmosphere of the 'team', although working in dispersed mode at Ordnance Survey's head office, was one of humour, practical joke and at times rebellion, whilst working with great enthusiasm and initiative and innovation.

Colonel Gardiner-Hill, the project leader, was an extremely intelligent but rather eccentric and wily character. He was also very adept politically and in managing the messages to his superior officers to sustain their engagement and support for the work during challenging periods.

Mr Syd Hull, during his previous career at Ordnance Survey as a technician surveyor, effectively the second member of the team, embarked on developing digital cartographic techniques, was both a very capable systems analyst and an innovative programmer employed within the centralised Computer Unit. He had acquired, in his earlier role as a surveyor technician, a very considerable knowledge of Ordnance Survey's large-scale mapping. He was a classic example of the previously repressed technician groups at Ordnance Survey and one of the very few who had made the break, as it were, because of his aptitude for the new opportunities arising from the introduction of computing. He could be waspish in his criticism but always retained a great sense of humour for and with those working with him.

He nurtured strong feelings against the less competent, particularly those military officers who simply served their time at Ordnance Survey, and regularly kicked over the many tedious traces that were such a feature of contemporary life at Ordnance Survey. The writer of this account, Peter Wesley, who had come to Ordnance Survey under new arrangements for the introduction of the Joint Survey Service to Ordnance Survey, was the third member of the team at this time. The military management and the administrators of personnel were still reluctant to offer positions to graduates in the face of conflicting demands from military officers and the trade union of the few technicians deemed suitable to rise further. This third appointment to the team had been planned following an initial but quite lengthy orientation period in conventional cartography.

This orientation involved managing several large-scale map production units at senior technician level, engaged on the 1980 task using conventional scribing methods, and also managing the department charged with the meticulous function of large-scale map examination, before he joined Development Unit and the newly formed Gardiner-Hill 'team'. The unyielding and traditional conservatism of the Examination Department provided a very clear insight into the sheer size of the future task of introducing such radically different production techniques and possibly maps of different appearance on the back of computer-compatible data.

All three members of the team, from very different backgrounds, were quite 'unconventional' in different ways, certainly by Ordnance Survey standards. All had the essential advantage that what Ordnance Survey traditionalists called the obvious, was not necessarily taken for granted. Because of the very tight structural lines along which military Ordnance Survey was managed, it wasn't a team in the sense of a group, collocated and working together, with all the benefits such a structure brings. Late evening sessions with visits to local hostelries for refreshment frequently solved problems and served to retain high morale despite the generally unfulfilling atmosphere of the department at large.

The modus operandi of the team and its 'let's try it' philosophy in turn led to a large degree of 'creative tension' with senior managers of the overall structure and especially with the guardians of standards and traditions within the organisation. Ordnance Survey was, at this time, intensely conservative in its outlook and in its attitude to change. Its stultifying atmosphere, however, failed to overcome and to subdue the approach of the small team working on the development of digital mapping techniques. Gardiner-Hill's great gift was an ability and drive that broke with well-established practice at Ordnance Survey. His accepted unconventionality helped him to break into the management hierarchy of other commands at whatever level he deemed appropriate. His preference was for informal and unannounced 'walkabouts', often in commands other than his own, when he would go and seek facts, opinion or resources from wherever they might be found, and he encouraged his staff to do likewise.

This aspect of his personal style, which ran contrary to established practice, created considerable tension within Ordnance Survey, particularly among the managers of resources that he perceived he needed and sought. Many of the more conventional managers within well-established structures, who were engaged with conventional 1970 technology, became very defensive of their empires and simply dismissed the digital mapping venture as unworthy and a distraction from the main task. This widespread negative reaction to the experiments simply served to tighten team spirit within the project.

Toward the end of 1971 some of the results achieved in digitising, processing and plotting map data had proved sufficiently persuasive to suggest that there might indeed be a way forward with automating large-scales cartography as a viable production procedure. Meanwhile, Gardiner-Hill's vision was already extending to the possibility that there might also be something in it one day for customers with the supply of digital data that they could manipulate for themselves. His Professional Paper Number 23: The 'Development of Digital Maps', which was eventually published in 1972, effectively summarises 'the state of the art' and a vision of the future at this important time.

Gardiner-Hill's own enthusiasm, his confident attitude and his 'control of the message' upwards all served to achieve at least qualified support for further effort and resources to be committed to the automation project. Once again and almost 10 years after Director General Henley Dowson's initial and visionary statement, the Director General at this time, Major General B St G Irwin, produced an important and a defining internal paper in November 1971, over his personal signature block. The Development team worked long hours on preparation and collection of data for the upward briefing. The paper eventually presented by the Director General was of considerable significance and would serve to chart the path for the future with regard to automated cartography. The statement, as well as being an agreement to proceed apace with development, was aimed at those areas of Ordnance Survey that were still very sceptical about any further development.

The Director General's formal paper presented to his most senior executive committee in late 1971, began with a statement of aims: 'The aim of this paper is to summarise the present position and to outline the policy to be followed in the short term, in respect of automated cartography. Automated cartography includes the recording of topographic data in digital form, the subsequent processing of the data and its eventual output in whatever form it may be required.' He then summarised the present position.

'Experimental work has developed the technical process to the stage at which it is now possible to apply automated cartography to the production of mapping at 1:1250 and 1:2500 scales. The quality of the product is such that its acceptance by users for all present purposes is not seriously in question. In addition, the flexibility of the system enables special requirements to be met more easily than is now possible, so that all in all automation is now capable of improving the service to the customer. In so far as the bare costs of initial production of large-scale mapping are concerned, the evidence so far available shows that automated techniques are more expensive than current practice. Specifically in the case of 1:2500 scale mapping would, it is estimated, lead to an increase in overall production costs of the order of 10%. This, however, takes no account of the likely reduction of maintenance and storage costs, nor of the advantages stemming from the establishment of a databank. Furthermore, as experience is gained and flowline procedures are improved, production costs can be expected to decrease.'

The paper continued with great vision. It next summarised the long-term objective as follows: 'The full potential of an automated system will not be realised unless and until all required topographic data is banked in digital form and continually updated and is readily accessible for presentation in any required form of output. Before this stage can be reached, which cannot be for a number of years, much development work needs to be done. Its attainment will also involve a very large labour effort and a very large capital expenditure, all of which will require justification in financial terms. The human implications too will need careful study. Nevertheless, it is a proper long-term objective for the Department and will remain so until such time as further study or development, or changed circumstances, may dictate otherwise.'

What was most important about the paper was that it at last established a short-term policy that enabled those engaged on the development project to break out from the strictures of the level of resources previously allocated to it and the cranky equipment that had been acquired up to that time and used for an intense period of experimental development. The short-term policy was therefore agreed and declared to be: 'The stage has been reached where further progress in the development and evaluation of automated techniques can only be made with the aid of a pilot production project. This should lead to the evolution of more economical flowline procedures, to the stimulation of user interest and demand and to the exploitation of those by-products which will begin to come within reach.

'Thereafter a more realistic assessment of cost benefit may be made. The Department will therefore undertake the following operations, using automated techniques as soon as circumstance permit, the production of a defined area of standard 1:2500 scale overhaul mapping. This scale is preferred to 1:1250 on account of the size of the residual field programme, the scope which is afforded for experimenting with derived mapping and the lower costs in preparing 1:2500 scale mapping by automated methods and limited projects at any required but preferably large scale of mapping on a cost-sharing basis in conjunction with outside bodies. Arrangements are in hand for the purchase of enough equipment to carry out this work, and to enable development to continue at the present level it is an essential objective of the short-term policy so to improve procedures and develop outlets such that the financial advantage of automation can be established beyond doubt. Until this can be done, no further progress towards the long-term objective can be contemplated.'

This very clear and concise lead from the top of Ordnance Survey with regard to what was soon to be called digital mapping had followed almost a year of internal debate, as development continued. This debate extended to areas of wider concern. One such concern centred on copyright protection if there were ever to be digital data products. In the epoch before the Government's Whitford Commission was assembled to consider intellectual property rights, the question whether a tape containing digital data could be represented as an artistic work remained unresolved. This Commission eventually led to the emergence of the modern Copyright, Designs and Patents Act, which has enabled

Ordnance Survey to manage its intellectual property to the mutual benefit of customers and itself.

Another major aspect of the internal debate concerned who else might be authorised to digitise their maps if Ordnance Survey didn't. A memo from the Director General in May 1970 read 'detail which we have digitised can of course be sold in the normal way and may be the basis of an expanding trade. I would prefer it to be done in this way rather than by forcing others to do their own digitising, which is all the more reason for pressing ahead with a viable digitising system and the formation of our own databank as soon as equipment and "know-how" is at a sufficiently advanced state.' By taking this approach Ordnance Survey ensured a consistent national standard for the data and, whatever the rights and wrongs of copyright enforcement, it meant that the national mapping organisation could steadily, albeit slowly, construct a business around the emerging technology and by-products.

Ordnance Survey's approach to almost anything of significance that it attempted to do was, by traditional practice, still regulated and governed by a series of brief one topic 'policy statements'. These statements were reviewed by directors sequentially over the years for their continued relevance and currency. In effect, automated cartography was brought into line following the release of the policy statement. It was all the more surprising, even despite the underlying culture of the department, therefore, that the successful formulation of policy led next to a surprising and protracted debate amongst senior management about its release and propagation, either inside or outside the organisation. It is almost beyond belief, in retrospect, that the Director General's Committee decided that there was, indeed, no need for wider circulation and explanation of the policy statement.

It was this inclination toward secrecy and a profound unwillingness to communicate policy, for no real purpose whatsoever, that was to lead to continuing criticism of Ordnance Survey through the 1970s and into the 1980s. The policy statement, for those within Ordnance Survey who at least were aware of its existence, did lead to a clear demarcation of several aspects of responsibility for digital mapping as it entered a pilot production trial phase. The Director of Map Production was given clear responsibility for all aspects of the production and publication of 1:2500 scale mapping using digital techniques. The Director of Establishment and Finance, the most senior civil servant, who, the records show, was the major advocate of keeping policy under wraps, was given responsibility for staffing, training and so on.

The Director of Field Surveys, who already held responsibility for the Computer team was tasked with all computing aspects associated with digital mapping. Colonel Gardiner-Hill, still as Deputy Director of Planning and Development, was tasked with advising production on techniques and with continuing development work as directed by the Director General's Committee. It wasn't very long, following the internal release of the policy statement, before the Director of Map Production, Brigadier EPJ Williams, identified a need for an injection of middle and senior management who were aware of these developments and a further need for planning staff.

The development and release of the policy statement for digital mapping, despite the decision to keep it 'under wraps', was a major milestone for the project that would, in time, lead to the digitising of the basic-scale mapping archive of Great Britain by its original creator, Ordnance Survey. The policy statement set in train the pilot production project, which ran for almost 10 years before any substantial conclusion was to be drawn from it. The pilot production project fortunately was not limited simply to an evaluation of the production of a block of mapping as originally envisaged, but by staying in 'pilot production mode' for almost 10 years, a substantial quantity of mapping was captured as successive but disappointing cost-benefit analyses of digital production methods were made in parallel with slow-to-grow evidence of user requirements amongst Ordnance Survey's larger traditional customers.

During this period, when policy for the future of digital mapping was being developed within, a further external review of the nature and the operation of Ordnance Survey was established in 1970. This was the 'Janes Committee', which concerned itself mainly with questions of the services it should offer to potential customers, how these could best be provided and the clear need for Ordnance Survey to be more 'commercial' in its approach. Surprisingly, this formal review of Ordnance Survey failed to publish – in the conventional sense – any report at all, of its findings. However, in 1973 Sir Geoffrey Rippon MP, who held ultimate responsibility in Government for Ordnance Survey, eventually published the Committee's recommendations.

While not addressing any of the key issues associated with automated cartography, recommendations were made that would come to bear ultimately on its future. The most important of these recommendations was perhaps the release of Ordnance Survey from a previous obligation to publish each basic-scale map in chart paper form, as it was produced under the 1980 Plan or during its subsequent revision. The major conclusion from the Janes Review was that Ordnance Survey 'should make the survey information it collected available at basic scales, in such forms as may be appropriate to the needs of users'.

The Review also served to permit flexibility over the scale at which such maps were to be published. An indirect and perhaps unwitting result of this Review was that in setting more demanding cost-recovery targets for Ordnance Survey, amongst other things, for basic-scale mapping, it meant that the goal to achieve cost reductions and parity of costs between digital and conventional methods would be more difficult and the imperative to find customers for digital map data became substantially more pressing.

The year 1971 saw the start of planning and preparation for the pilot production phase of digital mapping. The textbook sequence of the first phase of experimental development to produce a workable production system was at least theoretically completed. The policy statement from the Director General in 1971 heralded the second phase, which would provide for the deployment of the results of experimentation in a formal pilot production trial. The pilot project was designed to enable the system, which had been developed and used by specialist and highly motivated staff, to produce results more routinely using the mix of staff to be found in a normal production environment, in a routine, disciplined production environment. The very act of creating the pilot and the selection of suitable staff to man it simply served to create a 'halo effect' on the staff chosen. Potentially at least, the act of selection tended to deny the 'normality' that the project sought.

Chapter 5
The role and impact of the ECU

It is all too easy, when looking back in review at the end of a project spanning almost three decades, to dismiss defining aspects and other influential factors in the very early and formative years as of limited impact on the eventual outcome. This certainly applies to the basic-scale map digitising project of Great Britain that Ordnance Survey undertook, simply because the start was so slow and hesitant and only yielded a very modest production contribution to the eventual outcome. The undoubted and ultimate success of the project grew out of an unspectacular lack of direction or real sense of purpose at the start. The early years saw a very modest commitment to the project, relative to the total resources available to the Department at the outset. The project in due course grew into an all-consuming industry involving a large proportion of Ordnance Survey's own production resources as well as most of the capacity of a network of successful private-sector digitising contractors, which Ordnance Survey had itself worked to create.

At the time when the seeds of this project were first sown, in the late 1960s and early 1970s, the impact of Ordnance Survey's more immediate past and its contemporary culture and attitudes were significant influences on the way in which the digitising project was conceived, implemented and driven forward in those early years. Ordnance Survey was fully committed to its current tasking, was extremely inward looking, very conservative, somewhat over planned and quite inflexible. It had become hostile to any external influences that came to bear on the Department, particularly if these were seen as likely to pose a distraction from its core task.

The post-war task had been established by the pre-war Davidson Committee and Ordnance Survey's considered implementation of its main recommendations. The technology and methodologies deployed continued to evolve and develop very slowly through the 1950s and 1960s. Generally, Ordnance Survey received resources adequate for this tasking from successive governments and was able to meet its self-imposed obligations with respect to the basic-scale map archive of Great Britain. Successive cycles of detailed and centralised planning made clear that the accomplishment of the end result, due in 1980, of the complete modernisation and metrication of the basic-scale mapping was assured if followed through without any significant distraction or diversion of resources from the planned programme.

These circumstances contributed to an overall environment of complacency with the ever-attendant risk that alternative approaches or different outcomes could easily be ignored or overlooked by those within Ordnance Survey, whose duty it was to deliver the chosen outcome. The constant comings and goings from relatively short-term military postings into almost all positions of influence or authority in the organisation and the resultant lack of long-term and visionary leaders apart from a very small number, served to sustain the negative and uncritical internal climate. It was therefore mainly to fall to outside influence or stimuli – of one sort or another – that could possibly trigger any fundamental change of approach to the task or the adoption of any additional burden.

The ECU came into existence as a result of sheer opportunism by its founder David Bickmore, in response to the rapid development of computer-based technology throughout the 1960s. The ECU, so utterly different in role, style and culture to the contemporary Ordnance Survey, proved variously to be an irritant, a stimulant and something of a conscience for Great Britain's national mapping organisation, particularly during the experimental phases of what became the national digitising project. The ECU, first created in 1967, had its origins in the Clarendon Press of the University of Oxford®, during the period from 1960 to1965. The seed for a unit deploying this new technology was Bickmore's 'Atlas of Britain' project. The atlas, although eventually published, contained widely acclaimed cartography but was criticised in respect of badly out-of-date information presented via the cartography of the atlas.

The information had seriously degraded following its collection because of the lengthy timescale associated with conventional procedures of drawing, editing and printing. The use of emerging computer-based technology to foreshorten production schedules was seen by Bickmore as the panacea for this particular and recurrent problem in the wider cartographic industry. The ECU had neither tradition nor track record, but it was relatively well funded initially and very well equipped, soon after its launch, with examples of state-of-the-art equipment, based on the rapidly evolving electronic computer.

The Unit was very much the brainchild of David Bickmore, who was to lead it for almost 10 years. He was a man of considerable charm: a well-connected establishment socialite, something of an academic in style despite his commercial experience with the Oxford University Press. As David Rhind has subsequently observed, he was adept at seeking and securing funds and support for his cause; he could quieten opposition very effectively and had the ability to fend off his detractors, given the newly elected Westminster Labour Government's increasing and prioritised emphasis on science and technology and their resolve to reform British science and harness technology.

Bickmore, with his influential contacts in the Royal Society, seized the opportunity to secure some of the new funding that was becoming available. His strong will, his widespread 'political' and academic contacts and his single-minded approach to achieving his goals, were all vital and instrumental in securing the necessary support and funding such that the ECU could be created. However, it was these self-same personal characteristics that were to contribute later to the uncertain relationship with Ordnance Survey as a possible client of, or collaborator with, his Unit. Further, the nature of his research and project staff, which he hired and with whom he surrounded himself, were also soon to contribute to the rather negative relationship with Ordnance Survey.

Almost all ECU staffers were fresh from university: well-armed with degrees and doctorates, all were very bright and able but most were without any real knowledge of the existing cartographic industry and its traditions, which their efforts were to be directed to changing. Most of Bickmore's staff came from sciences and backgrounds that were wholly alien to cartography as previously known and certainly to that traditionally deployed by Ordnance Survey. Cartography, by tradition, was an industry of conservatism and substantial discipline, usually characterised by slow change and very long lead times, the very characteristics which had contributed so materially to the failure of Bickmore's own atlas project.

ECU Project staff were in many cases quite 'unconventional' sometimes, in appearance and attitude, and appeared and acted rather differently to their counterparts in Ordnance Survey. They were innovative, questioning and independent in outlook. They tended to come and go from Bickmore's Experimental Unit, often in mid project, at times with quite serious damage to project schedules and results. The writer was personally present at one project meeting in the early 1970s when the ECU brought a small team to Ordnance Survey head office. One member of the ECU team, obviously very gifted and several years ahead of his time in fashion, sported both an earring and a 'pony tail' hairstyle. On appearance alone he was deemed by the brigadiers and colonels present not to be taken seriously by the best suited, 'short back and sides' senior military representatives of Ordnance Survey who were present at the meeting.

The ECU team in the years after its creation was relatively small in number and during the period of uneasy cooperation with Ordnance Survey, some 10 to 13 project staff were deployed at any one time on 6 or 7 quite different projects, many quite unrelated to the work of Ordnance Survey. Bickmore ran the unit autocratically but very much on project lines. He felt that his preferred modus operandi facilitated continuing customer contact (and hopefully continued financial support) through feedback on progress with each task, which afforded him regular opportunity to report his Unit's apparent successes in public.

Ordnance Survey, by well-founded and established tradition and a general lack of real opportunity over the years, was slow to make changes to the materials and the methodologies applied to its production tasks. Established practice was that the Department would only endorse and implement changes after laboured trials, in-depth review and prolonged consideration by an internal committee. The business that Ordnance Survey was in and its organisational structure and military management had always demanded great emphasis on individual craft skills of the technician work force. Ordnance Survey, of course, had always to consider the dominating demand of national mapping that the outputs from such a long-term task should be consistent in content and appearance within the discipline of the national specifications.

The investment cost of introducing new materials or equipment, the consequential costs and loss of output associated with retraining staff and the impact of change on the consistency of specification and appearance over an archive spanning some three decades of production effort, were all major considerations for Ordnance Survey, before any changes could be implemented. It is fair to conclude that Bickmore and his staff never really came to grips with such long-term considerations and values. He and his researchers neither grasped nor accepted this type of inherent cultural difference. Worse still, and because of the failure to create any real climate of trust between the two organisations, Ordnance Survey very soon came to believe that results and outcomes reported by the ECU were often not sustainable, based – as they frequently were on results of short-lived trials – generally using very small samples, which, on occasion, might be 'fixed' by very innovative personnel.

Many of the ECU projects carried out on behalf of Ordnance Survey were felt not to be pursued to the same rigorous standards normally associated with Ordnance Survey's own inhouse development trials and other investigations. Some critics concluded that results claimed by Bickmore and his project staff were overstated, often the outcome of what Ordnance Survey came to regard as non-rigorous testing of hastily written software and generally poor post-project evaluation. The reputation that soon came to bedevil the ECU and its clients the most, however, was one of very poor project timekeeping. Almost invariably, the previously agreed deadlines for various phases of each project were simply missed and often unreported by the ECU project staff involved. These sins of omission were most often associated with a natural tendency to overcommit resources on an ever-widening portfolio of projects, either inspired in-house or by unsuspecting 'customers'. Most project staff were not adept at 'customer care' and were disarmingly frank about the Unit's and their own shortcomings. All this was absolute anathema to Great Britain's national mapping authority.

The inescapable fact was that the reality of the relationship between Ordnance Survey and the ECU came from the mix between the extreme perceptions of the lumbering, jealous and suspicious Ordnance Survey and the dynamic, rather flashy research unit, which was desperately seeking a sustained role, ever more clients and increasing funds and a desirable reputation. Most of the friction and mistrust that eventually surfaced was the result of perceptions and misconceptions, but behaviour on both sides tended to confirm basic assumptions, prejudice, worst fears and deep suspicions. The ECU once created and, during its early mission and task-finding phase managed to create a genuine concern, if not fear, inside Ordnance Survey, that its long-established role and the funding for its fulfilment might somehow be challenged, weakened or subverted by these 'new kids on the block'.

Discussion of such a threat at the highest level inside Ordnance Survey is documented in contemporary records. This perception and consequent fear on the part of Ordnance Survey was heightened when the ECU had already quite successfully developed experimental facilities employing the new technologies that Ordnance Survey hadn't. It is necessary to question why the relationship between Ordnance Survey and ECU wasn't perhaps more productive. Maybe with different personalities at the respective helms, the two organisations might have succeeded in fulfilling complementary roles to their mutual benefit. The ECU had, unfortunately, arrived before Ordnance Survey had formulated any real plans to harness the new technologies of the computer age for cartography.

Internal investigations in this direction were vested in a very small number of relatively junior staff at Ordnance Survey. There was in parallel an absence of any top-down strategic direction ahead of those reported in the previous chapter from within Ordnance Survey in connection with such matters. The ECU continued to make rash and unsubstantiated claims for its prowess at a variety of public gatherings it organised. This caused genuine concern inside Ordnance Survey for fear that their government paymaster or even customer groupings might come to suspect that there was an alternative approach that might benefit them. In reality it quickly became clear that the ECU, its projects and their results typically suffered many major shortcomings, most of their own making. Deadlines, so beloved of Ordnance Survey, were frequently missed or simply ignored in a manner which Ordnance Survey staff came to regard as typical but no less cavalier. These failures largely stemmed from, overconfidence in the face of major problems and the innate optimism of the bright young people that Bickmore gathered round himself.

They simply regarded almost anything or any outcome as possible. The ECU leader and his project staff tended not to factor in to project schedules the inherent unreliability of contemporary hardware, and weaknesses in maintenance and support which were on a scale almost beyond belief and understanding in the context of the performance of latter-day technology. Much of ECU's project work either required innovative software to be developed or technology to be applied to the cartographic task that can best be described as at the 'leading edge' of development. Almost all tasks attempted in these early years were beyond the bounds of any past experience. There is no doubt that ECU project staff were guilty, on several occasions, of 'talking up' results which could not be confirmed following Ordnance Survey's typically rigorous analysis and review of results.

As the ECU cast about for a portfolio of more and differing clients and for different tasks, contention for the very limited resources available within the Unit certainly occurred. It was from such circumstances that missed deadlines most frequently occurred. Never subject to either rigorous discipline or effective project management, the ECU gradually lost any real focus and sense of direction in terms of the sort of task that Ordnance Survey wanted pursued. Although both parties continued to maintain some formal and informal contact, the tense relationship between the two organisations gradually weakened as they set off in quite different directions. The ECU was, from the outset, a research unit by definition and inclination. It suffered from its mixed agenda with generally inconsistent and often competing objectives. It most certainly never had the staying power, the resources or the discipline required for any lengthy and sustained digital production task such as that which Ordnance Survey would eventually define and implement over such a long period.

However, the concern which had developed within Ordnance Survey that the ECU might somehow either supplant Ordnance Survey's national mapping role or its apparent willingness or ability to conduct relevant and applied research, did stimulate in-house progress with automation. Ordnance Survey, sensitive and protective of its established role, feared that doubt might be raised within government itself by a successful and proselytising ECU leader. Ordnance Survey feared being seen as unable or unwilling to adapt to and to master emerging computer technology and all that was rashly claimed for it within the realm of its national mapping task.

The ECU did undoubtedly achieve substantial progress in harnessing the new technology and in making it work on cartographic projects. Their efforts by the very nature of the organisation soon lost focus on almost all that it attempted. Pioneering work was done in a variety of fields, such as data formats and structures and in terms of data standards. Much of this early work was never picked up again in later mainstream development work associated with digital mapping. Even on the ill-fated Ordnance Survey/ECU Bideford project, a variety of mapping was produced quite successfully by the ECU, albeit delivered much later than originally promised.

Upon rigorous examination, however, the results of this extended cooperation failed to meet Ordnance Survey's needs in terms of required goals or standards. Following assessment, Ordnance Survey quickly concluded that ECU software could not be 'production hardened' without a great deal of further investment and effort. Also, having continued to use 'stream digitising' methods as the standard capture technique, which Ordnance Survey had quickly realised was not the best approach to be applied to the needs of the more geometrical detail of urban large-scale mapping, the ECU production technique was not really seen as 'forward compatible'. It was this and a gradual but discernible shift by the ECU away from the type of work that Ordnance Survey needed to tackle (possibly stimulated by the backgrounds and interests of then current ECU staff) to a much greater emphasis on the mapping of statistical data of one sort or another that really brought the eventual break with Ordnance Survey.

David Rhind (eventually and until 1998 the Director General of Ordnance Survey) in a paper entitled 'The Incubation of Geographic Information Systems in Europe' identified a causal link between early ECU projects and the world's first digital production flowline that was created by Ordnance Survey in the early 1970s. To the writer, who was closely involved for some of the time at least in the liaison between the two bodies, the contribution of the ECU was limited to helping to create a clearer perception of what in fact might be possible, to assisting in building confidence in the few Ordnance Survey staff involved with the operations and to a nagging external challenge to keep going largely because the underlying ECU culture was to say that almost anything at all by way of development really was possible.

In an earlier review of the contribution of the ECU entitled 'Personality as a Factor in the Development of a Discipline: The example of Computer Assisted Cartography', David Rhind attempted to assess the nature of what he saw as the limited contribution of the ECU. In terms of Ordnance Survey and its eventual project to digitise the basic-scale mapping inventory, the ECU proved to be something of a stimulant and a catalyst, at times an irritant to Ordnance Survey complacency. The ECU was a very useful information source concerning the practicality and functionality of some of the early equipment on the market. Irrational concern about what ECU might do or say in public if Ordnance Survey chose to ignore the potential of the new technology should not be underestimated in assessing the role of the ECU in relation to the Ordnance Survey Digital Mapping Project.

Chapter 6
From experimentation to pilot production trials of digital mapping

In-house experimentation with automated cartographic techniques at Ordnance Survey head office, before the founding of the pilot trials, following the Director General's short- and medium-term policy statement in late 1971, lacked well-defined goals and realistic strategic direction from higher up the hierarchical management structure. Development work in connection with automating cartographic processes was disjointed and unsystematic in approach. Experimentation was driven generally by the individuals engaged on confronting its potential and challenges. The small 'team' that was involved tackled issues and aspects as they cropped up. At no time was there a broad research brief to design, develop and implement a system by a particular point in time.

Whilst in almost all other aspects Ordnance Survey worked in a very formal and systematic manner, in this particular case there was no feeling at all of 'top down' direction or control. Looking back to this period at Ordnance Survey, if it is possible to distil a wider departmental view from this time, the experimentation was seen initially almost as an eccentricity, or at best, a relatively obscure minor interest that could only really serve to distract from the real business of the Department. There was no evidence then or since of the existence of a concept of a long-term strategic objective to harness the power of the computer to assist with or even, eventually, remove tedious production processes. Possibly until Gardiner-Hill's arrival at Ordnance Survey there was no one of sufficient rank who could relate the results from individual trials and experiments to the wider departmental task.

The overall amount of effort put into experiments with automated cartography was contained at a very low level, both in terms of the minimal capital investment made and in the very small number of staff deployed on work connected with all experimental development generally inside Ordnance Survey. Records of meetings at this particular time reveal that when the topic of automation cropped up, a strong desire was usually expressed amongst members of Ordnance Survey's senior management, to let others (for example, the ECU or other organisations such as universities) first establish what could be achieved by the new technology. Such a strategy was seen to prevent disruption of the paramount task of the Department to complete the 1980 task established by the pre-war Davidson Committee. Eventually, the wider concern and scepticism about the ECU's often overstated claims, already described, about what it said it could do and, in a sense, describing what Ordnance Survey was felt unable, or unwilling, to do, did at least create some internal debate.

The vitally important 1971 policy directive from the Director General of the day marked the end of this initial and uncertain epoch. Scepticism about any benefits to be gained from automating production processes and the need to increase the pace with further development work and investment were, at last, put into a fresh and proper perspective. Whilst prejudice and bias – typically manifesting itself in criticism, lack of support and even lack of cooperation where conflict for resources occurred – persisted quite widely within Ordnance Survey for many more years, the Director General's policy announcement made it possible for those involved with automated cartography to claim legitimacy for their efforts. Materially, it meant that the projected use of automated cartography, its need for investment and a further allocation of resources, at last, began to appear in formal departmental planning procedures. This led in turn to the consequential allocation of resources, albeit at a very humble level initially.

The key objectives of the pilot trial were twofold. The primary objective was to develop and establish rigorous procedures for digitising, drafting and editing of rural map data at 1:2500 scale, thereby testing the effectiveness in production of the automated methods devised to date, whilst obtaining reliable production cost data. This objective was set with a view to the eventual sale of the data in digital form and the automated production of the final drawing, from which maps could be published. This goal of the pilot sought to determine the economics of map production in a more realistic production rather than an experimental environment performing a very substantial sample of work. The secondary objective sought to evaluate consequential computer loading arising from an enlarged digital mapping activity ahead of a future mainframe computer upgrade. The trial was further also seen as a catalyst in the stimulation of usage of digital map data by customers, either existing or new to Ordnance Survey.

At the time of the policy statement by the Director General, Ordnance Survey possessed only one rather unreliable digitising table upon which all the experiments to date had been conducted. This first very quirky digitising table was quickly augmented, following the Director General's late 1971 directive, by the purchase of two Bendix Freescan tables assembled and supplied by Ferranti, UK. Soon after this acquisition, a Ferranti flatbed master plotter with a light spot projector plotting head was also purchased, in April 1972. This particular equipment was chosen from an original 'shopping list' previously assembled and intensively evaluated during Ordnance Survey's thorough appraisal of digital mapping equipment that was considered suitable and available.

'Buying British' equipment was a major consideration imposed on government departments at this particular time. The Government's view of 'the white heat of the technological revolution' enforced this aspect of equipment acquisition. In any case, the prospect of reliable UK-based service and support together with competitive pricing were seen as deciding criteria. The all too familiar unreliability of contemporary electronic and electro-mechanical equipment, which had characterised almost all known uses at Ordnance Survey, other JASB departments and the ECU itself to date, meant that responsive support and service were issues of prime importance, if such equipment was to be deployed in a production, as opposed to a research, environment. Clearly any significant equipment 'downtime' would only lead to high levels of 'indirect' or non-productive time for production staff, who conventionally worked within a very disciplined system of recording their time in great detail to specific processes in conventional production flowlines. To date, staff employed on experimental work had simply diverted to 'other activities' when equipment failed.

Ferranti Ltd, with its works and head office in Edinburgh, had made rapid and sustained progress within the field of computer-aided design and drafting. Perhaps encouraged by the progress that Ordnance Survey had made, Ferranti managed to position themselves as a very credible UK supplier, both in terms of product development and system integration, following a significant decision taken by them a few years earlier: that there appeared to be valuable business to be won in this segment of the emerging electronics market.

There was almost no real guidance in the 1971 policy statement with regard to the scale, the duration and the level of investment to be made in the proposed pilot production trial project. However, following the initial equipment acquisitions Gardiner-Hill was soon to seek Ordnance Survey senior management approval to purchase a further six digitising tables later in 1972. Approval to upgrade the performance of the Calcomp drum plotter, which had been the 'work horse' for all graphic output from data up to this point, was also sought and won by Ordnance Survey's Development Branch. It was at this point in time that the decision was made to transfer the management and control of the pilot production trial from Development Branch to Cartography Division (the actual production 'factory' of Ordnance Survey).

With a few exceptions, this transfer was not practically welcomed by the hierarchy of the receiving cartographic management, who regarded the venture variously as 'nonessential', a 'distraction', a 'plaything' of indulged graduates and 'outsiders' or, at best, a system, that might well 'blow up' in their hands and with which, in the prevailing climate of blame at Ordnance Survey when things went wrong, they might well be associated. There was some considerable realism and truth here as experimentation and development had certainly taken place in the informal and 'rarefied' atmosphere of Ordnance Survey's embryonic research and development function. Almost inevitably 'everything worked very well when it left us' soon became something of a frequently heard joke between those directly involved with handing over the embryonic and soon to be scaled up facility and those receiving it.

This had the rather obvious connotation that 'it had all gone wrong' at or after, transfer. Support and cooperation at the working level by the folk in development after transfer, however, remained enthusiastic, with all involved committed to the project's eventual success. It was at times when there was very real contention for scarce resources or when outputs from automated cartography were critically reviewed that the more conservative minds inside Ordnance Survey, at all levels, indulged in destructive criticism. Development Branch, which had relinquished day-to-day responsibility for the project, was still tasked with liaison with

Computer Services staff and with troubleshooting and support for the pilot project.

However, the very limited personnel resources of two young graduate staff from the Joint Survey Service, on short-term tours of duty and who previously had been dedicated to matters connected with digital mapping development, were quickly diverted to what were seen as the important issues of map and detail 'generalisation' and the development of procedures to derive small-scale mapping from the basic-scale map data. Thus the concept of 'generalisation' (perhaps best summarised as the simplification and selection of images), long the 'holy grail' of traditional cartographers, once more diverted attention of those involved away from the fundamental task of capturing basic-scale map data in digital form. It was felt that success in employing computer techniques would add considerably to the cost justification of the emerging technology.

Mapping under the 1980 Plan, scheduled to be taken up first by the pilot project, covered some 60 square kilometres of 1:2500 scale mapping of an area of south Hampshire centred on the town of Waterlooville. The Director General's policy statement was timely in that it coincided with the eventual emergence of a customer interest dimension for a digital map data product. Increasingly, as time passed, customers would come to influence which areas that the pilot project would take up. A subsequent senior management committee decision to use the pilot flowline also to produce new additions (triggered by twin criteria of age since last published and the amount of change on the ground) proved to be somewhat antagonistic to the plan to complete blocks of mapping for this fresh initiative served only to produce the unwelcome 'pepper pot' effect of scattered maps in digital format.

Hampshire County Council and the Department of the Environment's Location Referencing Coordinating Committee (on which Ordnance Survey was represented by its Development Branch) had shown interest in the prospect of having a large block of digital map data in this particular area. This particular area was of interest to them for their own experiments using the map information. Ordnance Survey clearly had to balance such external requests, which were not firm commercial orders, with the demands of planning their own 1980 task production. With the prospect of a further six digitising tables being deployed and with the now pressing need to keep all tables fully loaded on a production flowline that, at this very early stage, included so many 'off table' operations dictated by the successive stages of the pilot flowline, additional areas of 1:2500 scale mapping in south Herefordshire and south Worcestershire were also soon allocated to the production loading of the embryonic digital mapping production capacity. The rather optimistic target date of June 1973 for both areas was set for the capture of all the point-and-line map detail and text contained in the mapping.

At this stage the use of symbols had not been included. Data capture was made on the digitising table from a 5:3 enlarged field document at 1:1500 scale, which gave the digitising operator a larger and clearer target at which to point the cross hairs of the hand-held cursor.

An interesting and early development associated with the digital mapping pilot project was the requirement to identify individual maps which had been produced by digital techniques. In 1972 Ordnance Survey's Planning Unit asked to be able to distinguish such map sheets for internal housekeeping purposes and to distinguish such sheets for customers. A typical in-house debate between the use of a footnote or symbol on each published map then followed. The latter prevailed and what became known as the 'digital snail' symbol was surprisingly quickly devised in Development Branch. It was implemented with almost no adverse comment from elsewhere in the Department.

The symbol itself purported to represent a reel of magnetic tape with the words 'DIGITAL MAP' positioned round the NW quadrant of the spool running out of a bolder outer' edge of the tape spool. The cynics and the many non-believers in the Department claimed that a snail was a very appropriate logo for a slow-moving project. It was also at this particular time that a formal call to abandon the old terminology of 'automated cartography' in favour of 'digital mapping' was finally accepted and implemented. Still largely reflecting the prevailing view inside Ordnance Survey that this new approach was simply an alternative cartographic tool, the digital symbol was only implemented top right and lower left on the standard grid and border master next to the symbol denoting a fully metricated map (an aspect of the 1980 plan).

It was into this master framework that the master plot of the digital data for the map sheet itself, up to the sheet's neat line, was then dropped during a final, reprographic process before the printing plate was made. From this point onwards all printed map sheets emerging from the pilot production flowline bore the 'digital snail' symbol.

It was at a relatively early stage in the pilot production project, as reliable feedback and suggestions started to come from operatives and their line management, that improved facilities were first considered and then developed jointly by Development Unit and Computer Unit staff. These improvements were implemented in the digital mapping procedures and software, but in a rather ad hoc and often undocumented manner. This in turn made the collection of data on production times and costs somewhat unreliable. Changes to software and production techniques, either to correct obvious shortcomings or to improve procedures, were applied as 'fixes' and not released in a disciplined fashion using 'version management'. This was to prove to be a material weakness, striking adversely at the prime objective of the pilot project to collect reliable comparative costing data between conventional and digital methods.

The first truly significant innovation saw the ingenious use of a conceptual mathematical 'spline' in a curve-fitting procedure, which had been picked up and the theory developed by Colonel Gardiner-Hill from published work by McConologue (see bibliography item 3 for references). This procedure replaced the need for the digitiser operator to encode dense but sufficient points along a curvilinear line on the map in 'stream' mode of digitising, whereby coordinate sets were captured at a predetermined time or distance interval, to define a curvilinear line on the map. To engage the curve-fitting routine in the post-processing software, the digitiser operator simply flagged the start and end of a curvilinear feature by depressing a key on the hand-held cursor and then needed only to select the key control points through which the mathematical 'spline' could be computed and passed, thereby providing sufficient data points to replicate the line on the map. This effectively ended the use of digitising in 'stream' mode at Ordnance Survey, which in turn led to the specification of simpler and cheaper digitising equipment.

This move also created a major difference of approach from that of the ECU. This particular enhancement alone achieved a 50% time saving in the capture of rural mapping and, at the same time, achieved a significant increase in the quality of representation of curvilinear map features only at the rather modest expense of some additional operator training and a modest increase in computer processing time. This proved to be a most significant and welcome improvement to the digitising task. In terms of practical development, this new approach to data capture must be ranked alongside the earlier development at Ordnance Survey of the 'feature menu' concept for applying numerical 'feature codes' to map detail during capture.

The delay between operator hand and machine gantry movement, particularly over large distance shifts on the original Dmac digitising table, precluded earlier development of the 'menu' system. The breakthrough in digitising efficiency on the new 'solid state' digitising equipment that the 'menu' had brought freed the operator from tediously setting keys on the digitising unit's controller before each different map feature was encoded. Under the new system, all the feature codes were set out individually and permanently on the digitising table by means of a small box for each feature code, but outside the area required for the map input graphic.

With the position of each particular menu box, in table coordinates already stored in the computer, by the act of moving the cursor to a box and selecting a point within it, the correct feature code for all of the same features on the map were assigned automatically to all subsequent map data. Work could continue on all similar features until the feature code needed to be changed once more by the same procedure. Other improvements to the digitising system saw further development work on the original concept of housing 'macros'. Following further work this concept was evaluated with checks on the ground and, indeed, was given much further consideration.

This particular concept involved the identification of identical house/building outlines on the mapping. The 'footprint' of the first house of its type was digitised as a 'macro', which was then used to encode all other houses of this type by a simple repeat command by the operator in all situations where it was found to occur. The house 'macro' simply needed the encoding of a position and an orientation. This was seen as a further means of speeding up and refining the data-capture procedure. Eventually, the use of a 'macro' was abandoned after a great deal of effort was expended.

The early months of the pilot project were characterised by the heavy demands placed by the pilot project's management on members of Development Branch and the staff in the Computer Unit. All such staff were fully engaged on systems analysis and programming to enhance the production procedures and software and, indeed, to 'troubleshoot' the many everyday difficulties and problems inevitably encountered by the staff selected to work on the first phase of the pilot project. Another major issue concerned the equipment performance and reliability when it was used more or less continuously in a production environment.

A problem of almost catastrophic proportions bedevilled the early months of the pilot project. It was originally laid at the door of the digitising equipment itself. However, this particular problem was eventually found to be caused by the mains electricity power supply to the production unit area at Ordnance Survey head office. The area was very prone to voltage 'spikes', which led in turn to very frequent losses of origin on the digitising table and a calamitous failure of the particular task on the table when the 'spike' occurred. These high voltage 'spikes' were eventually found to be caused by the tube lighting system installed years before in the drawing offices and also by the start-up of heavy equipment such as printing presses elsewhere in the building.

The first few months of the pilot trial witnessed many such losses. They caused a significant lowering of morale of all those involved, before the problem could be identified and remedial action taken to create a clean mains electricity supply to the digital mapping production cell. The Calcomp drum plotter, which was used extensively to produce 'edit plots' on the flowline, also continued to give problems, both in its reliability and its limited capacity. The search began with some urgency for alternative or further equipment for this purpose that could be deployed on the pilot task.

With the embryonic pilot production project firmly located within the most conservative 'heartland' of Ordnance Survey and with the array of never-ending problems and difficulties, it soon came to be regarded variously as something of a joke by traditionalists and a threat by others in terms of the loss of valued but traditional skills within 'cartography'. By far the most determined bastion of negative conservatism inside Ordnance Survey was the very substantial unit within the 'cartographic factory' called 'Large Scale Examination'. The writer managed this area during his initial period at Ordnance Survey. This unit, as well as having responsibility for the examination of all completed work issuing from conventional flowlines, and whilst serving as Ordnance Survey's quality control mechanism, also had responsibility for the 'classing' of cartographic draughtsmen and women as it was termed.

This was the name given to the monitoring procedure used during the development of cartographic staff from raw trainees right through to the stage of being fully trained and competent to perform production operations with limited supervision. Management's decision to treat the digital production effort no differently to traditional operations simply served to introduce a series of new problems and difficulties within cartographic production. The procedure of 'classing' involved the rigorous scrutiny, in infinite detail, of all work produced before a draughtsman or woman could be 'licensed' as fully competent. Even after this point was reached all his or her outputs received intense and detailed scrutiny.

Readers should be aware that beside this routine but rigorous examination of all outputs, the contemporary culture of Ordnance Survey still jealously preserved the long-established practice of the 'catch'. All levels of management in the hierarchy of the cartographic factory (some six grades in all, right through to the Director General) hosted a monthly 'catch'. A sample of the mapping that had been produced in the previous month, reducing serially in volume as it moved up the management grade structure, was scrutinised: 'plants' of errors to 'reward' ever more senior vigilance were a feature of this traditional practice.

The 'catch' was scrutinised formally in great detail at every level in the hierarchy and in the event of any shortcomings or errors being found, these were classified as either 'serious' or 'other'. In the case of large-scale mapping, it was in the Examination Area that 'examiner's remarks' were recorded formally for each task received, before being returned to the errant draughtsperson through line management for his or her education and for correction, before resubmission. The management of Examination Section also had ultimate responsibility for finding suitable remedial action for errors, however they were found, on published mapping.

The first large-scale maps bearing the 'digital snail' that passed though these conservative and well-established procedures took a very bad beating, and the pent-up conservatism and hostility of traditional cartography quickly spilled over. A digital map of this era certainly looked quite different in appearance. This was most notably so in respect of the type style used in digital processes. Also there was a variety of shortcomings on early maps, but most were very minor in nature. They were certainly visible when magnified as they almost always were through a magnifying linen tester, which had always been the 'iconic badge of honour' of the large-scale map examiner.

Early digital maps passing through Large Scale Examination received upwards of 300 examiner's comments, whereas 30 was more typical for conventional production of a two square kilometre map sheet at 1:2500 scale by a competent cartographer. As a result, a smouldering Gardiner-Hill. In both senses, because his route through Ordnance Survey could also be tracked as a result of his habitually smoking foul-smelling French cigars, led his team at very short notice into Large Scale Examination Section for the inevitable 'showdown'.

Following this robust meeting, some interim guidelines were issued to examiners, but overall there was almost no 'meeting of minds'. Just how the new approach to production could be adapted to traditional approaches and practices and vice versa exercised many minds and consumed much effort in the early days of the pilot production project, as outputs began to emerge in increasing numbers. The fundamental instinct of Ordnance Survey's senior line management remained, as ever, to 'force fit' the new approach to the tried and trusted processes of management, which had served the Department for such a long time. Ordnance Survey in 1972–73 was still largely an organisation of closed minds suffering from what could best be described as 'tunnel vision', explained, at least in part, by being borne down by the magnitude of its tasking, by its itinerant management and by its very traditions.

Meanwhile, work on further improvements to digital mapping production procedures continued. A series of enhancements to procedures were introduced early in 1973. These changes included a software routine for house and building 'squaring' in all cases that occurred on the map where the surveyor had not annotated detail as 'not square,' on the field document. A second enhancement provided, at least, a partial solution to the age-old problem of 'edgematching' the common edge of neighbouring map sheets. Because of these changes and for a wide range of other reasons, technical problems and delays beset and characterised production in the pilot project during these early months.

In truth, many problems that occurred in the early months were more to do with the transfer of the task from the experimental and 'fixing' environment of Development Branch to the more disciplined production environment that had traditionally implemented and operated only well-tested and well-proven methods and materials for production flowlines. In truth, and although uncomfortable for all concerned, this period of realism certainly justified the decision to 'scale up' to a pilot production project located in the true production environment of Ordnance Survey.

This transfer imposed a discipline and rigour on all concerned, and most importantly of all on those employees charged with continuing development and improvement. The small group of project operatives themselves, who had initially been selected by Development staff, generally remained enthusiastic but their fate was that they continued to operate within a wholly sceptical atmosphere of the wider Ordnance Survey cartographic production area. Many inevitably suffered a conflict of loyalty, but they were generally willing and, in some cases, quite innovative.

A very cheerful and personable character called Bernard Robertson, who had a solid conventional cartographic production background, assumed responsibility for the day-to-day management of the pilot production project. He quickly managed to build good team spirit, which, to some extent, helped to cope with the inevitable ups and downs in staff morale. The cartographers who had been selected or who volunteered to serve the future were generally young and in almost all cases brighter than their more normal duties had demanded. They soon identified improved procedures and techniques and embraced some of the characteristics of the development staff.

Day-to-day problems, if anything, increased at this time and further served to interfere with production output. A source of many of these problems initially was the reliability and the capacity of the Calcomp drum edit plotter as production levels began to increase. Turnround times for edit plots lengthened and scheduling work on and off digitising tables became increasingly difficult. As a result of these problems, an important purchase of a novel and a very fast flatbed plotting system, manufactured by an American company called Xynetics, was made after intense evaluation and trials at their premises. Once commissioned, it was hoped that this system would easily bear the increased load for edit plots.

It was at this same time in 1973 that the very first attempt was made to assess the cost of the digital production flowline. Because of the great many difficulties that had beset the project from the outset, the very low level of production output achieved by then and possibly the desire of some in quite senior positions to see the venture killed off, there was already a growing concern at this time about the economics of the digital approach and, indeed, about its very justification. But with great instability in the production flowline, largely caused by rapidly changing procedures and software and very limited outputs, this first attempt at costing the

97

production process was fortunately seen as likely to be unreliable and was soon abandoned for the time being and then rescheduled for the future. The encouragement and the perhaps ill-founded optimism of Gardiner-Hill and his staff and low level but sustained interest outside Ordnance Survey gradually began to have an effect on the attitude of the Department's senior management to the project.

Developments of digital procedures followed very quickly. The recently acquired Xynetics edit plotter, although very impressive technically with fast 'hover' bearing technology, continued to suffer irritating 'teething' problems. After installation at Ordnance Survey head office, the software, which ran on a Hewlett-Packard® computer, proved to be unreliable. At the end of 1973, following a decision by Ordnance Survey to expand digitising capacity for the pilot production trial, an important fresh technical approach was developed by Ferranti, which was adopted by Ordnance Survey.

This important development took account of the increased power, reducing costs and the increasing reliability of mini computers. It afforded the prospect of much cheaper digitising equipment costs. Six new Ferranti Freescan digitising tables were purchased, but instead of each having their own magnetic tape storage facility, the tables were configured in a processor-controlled digitiser (PCD) system linked to a Digital Equipment Corporation (DEC) PDP 11/05 mini computer. This controller managed and stored the production output of all digital map data from the linked tables. This configuration had capacity for further extension if additional digitising capacity were required for the pilot project. This first expansion at last provided a spare capacity margin for the training of new digitiser operators. This took about two months for each person who already had a previous background of scribing the conventional large-scale maps.

In 1973 a fresh approach to the digitising task was adopted with an evaluation of the 1:1250 task attempted in terms of its production by digital methods. Although much of the coverage at this particular map scale had already been completed under the 1980 plan, these maps portrayed the most dynamic parts of the country in terms of change on the ground thereby justifying frequent revisions. Ordnance Survey planned to publish serial new editions of such maps by tedious and time-consuming conventional methods, according to published 'age and change' criteria. Production methods had already been developed that precluded the redrawing of all unchanged detail. The previous vision of two Director Generals and Gardiner-Hill had predicted the use of digital techniques for this never-ending task.

For the initial evaluation, six maps at 1:1250 scale, with an eighty per cent 'density rating', which was felt to represent average data volumes for this map series, were selected. These sample maps were given to experienced Grade 4 draughtsmen and women and to some relatively inexperienced Cartographic Assistant operatives to digitise. They turned in times of 15.8 and 21.5 hours per sheet respectively for initial digitising. With tables at this time yielding only 33 hours production time per week, empirical rates of 1.8 x 1:1250 maps using all staff and 3.5 x 1:2500 maps again using all staff, per table per week were deduced from these trial digitisings and these rates were used for subsequent resource and output planning purposes by Ordnance Survey. Shift-based operations were not considered at all at this time, largely because of the sense of complacency and lack of urgency of the task.

It was also about this time that Ordnance Survey was becoming increasingly aware of emerging interest in large-scale digital map data by potential customers. The local authorities of Derby and Bradford and the commercial customer Marconi® Ltd all made early contact. These early potential users were soon to be followed by other local authorities at Washington (Tyne and Wear), Tamworth, Telford and Northamptonshire. Consequent upon this upsurge in interest by potential customers, the main issues of copyright in digital map data and its licensed use were first raised and considered in any depth at Ordnance Survey. Further, there was an urgent and continuing imperative coming from the top of the Department to cost the embryonic production flowlines within Ordnance Survey. However, the costing data collected to date was considered unreliable and therefore unable to guide the Department in taking important and necessary decisions in connection with the future of digital mapping.

A further expansion of digitising capacity by five more digitising tables on the PCD system, aimed at balancing outputs with existing plotter capacity, was sought and agreed.

Finally, a more stable unit of experienced staff was achieved by project management. This unit was felt capable of producing reliable costing data for both 1:1250 scale and 1:2500 scale flowlines by no later than July 1974. As this fresh initiative was launched, hopefully to document the cost differential between conventional and digital production methods, the Director General's Committee gave the management of the pilot production project surprisingly clear guidance. 'While acquisition of data couldn't yet be achieved without incurring extra cost, nevertheless data would clearly represent an additional asset potentially at least, with great value. The contemporary project initiated with PMA Associates, funded by the Department of the Environment (DOE), to re-engineer digital map data already captured, could lead to increased user benefits and, therefore, an increased demand for data.'

The earlier decision that, subject to the financial viability of the pilot production project, the next logical aim was to be full implementation to produce a national databank of map information was not felt to be appropriate at this time as justification could not be made in financial terms, and because the necessary mainframe computer replacement proposal didn't really have to be made just yet. The size of the eventual databank and the use expected of it would be key determinants in sizing the next mainframe computer system. However, whilst it was concluded that there was sufficient justification to continue with the pilot production project, vitally with a need to obtain reliable cost data for a much larger head of work, there was also clearly scope for greater cooperation with those local authorities that had already approached Ordnance Survey to obtain digital map data for their trials.

There was also felt to be considerable scope to achieve much greater economy in digital map production as staff became more experienced and the systems became evermore refined and efficient. At a time of flagging morale of most of those working on the digitising project, the Director General of the day concluded this rather uplifting communique with a call to his colleagues to redefine and to publicise the key objectives for the pilot production project.

The next stumbling block for costing the digitising project was the enforced three-day working week forced upon Ordnance Survey as a result of widespread and national trade union industrial action. As a result, a mains electrical supply was not available at other times. On a more positive note, some improvements to the master plotter system became available from the manufacturer. A new controlling computer, a new and greatly enhanced plot programme developed by Ferranti Ltd based on Ordnance Survey's previous experience and needs, which had been fed back to the supplier during productive liaison visits, and, finally, a rotational capacity in the plotter head designed to permit the rotation of symbols, all meant the situation with regard to final plotting of maps really did start to improve.

Persistent and previously intractable production problems associated with consistent and reliable edit plot production on the Xynetics plotter were solved by the introduction of pressurised Fisher® pens, a spin-off from America's space exploration programme. Given these improvements, which were implemented in an ad hoc manner, results achieved in this first phase of costing trial were:

Map scale	1:1250	1:2500
Number of maps digitised	42	1160
Number of maps printed	162	357
Unit cost of production September 1973	£312	£509
Unit cost of production July 1974	£302	£512
Conventional cost July 1974	£168	£299

This first phase of the pilot production project coincided with a period of very substantial wage inflation in the national economy of Great Britain. Ordnance Survey's production costs rose disproportionately because of its labour-intensive processes; and worse, but in parallel, the organisation suffered severe losses of experienced staff to other employers in the public and private sectors. Throughout the period of disappointing cost comparisons and perhaps coming as something of a distraction from that issue, hopes were again raised or rekindled of the prospect of cheaper derived mapping at 1:10000 and 1:25000 scales using the underlying large-scale digital map data, once it had been produced for large-scale purposes. However, this expectation had neither been justified nor proven by the end of 1974.

Throughout this period of critical evaluation, improvements to equipment, software and production procedures came thick and fast. They were introduced as soon as they became available, in a rather undisciplined manner. Really at no time could the digital map production system be described as either stable or mature. Pressure remained on all staff involved to achieve faster throughput times with consequential cost reductions. It soon became apparent that the Xynetics plotter had spare capacity for edit plot output. It was at this time that production output on the edit plotter was switched to colour as an aid to more efficient edit and correction.

In previous monochrome output mode, on dense sheets where line detail and unique feature serial numbers clashed, editing operatives found the task very difficult. Similarly, the master plotter also had spare capacity following a recent series of enhancements. The production flowlines had developed into a series of stops and starts with volume 'bulges' at bottleneck places. Flows of work through to completion were very uncertain and irregular. As a result, the previously and highly valued concept of providing job satisfaction, with one operator seeing through all processes for one map sheet, became increasingly difficult to manage. The perception of the passage of any one map sheet down the flowline was, at this time, one of slow and irregular progress. Traditionally, even if lengthy, tight flowline management and control had always been the hallmark of Ordnance Survey's production control on conventional operations.

The outstanding difficulty in making valid and legitimate cost comparison between digital and conventional methods was one of establishing reliable 'work measurement'. The concept of plan assessment rating or 'par value' on 1:1250 scale resurvey sheets by assessing map density' had always been employed in all areas of Ordnance Survey, as an aid to forecasting and monitoring throughput times in production.

This was seen as a common and balancing mechanism for widely differing map sheets to be digitised. It was also seen as the legitimate basis on which conventional and digital production costs could be compared. Unfortunately, no similar mechanism existed for the 1:2500 scale mapping, which was subject to much greater margins of variation in volume and density of map detail. The next formal attempt at costing digital map production took place in February 1975, with the following data recorded:

Map scale	1:1250	1:2500
Number of maps digitised	205	461
Number of maps printed	150	519
Cost of digital production	£383	£508
Percentage change	+26%	-1%
Conventional cost	£191	£342
Percentage change	+14%	+14%

Still not profiting from previous experience, these results were achieved not only during a time of further and perhaps inevitable flowline instability, but also during a time of rapid wage inflation. The results in the case of the production of 1:1250 scale resurvey maps by digital methods, in comparison with conventional methods, showed that the situation had clearly worsened since the previous assessment. The major cause of this problem was seen as the heavy commitment of supervisory time by the Grade 3 supervisor to check and to assure quality on the digital production line, particularly during a period of training of new recruits. The digital method was clearly more expensive and equally as labour-intensive.

If these new production techniques were ever to be justified, it was increasingly felt that it would need to be justified by factors other than lower cost of production. Interestingly, it is at this point that the concept of 'national interest' begins to emerge in the debate. This really does mark the emergence of realistic, strategic thinking at Ordnance Survey in terms of what digital mapping might possibly become as a key 'fuel' for a multiplicity of external users and for Ordnance Survey itself.

It became accepted that the previous approach of producing sporadic cover was neither an effective way of compiling a national topographic databank nor of facilitating derived map production, while also failing to satisfy emerging customer needs. However, the conclusion was drawn that to complete a national databank with so many maps already produced conventionally under the 1980 production plan, with each needing to be digitised, would, at current rates, prove to be very costly indeed. Any such task was seen by many, at this time, as merely duplicative effort.

Plans laid at budget-making time provided for a further increase in digitising capacity, with five further tables to supplement the PCD system and for one further edit plotter. The Director General's Committee, faced with unequivocal evidence of a worsening trend in digital flowline costs, finally concluded 'no new investment could be made unless it was justified by cheaper National Grid plan production (the 1980 plan) or until the decision is made that digital mapping is advisable in the national interest'. Surprisingly, there was widespread internal condemnation of the way that the performance and accountability report (PAR) value rating of the effort required for each digitising job had been applied. Those seeking to progress digital mapping felt that a well-established system had been badly misapplied in the case of the digital task.

The Director General attempted to 'shore up' the project and concluded 'the concept of digital mapping and the acquisition of a national database was a right and proper objective for Ordnance Survey. Increased effort should be put into tackling the problems. The following conclusions were drawn: digital mapping couldn't compete with conventional methods on cost grounds as an alternative production method but this had never been a sole objective. Further, if the creation of a digital databank or database of survey information as an alternative to the graphical record held on glass sheets were an objective, then the cost equation could be favourably modified.

The database could be viewed as having an asset value distinct from the value of graphical output. Limited experience to date indicated that the continuous revision of the digital database would be considerably more expensive than the conventional alternative. At the present time and state of the art, the flexibility of using a digital database as a resource for derived mapping appeared not to be as great as previously thought. A four times automatic reduction in scale was seen as the maximum possible without extensive redigitising or considerable manual intervention. With regard to savings on storage, any new digital system would have to run in tandem for a great many years with obvious duplication of costs, and the use of magnetic tape had the essential overhead costs of cyclically rewriting tapes to avoid deterioration of the magnetic image.

Undoubtedly a potential market for digital data beyond the conventional graphical products existed, but it would prove very difficult to quantify. It is for consideration whether Ordnance Survey should produce large-scale maps in digital form centrally or by others under licence. If demand for digital data grew significantly, outside help might be needed to assist. There existed a clear need to evaluate and gauge market demand for digital data as most external user applications to date had anecdotally at least not been able to demonstrate proven benefits. In any case, Ordnance Survey probably needed a lead time of two to five years ahead of market demand.

Although the particular conclusions and emphasis in the 1972 policy statement by the Director General still stood, these more recent conclusions came as something of a 'show-stopper' to all those working on and for the project. Almost all staff involved on the project felt that they had seen and sampled the future, which was now cast into serious doubt. The only comfort to those managing and working on the pilot project was a call by the Director General for a fundamental review of the staffing of the project. The decision not to invest further but to continue the pilot – merely as a substitute for conventional drawing and publishing – came as a major blow to a very upbeat morale which had been sustained through all the uncertainty and the ever-present frustration with equipment. The conclusion that an 'act of faith' could not be sustained or fuelled further could neither really be challenged with clearly stated market needs or with valid cost comparisons. What seemed clear was that Ordnance Survey would need to make early decisions for major investment when and if any national requirement for a topographic database could finally and firmly be established.

In May 1975, the Director General's Committee reignited the hopes of all concerned with a call to seek further cost-benefit information for the several factors in the original and rather damning internal report on the state of digital mapping. For the immediate future, production and cost data would be collected on a different basis. The new plan was that the work of an experienced production subsection would be monitored separately, when some system improvements had been implemented. Specifically, the performance of the unreliable, Xynetics edit plotter needed significant improvement and the average of two or three edit plot cycles for each map called for a significant reduction. Further digital mapping would in future have dedicated 'slots' on the Department's ICL 1906 mainframe computer to guarantee turnround times. Also for the next round of cost recording, the previously volatile feature coding structure was to be reviewed and stabilised. To accelerate progress, the need for a final 'clean run' to ensure 'cartographic elegance', often only visible through a magnifier but which many conservatives inside Ordnance Survey still prized so highly, was removed, but this would merely serve to lay up trouble for the future.

The directive that came from the Director General's Committee confirmed that there could be no further investment in digital mapping, at least until there was a successful outcome to the PMA project to restructure Ordnance Survey's digital data and at least one major user application was proven to be viable/ successful. Further conditions were made that a solution should be in sight for the economic maintenance of the digital database, compatible with the policy of continuous revision, that more of the problems associated with producing derived mapping from the basic scales digital data should be resolved. A clear call was also made to all concerned to pursue all of these issues, and this really posed a most daunting challenge, as almost all had cause and effect outside the organisation.

A further comparative costing of the pilot production flowlines with conventional methods was again made at the end of 1975. Costs still came out greater on the digital side of the equation. In response to this, the executive of Ordnance Survey simply noted the results and asked that the monitoring of production costs should continue. A new concern gradually surfaced concerning the costs of updating the digital data map files. Evidence from outside Ordnance Survey suggested that digital data, were it to be of use, must be as up to date as possible.

In terms of conventional mapping, such a demand appeared to be somewhat illogical, but it was to become an external demand with digital data that never really wavered or weakened throughout the two decades ahead. It was eventually decided by Ordnance Survey that an updating experiment be conducted and reported with the next six-monthly production cost report. Externally there was an increasing demand, largely from leading local authorities, for a digital revision service no less rigorous than the diazo-based product called the Supply of Unpublished Survey Information service (SUSI). The ultimate solution was still some six or seven years away and would have to wait for follow-up action to Ordnance Survey's belated Study of Revision.

Internally at Ordnance Survey a very dangerous practice had been adopted in digital production, which was caused by equipment shortcomings and the increasingly pragmatic approach adopted by management in pursuit of a favourable cost comparison result. Shortcomings in clarity at edit plot stage made it difficult to distinguish between digitising or plotter errors, and these could not really be pinpointed until the precision and clarity of master plotter output stage. Errors noted at this late stage in the flowline were simply logged and held on a correction file until a customer ordered that particular file, when, theoretically at least, these errors and omissions were corrected on the actual map data file supplied. This was perceived to be a very dangerous practice that was difficult to manage and one that broke all previous Ordnance Survey best practice rules.

The pilot production trial next reported a further round of costing data in June 1976. Typically, the main thrust of the original costing challenge was blunted by the inclusion of the revision of maps already in the digital databank. This was soon seen as 'shifting the goal posts' when under pressure. This additional dimension of the trial indicated that six each of fifty house unit updates were only marginally more expensive than the full three hundred house unit revision at new edition stage. The staged approach to revision of digital maps, if adopted in future, clearly had the additional benefits that there was always an up-to-date tape available for customers. Also, if derived maps were ever to be produced from the data, it would have to be on the back of the most up-to-date data.

The phased approach to revision of digital files also facilitated the capture of any specification changes. This was to be at some further cost but at an early date, thus helping to ensure that the databank remained as consistent as possible nationally, both in form and content. This most recent comparative costing indicated further improvement in the overall cost ratio between digital and conventional map production. As the years passed the residual remapping task became of less and less significance, hence the initiative to bring continuous revision into the reckoning. The earlier call to evaluate the less tangible benefits arising from digitising, particularly those that accrued from outside the Department, still didn't appear in the report. These difficult issues would have to wait for the ceremonial enquiries of the Ordnance Survey Review Committee, which was appointed by HM Government in January 1978.

The pilot production project of digital mapping, by now almost with a will of its own, survived the latest review and continued to produce map data. The list of feature codes was finally stabilised, the equipment deployed generally performed satisfactorily and the balance of resources, particularly between edit and final plot capacity, was adjusted further with a two-shift working pattern on the master plotter. The performance of the Xynetics plotter was improved by hardware and software upgrades from the manufacturer. Finally, in the 1976–77 departmental estimates additional edit plot equipment was, at least, planned, as the original Calcomp drum plotter began to fail to meet its operational specification.

Two other important steps were made at this time. Development Branch personnel were tasked with looking at the whole question of interactive edit as an alternative to the ponderous offline, off table 'edit loop'. The dangerous practice of not finally 'cleaning up' each map until customers purchased it, which had been introduced as a cost reduction measure, was finally eradicated from procedures and all tapes entering the databank were at least deemed to be error free.

It was about this time that real complacency overtook the pilot project and it simply became a routine aspect of Ordnance Survey's task. The 'stalemate' in any real financial or technical justification simply left the project in limbo, neither accelerating in a revitalised mode nor stifled out of existence.

Chapter 7
Ordnance Survey's first attempt to meet the stated needs of customers for digital mapping by software restructuring of the data

During 1971 and 1972 there was an emerging appreciation, at least amongst a small number of people at Ordnance Survey who were grappling with the many and recurrent problems associated with digital mapping, that there would perhaps one day be a national topographic database of map information. The emphasis in these early years of digital mapping was predominantly on servicing contemporary production needs of Ordnance Survey. These needs centred on the completion of the post-war resurvey of Great Britain, its maintenance by revision and, where necessary, the upgrade of scales where appropriate. By 1971 there was very limited external user interest in the computer-based mapping venture by Ordnance Survey.

The bulk of this initial external interest, resided within central government, mainly on behalf of local government in the discharge of its town and country planning responsibilities. However, when Major General Irwin, the Director General, issued his definitive and challenging statement about the emerging technology in 1971, which in turn led to the establishment of Ordnance Survey's pilot production project, it included an important aspect, which focused on the need to stimulate user interest, thus creating an eventual demand for digital map data.

Coincidentally, in 1972, during the very early stages of the project aimed at the development of digital mapping, one of a handful of external influences that would shape its progress and eventual outcome occurred in the form of a report, published by HMSO, which was rendered to central government. This report was entitled 'A General Information System for Planning' (GISP). This particular report described the need for all local authorities, the Scottish Development Department and the Ministry of Housing and Local Government (the forerunner of the DOE), each to comply systematically with the Town and Country Planning Act 1968. The report considered the range of mechanisms and procedures by which this need might best be met, but concluded that the best approach was to design and implement a nationwide planning information system.

The GISP report launched the concept of 'basic spatial units' and their derived geographical and mathematical 'centroids' as a basis for unique references for the planning, control and management of development. Interestingly and almost certainly because of the limitations of contemporary computer processing power, the report didn't pursue the more powerful concepts of boundaries and areas. However, it was the GISP report that highlighted for the first time the need for the property parcels contained within the basic-scale mapping of Great Britain to be held and made available in a machine-readable form. These events certainly represent the first statement of any external demand for digital map data. The report, despite the severe limitations of the rudimentary digitising equipment available at the time, was dominated by the concept of 'point referencing' of land parcels using 'centroids'.

Ordnance Survey had already been involved for a number of years with a large and ponderous national governmental committee (The Locational Referencing Committee), which had initiated the GISP report and which was tasked with considering the concept and practice of 'locational referencing' for government. Members of Ordnance Survey staff who were concerned with such matters, studied the GISP report with great care. The DOE had, in the interim, been created to deal with, amongst other things, local government and physical planning. A 392-page 'point referencing manual' was produced and published within a very tight timescale. Within the local authority community there was renewed interest and debate about how the goals of the GISP report could best be met.

Additionally, and in the wake of these initiatives, funds were made available by government for research into the need for suitable techniques in handling spatial data. A joint project between the DOE and the Local Authorities Management Services and Computing Committee

(LAMSAC), aiming to research the needs for an information system, was duly initiated. This initiative, not entirely by chance, coincided with publicity about the successful completion and publication of the very first digital map sheet SO 50–5152 at 1:2500 scale. Colonel RC Gardiner-Hill's professional paper published in 1972 described and publicised the production techniques which had already been implemented on the infant pilot production flowline. At this time of increased publicity about digital mapping, individuals within Ordnance Survey and outside first began to comment on the obvious shortcomings in the data that Ordnance Survey had struggled so hard to produce.

The 'concept of areas' was not covered in the original data design and Gardiner-Hill, in particular, was not willing to accord it any priority at this time. With domestic pressure mounting, his attention was necessarily focused on improving the tedious production procedures in the pilot project. There were also some expressions of concern outside Ordnance Survey that the digital map data might not be best suited to users with needs beyond simply redrawing the large-scale map from which the map data had originally been created. It was also at this time, that discussion about the merits of a more suitable data structure than that implemented by Ordnance Survey first really surfaced. This and the difficulty that those interested had in forecasting when large blocks of contiguous data, if ever, would become available, was the other aspect about which concern was increasingly expressed. These two apparent weaknesses were, in fact, to bedevil Ordnance Survey for almost the whole duration of the digitising project. The former was to prove an almost continuous 'distraction' from the task of capturing the data and remained the cause of several 'false dawns'.

In 1974 Ordnance Survey conducted its first comprehensive study of user needs for digital mapping, which tended, somewhat surprisingly so early in the life of the project, to confirm the limited usefulness of the map data it was striving to produce. This was particularly so in terms of any use of map data as a 'fuel' for large computer-based information systems, which increasingly users and commentators alike saw as the way forward for future mainstream user requirements. At this time and in view of all that had occurred on the local government front in the wake of the publication of the GISP report concerning the need for these information systems, Ordnance Survey approached the DOE for financial support for a data restructuring project.

The DOE had become the host ministry for local government. Ordnance Survey sought access to some of the funds that had been set aside for research under the LOGIS programme, into matters relevant to the development of physical planning information systems. The outcome of this approach was a contract for a feasibility study by a small software company called PMA, aiming to investigate the different needs of potential users of large-scale digital map data, mainly in local authorities but with concern for similar needs in public utility undertakings, central government and elsewhere. The study called for a review of the need for a possible methodology whereby Ordnance Survey digital map data could be 'restructured' to better fulfil user requirements, other than for simple cartographic replication. In the main, the local authority need centred on the ability to create and maintain large files storing an accurate representation of features falling within closed perimeters, to be held at the heart of a new generation of computer-based information systems.

The report of the feasibility study confirmed not only the need for 'restructuring', as it came to be called, but also the contractor's claimed ability to devise and write suitable software for delivery back to Ordnance Survey. The study concluded that Ordnance Survey itself should best manage and direct the data transmutation processes, yet to be devised, thereby standardising the approach into a national operation, thus avoiding wasteful duplication. This was to be the first of what was to become a recurring and familiar call from several external reviews which were wished on Ordnance Survey in the years ahead and throughout the life of the digitising project. The report of the PMA feasibility study helped to secure substantial funding for the project for Ordnance Survey from the much larger resources of the DOE.

Following broad acceptance of the feasibility study, PMA were, in due course, formally commissioned to develop and test software which would restructure Ordnance Survey large-scale digital data into a 'links and node' format. The objective here was to identify and extract the component line segments (links) of real life 'land parcels', followed by the computation of all intersections of perimeter line segments which were to be held as unique junction points (nodes). The secondary objective of the PMA contract was to develop and deploy a high-level user language called 'LAND', which had the capability of forming and extracting land parcels from the 'links and nodes' data by software, followed by the computation of a unique identifying and linking 'centroid' or reference point.

During the life of the contract, which ran from 1974 until 1979, there were many trials and tribulations for all parties concerned. The task was always to prove more difficult than the contractor or Ordnance Survey had envisaged and hence there was almost a continuing 'frisson' of tension and no little mistrust between them. The contractor eventually built and delivered a suite of Fortran and PLAN (machine language programme) programmes designed to run in 'batch mode' at Ordnance Survey head office on the ICL 1906S mainframe computer. A user panel was established under the overall auspices of the local authority host (LAMSAC) to monitor and direct the project.

Increasingly and because of the high level of external involvement, funding and interest in the outcome of the restructuring project consumed a great deal of effort and resources within Ordnance Survey. The software converted all map data at whatever scale to a common scale and then restructured it into three components: that is line and point data, text data and a text index. Low level files containing 500 square metres of map data were created for storage purposes, with high-level files comprising parcel formation and 'centroid' computation details for each low-level file also stored.

Full acceptance testing of the software was never satisfactorily completed by Ordnance Survey. By late 1976 a major problem had already surfaced. The somewhat ambiguous specification for the contract had led to the situation whereby, at conversion, the degree of successful parcel formation was open to very different interpretations. The DOE and Ordnance Survey not surprisingly sought 100% parcel and 'centroid' extraction whilst PMA, the contractor, felt that the overall success of parcel extraction should depend ultimately on the conversion process and the use of the user language, LAND. The end result of this quite acrimonious dispute was that two versions of the PMA software came to exist which, when deployed and run together, did nearly meet the specification that Ordnance Survey, on behalf of its user community, had sought from the outset.

Of the two versions of the software, one ran slowly and, at some considerable cost, created all the nodes with a 30-centimetre tolerance but with one reported exception condition, which was said to be rare in occurrence in the mapping. The fast-running version also created all the nodes with a 30-centimetre tolerance but was known to have five exception conditions, one of which alone occurred several hundred times within one 1:1250 scale map sheet. This of course in turn resulted in many fewer land parcels being successfully created. Beyond the incessant breakdowns in the software and the very poor yields of parcels in the early years, the charge that the basic position of data was shifted from its surveyed position by the restructuring processes was never adequately refuted to Ordnance Survey's complete satisfaction. Well ahead in time of effective interactive editing of map data, the project lapsed into something of a stalemate between Ordnance Survey and its contractor. This was possibly a foreseeable outcome in contracting out such an entirely novel concept.

Still within the realms of the very significant and external stimuli for the Ordnance Survey digital data capture project and following the call for Local Authority Information Systems capable of responding to the needs created by the 1968 Town and Country Planning Act, the combined efforts of DOE and LAMSAC led to the creation of two very significant trial projects. In Tyne and Wear a national gazetteer pilot study was initiated in 1974, which aimed to process spatial references from point digitising in batch mode of operation for local authority purposes.

In a quite different approach to the problem in Yorkshire, a Local Authority Management Information System (LAMIS) was initiated with the cooperation of the Department of Industry, Leeds County and the computer firm ICL. Here, using local authority datasets, online access to spatial referencing was achieved by digitising area boundaries. In 1975 the DOE commissioned a review by McKinsey and Co Inc, of both these approaches to spatial referencing for information systems. The principal conclusion of this review was that Ordnance Survey basic-scale maps were confirmed as the best source for extracting suitable references or for holding indexes for such purposes.

In retrospect, the protracted Ordnance Survey/PMA experience should certainly be assessed as innovative and visionary. It came, perhaps ideally, rather too early in the story of digital mapping. It arose more from external awareness and assessed need rather than from fundamental innovation within Ordnance Survey. There can be no doubt, however, that key staff at Ordnance Survey, aware of and alert to external circumstances through participation in the mainly local authority sector, did welcome and foster the initiative.

However, as well as in the sense of serving to clarify Ordnance Survey's thinking about the future for more refined machine processable map information and indeed about any other data specifications beyond the one already embarked upon, the PMA restructuring project did divert scarce resources of key staff and computer capacity away from the pilot production project. The PMA software was somewhat fatally 'tied' almost inextricably to the contemporary Ordnance Survey mainframe computer configuration. That said, the software did eventually serve to successfully 'restructure' the digital map data from the map stock of Dudley Metropolitan County, albeit with excessive tape handling problems and very substantial computer run times indeed.

The user language LAND was much less successful, due mainly to deficiencies in the original unstructured map data and to the need for the concept of a 'dark link' facility, which was never successfully implemented. This necessitated a conceptual link to ensure parcels were in fact closed mathematically. Beyond all that, the management of the database created by the project, was very complicated indeed and tied, without substantial rewriting to the hardware of the particular epoch. The project, although as it turned out not to be 'mainstream' for Ordnance Survey, did, at considerable cost, demonstrate to an outside authority and less so to its user community at large, that Ordnance Survey could act, reasonably productively, in partnership.

It could be argued that the PMA project ran for far too long without critical or indeed terminal review. However, in mitigation, Ordnance Survey was not the fundamental 'paymaster' for the project which, in total, consumed £1.3 million without counting the cost of the in-house resources which it consumed. Both the concept and the processes of the project itself were certainly 'at the leading edge'. The user need, beyond that of the limited Dudley project itself, was also very slow to consolidate and to become clear. Throughout the period of the project, a small consortium of staff elsewhere, already widely experienced in the needs of local authorities, had set out to achieve many of the stated goals of the PMA project, but instead of using restructured data they sought to use the raw digital map data that Ordnance Survey had embarked on capturing in the pilot production trial. This was the MOSS Consortium, which although it had its origins on the engineering side, it was to become one of the more potent external enabling influences on local authority requirements of Ordnance Survey for its digital mapping.

What can definitely be said of the PMA restructuring project was that it was an early and somewhat painful insight for Ordnance Survey into the hazards and difficulties of receiving and responding to users' needs. This may well, in part, have led to the regrettable failure, still at a very early and formative stage, by Ordnance Survey to address systematically the many shortcomings in the production procedures that they had adopted for the pilot production project. The rigorous examination of Ordnance Survey data provided by the restructuring software certainly served to illustrate the routine shortcomings in the final data product, such as overshoots and undershoots at junctions of elements and features, the over provision of data points, the frequent poor representation of curves and the significant volume of feature coding found to be in error.

These shortcomings were not detected in the less demanding environment of simple map production and replication of the graphic image. This sort of problem was simply not addressed and routine production continued as before. What the PMA project, and the run-up to it certainly did achieve was the confirmation that Ordnance Survey should be the sole focus for any attempt to capture digital map data, of whatever form, on a systematic basis. Increasingly, paths were beaten to Ordnance Survey's door and this outcome was to be of great significance for the future. Even when Ordnance Survey appeared to stumble in terms of progress or quality, there was never a serious attempt to deprive Ordnance Survey of its truly pivotal role in the overall task.

The long-running story of the PMA project and its aftermath was, in 1979, along with all other issues, destined to come under review by the Ordnance Survey Review Committee. The eventual outcome of this review served to accentuate the need for rapid progress with, and a significant cost reduction for, digitising by Ordnance Survey. The review merely served to confirm that most current and latent or contingent needs of Ordnance Survey's digital mapping could best be met from the specification which had initially been put in place after the long period of experimentation and before the commencement of the pilot production project, which by 1979 was already of seven years' duration.

The abortive PMA project and the software associated with it soon became 'stranded' by the technological progress with computing environments and the sheer cost of rewriting the software. It continued in operation in Dudley, but interactive operations started to become a realistic and affordable option for those users who wished to do more

116

than recreate the maps from which the data had been captured. The PMA project, by virtue of its high profile externally, certainly had several material consequences for Ordnance Survey and the digital map data project.

Chapter 8
A fundamental external review of Ordnance Survey and its activities led by Sir David Serpell, 1978–79: milestone or millstone?

The final Annual Report rendered to the Minister with political responsibility for Ordnance Survey by the newly civilianised Director General, Major General Irwin, for the year 1976–77, was generally 'downbeat' in tone. It reported a year of 'consolidation'. The foreword to the report reflected on the many problems Ordnance Survey faced and the potential threats to the organisation and its externally imposed task if Government failed to sustain the necessary level of resources. To a number of observers, this final report was seen as reflecting much more the needs and traditions of the past and they considered that it offered a limited vision of the future of Great Britain's national mapping organisation. Traditionally, Ordnance Survey had relied upon serial external reviews to effect radical change or to initiate a new sense of direction. Because of its traditional role and culture, Ordnance Survey lacked any effective internal mechanism to bring about profound change to its tasking or its sense of direction by critical review. Its traditional and distant relationship with HM Government, other than for estimates of expenditure or annual reporting, helped to ensure that Ordnance Survey was much better at looking back rather than to the future.

Mr Walter Smith was appointed in 1977, as the first truly civilian Director General, following an open competition for the post. His appointment brought an end to the tradition of military appointees to the top post. This important step meant at last that a much wider range of experience and expertise than could be bred within the limited military succession would become available to the Department. Walter Smith's previous experience and background were almost wholly outside government. In particular, he had never worked at Ordnance Survey.

He therefore brought a fresh mind to its many problems and difficulties. His experience consisted of working for and then managing a private-sector mapping company in the UK, followed by several years of service as the United Nation's Cartographic Adviser, based in New York. He brought commercial skills from his private-sector experience and his beliefs about management and communication were radically different to those of the military. His limited experience of Ordnance Survey was confined to public professional meetings in which some members of the military management had participated and from commercial and personal use of Ordnance Survey's products.

The function of Ordnance Survey, up to this point in time, had really been strictly 'governmental' in nature. The organisation itself was effectively rendered inaccessible to those outside by its nature as a government organisation of this particular time, but more by the attitudes and style of its itinerant military management. Communication with those in the professions and those users that maintained an interest in its role and products was most typically in the form of announcements. Genuine consultation was an untried form of communication at this stage in Ordnance Survey's evolution. The 1970s predated any serious concern for, or consideration of, markets and customers to anything like the modern degree, and there had only been very limited progress in moving toward a more commercial basis in the wake of the earlier external review.

'Outsiders' had always found it very difficult to get other than a very superficial grasp of the organisation, its mechanism for the allocation of resources, its programmes and methodology and, indeed, its internal behavioural culture. The traditional and very limited customer audiences were considered captive at well-rehearsed annual gatherings of the embryonic consultative machinery. Consultation did not necessarily herald a change in emphasis or strategy. Programmes set by Davidson pre-war were of extreme length for any organisation, and the government of the day decided the resource base on an annual basis, following submissions by Ordnance Survey through its political representation.

The previous external review, referred to above, which had become known as the 'Janes Committee', was initiated in February 1973 by the Conservative Government's Secretary of State for the Environment, Mr

Geoffrey Rippon MP, who sought to establish future aims for Ordnance Survey with a cost reduction and a more commercial approach. Using the pre-war Davidson Committee Review and the subsequent Serpell Review of Ordnance Survey as a base line for comparing impact on the Department, the 1973 Janes Committee Review failed fundamentally to redirect Ordnance Survey.

None of its recommendations were to impact immediately or materially on the embryonic digital mapping project. At the time of this public review, the digitising project was still only moving from experimentation to the pilot production project phase. What the review did achieve was to confirm that Ordnance Survey should remain as Great Britain's centralised survey and mapping organisation within the public sector and should not be sold off or dismembered. The Secretary of State, in accepting the report of the review by the Janes Committee, confirmed that there was no desire to lessen the contribution of Ordnance Survey to the life of the country. Further, he recognised that Ordnance Survey's products and services and its professional standards were justifiably held in worldwide high esteem.

What the review achieved, other than a lengthy and heated public debate about the future of Ordnance Survey's levelling and 1:25000 scale mapping services, was a clear recognition that the organisation needed to become much more enterprising in meeting the needs of customers with its products, as it pursued tighter commercial objectives founded on greater cost-recovery targets. This broad operational goal, once firmly established as a performance indicator and control mechanism, was in future to impact materially and adversely on the digital mapping venture, along with all other aspects of the Ordnance Survey task. One particular recommendation of the Janes Committee that the government of the day accepted and which became a planning factor, was the freedom granted to Ordnance Survey not to publish traditional chart paper copies of large-scale maps, unless they were justified by customer demand.

In subsequent years this was to have a material impact on the manner in which the digitising project was to develop. The emphasis of the Janes Committee on concern for customer needs particularly, was to apply increasingly in future to the department's plans associated with the production of large-scale digital data. It fell, however, to the Serpell Committee Review of Ordnance Survey to establish and reinforce the role of the customer and concern for markets, either current or emerging, in the outlook and psyche of the organisation.

Perceptions within Ordnance Survey soon developed that the newly appointed Director General, Mr Walter Smith, had been surprised and indeed disappointed at what he had found within the organisation upon his arrival. These perceptions developed rapidly and were never really corrected in the newly introduced staff briefing sessions on which the new Director General set such great store as a means of introducing two-way communication within Ordnance Survey for the very first time in its long history. His priorities soon became evident by the changes he was able to engineer from within. These early but significant changes addressed the need for a more appropriate management structure based on functions, regular and consistent two-way internal communication (certainly very novel and challenging at Ordnance Survey), a much higher emphasis on customers and their needs, the creation of the means to seek their opinions and much more reliable attribution of costs to activity.

However, the new Director General soon realised that the ensuing and relatively light hand on the organisation of the external Janes Committee review in 1973 had not established sufficient clarity of strategic direction. It had failed to give the new Director General and, indeed, a changing Ordnance Survey, the remit and security of resources necessary for the aggregated but very varied calls on the organisation. Contemporary records suggest that deeper and more sustained understanding of the organisation and its strengths and weaknesses increasingly swayed the Director General toward the mechanism of a further fundamental but externally conducted review. Such a review, were it conducted openly and thoroughly, with customers given a significant role in its affairs, would hopefully serve to direct the organisation in all aspects of its work and also help to secure, one way or another, the necessary level of resources, with predictability and some longer-term certainty about them. The Director General briefed staff accordingly that, if the future of Ordnance Survey were to be made more secure, then the future simply had to be determined other than by Ordnance Survey itself. This he felt was a fundamental issue because of the Department's track record and its deeply conservative culture.

In terms of digital mapping, the year of 1978 saw an aimless and faltering further prolongation of the pilot production project. Already in its fifth year, the pilot project had still not yielded any clarity of cost benefit or indeed of cost comparison with traditional methods. This was because of continued instability of production flowlines and also perhaps because of a reluctance by those most closely involved to draw the whole project to what might have proven to have been a final conclusion, with termination of the venture a strong possibility. Indeed, up to that particular point in time, it was clearly more expensive to digitise the large-scale maps than it was to produce them, under the 1980 plan, by conventional methods. The digital production system was still bedevilled with equipment reliability problems, with developing techniques, with ever-changing software and hardware; but it had proved capable, at a price, of capturing basic-scale map units in digital form and subsequently but somewhat tediously with their revision, but to what end?

By this time a small number of local authority and public utility customers, at least, were by now expressing some interest in digital map data. They showed interest, during the production trial, in certain areas of Great Britain, where customer needs and those of Ordnance Survey's map production had coincided, quite simply, by chance. More recently, there had been more specific consultation and planning. Whilst the many and profound problems associated with the future digital mapping epoch were normally confronted with sustained enthusiasm and optimism by the small number of Ordnance Survey staff who were involved with the project on a daily basis, there could be no overall sense of direction with so many issues and questions still unresolved. Within Ordnance Survey during this time, at the strategic planning level, digital mapping was still only regarded as an alternative map production technique with, perhaps, some still unproven wider potential. Left to its own devices and certainly without improved external communication and in-depth consultation and support for digital mapping, it could not be seen by those most closely involved how Ordnance Survey could itself move the question of the wider value of digital mapping, its use and its revision forward.

The long-term prospects for digital mapping had become bogged down in the pilot production trial. The way ahead for the project remained far from clear. An adequate level of resources to move it forward could not be found from within existing Ordnance Survey programmes – nor justified – without raising an outcry from those external bodies or individuals most affected at any switch of resources from other worthwhile activities, which had previously been legitimated by earlier public reviews. Possibly too much by way of resources had already been invested in the development of digital mapping. Abandonment of the project, somewhat surprisingly when looking back, was never really seen as an option. The strength of character and the persistence of those most closely involved with digital mapping at Ordnance Survey, who had been exposed to an insight at least into the potential of this new technology, helped to ensure that 'the flame would not be extinguished'.

Contemporary internal debate centred much more on how to improve processes and how to cut costs rather than whether the very approach itself should be sustained properly or abandoned. Production of digital data in 1977 was still far too expensive. It was inefficient and bedevilled with failures; the system still had many associated and complex technical problems that, despite all efforts to date, largely remained unresolved; its costs were still too high such that a switch over from conventional production methods could not be justified in pursuit of cost saving nor, at this time, from the standpoint of customers. The few customers that were found to exist were generally hesitant either in identifying real benefits to their businesses or in substantiating needs sufficient to drive Ordnance Survey on to any sort of public commitment to a long-term programme.

It was timely therefore in 1978 for the entirety of Ordnance Survey's role and operations to be subjected to a thorough and comprehensive external review. With prompt agreement by HM Government for such a 'root and branch' review, an early air of optimism ran through the Department. The likely prospects for, and the many problems still associated with, digital mapping would clearly come to preoccupy those conducting such a review. With so few external customers for digital data and with fewer still with any real experience of its use, it was always likely to prove most difficult for the review to identify and consult external market opinion. For this reason the Ordnance Survey Review Committee enlisted uncommitted academics and others to serve as informed surrogates for customers. This strategy was to prove, in the fullness of time, to be something of a two-edged sword.

In terms of the much wider issue of Ordnance Survey's future remit and role, and the narrower issue of digital mapping, it had become increasingly clear that a major external review was the best hope of identifying and reprioritising demands on Great Britain's national mapping agency. The new Director General saw the process of an organic review as the best means of securing sustained Government commitment to its recommended solutions. If this were true across the board of Ordnance

Survey activity, it was no less true with regard specifically to the future development of digital mapping. The project, which potentially, at least, had enormous implications for the future if problems could be solved, essentially lacked strategic goals and, indeed, any real sense of purpose. The inherent conflict between the concept of a domestic production technique or of a development offering a wholly new range of products for the future still remained. It was hoped that this dichotomy would be resolved finally by the conclusions of the external review.

The Rt Hon Peter Shore MP, Secretary of State for the Environment, in the increasingly embattled Labour Government, duly established the Ordnance Survey Review Committee in January 1978 and appointed Sir David Serpell to lead it. The other appointees to the Committee represented a very broadly based external body of diverse expertise. At least three or four of its ten members were reasonably familiar with Ordnance Survey's role and at least, in some cases, with experience of some of its more important activities. The terms of reference preoccupied the Director General in a lengthy debate with the Review Committee Chairman and the Minister responsible for Ordnance Survey.

They finally agreed on a suitably broad basis to admit almost any aspect of Ordnance Survey's role and functions as follows: 'Taking account of the views of users and all other interested parties, in the context of national surveying and mapping needs; to consider and make recommendations about the longer-term policies and activities of Ordnance Survey and ways of financing them'. Although asked to report early in 1979, the task proved more challenging than perhaps anticipated at the outset. Eventually, the Review was concluded with a substantial report that was delivered to the Minister and in confidence to the Director General in July 1979. Walter Smith, the Director General, who had first conceived of a holistic external review as the best way forward for Ordnance Survey, served throughout the Review as 'coadjutor' or adviser and clearly played an important role in influencing its deliberations.

Consideration of the report of the Review Committee and any timely reaction to its many recommendations were quickly overtaken by perhaps one of the most significant political upheavals witnessed in Great Britain. As a result of the general election later in 1979, which saw the departure of the Government that had set in train the Review, with its very simple terms of reference, the radical and reforming Thatcher Conservative Government duly took over. The Thatcher Government, in its pre-election statements, had sought to establish itself with a variety of policies which could only serve to impact harshly on the public and Civil Service sectors.

Public-sector spending cuts, a significant reduction in the number of civil servants, a drive to privatise public-sector activities, a desire to 'roll back the role and influence of Government' and a firm belief in the virtue of private enterprise were but a few of the new Government's stated objectives. These, if implemented, would clearly come to impact quite harshly upon Ordnance Survey at large, and in particular on the eventual outcome from the review, particularly with regard to the future role and the level of resources granted to Ordnance Survey. The Report of the Ordnance Survey Review Committee was therefore held for the arrival of new Ministers of the incoming Government. Messages soon came back to Ordnance Survey from London that the terms of reference for the Review clearly had not taken account of the new Government's inclinations and will; incoming Ministers therefore viewed its findings with deep suspicion that it had not gone far enough.

The 'Serpell Report', as it soon came to be called after its Chairman, recognised that the basic-scale mapping of Great Britain, the resurvey task, was nearing completion after some 30 years of sustained effort. This major and sustained activity had served to produce a significant 'archive' of topographic information largely held on glass or plastic sheets, which was widely used in paper form for almost all aspects of national life. Four major tasks for the future were identified in very general terms in the Review, and although general in applicability, they were to prove to be of great relevance and significance to the future of the stalled digital project.

The four tasks identified began with the archive of mapping that, if its value were to be maintained or even enhanced, needed to be kept up to date. Revision would have to be carried out continuously but systematically and economically. The second task was that Ordnance Survey should make the information from this updated archive available to users promptly and in forms acceptable to them as customers. The third task was that Ordnance Survey, in an era of rapid technological change, should be able to take advantage of progress, which would enable it to maintain or to improve its performance. The report had concluded that it was already clear that a growing demand for topographic data in digital form existed already, notably from local authorities, public utilities and research bodies. The review concluded that there was a real danger of incompatible systems being developed and introduced piecemeal, thereby wasting resources nationally. Ordnance Survey, as the national survey and mapping organisation, was directed not only to develop its digital mapping capability but also to provide a digital topographic database for universal use. The fourth task was that Ordnance Survey needed to transform itself from being a rather inward looking and conservatively run organisation into one that looked to the future and was responsive to change and developments elsewhere.

The review concluded that use of the map archive needed to be encouraged, if maximum value nationally were to be obtained from Ordnance Survey's work. All aspects of Ordnance Survey's role and work were reviewed and placed in one of two major categories of activity that had previously been identified and described. The first category comprised those activities which were so important that, to ensure their continued provision, government exchequer support should, if necessary, be forthcoming. These activities were described as 'core'. The second category comprised those activities which it was felt sensible and useful by the Review Committee for Ordnance Survey to undertake but which the exchequer should not normally be expected to support. These activities were described relative to 'core' as 'others'. The review referred in the report to the need for Ordnance Survey to be given a clear remit for the future. It concluded that Ordnance Survey would need to know which activities it was authorised to undertake and which of these were to be considered 'core'. The ground rules for putting forward its work programme and financial proposals, and the circumstances in which it should seek authorisation from the Secretary of State or consult its proposed advisory apparatus, were sought. The completion of the basic-scale archive and the many activities associated with it, such as maintenance and 'presentation', were quite clearly and unequivocally declared to be 'core activities' under the new definitions.

It was in section three of the report of the Ordnance Survey Review Committee that the major issues associated with basic-scale digitising were considered. The Review Committee took the view that 'in terms of digital mapping, Ordnance Survey was already faced with major policy and investment decisions and with the questions how fast and in what way to provide a complete digital topographic database for Great Britain'. The Review had clearly taken evidence both internally from Ordnance

Survey personnel and externally from customers and various other interested bodies that had foreseen the influence of emerging and cheaper computer technology on Ordnance Survey production and its products. It had taken evidence of customer demand for topographic information in a variety of forms, not least as digital map data itself.

The Review Committee Report drew very heavily upon the very frank summary, prepared by Ordnance Survey itself, of what had been achieved since experimentation gave way to the pilot production project in terms of digital mapping and the very modest achievements of the six years of its limited production activity. It must be remembered that the original goal of mere replication of the conventional basic-scale cartographic product had been the very modest aim established at the outset by Ordnance Survey. In summary, the review had concluded that 'digital methods used are more expensive and no quicker than conventional methods, and the digital data produced are little used outside Ordnance Survey'. Evidence given by Ordnance Survey to the Review showed that in taking the example of the digital production of a new 1:1250 scale map, conventional, production methods required 68 man-hours work in total, and digital production a total of 91 man-hours, as the tabulation below indicates:

Flowline	Conventional	Digital
Preparation	15	12
Digitising	Nil	13
Edit	7	35
Manual	39	22
Reprographics	7	9

Table of times (in man-hours) for production stages of a 1:1250 scale map.

The Review recognised that the digital flowline required 25% more labour in the cartographic and reprographic stages than for conventional production, with overall flowline throughput times still some 12 to 14 months in elapsed time from when it was first loaded into the programme. The Review identified the causes as the very large number of processes involved (some 14 in all as opposed to 8 on the parallel conventional flowline); the large number of conventional processes that were still necessary for the digital product and the costs and effort associated with checking, particularly of feature codes assigned to each element of digital data. The Review took a very broad-based view of the likely path and impact of technological development with regard to computing, as it might affect Ordnance Survey in future years.

The impact of ever cheaper and ever more powerful processors, particularly microprocessors, was seen as the key enabling technology. If allied with the growing realisation that customers would come to demand the flexibility of information itself rather than simply the use of printed maps, this must inevitably lead to the sort of needs for the future that were set out in the broadly supportive Chapter 10 of the Review's Report. Its recommendations were eventually to prove to be perceptive and persuasive. The supportive conclusions of the Review Committee were based less on clearly stated, tangible benefits either for Ordnance Survey itself or on the opinion of existing successful users. They were based much more on the optimism of potential customers with likely but as yet unproven benefits and on the commentary and support of cognoscenti amongst academic witnesses.

The role and the disproportionate influence of this group was at this time often quite considerable at such major governmental reviews. Academics were able to offer their generally better-informed opinion directly or more tellingly through the large and diverse networks of representative bodies and organisations upon which they typically seek to serve, although in no way being either committed or indeed latent customers themselves at this time, other than for free data for research purposes. It is acknowledged that a number of academics were, in fact, able to make significant representation to the Review Body. This representation typically seems to rank equally with the voice of actual or potential customers who would, in the main, be expected to fund such developments.

The Review Committee concluded that the not-so-distant future would see customers and, indeed, Ordnance Survey itself using a digital map databank compiled from the basic-scale map coverage of Great Britain in many diverse ways. They also concluded that, when they sat, Ordnance Survey had neither the most appropriate technology nor the most effective methods. The Review Committee, having taken evidence notably from equipment suppliers and from the organisation itself, raised and somewhat rashly supported the early prospect of either automatic or semi-automatic digitising but saw the real breakthrough for Ordnance Survey in these still very novel approaches allied to and supported by the much-needed ability to automate the tedious and time-consuming procedures associated with editing and correction of map data, once captured. They therefore concluded that the cost of producing new basic-scale maps by digital methods could be reduced well below present conventional map production costs.

Other conclusions were that the cost of updating map sheets digitally could also be reduced substantially, provided they were already in digital form and that improved systems should reduce the throughput time for new map editions to 3–4 months, with revision information produced much quicker, for example, after 50 house units (a long-established unit of work) of change. The Review also concluded that even if improved methods of digital mapping were confined simply to Ordnance Survey's domestic map production task, they still offered, potentially at least, substantial cost saving in comparison with current methods. In concluding that the current digital methods remained unsatisfactory on a long-term basis, being without time or cost advantage, the Review identified the concept of improved capture and edit equipment (semi- or fully-automatic it was hoped) as worth pursuing to achieve improved digital methods, with consequential savings in time and costs.

The Review Committee considered next the possible and likely uses of Ordnance Survey digital data, in the face of a very large volume of evidence submitted to it. The Review noted that a large number of organisations were already using or expecting to use digital topographic data in mapping or information systems, in both graphical and digital form. Greater selectivity and flexibility in the use of graphics and many possibilities in using computer-based data were all seen as likely prospects, with some of the latter applications calling for varying degrees of restructuring of the typical 'spaghetti' type data that Ordnance Survey had been producing. The data structure to date merely identified line and point elements and did not describe real-world features such as a road or a house, for example.

Many of those giving evidence to the Review saw one of the longer-term developments arising from the application of computer technology to Ordnance Survey's task, resulting in the ability to link other datasets to that of Ordnance Survey. Ordnance Survey had been in the act of organising a series of seminars for users of digital mapping as the Review Committee sat. These seminars were to prove useful as they shed some light on the plans and aspirations of actual users. The Review

Committee concluded that many customer organisations were not able to understand Ordnance Survey's present system and product and had remarkably little knowledge of what had been achieved to date in the pilot project. Very few organisations seemed willing to make serious progress in acquiring and using digital data, particularly when Ordnance Survey's plans for its preparation and sale remained so uncertain and unpublicised and when Ordnance Survey had proved unable or unwilling to forecast product cost or availability.

With resulting and current use not surprisingly very limited and sporadic, despite the wide range of uses and applications foreseen by the Review Committee, such a situation was seen as likely to continue until the large contiguous areas of digital map data, allegedly sought by users, could be made available. In other cases, where it was presumed that more highly structured data would be required, it was rather naively assumed by the Review that this could be produced in a routine manner by software then under development and trial by the contractor to Ordnance Survey, PMA Associates.

Quite perceptively, the Review Committee recognised Ordnance Survey's major dilemma. It could, on the one hand, quite realistically confine digitising, but using improved technology and methodologies in future, to those maps only that required redrawing, for whatever reason, but this would not for the foreseeable future provide contiguous areas of map data that customers said they needed. Alternatively, if large contiguous areas were to be captured on behalf of customers and to perhaps help Ordnance Survey itself with achieving derived mapping, many maps would need to be digitised that would otherwise not require redrawing in the foreseeable future. The Review Committee therefore argued that however much the cost of digitising and editing could be reduced, Ordnance Survey would, in pursuing the goal of producing large contiguous areas of digital map data, be forced inevitably to undertake a task that otherwise didn't need to be tackled, thus leading to an increased workload and increased costs to run the organisation.

The very conservative estimate that was obtained from Ordnance Survey itself was for an additional cost of some £15 million for a 10-year programme. However, to meet 'the wider use of the national map archive requirement' already referred to, the Review Committee felt that additional resources needed to be made available in any case and that subsequent decisions with respect to 'how', 'how fast' and 'in what way'

Ordnance Survey should proceed with digital mapping, were long overdue and should finally be decided and declared.

By way of response to this major dilemma in connection with further development of digital mapping by Ordnance Survey, the Review Committee eventually distilled out three major options, about which they consulted widely, for a way forward. The first option was to suspend digital mapping operations forthwith until clearer user needs emerged and until suitable and improved technology could be developed elsewhere and a market for digital map data more surely identified. The second option was for Ordnance Survey to embark on a major digital mapping programme at once in anticipation of the market, thereby seeking to reduce duplication of effort with digitising by others to a minimum. The third option developed was to adopt a two-stage approach, whereby for the next two or three years, Ordnance Survey would concentrate its digital resources on an investigation and development programme designed to provide, by 1981–82, a sound basis for decisions on how and over what timescale to provide a national topographic database.

Eventually there proved to be little support either in the marketplace or, indeed, on the Review Committee itself for either of the first two options. Option one was considered likely to lead, with some certainty, to wasteful duplication of effort and incompatibility of systems and data structures. Ordnance Survey itself would, it was felt, cease to gain further valuable experience of development and very possibly lose the ability to track developments elsewhere, upon which considerable but slightly naive hopes had been pinned by the Review Committee. Further, it was felt that in-house skills and experience would be dissipated or lost and any potential benefit for British industry in leading such developments would also be lost. It was felt that option two, if chosen, would be hard to justify.

Any deferment would benefit from anticipated and known developments of equipment, most notably in terms of automating the task of digitising. These exciting developments in equipment, largely touted by academics and optimistic equipment providers still largely remained to be proven and their cost-effectiveness established. A very large and rapid build-up in manual digitising equipment would, in any case, be needed for option two, with a consequent but rapid expansion in the numbers of staff dedicated to this slow and still non-cost-effective flowline. Option two also bore the other notable adverse consequence that it still remained unclear exactly what customers required in terms of the form, content and organisation of the data. This, almost certainly, could really only be determined by a series of cooperative pilot projects based on large contiguous areas of digital map data.

The Review Committee, sustained both by the evidence given by its many respondents and by Ordnance Survey's own thorough evidence, concluded that, given the prevailing uncertainties, the two-stage approach of the third option, was regarded as the best possible way forward. It was felt that an initial two- to three-year investigation phase costing approximately £1.5 million would permit current methods to be improved and costs reduced. The main hope here was felt to lie with an enhanced digital production system. Such an approach would also enable some of the existing digital resource to be reassigned to the task of providing contiguous cover of one or two whole counties, where user needs were already known. The value of such an approach was seen as providing both users and Ordnance Survey with the opportunity to assess the current approach and to establish, with greater certainty, the real needs of users.

Adoption of the third two-stage option would permit a major research and development programme using in-house, collaborative and contract resources aimed at developing new digital methods with greatly reduced costs. The objective of introducing an advanced digital system providing unit costs some 50% below present levels would ensure total national cover at a cost of approximately £16 million (some £5 million more than currently planned) but with the additional benefit of providing digital revision via the same approach. This development programme would also investigate user needs and appropriate data structures to meet these needs, improved restructuring facilities and mass data storage and data transmission.

The other major area of concern that the Review Committee considered carefully with Ordnance Survey was the likely duration and cost of the second phase of the proposed two-stage approach, assuming the first was broadly successful. The overall financial effects of the two-stage approach, where the second stage might have to be some 20 or more years in duration, was also considered. Many witness submissions felt that the Government itself should fund the assembly of the world's first topographic database. A very broad consensus was reached that the second phase should not exceed 10 years in total timescale if the wider benefits envisaged were to be secured. Detail of the cost and eventual duration of the second phase, and the revenue stream likely to be derived from it, could not be assembled with any degree of certainty, hence the need for the first phase. There was considerable speculation about the likely cost. Calculations were obscured somewhat by the Committee's parallel recognition that Ordnance Survey should also move forward on the issue of a small-scale database.

The Review Committee, with some novelty and imagination for the time, anticipated one of the aspirations of the future Conservative Government in Great Britain. They concluded that overall public expenditure might possibly be spread out over a longer period and in total be reduced by contracting out some of the digitising of the basic-scale mapping. Such a move would clearly reduce the need for capital investment in equipment by replacing it with contract fees, while another goal of the Thatcher Government would be met in further reducing the number of civil servants employed.

This approach was seen to avoid the relatively short-term build-up of labour and machines, but for the time being it had to remain as conjecture. However, it remains of considerable interest that the ultimate way forward in connection with resources to take the digital mapping project to a successful conclusion was in fact anticipated by the Review Committee. The Review attempted to project manpower requirements for the second stage and for the 'stable' state, once the digitising had been completed and when all aspects of the mapping and its revision were to be accomplished entirely by digital methods.

The Review Committee felt that if the first stage of the two-stage approach could be concluded by 1982–83, as proposed, there would then be greater clarity about the scope for major cost reductions from improved methods for initial digitising and for subsequent revisions. Also the nature and rate of growth of user needs and the willingness of major users to commit to the Ordnance Survey digital mapping service would be known. In addition, there would be greater clarity about the appropriate database structure, the effectiveness of the Ordnance Survey restructuring package and the level and frequency of revision required by users and the means of making it available. In addition, much improved estimates of the cost of improved computer technology could also become available, but the Review Committee accepted that the quantification of benefits would remain difficult to evaluate, although the report urged those involved to quantify resource savings in the longer term and also to quantify other benefits. It also concluded that, if stage one was carried out with the cooperation and commitment of actual and potential users, then at its completion sufficient clarity should exist to base judgements of whether how quickly and in what way Ordnance Survey should proceed with the provision of a national large-scale database.

The Report of the Review of Ordnance Survey concluded, quite forcefully in paragraph 10.46, that there was indeed a very clear need for a large-scale topographic database. The report had concluded that if Ordnance Survey itself failed to meet this requirement, then others would, by digitising national mapping to varying standards, specifications and accuracy. If such a scenario emerged, enabled by Ordnance Survey's actions, it would ensure that the clear benefits to the nation in avoiding duplication and waste, would be squandered. Ordnance Survey alone could deliver compatibility of datasets and increase the usefulness of the national map archive.

Completion of the 10-year second stage would deliver substantial manpower savings of nearly 300 staff currently envisaged for conventional operations. The Review Committee concluded that, on balance, a 10-year programme seemed desirable, but the investment of £1.5 million in the first stage would provide a much sounder assessment of the need and pace to proceed further. It also urged the early commencement and timely conclusion of stage one. It was felt that Ordnance Survey, because of the magnitude and impact of the decisions to be made and their ramifications, particularly for customers, should seek assistance in their evaluation and assessment, most notably by the soon-to-be established Ordnance Survey Advisory Board. The Review Committee urged the Government, which received its report, to make an early and very clear statement about its intentions with regard to Ordnance Survey's longer-term programme, once stage one's work had been completed and evaluated.

The Ordnance Survey Review Committee, led by Sir David Serpell, was extremely thorough in its approach. In respect of digital mapping, its report was eventually to prove to be a defining event for the Department and its customers. By consulting customers and commentators in such a thorough manner and by attempting to make a technology forecast, it was to prove to be a most significant influence on the future of digital mapping.

Chapter 9
Ordnance Survey itself takes stock of the digital mapping project as the Review Committee meets

Driven by the prospect of a thorough and searching independent review of its activities, Ordnance Survey took steps in 1978 to document, with a thorough internal study, where it stood with its digital mapping venture. The internal study, by a member of staff employed on development work, attempted to anticipate and to answer some of the questions that either the external Review Committee or witnesses giving evidence to it might well ask. The resulting unpublished paper represents a defining baseline in that it describes, with some care, the production procedures established during the lengthy and inconclusive pilot production project. This internal document provides an important historic baseline against which subsequent improvement and progress can be assessed.

The review documented the origins of the project and reaffirmed the four main aims of the pilot project. These were to evaluate the effectiveness of the methods so far devised in a production environment, to evaluate computer loadings for future mainframe computer capacity forecasting, to determine the economics of the production system and to stimulate existing and new users of map data to evaluate the benefits of the digital product. The capacity of the digital production system in 1978, available in the pilot production trial, permitted only some 10% of the total annual publishing task of basic-scale maps to be produced using this flowline rather than that based on conventional methods of manual scribing and so on.

The internal review of digital mapping concluded – based on all the experience accumulated in the five years leading up to 1979 – that conventional production methods were still some 30 to 60% more productive and that the form and content of the digital data produced was better suited to achieving simple graphical output. Perhaps this was not surprising as it was the original intention. The Review concluded that if the digital map product was to be of use in spatial information systems, the data needed to be restructured in some way. The Review document dealt quite harshly with the vision, which had always persisted, however simplistic and naive, that digital data would somehow provide an 'easy route' to the production of derived small-scale maps. This benefit had always been entered, by those concerned, under 'intangible benefits' in cost justifications for the new technology.

The Review concluded that this vague goal of achieving derived mapping more cheaply could only be served if all the map components were in digital form, itself a major logistical problem. Derivation of smaller scale maps would only be possible up to a point where 'generalisation', the cartographer's traditional art of simplification and separation of features, became significant in conventional terms. Experience in conventional map making had established that this threshold existed at a scale slightly smaller than Ordnance Survey's first derived map publication scale of 1:10000.

The internal review confirmed that the fundamental processes of digital production had remained unchanged for most of the pilot project, although software had been constantly amended and developed. These processes included the checking of source material on survey 'documents'; the preparations of documents for digitising initial data capture, on and off line the processing through Ordnance Survey-developed software on the mainframe computer; the checking and edit of map files; and finally the production of final graphics and data tapes. The actual equipment deployed on the pilot had been acquired in stages before and during the pilot production project. Of the 24 digitising tables available, 9 had their own magnetic tape writing capacity and 15 had their output managed by a host DEC/PDPI1 mini computer configured into the PCD system.

The tables were manufactured by the Bendix® Corporation of the USA, each with a stated resolution of 0.01 mm. The cursors on each digitising table had cross hairs to assist the precise aim by the operative, four control buttons and a warning light. Each operator had a keyboard with a text display, but most non-digitised information, such as feature codes and calls for processing sub-routines, were input through the table itself, using the 'menu' of choices laid out on the table. Text information was input 'offline' through a separate PCK sub-system.

At the time of this internal review the digital mapping system was essentially configured around Ordnance Survey's mainframe computer, which was an ICL 1906 S machine. This machine had total storage of 192 kilobytes capacity. It was purchased and employed by Ordnance Survey as a multipurpose facility. However, digital mapping soon came to be seen as, potentially, the most capacity-consuming task and consequently soon came to be regarded as a 'threat' in more traditional quarters of the Department.

For graphic output purposes, two offline pen plotters were deployed to create edit plots. Using these the operative concerned with that particular job could observe errors and omissions in initial digitising, before making amendments, more often than not, and tediously back once more on the digitising table. After early experimental and production use of a Calcomp drum plotter, two Xynetics flatbed plotters (models 1050 and 1100) had been purchased. Each plotter was capable of producing four-colour output and each was controlled by a dedicated Hewlett Packard 2200 series computer. Plot times averaged 30 minutes, depending on the nature and complexity of the map's detail and on the representation of features. Curvilinear pecked lines were the most exacting depiction. These machines had a floating head that hovered on an 'air cushion' above the table bearing the plot. The head with its pens was driven round the table at high speed under computer control, either in 'pen down' or' pen up' mode.

When the checking and edit stages had been completed to the demanding satisfaction of the large-scale map examiner, the mainframe computer prepared plot tapes that drove either of two Ferranti master plotters controlled by DEC/PDPB and PDP 11 computers respectively. These very substantial flatbed machines employed a beautifully engineered light-spot projector that moved relatively in x and y on a gantry above the table surface. The map was drawn by a computer-controlled light beam onto reprographic lithographic line film, in complete darkroom conditions. These high-precision machines, by the very nature of their operation, were found to have contributed significant production problems throughout the early years of the pilot project.

In terms of personnel, at the time when Ordnance Survey itself took stock, two 'sections' of cartographic staff were deployed on the digitising task for the pilot production project within Ordnance Survey's cartographic 'factory'. Each section comprised a number of cells of four staff, each with one supervisor per digitising table. These arrangements permitted the operative to complete all 'off table' procedures associated with the individual map production task. It was felt, from the inception of the pilot project, that job satisfaction would be maintained best with this approach, which replicated traditional production by conventional methods.

This arrangement had actually evolved in pursuit of job satisfaction, but it did also offer full accountability of the individual for the whole map task, whilst at the same time optimising the use of tables on a 'one shift per day' basis. The relatively low capital investment actually made by Ordnance Survey in the 24 digitising tables had always been held not to warrant a more industrialised arrangement involving multi-shift working, largely because of the considerable additional costs associated with shift pay anticipated under contemporary Civil Service conditions of service. The role of the supervisor (a grade three draughtsperson) was almost entirely to check and quality assure the production cell's output. The section leader (grade two) in turn had responsibility for all administration and an overview of the quality of the outputs of the section.

The processes associated with digital mapping always commenced with a 'preparation phase' before digitising commenced. With the imminent completion of the 1980 Plan to recreate the basic-scales mapping of Great Britain on the National Grid, the balance of the task soon switched to maintenance. The source and input document for digitising of almost all such maps was the master survey document (MSD) usually held in the Ordnance Survey field office nearest to its actual geographic location. The MSD represented an image of the most recent published version of the map, printed on either Astrafoil® or Mylar® in brown or blue dye, and on which the surveyor recorded deletions or additions in black or red ink as he worked in the field and office on the revision task. Only in the case of maps with almost no change since last published was a paper copy used, thereby avoiding the recall of the MSD to head office.

Typically, the MSD was checked upon receipt at head office for completeness, under Ordnance Survey's exhaustive rules, and for any physical damage, which was not at all uncommon. The grid intersections on each MSD were checked and enhanced, if not clear, as these served as the 'control points' for the transformation from digitising table coordinates to National Grid values during initial processing. The source document, upon completion of these processes, was next passed to Ordnance Survey's photo section, which produced a 'forward reading' 5:3 ratio enlargement of the MSD, using a process camera. Care at this stage ensured a well-balanced exposure with all detail clearly visible but with minimal 'line spread'.

The enlargement factor permitted the digitiser operator much greater pointing accuracy when using the aiming graticule on the digitising cursor. In addition, two diazo process paper copies of the input document were also produced. Upon return to the digitising section the documents were checked for any serious distortions. The use of a negative document had become standard practice because it was generally held by those concerned that bisecting a white line against a black background provided optimal accuracy. The negative was enhanced, where necessary, by cutting in any key line detail. The position and orientation of text was also decided and marked on the negative. On one of the diazo paper copies all text lines were allocated a serial number, detail lines were colour coded to show their feature codes, and boundary features were allocated a serial number. Text and boundary name data was next collated onto an 'offline' input form, which was then processed, along with the digitised file following its capture.

The overall digitising technique, which had been adopted by Ordnance Survey and deployed to date, used a point capture system, whereby a feature was described in digital form as a series of coordinates defining the ends of straight lines. For curvilinear line detail a routine within the processing software generated sufficient coordinates to define the curve, given four or more 'control' points along it. The coordinates of a point were detected and recorded in the table when one of the control buttons on the cursor was depressed by the operator. The work area on the table was divided into two parts. The major portion of the table held the stuck down negative input document and the smaller part the inter active input 'menu'. The 'menu' consisted of a film positive with columns of 6 m square boxes accurately positioned and fixed on the table relative to the table origin.

The table mechanism recognised a point digitised within one of the 'menu' boxes and interpreted this as a command to classify any following digitised points, within the perimeter of the negative document, as belonging to the feature type that the small box of the 'menu' represented. Digitising a point in other 'control command' boxes in the 'menu' invoked a variety of processing routines, for example, squaring, starting and ending jobs and so on, or to input numeric data to correct an erroneous serial number.

The procedures of digitising developed and refined by Ordnance Survey during early experimentation began with what was termed 'set-up'. This particular process served to effect the transformation from digitising table units to National Grid-related units by pointing to and recording table values for points of known value – for example, corner grid points and grid intersection points – within the negative of the map document. For 1:1250 scale maps, 36 such points were used for 'set-up', while for 1:2500 scale maps, 9 points only were used, unless at preparation stage the input document was assessed as badly distorted.

Each of the grid intersections were aimed at by the operative on four separate and independent occasions. In subsequent mainframe computer batch processing, the accuracy of set-up point digitising was checked and any out-of-tolerance observations made by the operative concerned were rejected. The transformation parameters were checked once the first processing had been completed. Invalid results did not cause the process to abort but a warning message enabled the operator to check the fit of map detail to the grid. The essential accuracy criteria here had been established very early on for digital mapping as 'no greater than half a line width' in any case if the discrepancy was larger than 0.1 mm, automatic rejection of the work took place.

The next stage of the digitising process served to collect all text information from both the body and the margins of the map. The operative completed an input form, which was then punched and entered into the computer through the PCK sub-system. The main data processing program next collated the serial numbers already allocated during digitising with the text strings, which had been input to the computer 'offline'. Positioning and orientation of text strings followed conventions, which took account of the needs of 'at scale' and of any derived mapping. It had been established that the collection of the text element of the data file demanded considerable care from the

140

draughtsman. The allocation of positions and orientation for all text and the actual encoding of text in the same sequence as the serial numbers on the offline form, had a direct and immediate influence on the number of edits, which it was necessary to limit if costs were to be contained.

With the completion of text input, the next step was to capture symbols, many of which were represented by a single point and were digitised as such. Some symbols on the 'menu' required 'orientation', in which case two points were encoded. Next the map detail itself was captured. A line was always read as a sequence of coordinates, either digitised or generated by the processing software, preceded by a feature code selected from the 'menu'. 'Pecked' lines were treated exactly like solid lines but with a different feature code. Lines enclosing features were always closed. For example, a four-cornered building needed five digitised points. An 'invisible' line feature was also available to the operator, to relate features that needed to be squared together.

The digitising of curves was made easier during the pilot project by the use of a button on the cursor, which set a flag that in turn invoked the 'curve fitting' routine during subsequent processing by software. Road and railway centrelines had to be interpolated by the operator. Boundaries were encoded to the type and text lying to the left and right of the direction of digitising, which was determined at the pre-edit stage. Further refinement of digitising procedures during the pilot production trial arose either from staff suggestions or as a result of an irregular series of reviews of methodology. Several aids designed to speed up or to ease the burden of the digitising task were evolved. These included a 'repeat feature code' facility by use of a digitising cursor button, a 'recall a point' facility via the menu (but not in curve mode) and the generation of certain forms of regular features during processing, for example, a circle, step treads and so on, as well as other processing aids which improved the overall appearance of the digitised map. These included the 'squaring' of square features, the creation of parallels and the alignment and internal edgematching between features on the two particular components of a two by one km format 1:2500 scale map.

All digitising up to 1979 was accomplished in what was called 'blind mode'. Suitable display screens that permitted real-time interaction with the data by the operative were only beginning to appear and at an affordable price. They were still very expensive, very slow and of very limited dimensions. The first available opportunity to check what had been produced during Ordnance Survey's digitising procedures was not provided to the operator until an edit plot was produced 'offline'. The operator customarily plotted his or her progress manually and diagrammatically on the second of the two diazo copies of the negative document as digitising proceeded. In marking up progress with digitising there was the ever-present risk of omissions and of 'double digitising'. These could not really be detected until the first edit plot was produced and examined critically. Once the initial digitising stage of data capture had been completed, the first processing run commenced on Ordnance Survey's mainframe computer.

The original magnetic tape-based processing system (DMA) had been developed during the experimental phase of digital mapping in the late 1960s. It was eventually superseded in 1979 by a disc-based processing system (DMB). The elements of the processing began with collective input of a magnetic tape from either the modular or PCD recording devices, text, offline edit, commands and requests input through the PCK sub-system and the files of parameters held in the computer's file store. Processing first allocated the data received according to a job (normally the individual map sheet) and initiated an appropriate control file for the task. The resulting input files were then passed through the main processing software and the resulting data sent to a map data file, which held it for output either to databanking or to plotting. The main processing software performed the following operations: the transformation of table coordinates to grid-related coordinates (based on the basic grid interval divided by 1024); the recognition of menu coordinates and the subsequent application of feature codes; the recognition and execution of commands, for example, the generation of curves, parallels and so on; the linking of text to feature serial numbers; followed by the linking of boundary information to digitised boundaries. The resulting data was stored in a map file on disc, which was subsequently dumped onto tape to fulfil carefully prescribed and disciplined security arrangements.

At this point in the process, with a complete file for each map initiated, checking and edit stages began. All first-generation edit plots were normally produced on one of the Xynetics plotters. As the two plotters available had differing input and control commands, the operating system allocated the job to the next plotter available. This proved something of a constraint if jobs failed. Plots of 'two by one' 1:2500 scale maps required internal 'edgematch' on the common edge, and these were normally allocated to the plotter with automatic paper feed. Next, the edit plot itself and the associated listing of coordinates of the start and end of each feature were returned to the digitising cell where checking by the supervisor and, whenever possible, correction by the original operative took place.

The main elements of the map were examined: for example, text, its spelling, size and position; boundaries and boundary text; feature coding; positional accuracy; omissions and double digitising; and a review of the more general appearance of the map (continuity of lines and smoothness of curves). The four-colour enlarged edit plot, on paper, was not capable of providing a rigorous accuracy check on the digitising itself, and if it contained anything more than average density of detail was often very difficult to read and decipher. Although the depiction of map detail was laid down within a set of rigorous rules to ensure that, as far as possible, work was generally to a consistent national standard, inevitably, a degree of judgement crept into the task. With errors and omissions duly marked up as an edit guide, the original operator typically rectified them either by redigitising or by offline input of a series of edit commands. These commands included 'change feature code', 'join ends of a feature', 'delete feature', 'square or align a feature', 'insert text' and so on. Table facilities for editing the map task included 'adding or deleting features', 'dividing features' and 'adjusting part of a feature'.

Once all corrections to the map file had been made, the processing cycle continued with a second edit plot produced as required and the edit cycle began again. It continued until the supervisor was broadly content with the most recent output. During the early years of the pilot project, residual and minor corrections – after several turns of the 'edit loop', as it was called – were normally held over and completed by hand on the final film positive produced on the master plotter. In parallel with this, step amendments to the map data file were also made during a final correction run. Where maps coming forward did not qualify for new edition publication treatment, that is as 'category C' maps, the data was at this stage simply databanked.

Where a new edition had to be published, the data file was then processed into a suitable plot file format, which was then 'queued' for plotting on one of the Ferranti master plotters. Again, because of incompatibility between the two plotters purchased by Ordnance Survey at differing stages in their development by Ferranti, the scheduling of tasks became something of a nightmare, particularly during periods of recurrent breakdown of one or other of the plotters. The light-spot projector on the plotter drew the contents of the map data file onto reprographic 'line film' on to which the standard border for the particular map series had already been exposed as a latent image in a contact frame. These arrangements permitted the film base itself, on which the map was to be drawn by light, to be preconditioned to the air-conditioned environment, thus ensuring greater accuracy but with the attendant and ever-present risk of 'losing accuracy of register', in turn leading to the need for replotting. These arrangements saved one photographic combination and normally produced acceptable results. Processing of the two latent photographic images was completed in a standard processing machine with concern for equal weight of grid lines in development.

The master plot and a diazo copy were then returned to the originating cell, thus providing the first valid accuracy comparison with the original MSD of that particular map. Inevitably, there was still a level of minor errors found during routine checking of the stable-based positive. Necessary graphical corrections were made to the positive by pen, scraper or by text on clear film which could be stuck down for corrections. When these had all been completed the map data file was similarly amended.

The final stages of production of the soon-to-be published map included the production of a combined negative with a 'stipple' mask cut to depict the infilling of buildings. The enhanced positive of the map led eventually to the production of a final positive, its examination and final correction; the microfilming of it for Ordnance Survey's microfilm revision product, Survey Information on Microfilm (SIM); the production of a new MSD to start the revision cycle again in the field; and eventual plate making for lithographic printing, by which the map itself would be published and made available on chart paper to customers.

The final product in the digital mapping system was the five copies of the digitised map data, held on magnetic tape, in three different geographic locations. This was considered to provide an adequate level of security and 'back-up' for the map data. One copy of each of the previous generations of the map were also stored to provide additional 'back-up', in the event of a disaster. At this point in the essential housekeeping, the disc-based map file was normally erased. When and if sales of map data occurred, conversion from the DMB databank format into a Fortran readable character form (DMC) in a customer-specified tape format took place on receipt of the order.

The internal review of Ordnance Survey's digital mapping processes reported whilst the external Serpell Review Committee sat in 1978. The internal review noted that in terms of accuracy achieved against that of the surveyed input, digital methods were comparable to conventional production methods. Any detail differing by more than one line width (typically 0.2 mm) was rejected. The standard error of degradation found arising from all production stages was in the range of 0.05 to 0.1 mm. This tolerance was found to accrue similarly from digital and conventional production systems alike. Itself it represented only a small portion of the total 'error budget' arising from the initial survey process.

Examination of the reliability of feature coding was afforded by the process of data restructuring programme described in Chapter 7, on which Ordnance Survey had already embarked, initially in experimental mode. The restructuring software suggested that coding errors were in fact quite common and this has proved a source of significant problems right up to the present time. The advent of interactive edit would in due course provide a solution to and some relief from this troublesome and inherent weakness.

By 1979 Ordnance Survey already had this significant development of interactive hardware under trial, along with an investigation of new digitising and plotting systems. The restructuring of digital map data using PMA software was at the stage of user trials in 1979. These user trials were being actively supported with Ordnance Survey's own resources. The concluding view of the internal report was rather critical in that the digital mapping system had progressed during the pilot project without a strategic plan and had already become a routine production system, albeit at greater cost than production of basic-scale mapping by conventional methods. The associated databank was considered in the review document to be of little use, other than to produce graphics. Only with significant additional input by Ordnance Survey itself or by others could its use be fully developed and optimised.

Chapter 10
The long aftermath of the Review Committee report

The 1978 Review of Ordnance Survey was conceived and managed as a thorough, holistic review of all the activities and interactions, internal and external, of Great Britain's national mapping organisation. It was the first of all the many public reviews of Ordnance Survey wished on Ordnance Survey in its time that had a genuine predisposition to seek out the views of customers and to reflect their stated needs in its recommendations. This was perhaps nowhere truer than with the approach the Review recommended for the future of Ordnance Survey's now languishing digital mapping project. Importantly and because the Review sought radical and profound changes at Ordnance Survey, it concerned itself very much throughout its findings with the attitudes and behaviour of the Department and its staff.

The 356-page report of the Review Committee dwelt at some considerable length on the views of the Department's actual customers and users. By inviting evidence from a wide range of representative bodies and academic commentators, for the first time in its history the potential or latent demands of future customers were at least speculated about. These needs were not therefore defined simply as mere extensions of all or any of the then current demands on Ordnance Survey. This applied particularly to the topic of digital mapping and the topographic database, which were seen, rather speculatively, as vital needs for the future.

There is no doubt that there was a very radical and challenging edge to the recommendations in the Report of the Ordnance Survey Review Committee. The report was published, slightly later than originally planned, in July 1979. The determination of what Ordnance Survey should in fact be doing by way of 'core' and 'non-core' activities was not simply rooted in meeting the needs of existing and already committed customers. This carefully considered approach contained in the report had investment and appropriate technology implications. It was perhaps these aspects of the Report that made it something of a 'hostage' with the newly installed and reforming Conservative Government, in which political dogma and economic theory appeared to play such a dominant influence.

In general, the emergence of the main thrust of the Report itself, still on a necessarily restricted basis because of the tardiness of the Government's response, brought a feeling of some relief to senior management inside the Department, despite the several quite critical 'sociological' conclusions. This was so because the Report had the potential, at least, to provide a clear sense of direction to Ordnance Survey in future and, hopefully at least, the mechanism to secure adequate resources to pursue it. This feeling of relief applied not only to those internal proponents of digital mapping who had always anguished about it but especially so to those members of staff already deeply involved with the project who had, over many years, remained committed to its successful future.

The delivery of the Report to Ministers of the Crown was indeed something of a triumph for Walter Smith, the first civilian Director General. More recent history following the establishment of the Review Committee and the creation of its Report must surely bestow on his 'steering' and 'management' of the Review the accolade of having been very successful indeed. It was certainly not his fault that Ministers of the Crown, to whom the report was actually delivered, were of a quite different political persuasion to those who had commissioned the Review. In quick succession, a series of junior ministers in the new government, who held responsibility for Ordnance Survey, were constrained from taking necessary and consequential action by the Thatcher Government's inflexible and rather dogmatic approach to the public sector.

Many of the conclusions drawn and recommendations made in the Review simply failed to conform to the new political economic order. Simply put perhaps, the most fundamental concept in the Report of a 'core activity', whereby the State (the Government) should provide support for any uneconomic aspects of Ordnance Survey diverse activities that served national needs, had suddenly become a totally alien concept following the national elections. Certainly, none of the many 'small men' who sat in the relevant Minister's chair at the DOE head office in Marsham Street, London, in the four years following the completion of the task of the Review Committee, could either approve or implement such a concept.

The contents of the Review Committee Report were, of course, already well known to Ordnance Survey through the active supporting role of the Director General, Mr Walter Smith, on the Committee itself, as 'coadjutor', but also through the conventional public-sector courtesies of clearance of the final report with him in advance of publication. Clearly Ordnance Survey was unable during this frustrating period to implement either any major policy changes or commit to any significant redirection of resources. This would undoubtedly have constituted 'contempt of parliament'. However, foreknowledge of the thrust of the report, described above, did permit a gradual repositioning toward the paths for the future that the Review Committee had commended.

As the months of silence from Central Government passed into years, the frustration of the Director General concerning Ordnance Survey's future in general and its digital mapping programme in particular became increasingly visible. Following such a high profile and public review, but without a formal Ministerial response, neither public statements of commitment to the digitising task nor the reassurance that adequate resources would ultimately be provided could be made. Fortunately, this obvious sanction was not permitted to inhibit several important investigations by Ordnance Survey from within its existing resource base, which sought to inform the future. It was perhaps fortunate that Ordnance Survey, throughout the four long years of indecision about its future, despite almost 'ceremonial' government-led manpower cuts, had generally continued to receive adequate resources for its pre-Review remit.

What became increasingly clear was that the previous Labour Government, in establishing terms of reference for the Ordnance Survey Review Committee, had presumed that Ordnance Survey would remain a government department, continuing to draw down its annual vote of funds to support a large proportion of its activities. The Thatcher Government, in receiving the Report of the Review Committee, had clearly found it wanting in that the radical and mandatory options for contemporary reviews of public bodies simply had to include those of 'closing down', 'outsourcing', 'dismemberment' and ultimately, 'privatisation'. Thus it was that the business and technical future for Ordnance Survey, so well mapped out by the Review Committee, had become mired in the doctrinaire approach of the Conservative Government for much of the early 1980s.

The considerable volume of material taken during the Review's evidence sessions, in connection with the current state of and likely future demands for digital mapping, both from actual users and from many varied contributors, often on behalf of potential users, genuinely suffered from a lack of focus. Indeed, the evidence collected by the Review Committee was frequently argumentative and conflicting in terms of stated needs for, and the potential benefits to be derived from, digital mapping. Reviewing all the evidence tendered to the Review Committee, even some twenty years on, leads the reader to conclude how thin and inconsistent the actual evidence of the external need for digital data actually was at that time.

It remains quite remarkable that the Report itself contained such an important vision for the future, certainly on the basis of the actual need that existed then. There had been a strong feeling expressed in some evidence, particularly by academic and other commentators, that up to 1979 Ordnance Survey had almost wilfully 'missed a trick' by not taking digital mapping forward much more quickly than it in fact had. In fairness to Ordnance Survey, although the pilot project had undoubtedly been allowed to 'drift', it really hadn't been possible to increase activity significantly, either from the standpoints of resource availability or actual technical feasibility. Ignoring any internal benefits that might have accrued to Ordnance Survey from improved or increased activity, it most certainly would not have been a valid response to any clearly stated or coherent external user need.

To a very large degree, the Review Committee found themselves in a starkly similar position to that of Ordnance Survey's senior management in the months just prior to the Review. The long years of experimentation and the pilot production project had signally failed to deliver a sufficient breakthrough, either in time or cost of production of map data in comparison with traditional and conventional map production methods.

Even in 1979 there was insufficient evidence of any real user demand or, indeed, even of what specifically was required by customers from digital mapping. This remained so for the short and medium term. Experience of actual beneficial use of digital map data simply didn't exist. Most of the very few actual users of digital data at this time were themselves struggling to justify innovative information systems for which digital map data was but one of the necessary information ingredients. It was clearly easier for those who had experimented as early users of map data to point to apparent shortcomings in the performance of Ordnance Survey rather than to admit that they still had a very large hill to climb themselves with internal justification of embryonic information systems.

The limited evidence taken during the Review on the price potential of digital mapping serves as an interesting case in point. Users who responded still saw the price potential of digital map data as no more than that of a paper map. Whilst such a view persisted, it would simply not have been possible for Ordnance Survey to increase substantially the availability of digital map data. Domestically, the extra resources to produce more digital map data had simply not been available without reallocation of resources, which inevitably caused material damage to other programmes that were held equally important by other respondents to the Review Committee. Most thinking at the time of the Review was still locked into a culture of government's provision of an essential national service. There was, at the time of the Review, a clear need for a very radical and far-sighted approach if the national mapping organisation of Great Britain was to emerge from what was effectively a 'straightjacket' imposed by its past, in terms of both resources and tasks.

The Review Committee had also documented Ordnance Survey's slow and limited progress with digital mapping. This is best illustrated below by production output levels during the life of the long-drawn-out pilot production project. At the time of the external Review the pilot project had already run for most of the 1970s. It had become apparent early on in the story of digital mapping that Ordnance Survey would, for many years, have to face a significant dichotomy of purpose, which at different times would pull Ordnance Survey, strategically, in significantly differing directions. This dichotomy is best represented by the differing goals of an internal production process striving to establish its viability and legitimacy and a means of meeting alleged customer requirements for digital map data.

These requirements were painfully slow to emerge with any clarity and certainty. General Irwin, in his 1974–75 Annual Report to stakeholders, had said: 'Whether the young plant (the topographic digital database) flourishes or withers will depend in large measure upon the encouragement we receive from users. The resources which will be needed to extend the system over the whole country must be shown to be justified'. To offer a balanced view, it was not just outside Ordnance Survey that there was a growing realisation that Ordnance Survey's efforts to date with digital mapping were simply neither credible nor acceptable, neither as a cheaper production technique nor as a means of providing a new product in the marketplace. However, the charge could fairly be levelled that Ordnance Survey senior management had apparently and signally failed 'to kill or cure' the ailing digital production unit. They had neither effected significant improvement, nor critical evaluation with a suitable and well-founded strategic framework. This duty instead passed to the public review mechanism of the Ordnance Survey Review Committee.

The tabulation below illustrates very clearly the scale of achievement of digital map production during the years of the pilot production project. The volumes are consistently low and any acceleration is limited. Generally low levels of resources deployed and technological shortcomings remain the major causes of the progress achieved.

Year	1:1250	1:2500	1:10000
1973–74	94	171	
1974–75	298	850	
1975–76	460	1015	
1976–77	411	1566	
1977–78 (1)	438	1236	
1978–79	579	788	10
1979–80 (2)	659	883	5
1980–81	436	416	17
Totals (3)	3375 units	6925 units	32 units

Digital maps produced annually by Ordnance Survey from 1973–1981.
(Source: Published Annual Reports by HMSO)

Notes

1 It was at this time that Ordnance Survey first used the digital flowline to produce new editions.

2 At the time of the Review Committee Ordnance Survey declared the following totals in the map series:

1.1250 scale – 54,365 map units (each 500 m by 500 m).
1:2500 scale – 158,020 map units (each 1 sq.km).

3 Ordnance Survey's policy of producing new editions of revised maps by digital methods, led increasingly to a 'pepper pot' effect, which ran counter to achieving blocks of contiguous data, which customers could make use of.

In addressing several of its recommendations to the need for change in Ordnance Survey's attitude and approach, the Report of the Review Committee – wisely, in retrospect – triggered the future for digital mapping, which indeed has since come to pass. In stressing the need to look outward much more in the future than in the past, several guidelines for the future of digital mapping were prescribed. The first was that the data structure for the future needed to be as independent of equipment or application as possible. It was felt that it should be capable of adaptation to changing needs and the many demands likely to be placed upon it in future.

The second guideline was that national standards for data coding, data structure and data organisation should be developed, but in close consultation with as many users as possible. The third guideline called for the establishment of a 'club' of real customers for digital map data. The 'club' would serve both to advise and to guide Ordnance Survey, and once formed should be encouraged to succeed. It was recognised that this would demand quite profound changes in attitude by Ordnance Survey and its staff to cooperation with external groups and to seeking and valuing their opinions.

This approach demanded radical changes to Ordnance Survey's corporate style and persuasion, from one of 'telling' to one of 'listening' before reaction. The fourth guideline was that Ordnance Survey should not remain aloof from possibly many small and first-time users, but it should strive to make digital mapping both accessible and affordable. Advice and support with respect to hardware and software needed to be given freely by Ordnance Survey to facilitate much wider use of digital map data than in the past. The Review recognised that the need existed for greater dissemination of information by Ordnance Survey in connection with digital mapping, with far less secrecy about its plans for the future.

The Review also concluded that improved communications should include close and regular contact with manufacturers and suppliers of hardware who aspired to sell to Ordnance Survey. The Report of the Review had commented favourably on the user panel gatherings, which Ordnance Survey had initiated while the Review Committee itself was actually sitting. The guidelines next addressed the task-oriented, craft-based workforce of Ordnance Survey, which had buckled down so well under its inflexible military management to the post-war task of remapping Great Britain. The Review concluded that the existing large workforce was unlikely to be appropriate for the task in future. A much greater role for graduates from different backgrounds was anticipated and indeed demanded in the Report.

A quite differing mix of skills and experience was seen as essential for planning, developing and managing the future, although it was felt that a production workforce, with much greater flexibility than ever before, would still be required, either in-house or, more radically, under the direction of suitable contractors to Ordnance Survey. It was this particular approach which brought innovation and novelty to the recommendations of the Review. Through lack of investment and by conducting only limited research and development work generally, Ordnance Survey had not managed to keep itself up to date with all the relevant advances, particularly in the application of computer technology to its business.

By raising the status of Ordnance Survey's Research and Development to that of a 'core activity', with adequate levels of resources assured, the Review called for a much sharper focus for its programmes; the allocation of substantially more resources of the correct type; and greatly increased cooperation with external agencies and suitable individuals who could contribute to the overall development task. Lastly, the Review demanded that Ordnance Survey should break with the past and prove willing to accept data from other bodies while cooperating 'comfortably' with commercial companies, universities and so on.

To sum up, the conclusion of the Review Committee was that Ordnance Survey had become a very inward-looking organisation, which remained unwilling to share its often poorly laid plans for the future. This was certainly true in respect of digital mapping, with Ordnance Survey generally giving low priority both to determining and meeting the needs of customers. The Review Committee found Ordnance Survey less than fully aware of what had been happening in the world at large, particularly with regard to technological developments. This generic criticism was, in some respects, unfair.

The workforce at large that had long been frustrated by the lack of opportunities for development whilst performing the often-routine tasks, prescribed by Davidson in far off 'before world war two times'. The organisation had become task-oriented and complacent at that. The depth of talent to be found within the workforce at Ordnance Survey, which had generally been underutilised, was soon to be revealed in the years after Review Committee reported, primarily as the old culture slowly unravelled under the stimulus of ever-increasing civilian management. Ordnance Survey had been found by the Review to lack any effective machinery for influence by those outside the organisation, most notably by users and customers. They in turn had only very sketchy knowledge of Ordnance Survey's problems and aspirations and more specifically its plans.

In the case of digital mapping itself, the Review found its use outside Ordnance Survey to be very limited indeed. This was most often because there were very few areas of substantial contiguous map data available, despite all the effort expended on the pilot production project up to that point in time. The original and continuing hope that had been pinned by Ordnance Survey on the restructuring of data by its contractor had in fact, by the time of the Review, still not been realised. Indeed, it had become clear to those most closely involved that the complicated processes of post-processing were rendered vulnerable to the inconsistency and weakness of much of the original map data produced by Ordnance Survey. However, the self-same map data had in fact proved only just acceptable for the original purposes of cartographic production.

With all its many recommendations and plans for Ordnance Survey's future, the Review Committee Report received absolutely no response from Central Government whatsoever. It soon became clear, to the enormous frustration of all concerned, that government officials in Ordnance Survey's parent ministry in London were simply not able to commend the unanimous Report of the Review Committee to Ministers of the Crown in the radical, reforming Thatcher Government. Reductions in public spending, rolling back the role of government and privatisation all ran counter to the strategy that had been set out by the Review.

The hopes of the Ordnance Survey staff and management for a clear route ahead and particularly those of Walter Smith, who had, from the outset, sought an unambiguous mission underpinned with an adequate level of resources to accomplish it, were to be dashed by the total absence of any sign of action at all from government. In response to the Review Walter Smith, quite refreshingly at first had sought to lead the Department into a much more open and interactive style of management, with top-down formal briefings to all levels, from a much more visible and approachable management team that he had begun to select. Months

154

eventually gave way to years with still no reaction from Government to the Report of the Review. The Director General became visibly wearied by being unable to bring any news of the outcome of the Review that he had sought and encouraged. It seemed at the time that the exercise may well have been all in vain.

Ordnance Survey first really became aware that it had been caught in the 'crossfire' of politics when Mr Robert Adley MP tabled a Government-inspired question in Parliament in July 1981. This provided the Secretary of State for the Environment, Mr Michael Heseltine MP, with an opportunity to respond as follows: 'The previous Government assumed that Ordnance Survey would remain as a government department and so the Review Committee considered no other structural possibility. Government now needs to consider the long-term future of Ordnance Survey against all other possible structures, either inside or wholly or partially outside the Civil Service'.

It was at this point that he introduced the proposal for 'Trading Fund' status for Ordnance Survey, which was later rejected in the House of Lords in a surprisingly high-profile defeat for the Government, inspired by Lord Shackleton (a Labour peer with a lifelong interest in mapping matters acquired from his forbears). New cost-recovery targets for Ordnance Survey of 30% for large-scale products and 100% for small-scale products, were imposed arbitrarily. Helpfully, the Secretary of State's statement to Parliament concluded by recognising the need, above all else, for Ordnance Survey to make progress in keeping up to date with new technologies. In accepting this need, he said that he awaited formal proposals from Ordnance Survey in connection with the Review Committee's first stage, but he acknowledged that speed had to be tempered by the availability of resources.

The 'Whitehall dam' continued to hold fast despite any ploy or strategy, which included the arming of external participants in the Review with suitable 'barbs' in an attempt to goad the Government into action. Ordnance Survey tried almost everything to dislodge the Report from the mandarins and their political masters in London. In fact, four full years passed before any real sort of response was received. This ridiculous delay brought mixed blessings, particularly with regard to digital mapping, where breathing space enabled development work to proceed but on balance, the consequences of this delay were overwhelmingly unsatisfactory and damaging.

The delay brought considerable doubt and frustration in-house, which simply served to lower morale even further. Profound and continuing uncertainty about the future within Ordnance Survey's user community, perhaps nowhere more so than the small group concerned with digital mapping, merely served to damage Ordnance Survey's credibility still further. It must be remembered that the stalled Review coincided with the often-repeated messages from HM Government that dismemberment, contracting out, privatisation or closure were all possible options for the activities traditionally the preserve of government.

Ordnance Survey was but a relatively small and insignificant aspect of this political drive. Positive messages for customers involving government activity being sustained, long-term commitments being made or funds being made available for essential services had all ceased to emerge very soon after the Thatcher victory in 1979. The 'sacred cow' for all of the four years whilst Ordnance Survey and those interested in it waited was, quite simply, a year-on-year goal set by the Government with targets to reduce public expenditure and Civil Service manpower. The cause of digital mapping and its progress, the importance of which the Review Committee had recognised so clearly, was completely and utterly stalled by way of any response by central government.

That, fortunately, did not mean that Ordnance Survey simply did nothing during this period of waiting. Made aware of and armed with the Review Report's conclusions and recommendations, Ordnance Survey, within the constraint of its tasking and its declining resources during each year of the Thatcher Government, was able to move on some aspects in pursuit of goals set out in the Review's Report. In many cases valuable preparatory or investigation stages were initiated and, in some cases, actually successfully accomplished from within Ordnance Survey's limited but discretionary annual spend, during this otherwise sterile period of inaction by government.

The Conservative Government's goal of reducing the overall size of the Civil Service, in Ordnance Survey's case at least somewhat ironically, set free some cash in successive public expenditure surveys, which otherwise would have been committed to cover staff salaries. Ordnance Survey also became increasingly adept at managing its separated capital expenditure budget each year. Somewhat surprisingly and ironically, in the early 1980s, this resource stream was never placed under anything like the same scrutiny as that of central Government's salary provision for manpower in the Civil Service.

On several major aspects of the Report that seemed to Ordnance Survey's management to make good sense, almost irrespective of the eventual outcome of the Review, action was taken to initiate relevant activities. These initiatives concerned the development of worthwhile and productive external contacts, an increasing role for customers, more effective map revision methods at large, particularly those of digital map files, an assessment of the likely benefits to customers from accelerated progress with digital mapping and a recognition of the need for rapid enhancement of digitising and data edit methods.

The latter included trials of equipment that met the so-called first-stage needs for improvement of enhanced digitising, as suggested by the Review itself. The interim period between the Report's issue and the first signs of the Government's reaction enabled Ordnance Survey to consider the steps by which external contractors could be encouraged and eventually 'harnessed to the Ordnance Survey yoke'. The four long years of uncertainty undoubtedly saw an increase in volume and diversity in external uses of digital mapping, and this rather debilitating period did at least serve to underpin and advance the rather weak and ill-defined customer requirement that both Ordnance Survey and the Review Committee had wrestled with. This inordinate delay whilst awaiting the Government's response undoubtedly caused many problems to users and Ordnance Survey alike. Major progress would not prove possible until additional resources could be provided on the back of a positive response from HM Government to the Review Committee's Report.

One important recommendation made by the Review Committee, which was taken up quickly by Ordnance Survey, was that an externally populated advisory board of management should be created. The concept behind such a move was that business experience and expertise from outside Ordnance Survey could interact with and influence and guide the Ordnance Survey senior management team whilst also serving as an independent source of advice to government Ministers, a function previously and traditionally the sole preserve of the Director General. The Advisory Board was implemented, with Ministerial approval, in 1981.

Sir Robert Clayton CBE of English Electric was appointed Chairman. Membership included Mr M Montague, Chairman of the English Tourist Board, Sir A Muir Wood, a partner of Sir William Halcrow, Mr D Barber,

Chairman of the Countryside Commission and Lord Chorley, who had served on the original Serpell Review Committee in 1978. All were appointed by the Government on a personal rather than a representational basis. This move to establish a mixed Board indicated a significant change in the affairs of the national mapping organisation in Great Britain. The feeling inside Ordnance Survey at the time was that this was something of a gamble by the Director General to seek legitimacy for his plans before they were submitted to central government.

The price was to be a loss of 'sovereignty' that previous Director Generals had enjoyed. The presumption was that a body of the 'great and the good', serving as non-executive directors, able only to devote limited time to this new function, would at least be persuadable by the executive directors. Most of the appointees turned out to be very strong-willed individuals, used in their normal business lives to having their own way. They judged Ordnance Survey and its approach to issues by their own values and business methods. Overall, it is fair to say that they tended to fail to grasp the significance of the public sector, national interest values, which the executive directors were likely to pursue because of their role, beliefs and values.

This situation, at least from afar, provided a most interesting cameo of conflict of values and approach. The ensuing friction and mutual mistrust between the Advisory Board and Ordnance Survey's contemporary senior management soon 'gave the lie' to earlier expectations. Meetings became increasingly adversarial between the 'two camps' as mutual suspicion and mistrust grew. This was particularly so in respect of feedback from the Advisory Board to Whitehall. However, it could be argued that a body such as the Ordnance Survey Advisory Board was perhaps a necessary and inevitable step in the vital transition of Ordnance Survey, from the old-style, inward-looking directorate-based corporate management to that of more modern times with a management board of executive and non-executive directors, working together to manage Great Britain's national mapping agency, in the style of a well-founded business.

In the following three years a whole series of further reviews and investigations took place in connection with the future of the digital mapping project, the importance of which the Review Committee had recognised and endorsed so strongly. Ordnance Survey had itself embarked on a series of investigations representing the first stage of the two-stage approach. With tension already developing in relations with the Advisory Board, one of the Advisory Board's early actions was to press for an independent review of Ordnance Survey's progress with stage one. Dr RAS Whitfield of Triad Computing Systems was duly retained at the end of 1981 for this review task, on behalf of Ordnance Survey, by central Government's computer unit, the CCTA (Central Computer and Telecommunications agency).

Whilst many of Whitfield's conclusions mirrored the broad thrust of the Review Committee's findings, some very significant differences soon became evident. The difference was indeed most extreme in terms of what the marketplace appeared to require by way of large-scale digital map data. Such a substantial difference of opinion, emerging so soon after the Review Committee took evidence, can really only be explained in terms of the impact of misleading evidence given to the Review Committee itself – only two years before – by academics and other commentators.

These alleged demands on Ordnance Survey appear to have held sway with the Review Committee, essentially in the absence of any great volume of hard evidence of actual and beneficial use or, more plausibly, the actual demands of real customers and users. In slight mitigation, the two years of additional experience, post-Review, by the very few organisations which had initiated trials and pilot projects, had also served, in small part at least, to better inform the enquiries made by Dr Whitfield. Dr Whitfield determined, with some clarity, that the majority of users of digital data in future were likely to be in the public sector, mainly represented by the utilities, local authorities and various departments of central government.

He also found that the very few actual users had in the main shifted – if indeed they had ever presented a realistic demand – from apparently requiring complex and structured datasets as 'fuel' for sophisticated, corporate information systems, to much simpler uses that more closely reflected their traditional, in-house cartographic-based practices. Whitfield confirmed the need for Ordnance Survey to continue with its development plans, along the lines suggested by the Ordnance Survey Review Committee, but with some significant changes in priorities. Recognising the paucity of additional resources that Ordnance Survey had been able to bring to bear in the interim, Whitfield accepted that the digital topographic database could not possibly be implemented in 1983 as previously suggested. His report back to the Advisory Board drew the following conclusions and made several key recommendations.

Whitfield found that there was a widespread external belief amongst users in the future value of digital mapping. He concluded that there was still an urgent need to reduce the cost of digital conversion of Ordnance Survey's large-scale mapping of Great Britain and also a need to speed up its completion. To no one's surprise, because of his private-sector experience, he concluded that the situation demanded a clear development strategy with detailed costings and the use of external expertise wherever and whenever it could be found. Other conclusions were that Ordnance Survey needed to introduce a new and more effective data management system and also needed to establish just how great was the demand for a full topographic database. This in the light of its likely cost and the near certain Government call for users, effectively, to pay for it.

Whitfield recognised a need to provide a means whereby digital maps could be updated digitally, but he acknowledged that this issue was already under active consideration by the Study of Revision team, which by this time was close to drawing conclusions of its own. He also found a very clear need for Ordnance Survey to stimulate user interest in digital mapping by means of customer-based pilot projects, joint ventures and so on. He had concluded that technical support and even funding by Ordnance Survey might be needed to 'kick-start' such projects, which would in time help to create further demand for digital map data. Whitfield concluded with a criticism of Ordnance Survey, which first appeared in the earlier Review Committee's Report. He concluded that Ordnance Survey needed to distinguish more clearly in future between development projects whereby solutions to problems were sought and implementation or 'roll-out' projects, particularly those undertaken in partnership with users. This serious corporate weakness was very much a throwback to Ordnance Survey's tradition of thrift and its inherent culture of fear of failure. It meant that innovations, particularly when new equipment was purchased, were eventually made to work after a fashion, often at great additional expense, rather than declare failure followed by abandonment.

Dr Whitfield's report, so typical of the product of short-term consultants, broadly confirmed the good sense and relevance of the strategy devised by the Review Committee for Ordnance Survey in terms of creating and exploiting digital mapping, although he discovered and highlighted a significant and apparent shift in terms of external use of map data. His report, compiled in a relatively short timescale, independently reassured the Ordnance Survey Advisory Board. They, in turn, were able to advise Ministers at the DOE accordingly but still with no apparent outcome in terms of the critical decisions that the report of the Review. Committee had hoped to trigger.

Dr Whitfield's report certainly helped to galvanise Ordnance Survey itself into a further flurry of investigative activity, the most important of which was, perhaps, a concerted attempt to seek from the public-sector customer base, identified by Whitfield, just what their future needs from large-scale digital mapping were likely to be. The Whitfield Report did, however, serve to provide further independent and, therefore, credible, external evidence of the need for accelerated progress and investment when the Government eventually came to consider the Review Committee's Report some two years further on.

The Ordnance Survey Review Committee had concluded that there was a very strong case for Ordnance Survey to proceed further with digital mapping, both for its own internal production needs and to support the growing and diverse external user requirements, about which the Review Committee had heard a great deal. These external requirements, at the time of the Review itself, were, in fact, hugely overstated. The Review Committee had found these claims difficult to relate to the reality of sales and usage of map data up to that point in time, which had been provided by Ordnance Survey. The Review Committee had to wrestle with arguments for and against small-scale data, the needs for richer, restructured data and calls for leaner, faster data.

However, their overall conclusion was, first and foremost, that such issues needed to be resolved before any major programme for digital mapping could be initiated. Also, without significant breakthroughs in production techniques and therefore costs and timescales, any significant progress probably could not be justified. The true picture in 1979 was that there was almost no significant or successful usage of digital mapping out there in the marketplace, least of all by organisations that were willing to pay anything like the realistic cost of producing the data.

Nevertheless, and despite all this, with substantial foresight and a great deal of faith, the original Review Committee had identified and supported the need, at some stage in the future. Incidentally, they foresaw the likely substantial lead time for compilation of a large-scale-map-based topographic database which covered the entirety of Great Britain. Quite interestingly and significantly there were few indeed amongst Ordnance Survey's contemporary senior management team that would have ventured that far, out loud, even within internal councils and committees. The first of the proposed two stages of the strategy adopted by the Review Committee was to be one of investigation with three principal themes.

The first was to improve internal data capture methods by acquiring and deploying suitable enhanced digitising and edit systems that had begun to appear on the market in more recent years, particularly those on the back of innovative screen technology. The second theme was to redeploy existing production resources to achieve digital map coverage of larger contiguous areas, such that Ordnance Survey and specific identified users, in those areas, could more reliably evaluate the benefits of digital map data. These particular areas were only to be taken into the production programme following careful consultation and, more particularly, where there existed a clearly stated user interest and firm commitment to purchase and to report the conclusions derived from user trials.

This particular theme demanded much greater cooperation between Ordnance Surveys and its customers than heretofore. This also raised the issue finally and fairly and squarely with digital mapping that there was more to marketing of digital mapping than mere sales. This represented a major cultural change for Ordnance Survey. The third theme dictated for this phase of investigation was to deploy a substantial joint internal and a cooperative external research and development effort. This programme was given several broad goals. These included developing new digital production methods: aiming to achieve much lower production costs for digital map data, whatever its form; creating a viable digital revision or 'update' service for the map data; investigating users' needs and their requirements of the data; and identifying the needs for and methods of restructuring of data facilities for mass storage and for data transmission.

The Review Committee's two-stage approach, the strategy itself and the suggested timescale for the completion of the first stage of investigation had been quickly 'blown off course' by Ordnance Survey's apparent inability – or unwillingness – to increase significantly the in-house R&D

effort, whilst constrained by general and continuing civil service manpower cuts.

It remains unclear whether the immediate but almost token increase from 8 to 10 in the number of suitable staff employed on R&D activities was simply a ploy adopted by Ordnance Survey's management to put pressure on the Government to make a response – and the desired one at that – or whether from a total manpower of nearly 4,000 employees such a modest increase was in fact the best possible that could be achieved. At a time of general staff 'wastage' out of the Department to meet Government-set manpower ceilings, there was little prospect of recruitment of suitable employees who could rise to these new challenges.

The Joint Survey Service was not able, in the short term, to deliver sufficient skilled graduates, but a reappraisal of the potential of existing staff and major changes in outlook with regard to their development and redeployment was at least and at last initiated. Both approaches were soon to bear fruit, with a supply of staff capable of meeting the most demanding challenges that the future of digital mapping, in all its aspects, would come to expect. This apparent inability of Ordnance Survey to equip adequately the vital in-house research and development function to the sort of level suggested by the Review Report was soon to develop into a broader and oft-repeated statement to Government that not a lot could be done until Ministers responded to the Review Committee Report.

Political strategy apart, it surely meant that even with increased levels of cooperation with universities, equipment suppliers and so on, progress with such a wide range of studies was very much slower than the original Review had presumed or demanded. That all said, the Ordnance Survey return to central Government on its R&D expenditure, for the year 1982–83 was shown as £800,000. It is fair to report, from personal experience, that this annual return should be viewed with some suspicion. It was always seen as a notoriously unreliable indicator of the health of Ordnance Survey's commitment to research and development. The return customarily included expenditure on a variety of quite routine activities that fell within the Treasury's loose definitions of both research and development.

The next significant event during this period of great uncertainty was a very thorough and wide-ranging domestic review, which led in late 1982 to an internal report for the Advisory Board. This report represents the next systematic documentation, post-Ordnance Survey Review Committee, of progress made and of the interim approach adopted by Ordnance Survey's senior management in the total absence of any indications, formal or otherwise, from Government. This report summarised what had actually been achieved to date in pursuit of the goals suggested in the external Review Report. Having played a substantial role in their formulation, Ordnance Survey clearly supported the approach set out in the Review's Report, given the required levels of resources and, particularly, fresh investment by some means or other.

While waiting for a formal response from Government, Ordnance Survey tackled tasks that clearly needed to be completed, if the broad thrust of strategy suggested in the Review was ever to be deployed. These important tasks were those that Ordnance Survey felt could reasonably be pursued without committing contempt of its political masters and parliament and without the vital extra resources and legitimacy, which could only come from central government's eventual and long-awaited acceptance and its general endorsement of the findings of the external Committee's Review.

The internal report summarised what Ordnance Survey believed it had achieved by way of various investigations and the developments undertaken during the three years since 1979, when the Review Committee first reported. The report summarised important progress in several fields of endeavour. The first concerned the search for enhanced digitising systems. Trials associated with the evaluation and development of interactive computer graphic systems had found them capable of alleviating the serious digitising 'bottleneck' associated with the tedious and labour-intensive 'edit and correction loop' of the digital map data production flowline. Equipment tested during this evaluation proved such a success that three sets of suitable equipment were purchased from Ferranti Cetec Ltd, of Edinburgh, as the original suppliers of digital equipment had become known.

These 'workstations' were commissioned and deployed by April 1982 with resounding success on the production flowline. It is interesting that Ordnance Survey's management was quick to take advantage in production of any improvements that came to light during the investigation phase following the Review. Forecasts of cost reductions arising from the use of interactive facilities were initially assessed at 15 to

25%. Savings indicated by early trials were much less than those suggested in the rather optimistic Review Committee Report, which possibly again were the result of academic evidence or that given by manufacturers who had a vested interest in the outcome. Estimated levels of savings were certainly not achieved initially, but even these levels of improvement served to bring digital data production times and costs closer to those of conventional map production methods.

The Review Committee had identified the urgent need for Ordnance Survey to make contiguous county-wide blocks of digital data available for customers who committed to purchase as a vital aspect of future development strategy for digital mapping. The internal report confirmed that by mid-1982, West Midlands county had been completed and Tyne and Wear county was 90% completed by the end of that year. The provision of full coverage for the London Boroughs of Haringey, Hackney, Tower Hamlets and Hillingdon was also almost completed by the start of 1983 and a start was made on the creation of a series of small urban blocks of map data to enable specific user evaluations to commence.

The Review Committee's Report had concluded very positively that the blend of manual and offline digitising techniques that Ordnance Survey had developed, and which had been the subject of extended production use in the pilot project, were not appropriate for the substantial future task of creating a national topographic database within a reasonable timescale. Ordnance Survey had in the intervening period reviewed and conducted trials on a wide range of advanced equipment available in the international marketplace. In the end the decision was taken to purchase semi-automated, line-following equipment from Laser-Scan Ltd of Cambridge. This equipment had been developed initially for and at the Atomic Research Facility at Harwell in Oxfordshire, initially for research applications in particle physics.

Despite the evidence given to the Review Committee to the contrary, raster-scanning-based equipment was assessed as unlikely to be suitable at that stage of its development. In point of fact, during the extended life of the digital mapping project, raster technology, despite persistent advocacy of its use, particularly by academic commentators, was never able to overcome its many problems. Problems included the inherent nature of Ordnance Survey's large-scale mapping of Great Britain. The advanced capture system, which Ordnance Survey eventually purchased, somewhat speculatively in view of its substantial cost, was called the Topographic Database Development System or TODDS, as it became known.

It was a configuration of a laser-line-following device called Fastrak, with two interactive workstations, all online to a Digital Equipment Corporation Vax computer 11/780. This cluster of 'high-tech' equipment, together with suitable software developed by the supplier, was duly installed for trials and evaluation but the period of its early use was be devilled by protracted hardware and software problems. The system's most significant shortcoming, in the context of Ordnance Survey's priority needs in connection with the 1:1250 scale map coverage already produced, was a general inability to cope with the short vector and geometric nature of Ordnance Survey's urban data. The close of 1982 had been nominated as the point in time for a final decision following the system's thorough evaluation.

The somewhat predictable outcome of these and other developments, although in themselves disappointing, led to the final demise of the moratorium on further development of Ordnance Survey's digital mapping production system, which had been self-imposed at the time of publication of the Serpell Report. Work also commenced on Ordnance Survey's 'next computer study', which traditionally ran in ever shorter cycles. At last digital mapping production and the secure storage of map data were, in the new climate, able to stake their own important influence on the size and functionality calculations that had almost always seemed to create such a major headache for the organisation.

The Report of the Review Committee had identified the continuing need to keep the digital map data up to date, once created, as another important aspect of Ordnance Survey's future strategy. The Review Committee had received a good deal of evidence of the muddled state of Ordnance Survey's thinking and activity up to that point. The subsequent Whitfield report, armed with insights and user experience drawn from a further two years' experience, but still very limited at that, provided a focus for internal and external concerns that had not really been addressed adequately. Ordnance Survey, without any real call for anything else, had, during the later years of the pilot production trial, simply embarked on a policy of digitising revision data when some fifty 'house units' of change had accumulated on any one map sheet file.

The cost and organisational difficulty of such an approach soon became quite obvious. The lengthy elapsed times associated with this approach were generally felt to be unlikely to meet user requirements for up-to-date digital map data. Ordnance Survey, following early sight of the Serpell Report in 1980, had itself launched a major Study of Revision to consider all aspects of revision, which included a possible fully digital operational environment for the future. In reality, this internal study was a bit late in the day. It really ought to have been done some years before the completion of the resurvey programme prescribed all those years earlier by Davidson's Committee.

Peter Wesley, the author of this account, who had been involved with early digital experiments and the establishment of the pilot project itself, was appointed from the Joint Survey Service on his return to Ordnance Survey, to lead a small in-house team. The Study was to consider with users, through a market research campaign managed by external consultants, how all aspects of revision could be best accomplished in future years. The issues of field office versus head office update, the development of appropriate systems and suitable equipment all required consideration and resolution. It was hoped that rapid progress with such matters might follow the issue of the timely report by The Study of Revision team.

From this particular point in time the need for and the impact of the task of revision was to have a major and continuing influence on Ordnance Survey's approach to the future of digital map data.

In 1982 the Study of Revision reported internally to Ordnance Survey. Two major and urgent initiatives for experimental development were recommended and quickly launched. Both developments were eventually to have profound effects on the totality of Ordnance Survey operations in future years. Both were to demand very considerable investment, fundamentally different procedures and the reskilling of large numbers of staff.

The first initiative called for the development of a low-cost 'because of numbers required' customised workstation for field offices on which revision information drawn on the MSD by the surveyor could be digitised and edited. The ICL Perq computer, with digitising tablet and plotter linked, was the chosen hardware platform for the initial development. At the outset data transfer would be achieved by the use of tape cassettes, but an ISDN (integrated services digital network) data linkage from field office to head office was very quickly seen as the means by which eventual deployment of the system in field offices might be accomplished.

Staff could capture their revision work digitally on return to the office, before despatching it overnight for storage at head office. The trade unions and cartographic staff sought to have all digitising performed within head office, but this was never really a practical solution. This development very soon led to the equipment being called the Digital Field Update System or DFUS. The second initiative sought was in many respects even more demanding and called for instrumental field survey observations of control and associated map detail to be captured digitally and directly from electronic field instruments. This data could then be sent to head office for automatic computing and plotting, with eventual assimilation into the digital data file for the respective map sheet on which it was located, without a further graphic stage and consequential loss of accuracy.

Both initiatives were pursued to a very successful conclusion in-house. Staff who had previously languished in the world of craft skills, whose potential had been identified and developed with advanced training, worked with the increasing number of graduates on the payroll. Both developments did much to raise self-confidence and pride in the Department and its modernisation amongst the field survey staff, who had up to that point been held very remote from the digital revolution.

The Ordnance Survey Review Committee was undoubtedly 'dazzled' and distracted by a considerable body of evidence that purported to illustrate confirmed user needs for digital data. On closer and later examination, many of these claims could be seen to flow mainly from academics and other wise 'commentators' rather than from already established or future users, who were able and likely to actually purchase data for cash from Ordnance Survey. This was certainly true of the claims that users were demanding high-grade restructured data. Ordnance Survey had, throughout the Review, remained sceptical of such claims, but as a consequence was seen as unwilling or even reactionary.

Ordnance Survey itself, disappointed indeed with the poor quality of the market research conducted by consultants for the Study of Revision, therefore embarked on a subsequent investigation of the market for large-scale digital map data. An initial wide-ranging quantitative assessment of the market distilled out for the qualitative stage a very limited contemporary market of but a few forward-thinking public-utility

168

undertakings, some adventurous local authorities, a few departments of central government and a very small number of commercial companies. The Whitfield Report identified a significant apparent shift in actual methods of utilisation of digital map data since the overstated claims that had been put to and which were amplified by the Report of the Ordnance Survey Review Committee.

This important conclusion by Whitfield generally served to support the view that the Review Committee had been misled by much overstated claims of the likely uses of digital data. The reality was that large, corporate, multi-purpose information systems that required intelligent, 'structured' data were still possibly 10 or more years away and that most applications built to date, and those under development, simply aimed to use digital map data to replicate previous cartographic functions but, hopefully, in a faster and more cost-effective manner. This picture – developed and presented by Whitfield – of the overall adequacy of the map data produced almost unwittingly by Ordnance Survey and the limited size of the market together represented a much less compelling case for a major investment and for an organisation-dominating production programme.

However, the case made by the Ordnance Survey Review Committee remained with Government whilst Whitfield stressed yet again to Ordnance Survey the compelling need for collaborative programmes with more advanced users, thereby stimulating wider user need and better mutual understanding of actual map data product requirements. His view remained that the market for this type of product needed to be stimulated but was capable of being developed over time. The most significant outcome of all this was that Ordnance Survey's domestic production requirement was found, very generally, to correspond with what leading external players appeared to need for their own purposes. This particular conclusion differed from the need apparently identified before and at the time of the more profound Review Committee.

In May 1982 Ordnance Survey had only one person fully dedicated to marketing digital map data, including all user and customer liaison, within its small Development Unit. This slender resource was tasked with conducting a study into specific user requirements for digital mapping for the coming decade. This, it was hoped, would be very much in contrast to the non-specific evidence received by the Review Committee itself. The Director General for some time, in the absence of a formal response to the Review Committee's Report, had planned to approach Ministers by no later than mid-1983, thereby seeking increased resources commencing in 1984–85 for digital mapping as a 'core activity'.

This was, in effect, the minimum financial planning horizon within Government departments. He also expressed the hope that simultaneously he might finally trigger a suitable response to the many wider issues contained in the Report of the Review Committee, if indeed none had emerged by that date. In initiating this study, it was acknowledged that any predictions beyond the 10-year horizon would prove difficult and therefore unsafe. Requirements of the study of the market for digital map data were, in fact, twofold. It was seen as essential to explore with real users the many possible cartographic uses of the digital data in conjunction with the client's own information. Second, those actual blocks of mapping, which they would need and commit to, needed to be identified and brought within the limited Ordnance Survey digitising programme as quickly as possible. The basis of the market research was first established as the contemporary digital mapping product known as DMC. The methodology adopted for the study was to conduct a small number, about 10 in all, of in-depth interviews, selected carefully, with the cooperation of existing utility and local authority liaison contacts as a first phase. These studies were considered necessary to develop and refine a suitable questionnaire, which could be sent to the total target population of customers, actual or potential.

This important user-needs study was conducted with considerable energy and enthusiasm by one of the remaining junior army officers, Captain Tony Vickers RE, who had previously fulfilled the functions of digital mapping customer liaison within Ordnance Survey's Development Unit. The study ranged quite widely, but the need for reliable information, listed below, was stressed in the letter that accompanied the questionnaire. The letter made the point that it was Ordnance Survey's wish that committed users should drive any future digitising programme. The major questions posed included who would be buying digital map data and who was already digitising information from Ordnance Survey mapping. Other information sought was where and when data would be required and whether the current product was in fact suitable for most purposes. The customer's need for revision information and whether the Ordnance Survey digitising programme was significant to user plans for the future was also to be determined. Lastly, the letter sought to identify which users were rejecting Ordnance Survey large-scale map data and on what grounds.

Because of the overall level of care taken and guided, as it was, by selected user involvement, the Digital Mapping User Needs Study eventually received almost a 90% response rate. Market research consultants, who were engaged to advise on data processing aspects, described the response as remarkable for such a study. Ordnance Survey had made it clear at the outset that it had concluded, via the Review Committee, the Whitfield study and from its own regular contacts in the market that the rate of digital capture had to increase very rapidly. This was most likely to be achieved by the employment of suitable private-sector digitising contractors. Without any doubt, such a helpful response to the User Needs Study was brought about by an awakening interest in the public-sector market segment that had, in pursuit of their various core businesses, traditionally been large and committed users of Ordnance Survey basic-scale mapping on paper.

The results of the study, once processed and published, were discussed with users at a series of seminars. The timing certainly met the Director General's stated timescale. The study produced some very clear indications for the future of digital mapping. By any standards, this first credible approach to customers and users in connection with digital mapping can be viewed as an overwhelming success. The study confirmed the following key points. It was found that there was a broadly based external demand for large-scale digital map data that, it was felt, Ordnance Survey should strive to meet with significant increases in output. All new editions should be produced via the digital mapping flowlines, thus avoiding costly digital conversions at a later date. Further, it was found that Ordnance Survey should establish a rolling five-year digital production programme. Such a programme should contain suitably sized blocks, for which there was at least one or more firm user commitments to purchase the data. In addition, a long-term programme to achieve full national cover should also be planned and published.

Such a programme needed to be based on known resources, be subject to regular review and although likely to stretch very far into the future, it would make at least a token commitment and thus in turn enable users to make their plans for the future. It was felt that such a plan would also help to trigger an accelerated progress. It was accepted that such an acceleration could really only be achieved by contracting out and by third-party digitising initiated by utility companies, with the map data thus produced eventually being incorporated into Ordnance Survey's central databank. A much stronger marketing effort and presence was required, which, with suitable staff employed, would serve to release hard-pressed development staff who were urgently required to devise fresh technical developments.

The study also found that pricing and copyright policies needed to be revised with a view to maximising income derived from digital mapping. In the face of a price increase to £30 for the purchase of a single map file, also with an increase in the standing charge per sheet, this particular price hike was to prove the start of a long campaign of attrition by users to secure actual price reductions. What users there were for map data were already beginning to call for bulk-sale discounts for large users, discounts for first-time buyers and on firm orders with firm financial commitments.

A programme to create micro-blocks of digital mapping to supply new customers who were engaging in trials was also devised. It was felt that Ordnance Survey should work with software and hardware suppliers to encourage them to develop interfaces such that digital mapping would play with ease on systems offered by suppliers. The need for collaborative projects seeking to develop uses and to cost-justify the acquisition of map data, which had been initially raised by the Review Committee Report and then confirmed by Whitfield's conclusions, received further endorsement. As an example, local authorities sought joint development with the MOSS Consortium that their particular industry had given rise to. The marketing study by Ordnance Survey also found a stated need for a level of digital update service, which was to be more responsive than the 50 house-unit service associated with the analogue microfilm service (Survey Information on Microfilm or SIM). It became clear that the desired revision service would replicate the widely accepted SUSI normally available with conventional mapping but which could not yet be realistically offered at this point in time for digital mapping as such a service needed to be established in Ordnance Survey field offices.

A plethora of other requirements were also identified during this review of the marketplace, some of which were articulated to Ordnance Survey really for the first time. Some of these needs had really only come out of the increasing and more recent use of map data in trials and pilot projects. Some of the functionality sought of the digital map product would take many years before it could be developed, if at all. This additional functionality included better header information for 'part and part' sheets (that is where two scales of mapping existed within one square kilometre), alternative transfer media and formats, multiple feature coding for those seeking object data (for example, front of house and edge of road), edge match between abutting map files and creation of polygon facilities (for example, building features), the need to preserve the feature serial numbers (FSNs) and the apparent need to archive data that would eventually be overtaken by physical change on the ground.

Investigations following the Ordnance Survey Review Committee Report established that the existing data structure, already well proven in production, had the admirable characteristic that it could easily be converted to a wide range of other formats, such that digital map data could be utilised on a wide range of computer systems. The conversion software had been established as the basis for customer service from Ordnance Survey for all existing users. Studies had already been put in hand to address a number of known weaknesses or deficiencies in the existing data structure. These weaknesses demanded multiple attributes for features, the restructuring of data into a links and nodes structure, a review of attribute coding to better describe geometric objects, a facility to permit the logical connection of features, the need for data compression and better data validation. Although any or all of these developments were bound to further increase domestic production costs, decisions about them needed to be taken, if feasible, toward the end of 1982. In a sense the need for these enhancement represented the ever-present conflict between cost and value.

The PMA restructuring project work, initially commissioned from a software house by Ordnance Survey, had commenced some years even before the Review Committee was assembled to consider such issues. That project came about because of alleged shortcomings in digital map data which had been highlighted by early users and collaborators. The lengthy restructuring project was eventually brought to a head through a collaborative venture between Ordnance Survey and Dudley Metropolitan Borough, whereby this Midland Local Authority sought to acquire and use land-parcel data produced by restructuring in a data-base application. With a 60% success rate only achieved in parcel formation from the underlying digital map data by the use of specially developed software, the whole procedure became non-viable when a costly edit phase had to be deployed to get to 100% success rate for all land parcels.

Serious bugs in the software persisted and these were never properly eradicated, but the most significant cause of failure was the inherent poor quality and consistency of the underlying map data, which Ordnance Survey had struggled to create so expensively. The act of parcel building provided an intensely critical review of both the data's geometry and of its feature coding. What had become apparent was that if ever a higher grade of data 'fuel' was to be demanded of Ordnance Survey by significant paying customers, then the PMA approach simply had to be reconsidered. It soon became clear, following early and initial work on mass data storage and transmission, that neither of these topics were likely to give rise to any significant problems for Ordnance Survey in the more immediate future. Neither subject really threatened, on superficial consideration, to damage any particular future strategy for digital mapping. They were both therefore held in abeyance until specific problems appeared likely to surface.

The presumption that 'technology would eventually come to the rescue' did on occasions become something of a dangerous 'catch-all' escape from some of the more immediate problems confronting the further and rapid development of digital mapping at Ordnance Survey in the balance of the 1980s.

This very active but worrying chapter in Ordnance Survey's digital mapping story eventually culminated in June 1984, when the Secretary of State for the Environment – after five long years – finally pronounced on the Government's plans for the future of the organisation in the aftermath of and in response to the previous Government's Committee of Enquiry into its future. Considerable effort had been expended by those from within who were engaged on development work and by a number of outsiders.

The four-year period, between Sir David Serpell forwarding the report of his Committee's deliberations and its recommendations and the Government actually making a formal response, had afforded valuable time for Ordnance Survey itself to seek answers to the many and complex issues raised during the Review. It was, however, somewhat ironic that the Report of the Review had been sent under cover of a letter urging the Government to take prompt action, perhaps nowhere more so than in establishing the future of digital mapping, where serious risk of wasteful duplication and non-conformance to national standards, had been so clearly anticipated.

The four-year interval, frustrating as it was for the relatively few real customers 'at the leading edge' and to those staff at Ordnance Survey who were most aware of what was really needed for the digital future, afforded adequate time for a series of quite fundamental internal investigations to proceed and most certainly allowed the future requirements of users to be hardened up and confirmed. Nevertheless, progress in producing digital map data had slumped during this period of great uncertainty as the following table illustrates:

Year	1:1250	1:2500	1:10000
1981–82	395	202	25
1982–83	428	96	29
1983–84	295	83	26

Digital map outputs produced annually by Ordnance Survey, 1981–84 (Source: Published Annual Reports, HMSO).

The sharp decline in outputs in 1983–84 was occasioned by major specification changes associated with the demands pursued, in the main, by utility undertakings. Thus, by February 1983, Ordnance Survey had been armed with a very thorough perspective of the most certain segments of the market for digital map data. Production outputs had clearly slowed in the wake of the Review Committee findings for a variety of reasons, as the table, above, illustrates.

During this lengthy period of waiting, there was further and continuing evidence of self-doubt by Ordnance Survey as the Director General began to prepare his case for funds to Government. With quite limited resources already dedicated to the actual task of digitising, most of the weaknesses observed by the Review Committee were still very much in evidence. This was partly because of the lack of self-confidence in its own judgement and partly because of the need to gain credibility from an independent consultant's endorsement of its proposals. Ordnance Survey embarked on yet another study. The same Dr Whitfield, this time working in association with David Rhind – who was eventually to play a significant role in completion of the digitising project as Director General – was engaged to review Ordnance Survey's proposals for finally digitising all the large-scale maps of Great Britain. The threads for the future were at last being drawn and spun together, but there was still to be further delay and protracted uncertainty.

Chapter 11
Gathering momentum but still awaiting a response from central government

Previous chapters document several avenues of progress made by Ordnance Survey following the deliberations of the Review Committee and during the long period whilst the Central Government of the day sought an acceptable way forward for Great Britain's national mapping organisation. By late 1982 the Ordnance Survey Advisory Board – originally proposed by the Review Committee to bring business expertise to bear and to stimulate what was seen as a defensive, slow moving civil service department – was recruited and had met for the first time. From the outset the Advisory Board and the serving executive directors managed to create an uncomfortable relationship with mutual suspicion about the motives of each.

Ordnance Survey had already committed the slender resources it chose to muster for the Review Committee's first phase of investigation and development in connection with digital mapping. Bearing in mind the total resource capacity of both cash and staff of one sort or another of Ordnance Survey in the early 1980s, it was a relatively modest level of resources which had been deployed on the digitising project. A stubborn scepticism of Ordnance Survey about what new technology might actually achieve still existed in many quarters, not least amongst some members of staff occupying senior positions in management. The sentiment persisted, despite the Review Committee's conclusions, that the new technology was not considered strategic for the core business of preparing and publishing paper mapping.

The very limited resources allocated to phase one of the future strategy were due in part to the limited availability of suitable and talented people, which the Review Committee had previously commented upon with some feeling. For example, in the key area of Ordnance Survey's centralised Computer Unit, almost all of the system analysis and programming staff that had stayed through various waves of government-inspired vilification and pay freezes, had come from within Ordnance Survey itself. Very few of the staff concerned had any relevant external experience and few had the ability and enthusiasm of Mr Syd Hull. He, although self-taught, had consistently proved to have been one of the few inspirations behind many of the initial and subsequent developments that had taken place in the already lengthy digital mapping project.

The culture of the Department, even as late as 1982, meant that the small band of staff who were tasked with innovation and development were located and managed elsewhere, while the staff of the Computer Unit existed simply to manage and operate the status quo and to plan and implement future developments only when they had been investigated and recommended for implementation by the few innovators and their line management.

Typically for almost all of Ordnance Survey, this attitude still unfortunately led to a climate of defensiveness. Innovation, in this case with software or systems, was not encouraged. The very clear need for a greater number of suitable graduate staff with varied experience deployed in Ordnance Survey's embryonic Development Unit was frustrated by the old social order within the Department at large. The sensitivities and rivalry 'for a place in the sun' of the small military contingent that still served at Ordnance Survey and the fears of the much larger and largely unfulfilled technician cadre at Ordnance Survey, served equally as major constraints on the required build-up of the numbers and quality of suitable, talented graduate staff that the investigation and development phase really demanded.

It was at this time that there developed among the small band of personnel actually engaged on making progress with digital production methods within Ordnance Survey – whether working in the Computer Unit – managing production itself or within the Development Unit, a growing sense of frustration and despair. Expectations of imminent and fundamental technological breakthroughs had been almost assured by those giving evidence to the Ordnance Survey Review Committee, and these assumptions duly appeared in the final report. The Report of the Whitfield Study had served to underpin and to confirm these same expectations as still being quite realistic.

Yet, despite much shared enthusiasm and ingenuity by Ordnance Survey staff and the suppliers of the new technology, which soon became known as TODDS, this, the best of the likely novel solutions available in the three-to-five-year time horizon, was found to be seriously wanting when employed on the specifics of the Ordnance Survey large-scale digitising task. Incremental improvements to the rather tedious manual production methods employed to date on the pilot production flowline had been introduced on a continuing basis between 1980 and 1983, once justified, developed and tested. Individually, these were only rather modest refinements of the manual system and collectively they neither significantly reduced the still-too-high production costs nor significantly reduced the likely timescale if the task was realistically ever to be completed.

The reality was that the much-touted prospect of a 'significant and fundamental breakthrough' was simply not there to be taken. Perhaps the most positive aspect of this, the first real phase of progressive and non-incremental development with TODDS, was the increasing certainty of the contribution of the interactive graphics workstation such as MADES (map edit data system), which was an integral part of the prototype system. This sub-system had come about as a result of widespread and fundamental display screen technology development. These workstations were the subject of rigorous trials and evaluation in connection with the TODDS project for semi-automatic digitising, but they were soon to provide a breakthrough in their own right.

The charge could fairly be levelled at Ordnance Survey that the Fastrak digitising trials took far too long before conclusions were eventually drawn, but the equipment was extremely unreliable in performance and Ordnance Survey had long since harboured a culture whereby equipment, once purchased, simply had to be made to work to justify the initial expenditure. This was an integral part of the 'blame culture' that had always been so pervasive within Ordnance Survey. Risk taking had never been part of the in-house culture.

The newly-appointed Advisory Board received serial reports from Ordnance Survey directors of technological difficulties and increasing scepticism and doubts about the possibility of technological breakthroughs. They and executive directors were seized with increasing suspicion and doubt about any beneficial outcomes. Because of the worsening relationship between the rather pompous and suspicious

Advisory Board external members and the Ordnance Survey executive directors of the day, the Advisory Board quickly sought further external and alleged independent advice.

They arranged to have Ordnance Survey's technical proposals for future digitising of large-scale mapping reviewed by means of a short external consultancy. They wished the study to pay particular regard to the technologies proposed for data capture and to the suggested target data structure as well as the series of enhancements to it that Ordnance Survey was proposing to implement. David Rhind, an academic, and Dr R Whitfield once more, by now with ICL Ltd, were hired to conduct the further review study. A report to the Director General was demanded by September 1983. Access was duly granted to the reports of all the studies conducted by Ordnance Survey post-Serpell Review and to those of previous consultants. Interestingly, in the final report the consultants saw the need to stress their independence of Ordnance Survey and its personnel.

The Rhind/Whitfield Study, as it soon became known, was tasked with giving a further view on Ordnance Survey's plans, which sought to digitise all basic-scale maps of Great Britain by the year 2000 but with urban and peri-urban areas to be completed by 1990. In this approach Ordnance Survey planned to produce digital map data in a form similar to that which had been captured to date, but with progressive improvements to it as the programme proceeded. This was to be achieved by combining in-house resources with those of selected contractors using increased levels of automation as and when they became available and affordable. Other plans developed by Ordnance Survey included the introduction of a digital map revision and update service along the lines suggested by the Study of Revision. This called for revision information made more frequently available than under current mapping supply services and the eventual upgrade of map data to a more highly structured form suitable for a range of non-graphic uses at some stage in the future.

The report produced by the consultants concluded that Ordnance Survey was indeed justified, on behalf of users, in pressing ahead with their plans to accelerate the digitising project. The disadvantages of Ordnance Survey not providing leadership were confirmed as damaging and expensive to the national interest. Ordnance Survey plans were seen to represent a reasonable compromise between rapidity of coverage and of geographic priorities. Starting and completion dates and the timing of completion of urban and peri-urban mapping were found to be soundly based. The consultants accepted that Ordnance Survey's approach in seeking to harness more automated techniques had been conducted in a thorough and comprehensive manner.

The use of the current manual digitising methods suitably enhanced when possible were considered justified. Implementation schedules for improvements to the data product were generally felt to be too slow and likely to lead to the need for tedious rework. The consultants confirmed that user needs should dictate both data structure and content in future years. Further, they felt that it simply had to be accepted that user needs would change over time. The list of proposed enhancements to the data would undoubtedly serve to provide a more useful product for most customers.

The Rhind/Whitfield Study Report also served to confirm the major findings of the in-house user needs study, certainly in respect of the majority of the 'near future' users. They chose to remark that the longer-term needs identified by Ordnance Survey should be assessed with a good degree of care before they are met at some stage in the future. The review of this study purported to highlight some methodological weaknesses in the work of the in-house study with regard to weighting of samples and the need for further cross tabulations, but they did also recognise the many difficulties those conducting it had faced, with so very few actual users and with most of those really only just starting up the 'learning curve' of experience of using digital map data. The great 'fragility of the market' and its weakness at devising and nominating its needs with any real reliability up to this point in time is perhaps best illustrated by sales statistics.

Period	Digital sales	Cumulative sales
Up to December 1976	279	279
December 1976 to June 1981	963	1 242
June 1981 to October 1982	625	1 867

Growth in sales of large-scale digital map files (all scales).
(Data from actual sales figures to date)

These sales statistics portray a very small existing market in total, but one with a rather sudden burst of awakening interest by actual customers.

At this time, with the exception of the necessary investigation and research – detailed elsewhere – into the prospects for employing private-sector companies to work under contract to digitise Ordnance Survey mapping, if feasible, almost all the necessary groundwork of enquiry and investigation demanded of them, post-Serpell Review, had been completed by Ordnance Survey in one way or another in the ensuing four years.

The next milestone for the digitising project at Ordnance Survey was the first of two further external reviews, which took place in 1983. The first review was at the behest of a House of Lords Select Committee. The second review flowed from the first, but it was conducted as an enquiry into the needs for and the handling of geographic information a few years later on. The seriousness of impact and the material contribution of both external reviews is still, even with the passage of time, quite difficult to assess. Whether defining, catalytic or simply influencing can perhaps now be assessed objectively from this more distant perspective. However, both reviews should certainly have a place in any account of the history of Ordnance Survey's digitising project.

Public reviews of this nature, by their composition and modus operandi, seem to get 'steered' by the sheer volume of witnessing voices, many of whom most frequently seek to serve a rather narrow self-interest. Such reviews tend to seize upon what they are given rather than seek to think things through from fundamental principles. Such reviews are often pulled in a particular direction by those who are motivated, for whatever reason, to tender evidence. In the case of the first of these two external reviews, academics and a small number of active users of digital mapping, who were in the forefront of the development of pilot information systems, just as they had with the Ordnance Survey Review Committee before in 1978, managed once again to an extent to misdirect the review on a number of important matters.

Most notably these were the likely positive impact on the project from alternative technologies and the wildly exaggerated state of the development and readiness of the market for digital map data. At the time of both reviews, Ordnance Survey still retained much of its relict culture. It appeared to listen but, internally convinced that it knew best anyway, it tended to resume its own previously chosen course of action. Overstated claims made by 'outsiders' to external reviews merely served to confirm and indeed entrench this obdurate corporate culture. Whilst Ordnance Survey pursued its chosen policies, there was an increasing number of staff, albeit still small in overall numbers, within who, whilst they respected the Department's past achievements, were increasingly uninfluenced by the yoke of its history and its traditions.

Those, at different levels, who were involved with the digitising project strove to drive it forward in the best interests of all Ordnance Survey's stakeholders. In the period following the publication of the Report of the Ordnance Survey Review Committee in 1979, there was a growing belief within Ordnance Survey in the need for the digitising task to be completed and certainly within a more realistic timescale. However, caution and scepticism about such goals for Ordnance Survey still had a very large and influential constituency inside the Department, particularly within the senior management team.

With a full and considered response to the 1979 Review Committee Report still awaited from HM Government and following sustained pressure by Ordnance Survey on key friends in high places, in 1983 the House of Lords Select Committee on Science and Technology set out to conduct an enquiry into the development of remote sensing and digital mapping. The Committee was chaired by Lord Shackleton, who on a previous occasion had demonstrated his interest in such matters and his support for Ordnance Survey in opposing HM Government's wish to impose Trading Fund status prematurely on the Department. David Rhind, by then Professor of Geography at Birkbeck College® of the University of London®, was appointed as a specialist adviser to the Committee.

The Select Committee rendered its report in December 1983 and the House of Lords debated it quite promptly, in April 1984. David Rhind's influence on the Review, both in its deliberations and on the nature and content of the Report itself, should not be underestimated. The twin themes of the enquiry were, in point of fact, uneasy technological 'bedfellows'. Their only common strands were the inherently 'geographical' nature of their outputs and their shared dependence on computer technology and high-volume-information processing that was, at last, becoming universally available. Most witnesses who tendered evidence to the Select Committee and the Report of the Enquiry itself signally failed to weave the twin threads together to any great extent.

Remote sensing was inevitably trapped, at this particular point in time, within a much wider debate about the need for and the basis of Great Britain's continued interest in space research and the clear unwillingness of the Government to invest adequate resources in space-based research. Digital mapping had already been considered at considerable length and with great care during the deliberations of the Ordnance Survey Review Committee chaired by Sir David Serpell. The digitising project at Ordnance Survey had already featured at some length in the Review Committee's Report, which was produced in 1979. The main virtue of the House of Lords Select Committee deliberations and its Report was that, because of its timing and because of the Government's failure to respond to the original Review Committee Report, it was able to project and, to an extent at least, verify the results of Ordnance Survey's stage one enquiries and investigations.

Many of these studies had been completed in the interim, within the budget of the limited resources that Ordnance Survey had managed to invest. The Select Committee, by its very nature, had a positive role to play in applying further pressure on dilatory Government Ministers by urging them to make some response at least to the Review Committee Report. The Report of the Select Committee coincided with the preparation of a plan by Ordnance Survey that, if deployed, would see the acceleration of the completion of digital mapping of Great Britain, given that a suitable level of resources for the programme's duration could be found.

The House of Lords Select Committee, perhaps not surprisingly, reran many of the issues raised earlier. It concluded in its report that the demand for digital map data would continue to expand but that actual requirements of users were almost certain to change, as further experience was gained. Their report concluded that the costs of producing digital data would decrease substantially, on the back of differing technologies, and that new products could be made by Ordnance Survey and others from the data. The report, in general, reiterated much of what the Ordnance Survey Review Committee had already diagnosed as problems by way of progress to date. These included the lack of availability of data, poor advice to customers and lack of information about the benefits to be achieved from using map data, the still unresolved copyright problem with computer data products, the ultimate form and content of the data product, the lack of published standards for capture and exchange of digital map data and the lack of height data.

The House of Lords Report concluded very forcefully: 'Ordnance Survey is, to a degree, a prisoner of its history. Instinctively, it is tempted to carry on as before, producing the same maps to the same high quality but employing digital techniques as a direct substitute for manual methods. It is also geared up for this with all its staff concentrated on map production. The Committee recognises that the Director General wishes Ordnance Survey to become something more than a mere map factory, but the obstacles to this are considered severe. He does not have the R&D numbers or strength to adapt fast enough, and the shift to digital mapping after two centuries of paper mapping calls for a revolution in methods, attitudes and skills.'

The writer believes that the Director General was already heavily engaged in 'brinkmanship' with government to secure an adequate level of resources for any significant progress and acceleration of digitising. Between 1979 and 1983, with a total payroll in excess of 3,000 and an annual budget of around £40 million per annum, higher levels of investment in the digitising project could surely have been made.

The House of Lords Select Committee in its report indicated very strong support for Ordnance Survey to accelerate progress to achieve national digital map cover of Great Britain, as directed by the original Review Committee Report, with the second stage of the recommended two-stage approach for the future. The Select Committee called for the agreement and publication of a definite end date for the project, some 10 years hence; to forecasting a large upsurge in demand for large-scale digital map data, they felt that the 16 or more years, suggested by Ordnance Survey itself, was far too long for users to wait. Further, the Select Committee called for a clear programme of work to be planned and published, right through to completion; such that, through the life of the 10-year programme, customers could interact with Ordnance Survey in seeking to modify the overall plan, to change priorities and, where this was not feasible, to adjust the published timescales.

The Select Committee endorsed the Review Committee's and Ordnance Survey's plans for much of the residual digitising task to be 'contracted out' to private-sector companies whilst emphasising the value of the added prospect of creating a new industry in Great Britain. Their report called for much closer cooperation between Ordnance Survey and leading major customers to produce and justify positive cost-benefit studies for the successful and beneficial use of Ordnance Survey's digital map data services. Perhaps to no one's surprise, the criticisms of Ordnance Survey's user-needs study, first voiced in the earlier Rhind/Whitfield Report, were again highlighted. In point of fact and contrary to views voiced by external reviews, history soon showed this to have been a very thorough piece of work and a most reliable indicator of what actual users, as opposed to academics, were coming, increasingly, to demand.

The increasing focus in the marketplace on the trade-off between cost and functionality of the data was already beginning to bring some realism to the demands made of Great Britain's national mapping agency in terms of digital map data. The Select Committee Report concluded that 'the success of digital mapping would ultimately be conditioned by the understanding which users have of what it can do for them'. Other aspects that the Report of the Select Committee addressed concerned the content and organisation of the digital map data itself that the market demanded and the very real risk of the duplication of effort, resulting in data produced to wildly varying standards, if Government and Ordnance Survey continued to fail to impose a real sense of purpose and direction. The report recognised the very real dilemma that Ordnance Survey faced with the future of digital mapping. The choice realistically appeared to fall between carrying on as before with 'more of the same' or whether Ordnance Survey should adopt an entirely new approach to the task before it. With only some 10% of national coverage completed up to this point in time, and this to inconsistent and unreliable standards, the latter was still a very real option, especially if new technologies were, in fact, likely to become available.

The question of the suitability of the map data produced thus far and the role of raster data, again, perhaps not surprisingly, came to the foreground once more. A very great divergence of opinion was evident from the evidence taken by the Select Committee on the form and content required of the future map data product. Also, the very restrictive storage and supply of the digital map data, on magnetic tape, which the Committee felt only really provided Ordnance Survey with simple whole map extraction, was also recognised as a major constraint on future developments. There was really no overwhelming or conclusive guidance for the future from the evidence taken. The Select Committee did, however, call for some national standards to be prepared and published for the data itself and for its exchange. Ordnance Survey's efforts and the progress made to date, with these issues, was duly acknowledged and received approval from the Select Committee.

The Report of the Select Committee served to broaden the issue beyond the question of whether, how and at what speed Ordnance Survey should create national digital large-scale map data, by urging the Government to establish a suitable committee of enquiry to examine 'the handling of geographic information in the UK'. Quite clearly the Ordnance Survey digitising project would be material to any such enquiry. The Select Committee Report also called for the creation of a 'national geographic information centre' as the eventual focus for all related activity. In this context the report concluded furthermore: in addition to being responsive to change, Ordnance Survey must actively lead it. It felt 'the groundswell of change in information technology is apparent and, with the movement away from paper maps, old constraints and attitudes are weakening.

The advent of digital mapping creates new opportunities for information systems incorporating spatial data and using the national survey as a common reference point; indeed, the usefulness of digital mapping depends on such systems. Because Ordnance Survey provides the foundation for spatial databases, it should not remain passive while information systems grow up around it. Instead it should actively engage in their development.' Ordnance Survey had certainly not, by the time of the Select Committee Report in 1984, come to share or endorse such a broad perspective for the future.

The Select Committee, in its Report, recognised very clearly the importance of the large-scale map archive of Great Britain. It supported and reiterated the view, already put forward before by the Ordnance Survey Advisory Board, that 'it could see no basis on which responsibility for the essential archive maintenance, updating and modernisation work of Ordnance Survey could become a commercial operation'. However, the Select Committee concluded that the balance between costs and benefits of digitising for Ordnance Survey would turn out to be favourable by avoiding wasteful duplication of effort and, in a quite short timescale, should meet the needs of local authorities and the utility undertakings, who themselves were under mounting pressures to modernise their information systems.

Turning finally to the vital issue of who should pay for the 10-year digitising programme, which they demanded, the Select Committee regarded the task as an essential national activity which surely called for exchequer support through grant or loan. The Report concluded that 'the digitising programme should not be delayed by short-term cash limitations'.

The Government's response to the Report of the Select Committee was duly made by the Secretary of State for Trade and Industry in association with the Secretaries of State for the Environment, for Education and Science and for Defence, in July 1984. This public response confirmed that Ordnance Survey had indeed put forward proposals to Ministers for an accelerated digitising programme that would complete urban areas by 1990 and the rest of the country by the year 2000. This statement served at least to link the Select Committee findings with all that had gone before in the wake of the Serpell Review, which had been stalled by central government for so long.

The joint ministerial statement suggested that the 10-year programme was not, on the advice of Ordnance Survey, really seen as realistic or achievable even though, as already planned, much of the task was to be contracted out to a new industry to be encouraged and established within the private sector. The Government's response did however firmly put Ordnance Survey at the very heart of the programme, by urging all public bodies to follow the Ordnance Survey approach, rather than act on unilateral programmes, which would only serve to debilitate the desired national programme, by way of differing standards or specifications. The Government response endorsed moves by Ordnance Survey to promote actively the benefits of digital mapping through joint ventures and partnerships, initiated by what was still a very modest in-house marketing operation.

It also confirmed and stressed the need for a clearly publicised programme for digitising and for agreed public standards for the production and exchange of digital map data. The Government response projected the view that had come forcefully from within Ordnance Survey, but not from evidence given to the Select Committee largely by academics. This was the view that there were few internal or external needs for a more elaborate specification and data structure. The balance of opinion and direction had finally swung behind the 'more of the same until completion' opinion that appeared to offer the best approach for customers and for the Department itself. Indeed, the drive, which eventually became irresistible, was for Ordnance Survey to simplify its data specification for digital map data, which was already becoming predominant, at regular meetings with key utility industry customers. Finally, the Government's response to the House of Lords Select Committee confirmed that the Secretary of State for the Environment would appoint a committee of enquiry to report on the handling of geographic information in Great Britain.

The Select Committee, whilst conducting its enquiries and publishing its report, found that Ordnance Survey was already seriously 'review weary'. The issues that the holistic review of 1978–79 first raised had still not yet been resolved or graced with a formal response from HM Government. The period from 1979 until 1983 was generally a period of considerable frustration for Ordnance Survey and for the handful of customers already committed to a digital information future. There is no doubt that the very existence of 'a House of Lords Select Committee' retracing the steps and largely confirming the findings of the previous Review Committee did help to bring some pressure to bear on Government.

It certainly helped to publicise the results of the first phase of investigation that Ordnance Survey had embarked upon and the likely best pace at which the Review Committee's phase two could be implemented. The Select Committee enquiries and its report also served to widen the debate beyond the question of the speed at which Ordnance Survey should produce digital map cover of Great Britain. For the first time, at least in a public forum, it raised questions about wider issues arising from the opportunities that the completed capture of digital map data would create in a future of much wider and ubiquitous information processing and supply. Such a world would present Ordnance Survey with a fresh set of issues and challenges.

At long last and arising from further consideration of the original Review Committee Report, following sustained pressure from customer groups, a House of Lords Committee and Ordnance Survey itself, two statements did eventually emerge from central government. These at least served to clarify the future for Ordnance Survey. The first statement was made on 20 January 1984 by Rt Hon Patrick Jenkin MP, Secretary of State for the Environment, who announced: 'Following earlier consultation with the Ordnance Survey Advisory Board by my predecessor (Mr Heseltine) about future financial structures, in particular that of trading fund status for Ordnance Survey, I have decided not to proceed with that option'.

The reality was that the Government, perhaps somewhat surprisingly, had already received a significant rebuff on this subject in the House of Lords, with a majority galvanised into action, largely through the efforts of Lord Edward Shackleton, who had sustained a long-term interest in matters concerning mapping and charting, and Ordnance Survey in particular. The statement went on to confirm that Ordnance Survey would remain a vote-funded civil service department of government with targets set and monitored for financial performance, with obligations for annual trading accounts and a rolling five-year policy and plan.

The statement concluded with the announcement of the appointment of Mr William Waldegrave MP as Minister with responsibility for Ordnance Survey. This was, in fact, to prove to be of some considerable significance in seeking a satisfactory future for digital mapping at Ordnance Survey, for he was to prove an intelligent and informed Minister at a time when these matters at last came to a head. The statement concluded with a formal public acknowledgement of the Advisory Board's urgent call for a full response to the Serpell Committee recommendations. The Secretary of State made clear that in accepting the main thrust of the Report by the Serpell Committee a full and detailed response would be issued. This first statement from Government therefore settled the major structural and financial issues for Ordnance Survey.

The second statement was made by Mr William Waldegrave MP, Undersecretary of State for the Environment, on the 13 December 1984, in which he acknowledged that Ordnance Survey, whilst taking account of Serpell Report recommendations, had, as a result, made considerable progress on many fronts. This progress was, he said, reflected in the Government's full response to Serpell which, that day, he was making available. Paying particular regard to the future of the long-term digital mapping project, he announced an increase in the level of resources and activity from 1985–86 onwards. These additional resources were to be deployed on what could be identified and accepted as a 'core task' with an accelerated programme to digitise Ordnance Survey large-scale maps. He closed the statement by announcing the completion and acceptance of what was the first of Ordnance Survey's rolling five-year plans.

Chapter 12
Gathering evidence of the need for a big push forward by Ordnance Survey

The conclusions contained in the Report of the Ordnance Survey Review Committee, subsequently confirmed in the Whitfield Report, called for the development and expansion of the digital mapping project. In parallel with these two external reviews, Ordnance Survey, through its own user-needs study, had developed a clearer vision of what customers for digital mapping would be seeking from Ordnance Survey. However, customers who had actually made purchases of digital map data were still very few in number, with most of these still only at an early experimental stage in developing uses of digital map data and therefore in identifying realistic needs. The first of two phases of investigation, called for initially by the Review Committee as key stages of a development strategy for digital mapping, had, in the main, been completed satisfactorily.

One of these phase-one studies by Ordnance Survey itself, duly confirmed in turn by an independent external review, had made it clear that alternative technologies for data capture were, in fact, not yet available. Thus it became clear that the key goal of speeding up initial data capture, in turn significantly reducing costs, could not be realised in the foreseeable future. The Ordnance Survey consultative machinery, particularly those bodies representing local authorities, the utilities and other government departments, a House of Lords Select Committee and the relatively recently appointed Ordnance Survey Advisory Committee had each indicated a very clear need for Ordnance Survey to press on rapidly with the digitising of the basic-scale map archive of Great Britain.

Early in 1984 only some 22,000 map units (some 10% of the total) had in fact already been databanked. Some of these, which had been held from the very beginning of the project in original DMA format, would, in fact, eventually be found to need redigitising from scratch, largely on account of many major specification changes introduced since their initial capture and the generally poor curvilinear data captured before modern curve fitting techniques had been deployed on the production flowline. Consistency of data specification became a major issue for Ordnance Survey whilst the digitising programme remained so protracted. The conundrum that constantly had to be addressed was whether to maintain the specification used from the outset or to respond to customer and domestic needs for changes by backtracking over and reworking files already stored in the databank, to meet contemporary needs.

Armed with most of the evidence it needed and driven by the breadth of support from the various reviews and investigations, Ordnance Survey next sought to prepare a suitable case for submission to central Government for an accelerated programme of digitising, which had to be accompanied by a statement of the increased level of resources which were felt necessary to accomplish it. Ordnance Survey's own user-needs study findings were soon backed up by increasingly strident demands from the increasingly effective consultative committees most concerned. The justification for the rapid acceleration of the Ordnance Survey task was essentially twofold. On the one hand, rapid acceleration of progress with the task would remove the risk of customers attempting to create map data themselves, with all the attendant concerns of differing standards and specifications. On the other hand, those organisations that needed digital mapping but that could not afford 'to go it alone', should not be deprived of an essential element of information technology in the task of managing vital map-related information for their various businesses.

The major problem that Ordnance Survey needed to resolve was the near certain 'mismatch' that was likely to exist – for many years to come – between the costs incurred for an accelerated programme and the revenue stream that ever-increasing government-set cost-recovery targets demanded by way of pricing of the map data that most customers could or would afford. Coming from its past, where customers were only expected to pay the costs of printing maps, to a future where the cost of creation of the data had to be recovered from those demanding it, was certain to lead to sustained mistrust and antagonism.

The calculation of the likely costs and effort to achieve an accelerated national programme by the Review Committee could, by 1984, be clearly seen to have been wildly optimistic with regard both to the likely total cost of £15.8 million and to the 10-year timescale. This was not wholly surprising as the second stage of the suggested two-stage approach by the Serpell Review had been predicated on suitable advanced digitising techniques becoming available. Indeed, it had quickly become apparent that no such breakthrough could be found and any plans for the future simply had to be based wholly on existing manual methods enhanced whenever possible by incremental improvements in techniques or newly developed hardware facilities.

The case that Ordnance Survey sought to prepare and submit was, in fact, based on a programme that the Ordnance Survey user-needs study had helped to formulate. This case demanded that urban and peri-urban areas should be completed by 1990, mainly to meet the needs of the utility customers. The balance of the country could therefore not be completed before the year 2000. The cost of such a programme, assuming that sequential improvements to techniques and upgrades to equipment were achieved, was assessed at an additional £78 million after current planned levels of expenditure totalling £25 million were deducted. It should be noted that in continuing with this lower, level of resources dedicated to digital map conversion without an increase of the size eventually to be sought, Ordnance Survey would not have achieved full digital map cover for Great Britain much before the year 2048. Clearly at some point, differing technologies would have been applied leading to a quite different outcome. The timescale using only existing methods does serve to illustrate the magnitude of the task.

In the early part of 1984 Ordnance Survey's senior management team produced a paper arguing the case to justify a rapid acceleration of digitising. Much thought was also given to the best strategy for taking it forward for approval and support by central Government. Following soundings taken with suitable contacts at the DOE and HM Treasury, Ordnance Survey prepared to submit the case to its new Minister, the rather dynamic and generally supportive Mr William Waldegrave MP.

The case, bearing in mind the Thatcher Government's underlying philosophy, rather dangerously projected a very slow flow of revenue arising from the project. This was to prove to be something of a 'two-edged sword'. By making such a projection, Ordnance Survey sought to avoid the imposition of a 'revolving fund' concept for funding the digitising. But with a slower than anticipated take up by customers, progress would need to be slowed and this would have tended to militate against the need for a well-publicised and long-term programme for data availability, upon which major customers could plan their acquisitions. After all, this particular requirement had received emphasis in all of the studies and enquiries in the four years following the Review Committee Report.

The case that Ordnance Survey prepared and submitted duly emphasised the fact that the level of investment required could not be met from the resources dedicated to existing operations. Other obligations confirmed as essential and therefore categorised as 'core activities' by the Ordnance Survey Review Committee or those which were essential for revenue earning would need to be curtailed or closed down. The planned approach to central Government, at a time when the Thatcher Government's opposition to investment in government activities was uppermost in her Ministers' minds, quite obviously posed serious dangers that the plan would simply be rejected or stalled for a further period.

However, the proposed strategy had some attractions for the radical thinking Government of the day, in that it made clear that there would be no increase in the workforce of Ordnance Survey itself, with the digitising task to be placed under contract to the wholly private-sector companies. Despite consistent and persistent opposition by Ordnance Survey's trade unions – led in this particular case by the Institution of Professional Civil Servants (IPCS) – to such proposals, the case was founded on plans to contract out the greater part of the increased activity to private-sector companies. Whether the case was accepted or not, some financial provision had also been made in current departmental estimates for a vital series of trial contracts designed to engage and evaluate the private sector's willingness and abilities.

The House of Lords Select Committee for Science and Technology (Sub Committee 1) on Remote Sensing and Digital Mapping, when reviewing the likely role and contribution of Ordnance Survey had, in its wisdom, concluded that a total programme of some 10 years' duration was essential for the completion of the digitising task. This was clearly at odds with much of the evidence assembled up to that point in time, but such a claim – particularly from such a body – undoubtedly had a 'sanctifying' effect on the case eventually submitted by Ordnance Survey to government. The reality was that neither Ordnance Survey nor the wholly embryonic digitising industry in the private sector could reasonably be expected to 'ramp up' and 'ramp down' in such a short timescale. The account of the development of the private-sector digitising industry under Ordnance Survey's patient stewardship, told in the next chapter, only serves to justify the view that the House of Lords Select Committee's ten-year total timescale was indeed much too ambitious.

The case eventually submitted to government by Ordnance Survey was based on a plan to complete urban areas by 1990 and the balance of the country by the year 2000. With levels of in-house resources to be held broadly at the level of those provided for 1984, the rapid expansion called for was to be placed with the presumed much less risk-averse private sector. It is fair to say that there was a high level of cynicism about this particular aspect of the strategy within Ordnance Survey. This arose in large measure from the 'it is our job' type of prejudice, but there had already been some painful experiences of contracting out core operations. From 1982 onwards, there had been a series of generally unsuccessful mapping contracts, let in the wake of the Review Committee Report and the Report of Ordnance Survey's own study of revision.

This evidence remained the basis of the trade union's sustained opposition to an expanded programme founded on commercial contracts. When the case was actually prepared and presented, the role for private-sector contractors was entirely speculative as trial contracts, with all of the frustration and delays that they eventually brought, had yet to be planned and let. Ordnance Survey had concluded in its case that the timescale and the strategy of using the private sector would best serve realistic user needs and would make the best use of Ordnance Survey expertise in both digital data production and in matters of production control that had been developed over so many years. The position had been taken by Ordnance Survey that the private sector would eventually cope, and a shared production approach to the task would offer flexibility to Ordnance Survey if, as was likely, some contractors would fail in their performance.

The major attraction of the strategy suggested was that it obviated the rapid build-up and eventual rundown in staff numbers at Ordnance Survey for such a relatively short period. This was a time when successive and high-profile government 'manpower' cuts were the order of the day and while a 'career for life' was still very much the 'norm' culture for employees of Ordnance Survey. The respective roles in this proposed cooperative approach would, it was felt, serve to ensure that Ordnance Survey retained control of the project with full authority over the vital ingredients of planning and scheduling, specification and quality management.

The case eventually put to the Government considered four main options for funding an accelerated programme for digitising. The first was for 'full cost recovery', that is 'let the users who will benefit pay for the service', a doctrine in close harmony with contemporary Government philosophy. This approach was considered likely to preclude full single specification national coverage from ever being achieved, which, in turn, could lead to 'knee-jerk' responses in an unplanned manner with the attendant risks of customers digitising for themselves, to their own standards, to meet their own short-term needs. The likely outcome was therefore seen as one of ever-increasing prices with very limited usage of what data there was in the databank. The second option was the concept of a 'revolving fund', where revenue from digital mapping would be used theoretically to fund fresh activity.

This approach was felt likely to lead to undesirable outcomes similar to those associated with the first option. The third option was a case for investment based on full exchequer funding by central government to support a new, technology related presentation of Great Britain's national large-scale map archive. At a time of public expenditure restraint, it was considered that such an approach was unlikely to succeed. In any case, the Review Committee Report had also identified other aspects of national mapping that called for additional financial investment. The philosophy that, by seeking realistic charges, user demands of Ordnance Survey would be moderated, was again very much 'in tune' with the underlying philosophy of the ruling Thatcher Government. And so, with compelling arguments and the evidence of various reviews marshalled against all these options, Ordnance Survey pursued the final option vigorously in its submission. Government was asked to underwrite the cost of the accelerated digitising programme but with Ordnance Survey promising exploitation in the marketplace with full cost recovery to be achieved over the timescale of the accelerated programme.

The following tabulation shows the proposed build-up of additional funding that Ordnance Survey originally sought in its digital mapping submission, in relation to forecasts already made for Ordnance Survey's future financial performance in the first of the formal five-year plans that the Secretary of State had imposed on the Department when accepting the broad thrust of the Review Committee Report.

£ millions	1985–86	1986–87	1987–88	1988–89
Current vote	£57.3	£58.5	£59.4	£60.7
Extra funding*	£3.3	£8.4	£8.4	£8.4
New vote	£60.6	£66.9	£67.8	£69.1
New revenue projected	£30.2	£31.8	£32.8	£33.7
Exchequer support vote (%)	50.2%	52.5%	51.6%	51.2%

The financial basis of the case put to Ministers for additional funds

* These figures denote the increases in annual funding for the accelerated digitising programme continuing at the level of 1988–89, through to completion of the task.

The overall aim of such a plan was that even with the additional investment, Ordnance Survey would still manage to keep the percentage of government support below the 55% that had originally been set by Ministers in 1977 and which was only achieved for the first time in 1982. The greater part of the additional funding was to be employed on digitising contracts let to private-sector companies, with Ordnance Survey itself responsible for and managing national standards and the important processes of quality control of the contractor's work. Such a division of effort would, it was hoped, achieve competitive pricing, contain the need for increased Ordnance Survey capital investment and also ensure a smooth rundown in staff numbers.

Ordnance Survey staff, with or without the support of the trade union, would increasingly be diverted to the task of ensuring that contractors performed to specification and to agreed schedules. Ironically in the way of things, this reordering of the task for Ordnance Survey staff eventually came to suit the trade union, which, on another front, was battling with Government and Ordnance Survey to achieve higher professional status for its cartographic staff, with commensurate rewards for most of the staff concerned. Routine production work in the cartographic field did not generally support this other cause as it did on the surveying side of the organisation. Very gradually trade union and staff opposition to the use of private-sector contractors became weaker and weaker, until a genuine and productive partnership was achieved between Ordnance Survey and its considerable number of successful contractors.

An intense triangular correspondence next ensued between Ordnance Survey and officials at HM Treasury and the Department of the Environment about the preparation and sentiment of the case, before it could be put forward to Ministers. Most of the likely objections were exercised and eventually countered with suitable arguments. A slower investment and production schedule was soon developed. In the final analysis there was rivalry for funds between the Ordnance Survey's bid and that of the DOE itself. The DG, Mr Walter Smith, battled on and eventually wrote a very forceful letter, summarising, with dire predictions, what was likely to happen if the Ordnance Survey case for additional funding was not met. In the end the case went forward under cover of a letter from the DG in May 1984 to the ministerial office at the DOE, with the following revised model for additional funding for an accelerated digitising programme:

Year	1985-86	1986-87	1987-88	1988-89
Funds	£1.5m	£2.8m	£5.8m	£9.0m*

Additional funds sought by Ordnance Survey.

* Additional funding to continue at this level until completion.

Ordnance Survey, at the same time, circulated the case for additional funding for an accelerated programme to other government departments, thereby seeking to enlist their support. Of those contacted, the following responded quickly with very broad support for the Ordnance Survey cause and its proposal to complete digital map coverage of Great Britain in the revised timescale suggested. Her Majesty's Land Registry®, the Registers of Scotland, the Home Office, the Department of Transport, the Ministry of Agriculture, Food and Fisheries, the Office of Population, Censuses and Surveys (OPCS), the Welsh Office, the Scottish Office and the DOE itself all indicated their very broad support for Ordnance Survey's future needs.

Dr Martin Holdgate, the DOE's Chief Scientific Advisor, offered full support for the case, when consulted, and eventually Ordnance Survey's Minister, Mr William Waldegrave, annotated the submitted proposal as follows: 'Let us go into bat for an accelerated programme of digital mapping by Ordnance Survey'. This winning of ministerial support was the first major hurdle cleared, but there still remained HM Treasury to be convinced in the routine bilateral negotiations to secure the very substantial future vote funding for the DOE and, with it, the relatively modest increase in annual vote for Ordnance Survey. The fear, clearly foreseen at Ordnance Survey, had persisted that the additional level of support needed by the organisation to complete the digitising project would be subjugated, in these negotiations, to those of its very substantial 'parent' department. This, fortunately, did not come about. In reality, the enlarged Ordnance Survey vote allocation from HM Government was a figure so modest that it resided to the right of the decimal point of the many millions of pounds of overall allocation sought and won for and by the 'parent' department of Ordnance Survey.

It eventually became clear in October 1984 that Ordnance Survey's case had won the day and that the funding build-up, finally suggested above, would be made available to Great Britain's national mapping department. If the additional funding was to be available, the overall project timescale could only be met and promises to customers kept with a very significant and successful interaction between Ordnance Survey and private sector digitising contractors. In anticipation of increased funding, Ordnance Survey, in June 1984, began planning for the letting of trial digitising contracts.

A further influence on the digitising project was to be yet another committee of enquiry. In this case it came about from the original House of Lords Select Committee on Science and Technology, which had reported on remote sensing and digital mapping, with the Government's response eventually made in July 1984. The Select Committee had argued in its report that a need already existed to consider wider issues arising from the deployment of information technology and the yet-to-be-agreed programme and funding for Ordnance Survey's digitising project. The resulting enquiry into 'The Handling of Geographic Information' was duly established in April 1985. The Committee of Enquiry was chaired by Lord Chorley, who had appeared serially on the original Ordnance Survey Review Committee and the House of Lords Select Committee.

Both he and David Rhind were the main linkages and constants on and between the two committees.

Perhaps, not at all surprisingly, the issues and possible outcomes raised at the first were again played out at this most recent of enquiries. However, the issues were by then wider and the Ordnance Survey digitising proposals were but part of the new Committee's remit. The future role for and national expectations of Ordnance Survey in terms of digital mapping were covered in chapter four of the Committee's report. This was entitled 'Removing the barriers'. The report, which was published in 1987, concluded, in the face of much of the evidence given, that Ordnance Survey's large-scale digital map data was a vital element of future information-system needs in many customer organisations. The enquiry concluded that Ordnance Survey's new digitising programme, which flowed still somewhat uncertainly from the Government's response to the original Serpell Review Committee Report, was far too extended and would not therefore address adequately the mounting user needs for computer-based map information.

Ordnance Survey had in any case by this time already embarked on initiatives with private-sector contractors and with some of its more pressing utility customers, seeking to foreshorten overall project timescales. The Chorley Report, as it soon came to be called, was duly rendered to the DOE in 1987. It served to document that with some 30,000 map files in the databank at Ordnance Survey head office, some £22 million had already been spent, an estimate that most inside Ordnance Survey saw as deeply conservative.

Ordnance Survey still quoted, about this time, an average cost of some £800 to digitise, to check and to edit each MSD. The enquiry committee had received conflicting but very positive evidence of the imminence, yet again, of alternative technical approaches that Ordnance Survey could adopt. This concept persisted despite Ordnance Survey's disappointing evaluations and trials of the most likely systems and mounting scepticism about such rash and unsubstantiated claims. Those who favoured the alternative approach of raster scanning methods had managed to get their misleading and distracting message across to every single review of Ordnance Survey and its activities for almost a decade. HM Government, in pursuing other wider goals for Ordnance Survey, had, by this time, increased the cost recovery target for the large-scale 'core' activity, which included the digitising project to 40% for 1989–90. This necessitated a broad raft of price increases from Ordnance Survey who, at this time, were unlikely to expand the market without extensive digital map coverage being available.

This represented something of a catch-22 situation. The unavoidable price increases took the charge for a large-scale digital map file to £50 in April 1986 and to £85 in April 1987, but sales remained very limited. The enquiry committee certainly witnessed mounting pressure from actual and potential customers where they heard that map data needed to be produced to a reduced specification and be delivered by Ordnance Survey itself faster and more cheaply. The committee duly relayed this opinion. It called for a spirit of cooperation between Ordnance Survey and the utilities to resolve the apparent mismatch in specification for map data between Ordnance Survey's apparent wider and long-term needs and the more immediate needs of leading customers. During the enquiry some trial data, to a much lower specification, was actually produced by Eastern Region of British Gas®. An attempt was made to evaluate the likely cost savings. Ordnance Survey also attempted to evaluate the effort and cost to bring such data to the full specification that it firmly believed it needed for much wider future uses.

The report of the enquiry into the handling of geographic information covered a whole raft of issues such as the specification for the data, the creation of standards and the charging and copyright arrangements for map data. Early users had presented evidence on all these topics to the committee. By this time Ordnance Survey had become much more receptive to external comment and needs as well as responsive to criticism. Ordnance Survey already had a whole series of investigations covering most of the difficult issues arising from the accelerated provision and management of digital map data.

After many years of resentment and innate suspicion of customers and external commentators, Ordnance Survey had already moved substantially toward a much more open and consultative approach in its external relations. The value of close cooperation, which almost all external reviews had called for, was becoming an important feature of Ordnance Survey's ever widening external relations. Ordnance Survey still had its multi-strand business to manage within the demanding and often debilitating strictures devised by HM Government, but it had come at last to recognise the value of consultation before the event and true partnership. Both were in fact to play a still further and potent role in the final stages of the digitising project.

Chapter 13
At long last, gathering momentum with the help of private-sector contractors

The years between 1980 and 1984, following the work of the Ordnance Survey Review Committee led by Sir David Serpell, was a period of ever-increasing uncertainty for Ordnance Survey about its future roles and sources and levels of funding. During this lengthy period of great uncertainty, studies and investigations in connection with the future of digital mapping, which had been recommended in the Review Committee Report, were eventually all completed. The Director General had been prepared to admit that he had been unable to produce the necessary level of resources to expedite all outstanding matters. However, it increasingly became a matter of increasing urgency that HM Government should make a concerted response about the status, future role and the funding arrangements for Great Britain's national mapping organisation. Given central Government's thinking on those aspects would become clear, the future of digital mapping itself could hopefully, and at long last, be resolved.

With a much clearer picture of customers' requirements established and documented by Ordnance Survey's comprehensive user-needs study, the task to complete digital mapping, as laid out in the Review Committee Report, was increasingly seen to demand a finite time scale to achieve the completion of national coverage. The hopes of any significant technological breakthrough, in digitising times and costs, as suggested in the Report of the Review Committee, had soon been dashed in subsequent trials at Ordnance Survey of the technology which it had been agreed, as most likely to bring this about.

Despite stubborn advocacy to employ raster-data-capture technology by poorly informed academic commentators, who in many cases failed to understand the task, and potential system suppliers with an 'axe to grid' as the breakthrough most likely to succeed, it had become clear that, in the foreseeable future, there was no prospect of any significant or 'step change' reduction in digitising times, and therefore costs, from that particular approach. It is interesting to note here that this much advocated technology despite several visits to it by Ordnance Survey over the period, was in fact to play no part whatsoever in Ordnance Survey's digitising task before its completion in 1996. It soon became clear that the overall cost of the operation to convert a traditional map into a digital format was, therefore, most unlikely to reduce significantly, other than by relatively small incremental improvements to relevant equipment and enhanced working practices.

As a consequence, the overall timescale projected to capture the complete digital large-scale-map archive simply had to run to the year 2000 or, indeed, beyond. Most of the maps in early demand by customers covered the more densely populated areas of Great Britain, and these maps took longer and cost more to digitise. Hence there was little relief from high costs and long throughput times in early prospect for Ordnance Survey, when and if overall progress with the task could be accelerated significantly. The possible concept of a significant build-up of 'in-house' resources to complete the task, in terms of the equipment and the staff required, came increasingly to be seen as unrealistic and unachievable. This was most certainly so whilst the severe limitations, imposed centrally by the Government, on Ordnance Survey's overall employee numbers remained current and in force.

Prompted initially by the recommendation of the Review Committee Report, it became increasingly obvious to those involved with the digitising project's direction at Ordnance Survey that a considerable external force of private-sector contractors had to be recruited and mobilised as quickly as possible. A future and very significant contribution from contractors had to be found and developed, with what, by any standards, was still a very demanding task, if timescales and delivery schedules, increasingly demanded by customers, were to be met in future years. The wider view that the private sector alone could best invest, hire and fire staff and, indeed, tool-up quickly and very soon outperform the public sector, was very fashionable in the early 1980s.

Indeed, it was upon such beliefs that the doctrines of the Thatcher Government, seeking to suppress any demands from the public sector at this time, were in fact founded.

The resulting task of raising and developing a quality, private-sector digitising industry almost from scratch and capable of responding to Ordnance Survey's needs, in fact proved anything but simple and straightforward. Within Ordnance Survey itself there existed a fair degree of scepticism, based in part on traditional trade union philosophy and reaction to the attendant threat to members' jobs. The introduction of all new technology, but particularly that in pursuit of digital mapping, given the usual early and open prior consultation, had always been accepted and supported, very responsibly, by the key IPCS trade union within Ordnance Survey. This trade union represented the majority of technician and professional staff and had quite high membership levels.

However, and perhaps significantly, up to this point in time new technology had simply permitted more or different things to be accomplished. There was no real history at Ordnance Survey either of the introduction of new technology leading directly to job losses or of what were considered 'core tasks' being successfully sourced outside the Department. There had already been some recent considerable difficulty, both real and anecdotal, experienced with employing private-sector surveying and mapping contractors. On the surveying side of Ordnance Survey's production operations, private-sector commercial firms, specialising in surveying and mapping operations, had generally and recently proved themselves quite incapable of revising the 1:2500 scale overhauled mapping.

These maps had been produced initially by non-rigorous 'overhaul' methods adopted by Ordnance Survey for much of its protracted post-war resurvey campaign. Ordnance Survey technicians, over many years, had developed skills dealing with something of an art form rather than working toward a rigorous solution. After a series of contract lets, almost all contractors engaged on this work under contract appeared to lack any deep understanding of the nature of the task and all contractors fell well short of Ordnance Survey's standards, in terms of production control, attention to detail and thoroughness of completion. Indeed, all contractors, who had won such contracts, managed to get their 'fingers burned' very badly in financial terms.

To balance this unfortunate performance by the industry, it was also true that some of these same mapping contractors had, more recently, eventually managed the more straightforward and predictable task of mapping *abinitio* those areas of the country, as determined by Ordnance Survey, that demanded 1:1250 scale map cover. There is no doubt that, during 1984, following these contracts, word had got about that Ordnance Survey was indeed a difficult and very demanding client when it procured the services of contractors to help with its mapping task. As several of these mapping firms had at least an embryonic digitising capacity, it seemed likely in 1984 that any significant assistance with Ordnance Survey's large-scale map digitising task was, in fact, most likely to come from that same quarter. Eventually, this proved only to be partially so as 'sunrise' companies also began to succeed with the digitising task.

Before it became clear just how the Government would actually respond in detail to specific Review Committee recommendations in connection with digital mapping, Ordnance Survey had already made a modest financial provision in its future departmental estimates for some exploratory digitising contracts. Some effort had also been made, toward the end of 1983, by staff concerned with digital mapping in Ordnance Survey's Development Unit, to identify and to seek out possible future digitising contractors. It was at this time, when user requirements had already become clearer and indeed some commitments to purchase data had been received by the still embryonic marketing unit created for digital mapping within Development Branch, that Ordnance Survey's own level of domestic digital mapping outputs slumped somewhat alarmingly (see previous tabulations in Chapter 11).

This was due to a variety of causes, which included significant losses of experienced production staff into line management and amongst trained production staff as Civil Service pay levels fell significantly below those in the private sector. Such losses of experienced staff contributed materially to lower output rates per person/per table as did the negative impact of specification changes that had to be evaluated in trials and thoroughly tested before introduction to production flowlines. There was a major and inevitable constraint and diversion of hard-pressed resources associated with changing specifications during this time in that any significant changes led directly to another major backlog of work required to bring older map files to the new specification. In the face of the protracted uncertainty about the future and the funding of Ordnance Survey itself, the diversion of cartographic staff onto more lucrative repayment tasks in pursuit of ever-increasing Government-imposed cost recovery targets, further contributed to declining productivity on core activities.

Somewhat amazingly, in retrospect, throughout the long years of Ordnance Survey's in-house digital data production activity, no formal and comprehensive specification for the digitising task itself had ever been produced. Instead, a series of instruction manuals, table menus and non-systematic standing instructions, as well as the aggregate experience of key staff, had remained the basis of 'documentation' about how the task should be tackled and controlled. This plethora of information was certainly not systematic, was incomplete and in some cases was contradictory. It was found to be quite unsuited to the enlistment of companies and operatives coming new to the task and could not serve as the basis by which their efforts at digitising could finally be evaluated and judged before payment.

If contracting out much of the digitising workload was to be the way forward for Ordnance Survey to recover its lost production capacity and, indeed, to increase the tempo of compiling the databank, it became a matter of some considerable urgency that a formal specification and basic technical instructions for the task should be produced. This important task was tackled in a timely fashion by experienced Ordnance Survey production staff, who managed to create and publish a very professional and comprehensive specification and guide to digital data production for the very first time.

As the concept of contracting out the task slowly gathered acceptance, Ordnance Survey hopes were high that a straightforward specification of the task, for the private sector, would be based less on established domestic methodology but more on objective target standards set to achieve a desired product. It was hoped by those most closely involved that contracts might, in the fullness of time, lead to quite different and innovative approaches from the private sector. Although initially Ordnance Survey chose not to simply 'franchise out' its digitising task, it was perhaps almost inevitable that most companies – typically small in size and level of overall resources to be deployed – that became involved with the task would seek a 'safe route' to success by simply emulating Ordnance Survey equipment, software and production procedures.

Thus it was, in February 1984, that Ordnance Survey Directors formally made the decision that the task of digitising of the basic-scales mapping of Great Britain would increasingly be taken up by private-sector contractors. Some important criteria for contracting out were quickly developed and made known as a consequence of this decision. The main aim of contracting out was to maintain existing standards, to secure value for money, to ensure that contracting out made good management sense and would not harm Ordnance Survey's own future role and performance. Contracting out the digitising task would, it was hoped, also offer, a 'yardstick' in the fullness of time by which in-house efficiency could itself be judged. By offering some trial contracts initially, the capacity and performance of the private sector would be evaluated and, if successful, would help Ordnance Survey to meet its commitments to deliver digital map data to customers in future years, according to an agreed and published schedule.

Despite sustained trade union opposition within Ordnance Survey to the very principle of contracting out, an advertisement was eventually placed in the Daily Telegraph® for 8 May 1984, seeking bids for digitising services for up to 12 blocks of basic-scale mapping, each block of approximately one hundred map sheets. The hectic period between February and May 1984 had been used for the creation of the specification for the task and the necessary contract documentation. Despite the previous informal assessment of some 38 likely contractors, which had already been conducted by Development Branch over the preceding months, Ordnance Survey had, in fact, very little reliable knowledge concerning either the private sector's abilities or capacity. Ordnance Survey itself was, in reality, still very slowly finding its way forward with contracting out such a task. At this very early stage the robust and enduring procedures for contract letting and management, which were eventually put in place to evaluate contractors before they were appointed, had not, at this point in time, been fully devised and deployed.

So it was when the first round of trial digitising contracts was actually let. To provide the very significant increase in progress with digitising that was required, it soon became apparent that an atmosphere of mutual cooperation and trust simply had to be the mutual goal of Ordnance Survey and its contractors. Suspicion and mutual mistrust, although almost instantaneous when quite different cultures and attitudes come together, could not be allowed to play any part at all, if the task was ever to be accomplished successfully. A cooperative and mutually supportive spirit, which eventually became the basis of a lengthy and generally productive commercial partnership, had to be forged from a necessarily negative climate of mutual suspicion. The obvious twin risks of predatory pricing to win contracts initially and the longer term and much greater risk of excessive pricing by a small cartel that might eventually emerge as successful contractors, were almost inevitably anticipated by Ordnance Survey.

Tension was heightened at the outset over what proved to be very demanding technical and management standards of Ordnance Survey's routine practice and the early shortcomings, and indeed wasteful failures, by some contractors. Ordnance Survey necessarily planned to complete a 100% quality check when it embarked on contracting out the task. This check involved the production of a Xynetics plot at Ordnance Survey produced especially for this task. The initial round of contracts provided for sheets with residual problems, found during examination by Ordnance Survey, to be returned to contractors for reworking and eventual completion before resubmission. Certainly several contractors chose to adopt the cost-saving concept of hurried work and seeking for Ordnance Survey to provide the first line of quality control.

These initial contracts, and the subsequent feedback from the contractors concerned, highlighted very clearly the urgent need for Ordnance Survey to harmonise the specification of digitising standards and its long-term approach to quality management and control, such that, together, they sought to achieve a consistent standard of data irrespective of who had actually produced it. There was certainly a good deal of interest initially around Great Britain from firms who wished to be involved with the project. Most had very limited production capacity. The first round of contracts resulted in some 23 bids in total from amongst the 55 companies who were sent contract documentation in response to the initial advertisement.

Eight blocks of mapping, scattered round the country, where unfortunately, as it eventually turned out, Ordnance Survey had already accepted obligations to deliver data, were awarded to seven companies following a rigorous tender evaluation procedure. The companies selected were Comsult, Laser-Scan Laboratories Ltd (they were awarded two blocks because of their experience), Mason Land Surveys Ltd*, MW

Kellogg Ltd, Eclipse Associates Ltd, JA Story and Partners*, and Cartographic Services (Southampton) Ltd*. The * symbol denotes companies that could be regarded as traditional survey and mapping companies. The rest could best be described as specialist digitising bureaux which, in most cases, had typically grown from other core businesses involved with either system or software development.

The seven initial contracts were duly awarded for a total bid cost of £435,000, following keen post-tender negotiations. The total price for this, the first series of digitising contracts, was considered broadly comparable, for a similar quantity of work, to a detailed, in-house costing of the contracts which had been carefully prepared, totalling £449,000. The comparison was based on agreed detail densities for each map sheet included in the contracts. The suspicion persisted, perhaps not surprisingly in view of past trade union politics within Ordnance Survey, that the contract prices tendered for this first let had deliberately been bid low, to ensure that much of the subsequent digitising task would be given to private-sector contractors.

However, very few, if any, of the initial band of digitising contractors could really have envisaged just how rocky the route ahead would prove to be for them. In an embryonic, 'fresh start' industry it is difficult to see the means by which a common purpose, leave alone a cartel, could have been established quite so quickly. An alternative and more realistic judgement, in view of all the problems that lay ahead for most, would be that any low pricing in the range tendered suggests considerable naivety and a generally poor understanding of the task. Ordnance Survey, either because the headline message about the obvious need for contracting hadn't got down to middle management or more charitably equally naively, set out a demand for very tight timescales for completion and delivery of all the data; in fact, by March 1985.

It is true that Ordnance Survey already had committed customers waiting for data in all the contract blocks but more because Ordnance Survey had funds earmarked for these contracts in the fiscal year 1984–85. Under Ordnance Survey's annual parliamentary vote regime, it required that such funds for the contracts could be disbursed, without staged payments, within that particular financial year. Bearing in mind the severity of the learning curve that most companies had to achieve, coming as most were, new and untried to this very demanding work for a 'well educated' client, such a timescale was almost certainly doomed to failure. In response to growing evidence of the steepness of the contractor's learning curve, Ordnance Survey organised very careful briefings of contractors with informative open days held at their Southampton head office.

During these visits further explanations of the specification were given and individual contractor concerns and problems were dealt with. Demonstrations of in-house proven and successful techniques were given during visits to production areas. In the light of all the effort that Ordnance Survey invested during this difficult period, it is interesting to note that these early contracts, somewhat surprisingly perhaps, were not let from the outset on the basis of a 'franchise' operation, using carefully specified methods and technology.

Such a 'method-based specification', although perhaps easier to establish at the outset, would of course have been very limiting for the various firms concerned as most had already created their own systems by purchasing suitable hardware and software from the industry. However, a franchise arrangement, if it had proved workable, would undoubtedly have produced more acceptable results from these contracts at a much earlier point in time.

Almost free of any constraints as to how the contractors actually carried out the work, the 'results-based specification' served to create, for the contractors, a much more demanding and difficult task initially. However, over time it was hoped that such an approach to the digitising contracts would admit greater creativity and some serious innovation by the contractors with significant unit cost reductions. The reality, however, was that the most successful contractors continued to mimic Ordnance Survey's approach throughout, right through to the final completion of the task itself. No significant breakthroughs – either in technology or method – really emerged from contracting out the digitising task.

In truth, the private sector sought a task that they could 'industrialise' by which means they could maximise the return on their investment, largely by shift working and economies of scale. Most contractors struggled initially to achieve the standards of quality required whilst meeting the keen deadlines for delivery of map data to Ordnance Survey. Once contractors did begin to achieve a measure of success in meeting the client's requirements, on a consistent basis, they had become too focused and too gainfully employed to experiment with alternative approaches to the task.

The burden of quality assurance and quality control settled heavily and disproportionately at the outset on Ordnance Survey. Confronting the difficulty of managing what was, by any standards, a 'sunrise industry', at the start of each individual contract Ordnance Survey required each contractor to effect the satisfactory completion of a very demanding test piece of digitising, which consisted of a specially prepared graphic with complex detail included. This test had to be completed successfully before the specific contract digitising task itself could be commenced. The test piece was conceived to offer a rigorous examination of each contractor's equipment, production system and personnel. What of course the test couldn't possibly shed any light on was the contractor's skill at managing production control.

It was this management element which, in some cases, was to prove to be a fatal shortcoming. When, at last, the test piece had been completed to Ordnance Survey's complete satisfaction, the input documents for the first group of map sheets, already carefully prepared at Ordnance Survey head office, were despatched to the contractor, who was then free to commence digitising of the first batch of map sheets. In fact, one of the contractors selected initially actually failed at this prior test piece stage, despite repeated attempts at it. Ordnance Survey duly invoked contract break clauses with the company concerned. It wasn't in fact until November 1984 that the most successful contractors were set free to commence actual digitising production work.

A second contractor, which had in fact passed the initial test piece stage, next failed to deliver satisfactory results on the first small batch of map sheets attempted and that long after agreed schedules. Each map sheet to be digitised in each contract was entered, via job route sheets, into Ordnance Survey's mainframe-based online production control system, just as they would be for in-house work. With more and more commitments being made by Ordnance Survey's embryonic marketing unit to its customers for delivery of digital data to agreed schedules, it became increasingly unacceptable for scheduled timings of digitising contracts to be missed. This first let of contracts very soon demonstrated to Ordnance Survey's management that the limited capacity of the in-house production areas, which needed to interface with the contractors, were coming under very severe pressure.

This was perhaps nowhere more so than in Ordnance Survey's quality assurance area for digital mapping. As a consequence, it therefore became necessary for the internal resources planned for digital data production to be reallocated to support tasks associated with the letting of digitising contracts. This led almost inevitably to a further and serious spiralling down in Ordnance Survey's domestic production levels of digital data. It therefore became an ever more urgent imperative that contractors should not only succeed but should indeed flourish in their work for Ordnance Survey. Whilst this sentiment was increasingly proclaimed internally, Ordnance Survey's standards, which, in any case, most contractors were really still struggling with, could not be lowered despite inevitable pressure to do so.

The early months of the first batch of digitising contracts brought many trials and tribulations for Ordnance Survey and contractors' staff alike. However, despite all this, very positive relations were preserved, at what for most, was a very fraught time. The very fact that Ordnance Survey could obviously and successfully perform the task routinely in-house and at all times with a willingness to demonstrate how it was best accomplished, helped to retain a positive and constructive relationship with its contractors. This was all very much in line with the concept of 'partnership' that Ordnance Survey senior management had initially conceived, when it had first become obvious that Ordnance Survey alone could never really hope to meet the rising expectations of customers for digital data.

Despite the failure to achieve significant progress on the first round of contracts by the end of 1985, the imperative to succeed with contracting out a large proportion of the digitising task was already becoming ever more obvious to those concerned within Ordnance Survey. There was simply no alternative as the necessary domestic growth in hardware capacity and staff numbers was never a realistic option. Faced with falling domestic outputs and in the hope that almost all problems would, in fact, eventually be overcome, Ordnance Survey really had no option other than to prepare plans for subsequent groups of digitising contracts. Such a strategy was necessary if the initial momentum with contracting out was to be sustained and not lost during the period of initial difficulties.

The business interests of any successful contractors were best served by a spirit of partnership if the increasingly urgent goal of achieving complete urban and peri-urban coverage of digital data by 1990 was, in fact, to be met. Specifically, the second group of contracts to be advertised by January 1985 were duly planned and scheduled, despite continued domestic trade union opposition. Clearly almost all of the first wave of contractors were by then experiencing serious difficulties, not least in terms of cash flow, as incomplete jobs stacked up in their generally modest and, as yet, unproven production systems. Individual jobs were passed back by Ordnance Survey's rigorous quality control procedures for necessary rework by the contractors. This early and serious failure by the contractors to satisfy the client only lent strength to the trade union's argument with management on the very principle of contracting out Ordnance Survey's production work.

The contractors also had a much more profound problem. Without assurances from Ordnance Survey about both the continuation and the volume of future digitising contracts, most contractors, being generally small and poorly capitalised companies, could neither really afford to 'tool up' with 'state of the art' equipment nor assemble, develop and hold together dedicated teams of workers, in the hope that contracts might be won, in competition, in future. These were all rather unfortunate but unavoidable consequences inevitably associated with the start-up of such an operation, which still needed to establish its worth. Although the six surviving contractors fell further and further behind the agreed but much amended schedules, four of them did, at last, begin to achieve some acceptable results. As a consequence some digital map data began to trickle into Ordnance Survey's map databank.

In early 1985, Ordnance Survey, as part of its then current five-year plan, prepared a digitising contract expenditure model, which perhaps best illustrates the increasing urgency with which contracting out the digitising task was regarded. The following plans for what was a very ambitious contract expenditure in future years were laid:

Year	1986–87	1987–88	1988–89
Planned expenditure	£2.60m	£3.76m	£3.76m

Planned expenditure on basic-scale digitising by contract.

It was at this particular point in time that Ordnance Survey decided to create a dedicated unit called Mapping Contract Services Branch, which was tasked with managing the burgeoning surveying and digitising contracts. The new unit would, it was hoped, ensure that all the skills required for this demanding task could be retained within this unit, which would offer a fully professional service of contract management to Ordnance Survey's contractors.

Whilst almost all of the contractors involved in the first letting of contracts had sought repeated slippage in delivery dates, a second major batch of contracts for digitising was advertised by Ordnance Survey and duly let in July 1985. These contracts provided for 802 maps to be digitised in blocks of between 50 and 100 map sheets each. The smaller blocks were to be awarded very much as trial contracts, after the satisfactory completion of the initial test piece, to companies who had not yet performed an Ordnance Survey contract.

This was based on experience, gained in the first award, of the belief that a smaller number of sheets would help new contractors conform to agreed schedules. Four new contractors were engaged and duly commenced their trial by test piece. Work commensurate with their apparent abilities and capacities was awarded to five of the first group of contractors, who were, by this time, generally performing satisfactorily.

The total cost bid by contractors for this second wave of digitising contracts was £557,000. Against this the Ordnance Survey detailed estimate, again based on map densities, totalled some £756,000. Ordnance Survey responded positively at this point in time to contractors' reported problems with work in progress and cash flow, by initiating a two-stage payment for work satisfactorily completed. However, it soon became apparent that the 60% staged initial payment to the contractor, on first submission of a map file to Ordnance Survey, merely encouraged undue haste with all its attendant shortcomings and mistakes. This typically left Ordnance Survey with the onerous task of bringing maps to a state of satisfactory completion, as some of the less diligent contractors appeared to lose interest once the first progress payment had been received and presumably their overheads covered. It soon became clear that the concept of making staged payments to contractors needed further attention, leading to urgent changes to the two stages previously initiated, at the behest of contractors.

In January 1986 the initial momentum achieved with contracting out much of the digitising task was further accelerated with a third round of contracts. Some 13 blocks (each of 50–100 maps) – all either in London or Glasgow – were offered with completion dates to be achieved by September 1986. Three already proven contractors received two or even three blocks each and a further group of new contractors were engaged to broaden the industry still further.

Despite the clear demand presented in the Ordnance Survey Review Committee Report for urgent completion of the national databank and the belated acceptance of this goal by HM Government, a serious and conflicting message began to emerge from Ordnance Survey, which once more represented Ordnance Survey's relict culture and philosophy at its very worst. At a mass briefing of staff in September 1986 the following message was passed by senior management: 'Taking into account developments in technology and assuming the availability of a consistent level of resources, Ordnance Survey now expects to have completed digitising of all major urban areas by 1995 and all other "warranted" conversion within a further decade'. To those within who were committed to the goal of a national digital map databank, and to customers outside who came from what might perhaps be seen as 'unwarranted' areas, the instinctive caution in this statement was so typical of Ordnance Survey past and so damaging to the momentum that had been so hard won.

Even many years on, it is difficult to see why Ordnance Survey senior management chose to be so indecisive, given that they themselves, in their post-Review Report submission to Ministers, had stressed the need for national coverage. The decision to brief staff in this way is still incomprehensible and demonstrated a lack of vision that had so bedevilled the Department in the past. Although the briefing did also admit the possibility of technological breakthrough and stress the need to weigh the cost and utilisation of digital mapping in deciding the eventual extent of digital mapping coverage in Great Britain, it came as a surprise that the commitment to drive the project through to completion, with the benefits of 'spun-off' products, and the prospect of revision nationally by digital techniques, wasn't seized more positively. This indecision further empowered Ordnance Survey's many and varied critics at a time when a business model for the successful commercial future of Ordnance Survey should have been emerging.

214

Also in 1986, with the first three waves of contracts underway and the first of these eventually completed some thirteen months behind schedule, Ordnance Survey carried out its first internal yet formal review of contract digitising. Of the 21 different companies engaged to date, three only, by this time, had proven themselves to be fully reliable and capable of consistently satisfactory production work. Four more companies were also assessed as being well on the way to becoming fully competent. The review also concluded that up to that point, in general terms, contractor production systems had generally been 'cobbled' together and were neither consistent in terms of the levels of precision achievable between components of the overall system nor sufficiently robust.

The review found that almost all of the companies engaged to date had suffered from poor estimating and from weak or non-existent production control procedures. Staff training had generally been inadequate for what had proved to be a particularly demanding task, for a very experienced client. The early contracts, and lack of guarantees about future work levels, had also served to create something of a 'transfer market' between contractors for competent and experienced staff. Ordnance Survey, the review concluded, had been hugely overoptimistic and somewhat naive, both about the skill and the capacity of its contractors. The wide variation in prices bid by contractors suggested a failure by most of the companies to fully understand the true nature and the full demands of the task.

The review, whilst commending Ordnance Survey for its genuine attempts to educate contractors, advocated closer contact still between contractors and Ordnance Survey's production units, to their mutual benefit. The review also acknowledged the wisdom of Ordnance Survey's planned future move toward a fixed half-yearly letting of longer-term, high-volume contracts for the most successful contractors. Despite realistic and legitimate concerns at Ordnance Survey about the creation and possible impact of a 'cartel' populated by the relatively small number of competent contractors, this new approach was seen as the best way to encourage rapid and sustainable growth in the overall production capacity available to Ordnance Survey in the marketplace.

Such a move to what would become almost rolling or 'call off' contracts would, it was felt, enable competent and competitive contractors to equip and staff their operations adequately and without breaks in continuity of work. Only with greatly increased capacity available across this still embryonic digitising industry, could the very real benefit in pricing be obtained for Ordnance Survey from keen, competitive tendering. Where contracts had been formally terminated in the face of complete failure by the contractor, the blocks of mapping concerned were transferred to in-house loading to minimise any further disruption to the eventual customers for the map data. The review concluded that the management of these failures had proved to be a lengthy, costly and debilitating business for Ordnance Survey. It was recognised by all concerned that its contract procedures called for further sharpening.

By the time of its own first formal review of contracting out the digital capture task in 1986, Ordnance Survey was customarily submitting only a 20% sample of its inhouse production to the rigours of examination by its own quality control units. Early contracts had demonstrated a clear need for a full and rigorous examination of every job submitted by contractors. The unfortunate theory had been developed by some of the less able contractors that the best way to quality control their work was by the use of Ordnance Survey's quality control processes after the first submission of their work. This was perceived as a cheap checking procedure of their somewhat flawed production operations.

This theory was duly confronted with further and much clearer instruction to contractors about what the client expected of them. Nevertheless, pressure on Ordnance Survey's quality control resources continued to mount, consuming, as it did, the most senior and the most capable of Ordnance Survey's production staff. The best contractors, who had more truly adopted the partnership culture in seeking for themselves a longer-term commercially successful future, were generally much more compliant with such precautionary moves by Ordnance Survey.

The reality and the actual 'economics' of contracting out the digitising task were explored in much more detail in a further and subsequent review commissioned by Ordnance Survey, which was conducted by their Consultancy, Inspection and Review Unit (approximating to an operations and management unit) in 1988. As a result of this review, which included significant cost comparisons, two major features became evident. The tabulation, in the next column, of production costs per map sheet for the first few batches of work by contractors, serves to illustrate the very disproportionate balance of costs between the contractors and Ordnance Survey. It also illustrates that, throughout the early phases of contract work, the situation continued to exist whereby a map sheet digitised by contractors cost Ordnance Survey a premium in comparison with costs associated with wholly in-house production.

It should be noted that, very early in the history of digitising, Ordnance Survey successfully developed a system of density assessment and rating for each map sheet such that meaningful comparisons could be made in costing. Each map sheet, from an infinitely variable archive, could therefore be reduced to the same density criteria for the purposes of comparison of cost or effort required. This convention was fully accepted by contractors and it was to endure, more or less unchanged, for the duration of the task as the basis of assessment of the task and for eventual payment.

Contract	By contractor	By Ordnance Survey	Total costs
Group 1	£628	£674	£1 182
Group 2	£746	£456	£1 202
Group 3	£785	£508	£1 293
Average cost:	£720 (57%)	£546 (43%)	£1 259

Costs per map unit digitised. (All adjusted to average density rating 4.5)
All contracts predate major specification change of OS 87.

The cost of digitising a map using purely Ordnance Survey in-house resources, at the time of the last group of contracts shown, was £910. By far the largest proportion of Ordnance Survey costs in dealing with contracts were incurred on checking and quality control of the contractor's work. With infinitely variable standards of work presented by contractors, with only a very small number of companies considered fully competent, there appeared to be very few other options for Ordnance Survey. Rigorous quality assurance procedures at least ensured that the standard of data actually databanked was maintained, but only at a very high price, the Ordnance Survey share of which was largely expended on quality management.

The contractors therefore, by March 1987, still had a long way to go in terms of achievement. The significant signs of steady improvement in performance and the degree of increasing competition suggested that the initial faith placed in the contracting-out process would quite soon be justified, not only in getting the task done but also in terms of its overall cost to the Department. The further internal review conducted toward the end of 1988 clearly illustrated this trend. Having benefited greatly from the marginally reduced specification and the new quality-assurance procedures brought about by Ordnance Survey's very positive interaction with the utilities reported elsewhere, the cost of digital data production by inhouse resources and by contract had indeed at last begun to converge. The review further indicated that the two most recent blocks of digitising performed in 1988 had cost on average £616 and £613 per sheet respectively.

It was on the basis of this review that the senior management team at Ordnance Survey eventually declared that the use of digitising contractors would henceforth become routine. IPCS the trade union concerned, which had sustained vigorous opposition from the outset to the use of digitising contractors, had, in the intervening years adopted and accepted a very different 'agenda'. The Union was, by this time, seeking much higher quality and better paid jobs for its members, in the face of inevitable structural reorganisation within the Civil Service at large and in Ordnance Survey in particular. Jobs involved with quality assurance and contract management better suited this goal than did the initial and routine task of digital production itself. Traditional opposition to the use of contractors thus quickly faded.

It had quickly become obvious to all concerned that ways and means simply had to be found to reduce the burden of Ordnance Survey's quality management of contractor's work to a much lower level. The key to this lay with a major improvement in the standard of contractor's work. Ordnance Survey staff redoubled their efforts at this and a new pattern of strategy payments was devised to sharpen up contractor's performance by completing each task to an acceptable level without any undue delay. The complexity of the then current specification, which contained 165 feature codes when the third round of contracts were let, was undoubtedly a major contributor to many of the errors found in contractor's work.

Ordnance Survey quickly set in train a study to consider how the number of feature codes could best be radically reduced. No further contracts were let whilst this study was in hand. Under increasing and sustained pressure from the utility organisations, that had developed their own agenda to acquire digital map data more suited to their immediate needs and their budgets, Ordnance Survey worked well with them in partnership to develop a simpler digitising specification and a robust quality assurance procedure. Both elements would soon serve to facilitate the use of digitising contractors, which really was the only salvation for Ordnance Survey in achieving faster production and greatly reduced costs. Contractors who mastered the digitising task and its quality management were able to work directly to Ordnance Survey or indeed for utility organisations, who increasingly planned to take on a new option of 'third-party digitising' to secure coverage of their own areas of interest, ahead of schedule.

Ordnance Survey regarded many of these areas as a much lower priority, covering, as most of them did only very rural areas. How this came about is described below with regard to 'third-party digitising', which was led by the utilities. The impact of 'third-party digitising' was to become of great significance in connection with Ordnance Survey's management of its private sector contractors. In 1987 a reduced specification for digitising known as OS 87, which had been developed out of the close cooperation between Ordnance Survey and utility representatives, was modified further in 1988. It became known as OS 88 and this, together with the new quality assurance procedure (NJUG 13), again initiated jointly with leading utility organisations, soon became the basis for all digitising operations.

Ordnance Survey took the decision not to retain the superseded feature codes. Work in progress was to be corrected on Ordnance Survey LITES interactive workstations and banked map files were to be corrected at a future revision stage. Map files awaiting revision and reform were suitably tagged in the databank. The utility undertakings, which had played such a significant role in these developments, had either enlisted or planned to enlist some of Ordnance Survey's contractors and, indeed, some other companies to digitise mapping that they required and which would not have featured in Ordnance Survey's programme for a good number of years. The following tabulation illustrates a stage up to 1989 in Ordnance Survey's progress on the long march toward the goal of full national coverage of large-scale digital map data. It also illustrates very effectively the build-up with the increasing role of private-sector contractors and their sustained contribution.

It was significant that by 1989 Ordnance Survey had generally achieved its goal of building a partnership with a network of private-sector contractor's whose skills and production capacity had increased almost beyond imagination from the start of cooperation some five years before.

A procedure whereby smaller fixed-price trial contracts were offered initially, was introduced once the competence of the new contractor had been established by the now well-proven and accepted trial test-piece. This process helped to sustain the pool of approved contractors at a healthy and, therefore, competitive level. Once a trial contract had been completed and its product had passed the quality assurance procedure, the new contractor became eligible to join the band of contractors who operated on annual contracts. These were loaded to suit the needs of the contractors and their individual capacities.

Year	Total digital production annually			Production	Total maps
	1:1250 scale	1:2500 scale	Total all scales	By contract	Data banked
1985–86	2094	496	2590	c480	27,572
1986–87	4498	1302	5800	2124 (36%)	33,360
1987–88	8013	2362	10375	5676 (55%)	44,282
1988–89	10628	3924	14552	7700 (53%)	58,872

Annual progress with digitising basic-scale mapping and the role of contractors.

The accepted figures in 1989 for the size of the large-scale map archive that would eventually become available in digital map form was:

Scale of map	1:1250	1:2500	1:10000
Number of maps in the series	54,400	162,600	3,670

The actual management of such large numbers of contracts, although still undergoing sequential change and fine tuning, had indeed become a normality that all concerned had helped to influence. The judgement really has to be that after a very slow and problem-ridden start by the contractors themselves, Ordnance Survey handled this aspect of its business in a most pragmatic and professional manner. This in turn was met by a remarkable level of trust and constructive cooperation by almost all the contractors who became involved during a period lasting almost 12 years. The initial vision by Ordnance Survey's senior management of a mutually beneficial partnership with the private sector had become a reality.

An industry, mostly of small companies, grew albeit slowly at first, eventually to provide the required capacity in the market place. It did also become, under Ordnance Survey's stewardship, both competent and lean and came to represent a very successful enterprise from both the standpoints of the client and contractor. The flexibility, tolerance and ingenuity of the staff employed in Mapping Contracts Branch at Ordnance Survey should certainly not pass into history unremarked. Neither should the contribution of the private sector who continued with the task to the very completion of digitising. Representatives of contracting companies received invites from Ordnance Survey to milestone celebrations and publicity events devised to publicise progress toward completion of the national databank.

Chapter 14
Increasing stimulus and external assistance for Ordnance Survey to complete the digitising task

By the time of the Serpell Review of Ordnance Survey, some of the nationalised utility undertakings of Great Britain had already embarked on substantial investment programmes aimed at building undertaking wide management information systems, often with quite different goals. Some of the utility organisations in Great Britain had commenced these very expensive developments during the 1980s, while others had commenced work, in some haste, only during the actual run up to their planned privatisation. At this time in their existence, the 'sell off culture' of the Thatcher Government was at full steam ahead. These information systems, as a minimum, were designed to catalogue and to help with the management of utility plant and engineering records.

Some utility undertakings were, however, seeking very much more ambitious information systems that would include customer and marketing information. Most developments were driven by the need to produce reliable inventories of corporate assets, many underground, as their owners were prepared for eventual privatisation. Another stimulus to development of such systems was the long-cherished goal of plant information exchange amongst utility undertakings and other bodies with responsibility, for example, for road maintenance. Such a development was seen by the more visionary in the utility field as that most likely to facilitate an eventual and effective street works act, which might in turn minimise the serial excavation of Great Britain's streets and thoroughfares.

One of the common basic ingredient 'fuels' for all such information systems had already been recognised. This 'fuel' was to be the Ordnance Survey large-scale mapping in digital form serving as the geographic background and possibly much more. The utility industry was quickly recognised in-house by those involved with digital mapping as the most robust of the external catalysts involved with Ordnance Survey's map digitising programme. There is no doubt that the utility industries generally and increasingly sought to position themselves individually and collectively to place mounting influence on Ordnance Survey.

Almost all utility organisations that interacted with Ordnance Survey at this time substantially underestimated the very substantial task of creating, maintaining and eventually digitising their own domestic plant records. Realising this and with many areas of common concern, the utility industries set out to unite primarily to develop an effective consultative forum within the National Joint Utilities Group (NJUG) that could increasingly be used to exert pressure on Ordnance Survey – in a manner that had previously been unknown. Utility undertakings had traditionally been amongst the heaviest users of Ordnance Survey's past conventional mapping services. The future importance of digital mapping was soon recognised, particularly by a few individual utility 'champions'. In the main, they had been tasked with leading information system development projects in those utility businesses that were most advanced in these matters.

Even with the acceleration of the digitising programme by a late surge of in-house activity, further augmented by the modest but increasingly reliable output from Ordnance Survey's network of successful contractors, it soon became apparent to the utilities that it would, in fact, be many years before Ordnance Survey would be able to offer complete digital map coverage of their particular areas of interest. Many of the utilities had buried and surface plant, and not just in the urban areas of Great Britain. This particularly worrying prospect was further compounded by Ordnance Survey's ultra-cautious and equivocal position with regard to the long-term goals associated with the digitising project.

For much of the 1980s Ordnance Survey was very prone indeed to sending out largely negative messages about the eventual completion of the programme, either by intent or through ill-considered language. Certainly there were several members of Ordnance Survey's top team who had little or no faith in a digital future, even at this time. This climate of caution had tended to suggest that thinly populated areas of the country were most unlikely to have full coverage of digital data in the foreseeable future. This was a particularly worrying message for the emerging water companies, whose principal resource was collected and managed in the more remote water catchments. These constantly negative statements by Ordnance Survey were based on traditional and almost inherent caution and, in fairness to the management team, on whether resources for digitising complete map cover would be secured over such a long period from central government.

This negative output from Ordnance Survey demonstrated a lack of commitment at the top of the organisation and a failure to recognise the true long-term potential of digital mapping. Such signals from members of Ordnance Survey's senior management team thankfully and simply served to invigorate a pressure group that was becoming ever more demanding in seeking a quite different outcome. Subtlety of approach aimed at successfully extracting any sort of definitive commitment from the utilities cannot, in all fairness, be ascribed to the Ordnance Survey management of the late 1980s. The call for rapid and complete national coverage, as articulated by the various external bodies considering such matters, was certainly a key requirement for many of the utility bodies.

The major problem for almost all utility undertakings was the simple fact that they were not able to demonstrate internally a suitable return on the very substantial investment that such comprehensive information system developments demanded. This was certainly true, for example, of British Telecom (BT®), who at various times and with various degrees of commitment had expressed an interest in acquiring full national map coverage. Ahead of the strategically important move by Ordnance Survey, which led to the introduction of 'key account managers', Ordnance Survey had found it extremely difficult to keep track of BT's often faltering and wavering commitment. This wavering commitment was also typical from many of the nation's water supply organisations. These bodies were also increasingly expressing interest in acquiring digital map coverage, not just of the territorial extent of their actual customer supply networks but also of the much more extensive river basin territories. In fact, it was these generally extreme rural areas, with the alarming prospect of identifying very few other customers for the digital map data, that had inevitably been pushed to the back of the queue in Ordnance Survey's planning for digital mapping.

British Gas, somewhat earlier than BT and the water supply bodies, had already embarked on the development of its business-critical Digital Records System (DRS). This was an information system developed such that plant and customer records could be integrated and managed more effectively. British Gas was one of the first utilities to produce a real and consistent champion of digital mapping. It was this particular development and its management that, in the coming decade, was to have a significant role in persuading and influencing Ordnance Survey's response to the market. By 1987 many of the utilities had actually progressed well beyond experimental and pilot stages with their information systems. Many were already revealing plans for record or information system deployment, albeit in stages, of their territory-wide projects. All were conceived and designed to operate as a minimum against a background of Ordnance Survey's basic-scale mapping cast in a digital form.

This point in the history of digital mapping, witnessing, at long last, a rapid increase in significant long-term uses and applications, was to prove pivotal in the story of digital mapping. Strategically important changes in the digitising project happened, as such things often do, because of a timely juxtaposition of several circumstances. It had become clear from the time of the publication of the Report of the Ordnance Survey Review Committee onwards that the specification for digital mapping had continued to grow in complexity to the point where 165 feature codes were being employed in the most recent of several data specifications. This specification had, of course, grown with Ordnance Survey's sustained belief that, at some time in the future, the digital data captured from the basic-scale maps would ultimately be used in the construction of mapping at several smaller derived map scales, notably those at 1:10000 and 1:25000. Feedback from several of Ordnance Survey's emerging digitising contractors and from potential customers, particularly within the utility industries, all suggested that the digital map data could be produced much faster and more cheaply given a simpler content and data structure specification.

The flow of information outward to customers and for the first time more reliably and consistently back to Ordnance Survey head office, from major potential users, had itself been greatly improved with the deployment, by Ordnance Survey, of 'a small but vital network of key account executives' for each utility industry. This was largely a result of an initiative demanded by the more customer-focused external members of Ordnance Survey's highest executive body. These new posts were filled by Ordnance Survey middle managers who would spend much of their time within the host utility organisation.

As sole points of contact, they acted as consultants and advisers to the utility and were able, really for the first time, to gather reliable marketing information about Ordnance Survey's key customers. The role and impact of this small band of dedicated staff in the development of this important segment of the market for digital map data, whilst at the same time helping to steer Ordnance Survey into a more responsive attitude, should, most certainly, not be underestimated. This was one of the first genuine market-led initiatives that Ordnance Survey had ever taken and provides some evidence of a shift in its attitude to customers.

The slow and painful nurturing into life, by Ordnance Survey itself, of a private-sector industry capable of digitising to the required national standards, was to prove another enabling factor for major changes in attitude at Ordnance Survey. Just as the emerging industry had grown in response to Ordnance Survey's original call, so many of the more successful contractor companies involved were also able to grow their capacity to meet an additional demand for map and records digitising from the utility sector itself. Almost coincident with the imposition by Ordnance Survey of a long overdue price increase for digital map data in April 1987, came the growing realisation by the utilities of the full cost of obtaining complete data coverage of their particular areas of operations. At the time that the utilities began to mobilise their growing influence in seeking a significant reduction in the map data specification, Ordnance Survey had only completed and databanked some 40,000 map units from the total archive of approximately 230,000 maps awaiting digitising. This fact alone added great strength to the force of the utility argument.

Arising from the Report of the Ordnance Survey Review Committee, the NJUG Ordnance Survey Committee assumed responsibility for the representation of their constituent industries within Ordnance Survey's new look formal consultative machinery. This group soon proved to be a significant external catalyst for change in connection with the digital mapping project. Concerned most about the sheer cost associated with the acquisition of full digital map data coverage for their areas of interest, the representatives of member utility companies, particularly those with nationwide operations and those who had made most progress, increasingly formed the view that their particular needs could, almost certainly, be better met with much simpler map data.

These key utility customers, from their narrow perspective, concluded that such a reduction in specification should very soon provide Ordnance

Survey and themselves, in turn, with a major reduction in the cost of acquiring digital map data. When this sort of view began to surface, for a time at least, there was a very real 'dialogue of the deaf' with neither side really listening to, nor seeking to understand, the other's position. Ordnance Survey, on the one hand, was genuinely concerned whether a radically reduced specification, increasingly being demanded on the grounds of cost, would reasonably meet all the future and latent requirements demanded of it. An example of a possible other use by Ordnance Survey was in pursuit of less expensive derived mapping which had always loomed very large on Ordnance Survey's national agenda.

Indeed future uses of the data simply could not be foreseen at this time. Calculations were made within Ordnance Survey of the likely cost of 'two bites of the cherry'. On the other hand, if a databank of consistent and homogenous specification was ever to be achieved, any significant changes to the specification would demand retrospective re-engineering back through the 40,000 map files so expensively and already created. As this reworking almost certainly could not be achieved at this time simply by the use of 'reprocessing' software alone, any such task amounted to a further substantial call on Ordnance Survey's already hard-pressed production resources. As the number of map sheets databanked had recently started to grow quite rapidly, any such re-engineering was always likely to become a major burden. This fact alone therefore amounted to a major inhibitor of change, both to the form and content of the digital map data. The impending and planned move to a disc-based databank on the mainframe computer and the changes yet to be made in 1987 to the map file header information were likely to facilitate more effective re-engineering than had traditionally been the case.

The overall impact of central government's ever-increasing demands of Ordnance Survey for higher cost-recovery targets and their clear segmentation between 'core' and 'non-core' activities, following the advice of the Review Committee Report, presented Ordnance Survey with the predicament that prices for digital data could, in reality, never be reduced and indeed quite the contrary, would need regular price increases, unless other major customer groups could be identified and mobilised to make significant map data acquisitions. At the end of 1986, a small working group of the larger NJUG devised a much-reduced specification for the large-scale digital map data, which they felt would serve their joint purpose. It must be said that this proposed specification took an extremely narrow view of the data specification issue.

Ordnance Survey, with its wider knowledge, for example, of emerging local authority demands from the map data, simply felt that it had to resist. The new utility approach to the specification meant that the 165 feature codes then currently being captured by Ordnance Survey and its successful contractors, could be reduced to 15 only in total. The principle that the requirement for overall 'half line width' accuracy in digitising, which Ordnance Survey had sought from the very outset of digitising, was retained but the proposed specification did permit a relaxation in 'graphic quality' when the data, so produced, was finally plotted and examined. The greatest impact of this reduction in the number of feature codes fell on the nature and complexity of water, railway and road data that could be captured. Following submission of the proposed specification to Ordnance Survey by the NJUG working party, it soon became apparent from trial data produced that if this simpler specification were to be used, there would be a good deal of ambiguity and a very large number of anomalies in the data captured.

Quite independently, Ordnance Survey, during the time while this reduced specification was being worked up by the utilities, had in any case come to the conclusion that in fact two additional feature codes were essential for the wider purposes and needs of future national mapping. These two new feature codes were considered vital to indicate roofed areas or 'building polygons' and to indicate 'road centrelines'. It was during this time of discussion about a reduced specification that reports from the Topographic Database Study, already being conducted within Ordnance Survey's R&D capacity, were indicating that a move to more highly structured data would be required at some time in the future. Thus it was that calls for expediency and lower costs on behalf of one, albeit important, segment of the market had to be weighed by Ordnance Survey against longer-term functionality and, therefore, value for all of its potential market segments as well as its own domestic uses to which the data might be put. This fractious period has already been described as a 'dialogue of the deaf'.

Ordnance Survey, under considerable pressure, eventually agreed, without prejudice to future choices, to conduct a formal production trial of what, initially, was called the 'NJUG 12 (feature codes) specification'. The results of the trial shown in the following tabulation were obtained from a suitable sample of actual production work, which was duplicated using both the existing full and the suggested far simpler data specification.

	NJUG 12 specification	Full specification
Pre edit	37 hours	74 hours
Digitise	110 hours	123 hours
Examination	9 hours	19 hours
Edit	10 hours	24 hours
Checking	2 hours	5 hours

Comparison of production times using the current and the simpler NJUG 12 specifications.

The reductions in production times that were achieved when using the reduced specification, during each production stage, eventually summed to an overall 34% reduction in total production times and costs for one map file. The results of this trial, once received and digested, merely served to confirm the increasing and widespread concern of the leading players amongst the utility organisations about Ordnance Survey's costs and its apparent approach to pricing. Their calls for cheaper and faster digital map data became ever more strident. Ordnance Survey, as the national mapping agency, in response, defended and proclaimed its wider strategy and diverse requirements from the digital map data. However, Ordnance Survey next took the data, which had been produced to the NJUG 12 specification, and attempted to upgrade it to the minimum specification that it considered its much wider purposes actually demanded. This upgrade stage was eventually found, in a subsequent production trial, to incur an additional 16% of the total costs of' production when using the reduced specification that was advocated so strongly by the utilities.

After considerable further discussion and consultation with the NJUG sub-group, Ordnance Survey eventually produced a pragmatic and compromise specification for digital mapping, which only contained some 35 feature codes in total. Those concerned with these issues within Ordnance Survey felt that this compromise specification just about managed to achieve the essential data 'structure' and the necessary cartographic quality from the data, when plotted in graphic form. This data specification eventually became known as 'OS 1987'. It was first publicised by Ordnance Survey in a formal consultative paper. The data produced from this specification clearly met and possibly, in some cases, still greatly exceeded the rather basic utility industry requirement, expressed so strongly at this time, for a cartographic 'backdrop' to their plant record information systems.

The data obtained by using this partially reduced specification also fulfilled Ordnance Survey's wider needs. It certainly achieved the necessary graphic quality when the map data was eventually reproduced at the basic scales. It enabled boundaries to be depicted fully to meet Ordnance Survey's statutory needs, and road centrelines were still available to address a likely requirement for a future venture with a vehicle navigation dataset and other applications for the map data. Further, the building 'seeds' to be put in the data offered the potential for some form of automation of the rather laborious stippled filling of roofed buildings on published large-scale maps.

Significant progress with these matters was eventually achieved at an important meeting between Ordnance Survey and senior representatives of the utility Industries called at the behest of Ordnance Survey. In welcoming the chief executives of BT, Mercury, British Gas, The Electricity Council and the Water Research Council at a meeting in November 1987, Ordnance Survey's Director General, Mr Peter McMaster, who internally at least had always appeared somewhat sceptical about the future need for and value of digital mapping, made the following statement: 'Ordnance Survey is committed to digital mapping as a source of graphical images and of data for geographical information systems in future. The main question is one of timing. Ordnance Survey aims to complete 100,000 maps covering urban Great Britain by 1995, and this number, including all those maps previously published at 1:1250 scale, will become available as digital map data by that date. Work will, in parallel with this goal, also accelerate on revising and updating digital map data. The main constraints upon us are the necessary resources and the Government's controls on running costs.'

In fairness to the three Director's General (Major General Irwin, Mr Walter Smith and Mr Peter McMaster), who in sequence, had led the organisation through the long years since the days of the first digitising experiments, the most significant problem they all faced had been the sustained desire of successive governments to reduce the overall cost burden of Ordnance Survey on HM Government, without really looking at the benefits which accrued to the nation from the Department's work. The Ordnance Survey Review Committee, established in 1978, had attempted to document and publicise this link. As a consequence of such a link, yet to be accepted, the Report of the Review Committee sought to achieve a continuity of resources from HM Government for the yet-to-be-agreed task of the national survey and mapping organisation. The much more discriminating financial targets of 'core' and 'non-core' activities established for Ordnance Survey in the wake of the Government's response to the Review Committee actually made the reallocation of in-house resources even more difficult. It was this that led to the concern and scepticism expressed by the Director General to the gathering of utility chiefs at Ordnance Survey head office in 1987.

One positive outcome of the high-level meeting between the heads of the organisations represented by the NJUG and Ordnance Survey's senior management team was the establishment of another joint working party. This working party was tasked with seeking ways to accelerate the completion of national, large-scale, digital map coverage. Sub-groups of this joint working party set out to confront the plethora of problems that arose from both technical and commercial aspects of such a programme. The novelty here for a changing culture at Ordnance Survey was the opening of the commercial aspects of its business to 'outsiders'. The technical sub-group reported in September 1988. The product of their labours was to prove to be a very significant breakthrough indeed, leading in turn to a period of very productive cooperation between personnel in the utility companies and representatives of Ordnance Survey. A further modification to the digital mapping specification (OS 1987) to be called 'OS 1988' was therefore finally agreed and details of this specification were published. This modified specification more closely met both sides' needs.

A quality control procedure, to be called 'NJUG 13' (Version 1), was also created and publicised in June 1988. The procedure was based, in terms of sampling and 'pass criteria', on the emerging British Standard BS 6001. The reality and the difficulty of the digitising task ahead was fortunately well illustrated very early in this period, during which rapid acceleration was being sought by potential customers, following a seriously defective utility map digitising contract, from which Ordnance Survey had been excluded. In a sense, great good eventually came out of this well-documented failure. Eventually, serious non-conformance and failure had to be admitted, jointly by the client utility and the digitising contractor, which resulted in a fair degree of publicity amongst all interested parties.

The failure demonstrated most clearly that the care that Ordnance Survey had traditionally taken during all stages of such work was vital and that, in reality, there was no simple approach to the digitising task. The fact that the digitising of maps should, in future, really only be attempted using stable, Ordnance Survey-produced, input documents for each map, merely served to strengthen Ordnance Survey's position as the natural and vital 'hub' of such activity. This important position, with full overall control of standards, was to prove to be vital in securing Ordnance Survey's commercial and intellectual property-based future. The quality assurance procedure really came out of failure and was conceived and designed for assessing and controlling the quality of all large-scale map digitising.

The immediate intention was that the rigours of NJUG 13 were to be deployed by client and contractor alike on all utility-commissioned digitising contracts. It was also to be used by Ordnance Survey before databanking digital map data produced under any bilateral arrangements between utility organisations and their contractors. It was also to be used by Ordnance Survey on any data produced directly for them, using either in-house resources or those of Ordnance Survey's own contractors. Each map would, in future, be digitised in conformance with the OS 1988 specification, and each map file would also have a certificate attesting its compliance with the NJUG 13 quality assurance procedure.

Both publicised 'standards', which were to be used during and after digitising, had come from close and constructive cooperation between Ordnance Survey staff and representatives of the utility organisations. This important progress was very much a manifestation of the changing culture within Ordnance Survey itself. Whilst suspicions remained on both sides, there was a sense of resolve amongst those concerned at operational levels with the negotiations to build on these developments. In agreeing the procedures for utility companies to commission digitising, the output of which, if it passed the NJUG 13 quality assurance procedure, would be accepted by Ordnance Survey for entry into the rapidly expanding databank, soon came to be called 'third-party digitising'.

It was also agreed that Ordnance Survey would retain control and coordination responsibilities to maintain these agreed standards and thus avoid any wasteful duplication of effort. Further, the agreement with the utility organisations enabled Ordnance Survey to build on its previous experience and expertise in managing private-sector contractors that had been tasked with producing digital map data. However, throughout these lengthy negotiations that sought to accelerate the completion of digital coverage of Great Britain, Ordnance Survey repeatedly and successfully resisted the granting of 'exclusivity' to any one organisation that was responsible for producing data. This was to remain an enduring principle by which Ordnance Survey continued to operate.

Throughout 1988 pressure continued to mount on Ordnance Survey from the utility companies. They were seeking to put some arrangements in place for sharing the commercial benefits from having map data available, if subsequent sales to another party actually took place of map data, which they had commissioned, accepted and supplied to Ordnance Survey for databanking. A number of contracts had already been let somewhat prematurely by utility companies to digitising contractors, only some of these contractors had, by this time, succeeded in satisfying Ordnance Survey's own demanding requirements.

Sadly and wastefully, many of these initial contracts were performed during the time of sequential changes in specification (NJUG 12 to OS 1987 to OS 1988) and before the absolute insistence on an Ordnance Survey-produced, dimensionally stable, input map document had been agreed as a vital starting point to digitising and well before the rigours of the NJUG 13 quality assurance procedure could be brought to bear. The first and worst example of these failed contracts was a 1988 contract let for digitising some 900 maps in the Gloucester area by the Severn Trent Water® Company. Here inaccurate and unreliable input documents derived from unstable SUSI copies of the maps concerned were used by the contractor.

At last, in September 1988, Ordnance Survey agreed to conduct an evaluation of 140 digital map files that had been produced by six different contracts under embryonic 'third-party digitising' arrangements. Because of protracted timescales, a very high proportion of these maps, not surprisingly, were digitised to the previous specification, which, by then, had become something of a moving target. The following conclusions could reasonably safely be drawn from the evaluation of the product of this initial contract. If data could not pass Ordnance Survey's own large-scale quality control procedures, it would surely fail the NJUG 13 quality procedure. Also, data suitable for databanking at Ordnance Survey would surely pass the NJUG 13 procedure. Data that generally passed the NJUG 13 procedure required an average of 1.5 hours 'repair' work before successful databanking at Ordnance Survey head office could be achieved.

The methodology for third-party digitising (as it came to be called) with all its underlying processes, was next formally negotiated and ultimately agreed between NJUG and Ordnance Survey. The urgency of the need to seek ways by which the sheer magnitude of the quality control task for direct contracts at Ordnance Survey head office could safely be scaled down had already been apparent for some time. With the additional burden of third-party data, the whole concept and operation of 'quality management' needed to be addressed urgently. Where a batch of work by a contractor directly serving a utility company successfully passed the NJUG 13 quality assurance procedure, only a sample would then subsequently be checked at Ordnance Survey's quality control stage before databanking.

It was therefore with some urgency that Ordnance Survey attempted to develop the criteria and the procedures for acceptance or 'repair' of map data files. The key to this requirement was soon found to exist in the principle of 'self-regulation'. Suppliers, be they contractors or utility clients, needed to reassure themselves that digital data was of an acceptable quality before they indicated acceptance before onward submission to Ordnance Survey. Each map sheet entering the digitising procedure was to be assessed for its apparent 'density' on the basis of the number of house 'seeds' counted automatically. Categories of 'sparse' (below 250 house seeds), medium (251–850 seeds) and dense (above 851 seeds) were created. The quality evaluation consisted of eight basic tests which checked various aspects and characteristics of the map data. Elements to be checked were the data format, with the use of DMC, OSTF (Ordnance Survey Transfer Format) or NTF level one, all permitted as suitable data formats for transmission and storage of map data.

The number of data points held to define the correct position and shape of map detail were, in the specification, to be kept to a minimum and this aspect was checked. From a sample of map data to be checked, a limit of 25% 'own provision' was retained by the test as the maximum tolerated. Next the accuracy of feature coding was checked. The 32 feature codes retained in the Ordnance Survey 1988 specification were grouped into eight classes, and each of these classes were tested separately, using either a coloured edit plot or by interaction on a workstation colour screen. The next test checked the positional accuracy of map information. This particular test required the use of a high-accuracy digitising table, within a workstation configuration, to assess a minimum of 50 data points, using the stable-based input document that had been used initially for digitising.

Other tests provided for the apparent 'squareness' of buildings, which had to be checked visually by examination on a workstation and the 'fit' of line junctions, which needed to be examined at 1:350 scale for a 1:1250 map scale original, using a suitable workstation screen. Any gaps or overshoots of 0.2 mm or greater would certainly lead to failure of the map. Final checks provided for six aspects of text which needed to be evaluated on each of the sample maps, with differing sample sizes for each of the three density categories. Finally, the test of 'completeness' was to be achieved by superimposition of a plot from the data over the original input document and subsequent careful examination.

The specification for NJUG 13 itself dictated how big the samples needed to be for each of the three categories of density and how these should be selected. The quality assurance procedure established minimum criteria for the acceptable quality level (AQL). It also established a proforma to be used to record results of all such work and a model format for the necessary certification of the quality found when the map data was examined. The OS 1988 specification demanded line accuracy of the data to be within plus or minus half a line width (0.1 mm). For the first time in the lengthy life of the digitising project, the basis for assessing the accuracy of digitising was set out clearly and unambiguously for all concerned to see and to work to.

Vital guidance was also given in the agreed plan for NJUG 13 in respect of the input document for acceptable digitising, which needed to be both dimensionally stable and as up-to-date as possible. This convention essentially dictated the use of an enlargement produced expertly by Ordnance Survey of the MSD of a particular map. This working version of the large-scale map had traditionally been held in the local Ordnance Survey field office. This move served to create a daunting logistical and management task for Ordnance Survey itself. In due course, a suitable control machinery for this task was developed and implemented by

Ordnance Survey to speed up the production of up-to-date digitising input documents for an ever-burgeoning digitising effort.

The development of the OS 1988 specification and the NJUG 13 quality assurance procedure soon proved to be vital contributions to the increasing momentum of the programme to provide complete digital map cover of Great Britain at the basic scales. The impetus given to this by the utility companies, who were most anxious to document their inventories of plant, provided a great stimulus. The close of 1988 came with Ordnance Survey slowly developing a consistent feel for third-party work, The sponsoring utility and its digitising contractor were required to supply a quality control certificate for each map sheet. Ordnance Survey was then required to use the same quality procedures on a sample selected from the certified batch.

Upon the basis of this examination, Ordnance Survey could either accept or reject the entire batch from which the sample examined had been taken. Rejection necessitated a complete rerun through the production processes by the contractor and eventual recertification. Such a severe penalty soon brought about much more consistent conformance to the procedures, with outputs to published standards achieved regularly by most of the various parties involved. Third-party digitising, running in parallel with Ordnance Survey's own efforts, in turn greatly enhanced by the improving performance of its contractors, was increasingly seen as the vehicle which would enable utility companies to drive on with the population and completion of their information systems. In addition, third-party activity finally removed the lingering and residual doubt about whether those areas that had remained toward the bottom of Ordnance Survey's priority list would, in fact, ever be digitised.

The increasing prospect of successful use of the NJUG 13 procedure served to render the quality-assurance task routine and widely available to public scrutiny. This, in turn, served to lessen quite genuine external concerns about whether anyone could ever really meet Ordnance Survey's own high standards, which critics always said had been set well beyond what was reasonably required in the marketplace. In March 1989 there were 13 contractors working under longer-term arrangements for Ordnance Survey with some 90% of their output assessed as acceptable. Ordnance Survey had, by this time, also received eight batches of map data from the utilities that had been digitised under the control of NJUG

13 procedures. The learning curve had well and truly been entered by all concerned.

Initially third-party digitising was developed under bilateral agreement between Ordnance Survey, on the one hand, and BT and various water companies on the other. In their haste to proceed, contracts between utility companies and their digitising contractors initially ran ahead of the completion of definitive arrangements for the OS 1988 specification and NJUG 13 quality assurance procedure. Thames Water, Essex Water, Severn Trent Water, Anglian Water®, Welsh Water™ and South West Water all got into difficulties as a result but, generally, did not lose their sense of purpose in seeking to obtain full coverage of their 'fiefdoms'.

The BT contract with Ordnance Survey, whereby the national survey provided management control of their digitising contracts, became something of a model agreement for all other utility companies. Others seeking to accelerate the provision of digital map coverage of their individual areas of interest quickly followed in negotiating suitable contracts with Ordnance Survey, although individual terms varied. The fundamentals of each and every agreement were that, if map data produced by Ordnance Survey already existed, it would be purchased under normal commercial arrangements. Where it didn't exist, Ordnance Survey first committed to reviewing its overall digitising programme but as the utility needs (particularly within the water industry) were typically in extreme rural areas, permission to sponsor digitising was normally to be granted and the royalty normally charged for digitising would, in such cases, always be waived.

Ordnance Survey would next provide the stable-based digitising document at a standard charge and the client company would contract with an approved digitising contractor to produce data to OS 1988 specification under NJUG 13 procedures. The actual sponsor of any digitising was held responsible for the quality of data that had to be passed to Ordnance Survey in batches, all with a suitable quality-assurance certificate. Ordnance Survey was permitted in the agreement to retain the data for its own purposes. This was then entered into the national databank. Ordnance Survey was also then free to publicise the new coverage and indeed to market the data and make sales to others. The proceeds from any such sales to other customers were to be split equally between the sponsoring utility and Ordnance Survey. This innovative arrangement for sharing the benefits of any such sales was only for a finite period in every case. BT, Welsh Water, Wessex Water and British Gas were given four years of shared sales, British Coal, Anglian Water, Severn Trent Water and South West Water were given three years of shared sales and Thames Water only two years.

The scope and importance of these arrangements during 1988, 1989 and 1990 can be judged by the size of the arrangements agreed, for example, with Welsh Water, where annual digitising contracts were let for 2,130, 4,420 and 5,000 map sheets, respectively, in those three years. These arrangements came to play a significant role in the overall story of the large-scale map digitising task, certainly in those areas of the country previously accorded by Ordnance Survey a very low priority for take-up. Several production areas of Ordnance Survey, which provided vital contact with all digitising contractors, soon and predictably fell once more under intense strain. Very quickly there was a plethora of complaints coming back to Ordnance Survey head office. Contractors, who had won contracts, were anxious to make a start and needed quality input documents. The most serious stresses, however, soon mounted on the Department in the wake of the initial submission of the digital data to Ordnance Survey. In many cases long waits ensued before final acceptance of the data and, critically for the contractors, before the commercial arrangement between the commissioning client and the contractor could be finalised.

In review, the arrangements made for third-party digitising with several utility companies toward the end of the 1980s, with the ultimate goal of accelerating digitising, were undoubtedly innovative. They grew and flourished out of a negative climate of mutual suspicion. Overall, the deal was a very good one for Ordnance Survey. It created a substantial additional resource because the private sector rapidly increased capacity to meet the needs identified by the marketplace. In commercial terms, Ordnance Survey succeeded in achieving cheaper digitising, as it wasn't until the very last year or so of the various arrangement to share proceeds, that Ordnance Survey really had to make any sizeable disbursements to sponsoring utility companies.

The creation, albeit slowly and painfully at first, by Ordnance Survey of a private-sector contracting industry, was an essential prerequisite. Success at third-party digitising resulted from the running together of several individual strategies. With the advent of increasingly successful in-house contracts, the previous somewhat authoritarian approach to everything by Ordnance Survey that it alone could perform its task had already been softened, and the next steps which facilitated third-party digitising, as a consequence, were unlikely to be as difficult. Sustained pressure from the utilities, initially for lower specification map data and, subsequently, for reduced costs as well, certainly made Ordnance Survey reconsider the specification for digital map data and just how the quality assurance of outputs could best be described and rendered routine, instead of appearing, as it always had to everyone else, to be something of an Ordnance Survey 'black art'.

Ordnance Survey's eventual willingness to shift its position pragmatically and the genuine desire and indeed ability to forge successful partnerships were seen as welcome signs of greater flexibility in approach to issues and real evidence of quite profound but largely unremarked cultural change within Ordnance Survey itself. The appointment of and the role played by the Ordnance Survey key account executives, who were attached to the utility industries as a marketing innovation, were indeed a catalyst and a facilitating force in creating and making these arrangements such a success.

The 1990s began with a clear and unequivocal public commitment by Ordnance Survey, at long last, to complete the task of digitising the large-scale mapping of Great Britain. The task of keeping the digital map data of Great Britain up to date had also been factored into Ordnance Survey's corporate planning for the future. Indeed, a very subtle transformation was already well under way throughout the Department, whereby almost all routine operations were becoming increasingly based entirely on digital methodologies.

There were very substantial in-house resources at Ordnance Survey deployed on the campaign to complete the digitising task. These resources had been assembled over time. The additional resource of private-sector contractors, most by this point in time on longer-term contracts directly with Ordnance Survey, were further enhanced by the additional impetus provided by third-party contracting. The OS 1988 specification and the NJUG 13 quality assurance procedures greatly facilitated the completion of the map digitising task.

Chapter 15
The final push to achieve completion of the task of digitising the large-scale mapping of Great Britain

By April 1989 Ordnance Survey had developed a much clearer sense of purpose with regard to the task of digitising its inventory of large-scale mapping. Despite the substantial increase in financial resources for this task that had at last been won, following a lengthy wrangle with the DOE and HM Treasury on behalf of central government, and despite the gradual enlistment and output of private-sector contractors, the number of maps actually databanked by April 1989 still left a considerable task for future years. Ordnance Survey, at this time, still couched any statements about its ultimate goal for digital mapping in very cautious and conditional terms.

Some 67% of the 1:1250 scale series (38,373 maps) and some 13% at 1:2500 scale (20,461 maps) had been captured and were already available to customers. However, the predominance of sales of digital data that had taken place indicated a considerable bias of customers still in favour of the 1:1250 scale mapping of urban areas. Domestic effort that was put into digitising at Ordnance Survey itself tended to focus on this particular task, for which the target completion date of 1995 had already been established and publicised. In making its next iteration of the five-year plan to its paymaster for the period 1989–94, Ordnance Survey prepared to digitise 13 000 map units a year for each of the five years of the plan. For the same period, Ordnance Survey planned for the following profile of digitising by the utilities under the third-party arrangements:

1989-90	1990-91	1991-92	1992-93	1993-94
10,000	15,000	18,000	12,000	10,000

Profile of map units to be digitised on third-party terms.

The presumption was made and planning put in hand for the vast majority of this additional external digitising effort to be deployed on the most rural 1:2500 scale areas. Ordnance Survey continued to accord a very low priority to such areas where only several of the newly emerged water companies had expressed any interest at all. Because these remoter areas were so extensive and covered by generally low-density maps, if any real acceleration of Ordnance Survey's domestic planning was to occur, then quite large numbers of map units required scheduling.

This proposal presented additional problems for Ordnance Survey in work areas that were already heavily engaged with Ordnance Survey's own contractors. The work areas most stressed were those responsible for input document preparation, for production control and for quality assurance. The volumes of digitising that this profile demanded seemed a reasonable prediction, although the ability and capacity of the digitising contractors still continued to represent a serious constraint on Ordnance Survey's own contracting workload. Without significant increases in contractor capacity and sustained improvement in performance, further demands on this resource by utility companies were likely to have a major and deleterious impact on Ordnance Survey's higher priority task for urban areas.

The key contemporary question was whether a sufficient number of new private-sector digitising companies could establish their competence, retain their standards and then gear up their capacity to take a rapidly increasing share of the available workload. A second strand of doubt about the contracting companies prevailed, predominantly whether a number of those who were already performing satisfactorily could manage organic growth in capacity whilst retaining the acceptable standards that they had taken so long to achieve.

Following rigorous examination and evaluation by Ordnance Survey, the clearance and adoption of the NJUG 13 quality assurance procedure for all in-house and contract work was to prove a major breakthrough for all concerned. It provided contractors with what they saw as an objective standard to aim for and the certification and acceptance procedure freed the clients from the onerous task of monitoring contractors' efforts. NJUG

13 served to demystify the whole process and its adoption went a long way to remove the suspicion held by customers and contractors alike that Ordnance Survey still persisted in making the task difficult and unpredictable for 'outsiders'.

By June 1989 four contracting companies had been moved by Ordnance Survey onto the 'random sampling' approach that was used for all in-house outputs. Contemporary records show that this was a most significant and symbolic step. It provided, it appears, a desirable goal for others and it signalled further that Ordnance Survey had by then, at long last, made irrevocable choices in connection with the digitising project. It was during this period in 1989 that Ordnance Survey staff completed the preparation of the specification for digitising the 1:10000 scale basic mapping of 'the mountain and moorland areas' of Great Britain. Wider knowledge and understanding of this step provided further proof that Ordnance Survey was at last intent on the completion of national digital map cover.

Already, as 1989 drew to a close, some 4 000 maps had been allocated to utility companies who wished to arrange 'sponsored' third-party digitising. Initially, there appeared to be somewhat less interest amongst potential sponsors than had been suggested in various bilateral discussions, which had led to the publication of a very ambitious profile that Ordnance Survey had prepared for the current version of its five-year plan. By mid-1989 only some 500 map units had been returned to Ordnance Survey on first submission from this source; but of these, only 98 were in fact fit and ready to databank. Most of the rest required significant rework. This serves to illustrate perhaps the very real dangers inherent in individual and uncoordinated digitising initiatives by customers, certainly without an agreed specification and without the standards of discipline that were to be imposed by NJUG 13 procedures. This was the original fear that the Ordnance Survey Review Committee had foreseen when they threw their weight behind the argument that Ordnance Survey should retain full control of what would be a very significant and long-term programme.

From June 1989 onwards concern began to surface within several work areas of Ordnance Survey in connection with the integrity and security of the digital map databank itself. Further, preparatory modelling work for the Topographic Database Study had highlighted the burgeoning presence and use of digital data domestically within Ordnance Survey, in various production areas not previously accustomed to managing and using digital map data in anything like a secure environment. This had indeed become a relatively recent phenomenon. Traditionally, large-scale digital map data had been produced and then databanked, map file by map file, by a well tried and tested procedure in the one cartographic production area.

Data was only ever extracted from the databank with tried and tested security, to supply a customer or the same area of production, to produce a revised edition. Similarly, data was sent back to the databank by a well tried and trusted routine, which ensured security and integrity of the data. This vital issue of data integrity surfaced at a time when conversion of maps to digital form was rising to a peak, during the final push to achieve the complete coverage of Great Britain. The complexity of operations caused by the rise of third-party sponsors and contractors over and above the in-house digitising effort, and the increasing use of digital data, in house, all meant that transactions on the databank ran at quite unprecedented levels. It was against this background that the data integrity issue really broke cover.

During 1990 most of the long-term map coverage previously held at 1:1250 scale had been digitised and was now held available in the databank. However, the situation with regard to the size of the 1:1250 map series had become something of a moving target. A developing approach by Ordnance Survey to 'upgrading' the map scale from 1:2500 to 1:1250 – for those peri-urban areas where physical development was most intense – began to manifest itself. Pressure was also coming, not only from customers who had found flaws in the 1:2500 scale mapping that had been 'overhauled' by the Cotswold methods but also from Ordnance Survey field offices, where the shortcomings of the same 1:2500 scale mapping in areas critical for further development were best understood for field operations.

Faced with an up-welling in demand, those managing this decision-making process, already under pressure from Ordnance Survey management to contain costs associated with the national survey, developed the concept of 1:1250 scale 'blisters'. These 'blisters' were to be upgraded to 1:1250 scale from the traditional 1:2500 scale coverage by a resurvey using either photogrammetric or ground instrumental methods. These were irregular pockets of mapping that were planned to keep pace with development on the periphery of city and town survey diagrams. Any moves of this nature meant that it was difficult to estimate the size of the workload to complete the digitising task associated with 1:1250 scale map coverage and the volume of data to be held at this scale in the databank.

The benefit to be derived by the increasing use of digital production methods on the field survey side of the house, already referred to, meant that surveys, once captured at source, didn't need to be digitised again. However, with the situation in these areas of perhaps greatest importance to customers' extremely fluid, it became increasingly difficult to quantify the task. In addition, many maps contained 'upgrades' of areas to the 1:1250 scale of mapping, where planned development was not yet completely constructed on the ground or where development was scheduled to last for a year or two. A device called 'quartering' was eventually devised, which meant that one or more quarters per square kilometre of original 1:2500 scale mapping could be digitised at the larger scale. These 'upgrades', on regular half-kilometre sheet lines, needed formal line management approval. Eventually, the concept of mixed-scale coverage, within a square kilometre, became routine ahead of the digitising task and further use of the map data.

On 8 January 1991 the important milestone of 100,000 maps successfully databanked, was achieved. Third-party digitising alone, in 1990-91, accounted for some 6,000 map units. As the mapping still left to be digitised was generally of increasingly remote rural areas (and therefore much sparser in detail), so the take-up under 'call-off' terms by Ordnance Survey's proven long-term contractors, grew dramatically in volume. The overall total of map data banked by the end of 1991 represented a two-fold increase over the previous two years. This high level of output was achieved by the three main streams of production. By March 1991 the complete 1:1250 scale map archive was, at last, digitised and made available to users in the databank. It is interesting to note that by this time, in its reporting of results and achievements, Ordnance Survey had gone through something of a cultural revolution. Mere levels of production outputs had, by this stage in the digital mapping project, yielded pride of place in successive Annual Reports to matters about the development of actual products and reports of the successful use that customers were actually making of the data products.

Map scale	1:1250	1:2500	1:10000 (Basic and part basic)
Number of maps	57,369	163,366	3,684

In April 1991 Ordnance Survey reported the definitive extent of the archive as shown in the table

Even as late as 1991, the target for completion of all map digitising was still regarded within Ordnance Survey as planned to occur, during the year 1999–2000. The following is the tabulation of actual digitised outputs achieved from all sources in the years following 1990:

Year	Number of map units digitised
1990–91	25,809
1991–92	32,834
1992–93	39,766
1993–94	*40,610
1994–95	Task completed

Number of map units digitised annually.

*By December 1993, 38,800 maps were still to be digitised

The number of basic-scale maps converted each year into digital form had been selected and established as an 'Agency Performance Target' by the Ordnance Survey Management Board. It was to become one of a small number of very high-profile targets used in reports to Ministers and in consultation with customers following Ordnance Survey's first designation as an Executive Agency under the Conservative Government's reorganisation of government functions. These results in the last few years of the digitising project show a staggering escalation in outputs and productivity, albeit of ever sparser density map sheets. Such volumes of work in progress continued to pose a considerable burden on Ordnance Survey to manufacture input documents and to manage transactions on the databank, in particular.

Throughout the early years of the 1990s contract prices for digitising continued to fall dramatically, mainly on account of ever lower levels of density of detail on the maps to be digitised but also because, at long last, of the competitive environment that Ordnance Survey had sought to achieve from the outset, when letting contracts. The following were the call off prices per map unit paid by Ordnance Survey to its contractors:

Year	Price per sheet (reduced to average density)
1989–90	£319 per sheet
1990–91	£278 per sheet
1991–92	£178 per sheet

Prices per map sheet digitised under 'call-off' contract terms.

This climate of declining workloads and ever lower unit production costs eventually led to an approach from established contractors which was designed to overcome the continuing annuality of Ordnance Survey's funding and at the same time affording themselves continuity of employment. This move by a group of 10 of the most experienced contractors used by Ordnance Survey was also designed to ensure the continued use of contractors through to completion of the task, including the basic 1:10000 scale areas.

Their proposal, in 1992–93, introducing the concept of 'digitise now, pay later' was duly placed before Ordnance Survey. The idea was that the chosen contractors would continue to fill their capacity on a call-off basis at a price agreed in advance with Ordnance Survey, which would be asked to agree to pay for this work in the following year. By 1993–94 payments direct to its own contractors totalled some £2.83 million. The contractors had finally grasped and understood the heavy restrictions on investment imposed by the annualising of Ordnance Survey's funding by Parliament. The much more demanding work of digitising the 1:10000 scale maps to complete the full national digital archive was eventually included in these arrangements to speed the completion of this major task.

Despite its cultural traditions and its inherent reserve with external contacts, looking back, Ordnance Survey somehow managed to stimulate and to develop an industry within the private sector that really didn't exist beforehand, by deploying suitable levels of financial resources to make the prospect look attractive. The granting of these additional financial resources following the long delay by Government in reacting to the Report of the Ordnance Survey Review Committee and the necessary limitations on in-house capacity were significant influences that helped to create the Ordnance Survey demand and the private sector's response to it. Whilst slower than perhaps anticipated initially to build quality and then capacity levels, the digitising industry ground out the required result really without any great innovation in terms of equipment or production techniques.

The contractors found it necessary to embark on quality management and production control as never before, as throughputs mounted dramatically. The development jointly by Ordnance Survey and the utilities of the NJUG 13 quality assurance procedure was timely in managing the staggering increase in production each year. The importance of NJUG 13 in achieving the requisite levels of quality and the concept of certified outputs, which demanded the minimum of effort by the client (utility or Ordnance Survey) should not be underestimated. It came to fruition because of the ability of Ordnance Survey personnel to think with novelty and some risk and because of utility folk being unwilling to take what Ordnance Survey said necessarily at face value. Innovation by all concerned served this united effort very well indeed.

Upon completion of the digitising task, so far ahead of any of the several past predictions, suitable celebrations and launches in support of sales and marketing at Ordnance Survey were held in Scotland, Wales and England to mark this important national event. The last map to be digitised under the project proved to be NH78NW, in the north of Scotland. Further work did continue for some time in clearing up various map 'slivers' and sections that were very much part of the previous epoch of paper mapping to formal and rigorous national sheet lines. After so much effort and frustration the digital map database was fully populated and ready for exploitation. The capture of so much systematic map data represented the largest and most sustained project of its type anywhere in the world. It must stand as a tribute to all those who played a part, inside and outside Ordnance Survey.

Chapter 16
In retrospect – The wider impact of the Ordnance Survey digitising project

The preceding chapters describe the origins and the history of Ordnance Survey. It also provides the background that explains how the national basic-scale map archive of Great Britain came to be created. This map archive was the final product of well over 100 years of disciplined and concerted endeavour by Ordnance Survey. In turn, this map archive of mapping published in traditional form on paper but kept securely at head office on very dimensionally stable glass plates became the basic raw material for the digitising project, which this account has sought to document. This particular chapter will attempt to describe and document the considerable impact of the digitising project, which ran for almost 30 years, and the position that it has finally helped to establish for the contemporary Ordnance Survey as a 'miller' and supplier of various geographic information products and services at the turn of the 20th century.

The creation of systematic digital map coverage of a country, even as small as Great Britain, at the sort of map scales tackled by Ordnance Survey, was certainly a very innovative achievement and the first of its type in the world. Most other national mapping agencies have embarked on compiling map databases at substantially larger map scales. Almost all have turned at some time or other to Ordnance Survey for advice and details of their experiences. In seeking to describe and evaluate the benefits that have accrued from the creation of Great Britain's national database of computer compatible large-scale map information, it must be remembered that it is in this modern form very much the product of what already existed by way of the national large-scale mapping of Great Britain.

The evolution of the modern national map archive had a long and, at times, troubled history. When it came to be digitised it was far from perfect and, in a sense, not as well suited to many of the purposes to which it has since been put as an abinitio design of the database would clearly have been. The deeply ingrained and introverted departmental culture of Ordnance Survey, which persisted largely unchanged throughout most of the early years of the digitising project itself, did not afford much by way of self-critical review of the Department's major activities. It really wasn't until yet another external review of Ordnance Survey took place during 1978–79 that any significant external review of Ordnance Survey's efforts at digitising the large-scale mapping was indeed possible.

The compilation of the databank of map information had become quite simply the result of a conversion process to transform a large volume of topographic information from one storage and presentation medium to another. With very few exceptional items, the task for the project simply represented the conversion of map information from the traditional graphic form to a digital form which could be stored and managed by electronic computers. From time to time during the life of the digitising project, which spanned almost three decades, there was considerable thought given to, and experimentation with, several alternative approaches to this simple conversion process; but increasingly users of what data that had been produced by that time repeatedly demanded simply the acceleration of the conversion programme. Actual and potential customers for the map data consistently advised Ordnance Survey against any distractions from this simple goal.

From its very beginning, the digitising project was severely constrained by the many limitations imposed by the nature of the technology that was available at the time. As the objectives of the digitising project began to be modified with the painfully slow emergence of actual customers who were seeking to purchase and to use the map data that was available, and as the size of the digital map archive grew, it simply really wasn't possible to start again with a fresh concept or design. This applied equally to the end-product itself and to the basic methodology of its production. In a project lasting some 30 years in total, Ordnance Survey very much became a 'prisoner' of its history and indeed of the path that it chose for the digitising project almost from the very outset.

The task of the creation of the large-scale map information database (now called the National Geographic Database or NGD) has had a profound impact on Ordnance Survey itself and on its current operations and performance. The digitising project and its product have played a significant role in the more recent development and current status of what is called 'geographic information' in Great Britain and the associated growth of markets and industries that sustain it, all within a relatively short period of time. Ordnance Survey is widely acclaimed, despite its alleged 'hawkish' commercial attitudes for a government agency, as a key player in the modern geographic information industry, both within Great Britain and internationally.

In terms of the impact on Ordnance Survey itself, the principal outcome of the digitising project has been to establish the national digital map archive as a valuable and definitive information source for a very large number of purposes, in forms which offer, much greater flexibility than when it was held in its previous form as printed maps on paper. Under increasing pressure from successive governments to reduce its call on government funds via the annual parliamentary vote in a long march toward full cost recovery, Ordnance Survey had in 1999 finally achieved 'Trading Fund status' as a commercial business within government. Due recognition had, at last, been given to the demand that Ordnance Survey should be paid by the national government for effort and activity considered to be 'in the national interest' or which are themselves not commercially viable (the basis of the National Interest Mapping Services Agreement finalised in 1999). The completion of the digitising project and the exploitation of its rich vein of information has provided a secure platform on which a very large proportion of Ordnance Survey's income has been won in recent years.

This platform has afforded Ordnance Survey the opportunity for product and service innovation, which it has generally seized very creatively, although perhaps not as rapidly in delivery as perhaps might have been hoped. Delays and difficulties with product development occurred in most cases because of the unfortunate historical legacy found so often in the basic-scale map data. Inevitably almost, considering its history, the 'raw fuel' of basic-scale map information that was available for product formulation needed considerable levels of repair, correction and the addition of other information not previously held. Nevertheless, the digitising project itself and the resulting geographic information has provided the basis of Ordnance Survey's modern commercial success and diversity.

Now equipped with national and systematic computerised map information, Ordnance Survey's products and services have been able to adopt and indeed benefit from the many freedoms created by the concept of computer-based geographic information. These freedoms include the power to select and to customise for a particular area of interest, for the actual information content required and for the particular form of presentation or delivery, as never before in its entire history Ordnance Survey has been able to address the varied demands and the generally rising expectations of its many and diverse customers. This degree of freedom has fortunately come at a time when Ordnance Survey's stakeholders have placed increasingly challenging demands upon the organisation in both the commercial and the political sense.

As the digitising project gathered increasing momentum from 1985 onwards, the map data files (now called Land-Line®) were sold as a product under that name to customers who operated chiefly in the utility, local government and central government segments of the total market. Most customers that existed were either planning or actually implementing computer-based information systems to assist in the management of their various activities. With sales of the map data increasing steadily through the late 1980s and early 1990s, other products were devised and developed from the databank, either by selective extraction and packaging to meet the needs of customer segments or in conjunction with additional activity or other types of information. However, Land-Line still at the turn of the century remains the largest (by value) selling product in Ordnance Survey's modern portfolio.

The continuous maintenance and updating of the database together with the supply of the revision information to customers is an integral part of the modern Ordnance Survey digital operation. The additional data products that have only become available at the turn of the century because of the original digitising project include Superplan and Superplan Data®. These are respectively the bespoke graphic output for customers from the Land-Line data and an alternative map data product which is sold through agents and which targets the shorter-term needs of the professional and commercial market segments. Other products that have come directly from the digitising project include OSCAR, the road data product; ADDRESS-POINT, the address reference dataset; and more recently Landplan®, which replaces the 1:10000 scale derived maps printed on paper by computer derivation from the basic-scale map information, again customised for the user of the service.

These additional products and services have all been created during the 1990s, once full national digital coverage at the basic scales was more or less guaranteed. All of these products owe their very existence to the data produced by the basic-scale digitising project, that this account seeks to describe and evaluate. The other major modern activity arising directly from the opportunity created by the basic-scale map archive itself has been the careful stewardship, protection and exploitation of Ordnance Survey's intellectual property rights in the map data. While conversion of the large-scale maps to digital form has perhaps made misuse – wittingly or unwittingly – easier, Ordnance Survey has been particularly successful at controlling and licensing use of the data by its customers. This particular aspect of Ordnance Survey's business provided an increasing and vital stream of revenue that, under the financial regime imposed by HM Government, permitted the organisation to invest for the future in product development and in system development and integration.

A significant contribution to the task of managing its intellectual property was achieved with the concept and practice of service level agreements (SLAs) negotiated with most major customers, or groups of customers that shared a broadly common purpose (local authorities and utility companies, for example). This broad concept of SLAs first became a reality with the initial agreement with all local authorities in April 1993. This agreement, and the others that followed the trail this one had blazed, facilitated the wider supply and use of Land-Line and other products and included commercial arrangements for their purchase and their licensed use. What is important is the fact that the map data that accrued from the digitising project gave considerable freedom to Ordnance Survey to create and modify products without further huge investment costs. In that sense alone the digitising project must in retrospect be deemed a major and successful initiative.

The following statistics illustrate very clearly the importance to Ordnance Survey itself of the totality of the basic-scale mapping operation, of which the computerised database is now essentially the main 'engine'. In 1996–97 Ordnance Survey's total turnover was some £69 million. Its total staff at this time was some 1 880. A considerable proportion of Ordnance Survey's staff were engaged, either directly or indirectly, with the modern basic-scale operation, which is now wholly digital. 'Core activities', the name given almost exclusively to the totality of basic-scale operations by the Ordnance Survey Review Committee toward the end of the 1970s, yielded a total revenue in the fiscal year 1996–97 of £57 million; £24 million was derived from copyright licensing, largely of data. Expenditure on 'core activity' in the same year was £59 million. This brief outline serves to identify Ordnance Survey as an increasingly successful public-sector business with very important national responsibilities. Through its widespread and diverse application and use, the digital map database can truly be said to be at the very core of modern Great Britain's society and its organisation and management as well as much of its economic activity. The modern map archive has an important role in central and local government, defence and security, education, research and much of Great Britain's business activity.

It is important to set the Ordnance Survey digitising task and the resulting database in this much wider context. Beyond the impact on Ordnance Survey itself, the digitising project has also had a substantial impact nationally. JB Harley in his 'Ordnance Survey Maps, a descriptive manual' in 1975 initially said, 'Digital mapping provides the purchaser with the means of drawing a map he requires for any particular purpose instead of having to accept what the cartographer has designed as a compromise between many conflicting requirements'. In fact, the impact on the production of maps themselves was soon to be but a small part of the total impact from the creation of the database and its ongoing maintenance and supply.

Increasingly, the digitising project at Ordnance Survey enabled customers to contemplate fulfilling their plans to integrate map data with other spatially referenced information, including customer, plant or design records in the utility industries; land terriers and the management of planning and other services in the local authority community; and for a very wide variety of purposes within the realm of central government. The modern phenomenon of geographic information systems (GIS) was, however, very slow to develop. Besides the cost of acquiring the Ordnance Survey map information, the high cost and the limited functionality of appropriate hardware, the unreliability of contemporary software and the sheer cost of converting other information which was also required in digital form, in various combinations, all served to constrain developments by Ordnance Survey's principal early customers. Despite the efforts and dedication of various system 'champions' within

Ordnance Survey's customer community, it had still proved difficult to establish realistic cost-benefit justifications for these embryonic GIS.

However, it is not surprising that it was from these sectors that the greatest stimulus and support for Ordnance Survey's efforts with the digitising project came. The completion of the Ordnance Survey database of map information provided for Great Britain a standard basic 'geographic template' against which a great variety of other information could be held and related. This basic 'template', which is maintained by Ordnance Survey to reflect the current situation in the landscape, meant that unrelated information and datasets could be related by their 'geographies' and added value could be extracted by users from the process. Ordnance Survey now also maintains a historic perspective for the nation from the database as it is revised. Redundant information is stored to provide this perspective of the past.

The advent of digital data also meant that spatially referenced information held by users could be related and exchanged electronically on a common basis, really for the first time without the substantial efforts associated traditionally with drawing and representation. In effect, these new opportunities that were created by the Ordnance Survey digitising initiative helped, in a substantial way, to birth the 'sunrise industry' of 'geographic information' in Great Britain. The report of the House of Lords Select Committee on Science and Technology in 1983, which, amongst other things, reviewed Ordnance Survey's efforts to date with digital mapping, included a recommendation to government that an enquiry should be established into future arrangements for 'geographic information'.

As a result of this initiative, the Government established a Committee of Enquiry in 1985, chaired by Lord Chorley entitled 'Handling Geographic Information'. The Report of this Committee of Enquiry in 1987 provided a very real stimulus to many elements of the embryonic geographic information industry and acted, at the same time, as a catalyst to Ordnance Survey's burgeoning effort to accelerate the digitising project. The Report was timely in that it coincided with an absolute proliferation of suitable technology, which almost annually began to reduce in cost as its power and functionality increased. Despite the slow and stumbling origins of geographic information, the 1990s can certainly be described as the 'coming of age' for GIS and the associated parts of the whole industry.

It was, to an extent, timely therefore that this juxtaposition of circumstances saw Ordnance Survey well placed with its data products and wider expertise to achieve a pivotal position in an industry that was growing so rapidly. The conclusions drawn by The Chorley Committee of Enquiry also eventually led to the creation of the much-needed national industry body the Association for Geographic Information. The hope and plan was that it would stimulate, regulate and coordinate a very disparate 'industry'. The totality of this new industry, which is worth probably hundreds of millions of pounds per annum, includes equipment and system development and sales, software development and licensing, the creation and capture of other information and the trading in all of this and a very wide range of other services for end-users. At the same time the initiative, taken so uncertainly and hesitantly, placed Ordnance Survey in a pivotal position within the GIS business of Great Britain as the 20th century came to an end.

Chapter 17
The equipment and systems that were employed

Technology inevitably was to play a significant role in the story of Ordnance Survey's digital mapping project. It was to serve in a complex manner, both as a constraint and as a catalyst at differing times during the thirty years that the project eventually spanned. A key feature in the story, almost throughout, however, was the vitally important role played by a very small number of commercial companies and the close cooperation typically achieved between their software and systems staff and Ordnance Survey's project personnel, at different levels. Mutually beneficial relationships were established from the outset with the suppliers of equipment and systems, at a time when Ordnance Survey almost universally tended to be secretive and withdrawn in its relationships.

Development inevitably took place in 'fits and starts'. Throughout the project there was the constant and very real risk of the distraction that technology alone could provide the answer to contemporary problems, if Ordnance Survey simply paused and awaited developments that were 'just round the corner'. Ordnance Survey, in turn, was typically an organisation dominated by caution and thrift. It was risk averse in the extreme, this largely arising from its public-sector culture and, because of its 'command economy approach' to tasks that it tackled, it was slow to embrace new approaches and methods. On grounds of thrift, methods and equipment were typically retained beyond their expected and reasonable life, partly because of the retraining load and partly because of the resulting disruption to production outputs.

Ordnance Survey always struggled to maximise its return on its capital purchases before they were in fact scrapped. This was especially true of the 'blind' digitising equipment, the techniques for which were initially enforced by contemporary technology but which were retained even when a fresh approach with interactive assistance was already clearly available. The demands of the civilian cartographic world alone were never realistically likely to stimulate the development of equipment and systems that were required and which were always likely to be at the 'leading edge of technology'.

At the end of the 1960s, with the exception of the military and national security organisations, most notably in the USA, there was only a very limited amount of suitable equipment available that could be applied to the demands of automating traditional cartographic procedures. Much of that which did exist had been developed as a result of secret military programmes during the protracted cold war. With a suitable lapse of time in the interests of secrecy, exciting glimpses of what these secure organisations had been attempting by way of automating map production, were given, in a succession of papers published mainly in the USA. These papers, most often written jointly with system suppliers, tended to gloss over the many difficulties that had been encountered in the development.

However, these papers helped to raise the prospect of the removal, or at least a reduction, in the volume of tedious and labour-intensive work associated with the preparation and publication of mapping. It was this particular prospect that eventually engaged Ordnance Survey's attention following an initial contact 'from out of the blue'. Most of the drive for these developments, within America's Department of Defense, arose from the need for rapid response mapping of almost anywhere in the world. Senior staff at British Military Survey's head office, based mainly at Feltham, were privy, at least, to some of the details and outcomes of these projects but security consideration did not allow a cross flow of information to their colleagues serving at Ordnance Survey. Outside of this high-spending and secretive environment, this was a time when an individual with an innovative concept still sought out a manufacturer to build a prototype, just as Dr Boyle did in the UK.

To those of us at Ordnance Survey who became involved with early work on 'automation', irrespective of the very obvious differences in the scale of budgets, these publications from America's military agencies, with their bewildering diagrams of system configurations, did undoubtedly help to inspire the belief that there was something in it for the early steps that Ordnance Survey needed to take with automation. It is interesting, upon somewhat distant reflection, that almost all of these papers that were read with great care, never really reported a fully successful outcome for such projects and almost all such papers included a final passage addressing the need for further and future development. In almost every case within the industry, from commercial cartographic houses producing atlases to national mapping organisations with their own particular responsibilities, the traditional cartographic procedures employed had always been manual, craft-skill-based and traditionally were very consuming of labour, with products taking years rather than months to appear.

This was certainly the case at Ordnance Survey, where maps that took almost two years to appear from within the 'factory' at head office in Southampton, were then immediately seen by users as being out of date. Ordnance Survey was, by the late 1960s, already embarked on a major post-war programme to reconstruct and modernise something approaching a quarter of a million individual maps. This 30-year programme was the basis of a massively labour-intensive effort which was run like a soviet style command economy. By 1971, for example, this factory was producing a new map, under the programme, every 13 minutes of its one shift's working routine. The programme to complete the new National Grid archive of basic-scale mapping was, by then, still less than half completed, despite all the sustained effort that had gone into it.

The UK's inter-departmental JASB had, as we have already seen in Chapter 2, created an automated cartography sub-committee to share information and experience and to undertake joint initiatives. Ordnance Survey played a full and active role in this with colleagues from other government mapping and charting organisations. One of the Committee's very early efforts was aimed at conducting a review of equipment that could perhaps assist in automating cartographic procedures. At this particular point in time a company based in Scotland, Dobbie McInnes (Dmac) Ltd, had produced and marketed a cartographic digitiser, which was an electro-mechanical device that permitted an operator to digitally encode the position of a line or point, relative to an 'origin', as it was 'traced' from a map.

A coil round the cursor cross hairs or 'pencil' tip (hence the description pencil follower) was coupled to another coil under the table surface by magnetic induction. The lower coil was mounted on an x-y gantry, which could move in response to any movement of the cursor by the operator. Movements in x and y of the gantry with the lower coil attached to it were detected and relayed to rotary shaft encoders. These early tables suffered frequent positional errors and losses of the table's origin. The obvious frustration of the decoupling of the two coils, if the cursor was moved too quickly or too far in one movement by the operator, was ever present. The tables demanded frequent servicing but degradation in accuracy soon accumulated, following each service.

The ECU, with whom Ordnance Survey cooperated, claimed that they achieved a 0.01-mm resolution (10 microns) from later models of this particular equipment. In 1970 Ordnance Survey tested and evaluated a Dmac Mk 1B digitising table. This evaluation indicated that distortions of 0.6 mm had been recorded across the table during digitising operations. It was concluded that much of this error budget could be eliminated successfully from the map data in a post-processing computer run. Feature coding of line, point and text information was accomplished by the use of keys or buttons on the cursor as the slow electro-mechanical response, on which the device was based, would not permit the recently found 'menu' system of feature coding to be used. This particular novel approach to feature coding, with its inherent repetitive and rapid movements between map detail and the elements of the 'menu', had been adopted from advanced work, found by a literature search, on interactive computer graphics. But before this fresh and innovative approach could be implemented further technical progress was necessary on the hardware side.

The period of years at the end of the 1960s and in the early 1970s, when Ordnance Survey was still very much in experimental mode with cartographic automation, were, nevertheless, extremely defining and formative. Many of the conventions and practices that were developed experimentally at this time, in the face of severe limitations imposed by the technology then available, eventually endured for the two decades or more of this production project. Refinements and improvements, when proven and confirmed, were certainly introduced in the production processes of digitising and editing as technology developed, but the nature of the data and the modus operandi of manual digitising remained remarkably constant. The accuracy tests of the early electro-mechanical digitising table indicated a substantial element of inaccuracy.

This inaccuracy crept in even with a trained operator's ability to aim and to digitise accurately and consistently using a fine target of cross hairs on the cursor, which was held over the 'at scale' map image. Two early experiments by Ordnance Survey's Map Production Test Group were conceived and designed to address this particular problem. The first experiment was based on the use of the map image to be digitised being etched photographically into a thick surface coating on a stable medium. A pointed tool, rather like a scribing tool, serving as the target on the digitising cursor was constrained onto the map image below by the depth of the etching. This would conceptually have produced a very early semi-automated digitising system, which possibly required an operative with lesser skills and experience. This trial of what was dubbed within Ordnance Survey as 'groovy digitising', with its potential for deskilling the task, was abandoned after the need for the skilled operative's interpretation skills were again confirmed as essential and indeed following several failures of the coating itself.

The second experiment quickly established that the use of an enlargement of the map to be digitised (in the ratio 5:3), in right-reading negative form, was the most acceptable document to digitise from the twin standpoints of achieving the necessary accuracy of aiming and pointing and ease of reading the map image to be digitised.

The safety margin of the enlargement ratio meant that, at output, when the data was reduced to the original scale of the map to be published, 'pointing' errors by the operative at the time of digitising had effectively been eliminated. This procedure was to endure without any serious challenge other than calls for different enlargement ratios almost to the end of the project. It was only when 'at scale' digitising in the field survey office, on DFUS, established that modern digitising tables and clearer MSD documents did not really demand the enlargement ratio, which, throughout its existence, caused ergonomic problems for the operative with the larger size of tables that such an approach demanded.

In 1971, at the time of the one of Ordnance Survey's mainframe computer upgrades, to the ICL 1904 machine, a state-of-the-art Calcomp 'drum plotter', to be run in offline mode, was purchased. Its principal purpose was to produce experimental edit plots of digital data and other graphic outputs required by management, from other computer-stored information. Whilst not able to plot data to the high-quality level typically obtained from the large, expensive and slow flatbed devices already on the market, it was able to output map images relatively quickly. By 1972–73, with the pilot production project at Ordnance Survey already initiated, the technological breakthrough, required with digitising, had already occurred. Three versions of an 'electronic', solid-state digitiser were located and identified on the market. All three used the same basic digitising matrix, which was manufactured by the Bendix Corporation from the USA. The three systems were the 'flatagrid' by Bendix themselves, the 'Digi grid' by Dmac of Scotland and the 'Freescan' by Ferranti, also from Scotland.

The initiative and substantial investment by Ferranti Ltd to widen their marketplace, with new segments, by recognising the opportunity to develop new expertise and supporting product lines providing for the needs of the wider defence industry and government – in this case in the realm of automated cartography – was to prove very timely, both for themselves and for Ordnance Survey. A period of very close cooperation soon began between the small Ordnance Survey team and the Ferranti data equipment and support folk who worked at the Crewe Toll factory in Edinburgh. Given the green light by its management for a pilot production project, Ordnance Survey's initial contract to equip a small production cell with digitisers, computers and the plotting machine was duly won by Ferranti Ltd.

Their bid was successful on the basis of the suitability and compatibility of the equipment, its competitive price and the provision of suitable arrangements for servicing and support. The latter was a vital element in these early days of computer applications, bedevilled as they were by all too frequent equipment failure and all too regular breakdown of software. Eight Freescan digitising tables in all and one flatbed master plotter, with a light spot projector, were purchased and duly installed as the initial production capacity for the pilot project.

The master plotter system was a very substantial and extremely precise machine. It was controlled and driven by a Digital Equipment Corporation (DEC) PDP 8 processor with magnetic tape data input. The light-spot projector drew the latent map image on litho process film in a complete darkroom environment. The image was then processed to develop the positive map image from the digital data. The major drawback to this system was that if and when the plot programme stalled or there were data errors, the plot failed to complete and was therefore of no further use. Operation of the system demanded great discipline and enduring patience from all concerned with its use.

The successful relationship between Ferranti Ltd and Ordnance Survey soon developed to the point where the digital mapping software developed in-house by Ordnance Survey for digitising, editing, processing and plotting was actually marketed to third-party customers by Ferranti Ltd, but with only limited commercial success. The value of this very early joint venture was that a working system could be demonstrated and delivered without many of the normal system implementation problems typically encountered at this time.

Ordnance Survey continued to derive considerable benefit from access to Ferranti's software engineers and to the wider resource base available to a world-class, diverse and leading-edge technology supplier. Ferranti Ltd, which soon became Ferranti Cetec in a business reorganisation, came to dominate Ordnance Survey's equipment and system procurement for the digitising project, under successive central government 'Buy British' directions.

Initially, each of the digitising tables purchased from the supplier by Ordnance Survey for the pilot production project, was a free-standing system with alpha-numeric keyboard input, which recorded the data captured on an expensive 'slave' tape deck. In fact, this first commissioning proved to be a period of great frustration for all concerned. A succession of problems bedevilled the implementation of this new equipment. The solid-state digitising tables were found to be surprisingly vulnerable to a less-than-perfect electricity supply. This led to 'origin loss' on the digitising table in mid-task. After a great deal of tribulation, the solution to this was found to be a 'spike free', clean power supply, free of voltage fluctuations, to the digital production area. Soon after this solution to the problem was found, the whole country, facing the global energy crisis and widespread industrial disruption brought on by militant trade union activity, was reduced to the three-day production week.

It wasn't long before, however, in 1974–75, when the situation returned to normal, that Ordnance Survey took the decision to increase its digital map production capacity. Also by this time Ferranti Cetec had developed the option of a digitising configuration based on a 'cluster' of basic digitising tables each linked to a DEC PDP 11/05 mini computer. This provided an alternative to the 'stand alone' systems purchased initially, which necessitated an expensive magnetic tape unit on each table. A cluster system of five further digitising tables, each logging data on the micro computer, which in turn sorted and created the individual map files, was purchased. In 1975–76 this cluster system was further enhanced with four more tables. This brought the total of digitising tables engaged in routine production to 18.

It was at this stage in the life of the pilot production project that a very technologically advanced, fast-edit plotting device was also purchased to 'beef up' the capacity and throughput for producing edit plots. This was the Xynetics Corporation's plotter, which was flatbed in form and quite different in concept and design to the previously installed Calcomp drum edit plotter. The pen head on the Xynetics edit plotter moved at very fast speeds on an air bearing under processor control, across the platen supporting the drawing medium, rather after the style of hovercraft technology. It was an awe-inspiring item of technology.

Also, at this time, it became increasingly clear that one Ferranti master plotter tasked with producing the final graphic for map production and publishing, could, with enhanced memory for the controller, support the output from some 20 digitising tables. With two-shift working and one plot per overnight run, each night one master plotter was capable, with great care, of producing some 40 map sheets per week. This was a time of very rapid change away from the early experimental days with regard to several aspects of both methodology and software functions. This, however, did not apply to the actual manner of digitising as there were no realistic alternative facilities for working on the data in real time and interactively.

The digitising operative continued to operate in 'blind' digitising mode; that is the operative was not able to see the data he or she was producing, in real time, as it was captured. This obvious and serious impediment would continue to pose enormous problems with the continuing need for a substantial edit plot, correction, edit plot loop further down the production flowline beyond initial digitising. Such problems could not realistically be addressed and solved finally until interactive graphics became an economic reality, on the back of the development of cheaper and more effective screen technology.

In 1976–77, a further six Freescan digitising tables were purchased and added to the PCD cluster system. This brought the total production capacity available to 24 digitising tables, still all operated in 'blind' mode. Further, overall flowline capacity balancing was again achieved with the purchase of a second Xynetics edit plotter and a second Ferranti master plotter. Improvements to the plotting software by Ferranti for the latter also served to shorten throughput times and therefore contribute significantly to overall production flowline capacity. This stuttering development of the production capacity, retained for the pilot project –

still with no solid evidence of increased efficiency or real cost savings achieved by using digital production techniques rather than conventional cartographic methods – eventually ground almost to a halt. During the year 1977–78, the prospect of a successful outcome for the project was overtaken by a wave of introspection at the announcement of and the substantial turmoil created by the workings of the Ordnance Survey Review Committee led by Sir David Serpell.

It was also at this time that Ordnance Survey considered switching to new suppliers of equipment and systems. Further changes in technology and mounting pressures by its management to identify new and faster approaches to the tedious digitising task eventually led to fresh contact with new and innovative equipment manufacturers and system suppliers. Ordnance Survey's own recently created Research and Development Unit initiated an investigation of the likely benefits of interactive data capture and edit operations, using graphic screens. The vehicle for this study was the TODDS which comprised a Fastrak semi-automatic digitising system developed and manufactured by the very innovative Laser Scan Ltd of Cambridge and two interactive graphic workstations, all powered by a DEC Vax 11/780 mini computer.

This purchase of such an expensive system, which appeared to offer the best prospects of a breakthrough, was, without doubt, encouraged by the conclusions and recommendations of the Serpell Report, to which HM Government had still failed to respond. However, by 1981–82 there was gathering gloom all round at Ordnance Survey with little or no prospect of successfully achieving semi-automatic digitising by employing this system. The semi-automatic system proved incapable of providing faster, cheaper initial digitising, despite the optimism of the Review Committee Report. However, it had become apparent, with extensive use during trials of TODDS, that the technique of working interactively on the two linked MADES workstations actually offered substantial gains in production efficiency and reduced costs. This occurred not only during the initial digitising stage but certainly served to 'short circuit' the lengthy and tedious edit plot loop, by achieving one stage correction and verification of the map data.

Following trials of interactive systems, which appeared to achieve cost savings of the order of 10% on edit generally and up to 40% on the map revision flowline, Ordnance Survey developed a procurement and implementation strategy. Considerable changes were required to the established production procedures. Seven MADES workstations, each costing almost £45,000, were acquired initially from Laser-Scan Ltd and these were powered by a DEC VAX 11/750 computer, which also provided spare capacity for the further expansion, already planned, at a later date.

Even at this early stage there was mounting concern within Ordnance Survey about the wisdom of getting tied in to one particular supplier. Laser-Scan Ltd, although innovative and supportive, was still a relatively small and generally under-capitalised company located on the University Science Park at Cambridge. Its relatively 'high tech' business, spun off from Cambridge University research, demanded significant investment for continuous development and improvement of systems. The Ordnance Survey detailed plan for 1983 showed the number of digitising tables rising in 1984 from 24 to 34. This same plan showed MADES workstations increasing from 7 to 13 and the number of Xynetics plotters and Ferranti master plotters each remaining at two in number. The Xynetics were operated on a full two-shift regime and the master plotter on a 12-hour working day. Despite the trend to working interactively, in November 1984, Ordnance Survey purchased seven blind digitising tables from Laser-Scan at a cost of £86,000.

The tables were made by Altek, an American company, but were integrated into a system by the supplier for Ordnance Survey. This company in the USA had commenced development in 1970 and entered the market in 1978. The resolution of this digitising tablet was 0.001 inches with a similar repeatability. 'Backlighting' on the table was available to facilitate digitising from a negative master. By this time, some of the older tables, which had been in use for almost 10 years, were beginning to show signs of failure. Also in 1984 the VAX computer was upgraded by the purchase of an 11/780 machine and this also powered what became known as Laser-Scan's DigSys, consisting of eight digitising tables. Thus it was that Laser-Scan Ltd of Cambridge had managed to become Ordnance Survey's preferred supplier, particularly of workstations system to be deployed on the digitising task.

Ordnance Survey's Digital Mapping Equipment Procurement Steering Group next considered a range of options for further equipment acquisitions. In 1984 Ordnance Survey again sought tenders for interactive equipment by advertising in the *Daily Telegraph*. Bids were received from Applied Research of Cambridge (ARC), Computervision®,

Intergraph®, Contraves, Laser-Scan and Sysscan. The ARC proposal was eventually chosen in that it prevented Laser-Scan reaching a dominant supplier situation. They would install a VAX computer 11/750 controlling four twin screen workstations with Altek digitising tables. Already there had been a shift in Ordnance Survey's thinking, and these edit stations served to enable Ordnance Survey staff – who were often deployed on digitising contract management and quality assurance – to provide an additional production capacity.

Thus it was that by 1980 Ordnance Survey had assembled a very substantial head office-based digital production capacity, which, despite all efforts, had not been able to rival the costs of conventional methods of production in the remapping programme. This digital capacity was being loaded increasingly with the production of revised editions. Unfortunately, and to no one's surprise, this approach surely led to the now notorious 'pepper pot' effect, with widely scattered and non-contiguous digital data, which clearly flew in the face of the increasingly strident demand from users for coherent blocks of digital data, either for purchase or user experimentation. The Serpell Report, in recognising the proximity of an information age with demands for complete digital map data as one of its fuels, directed Ordnance Survey towards a major and quite rapid programme to convert all remaining non-digital map sheets with the increasing help of private-sector contractors.

The report of the Study of Revision soon followed, presenting a clear future vision of revision with digitising completed locally where and when change in the landscape was found by Ordnance Survey field offices. This necessitated a very substantial development and investment effort by Ordnance Survey, and these developments in maintaining digital data will be described in Chapter 23. With the ever-increasing volumes of digital data stored and the rapid rise in the number of transactions on the databank itself, Ordnance Survey's ICL 1906S mainframe computer was replaced in 1983 by a 2966 configuration, also by ICL; but the trend toward smaller and more powerful dedicated computers was soon to impact on the digital mapping project.

Frustration within Ordnance Survey and amongst customers with the overall speed of progress with digital conversion started to dominate discussions at senior management meetings. Ordnance Survey's Research and Development unit was duly tasked in 1984–85 with looking at the alternative approach of 'raster scanning' the remaining large-scale maps and the use of vectorising software to achieve the product of coded vector-based data. Customers continually reassured Ordnance Survey that this was the form in which they required large-scale digital map data.

In most cases the problem with raster scanning resided with the input document for which there was no economical alternative to the MSD, which inevitably contained varying amounts of hand-penned work by the surveyor. This and the inconsistent nature of the input document (the MSD) meant that the final interactive edit stage was much too lengthy and expensive, thus negating the advantage of the speed of initial raster capture. By 1987 this approach was found not to work and was seen as a distraction from the tedious task of manual digitising. It was also at this time that no further attempts were made to increase the head office-based digitising capacity. The somewhat painful emergence of third-party clients and the slowly increasing number of competent contractors working for them and for Ordnance Survey directly became the preferred strategy to increase production capacity. This obviated the need to purchase further equipment, the demand for which, if targets were met, would not be sustained.

The use of the two interactive graphics workstations configured with the TODDS trial development project had proven their worth routinely in the production of digital map data by established methods. In 1983–84 three further workstations were purchased for faster and cheaper edit of data. In pursuit of the long march away from the 'blind' digitising techniques of the past, eight new digitising tables were purchased, and these provided the operative with information and prompts during data capture via a visual display unit. During 1984–85 a total of 32 digitising tables and 11 interactive edit stations were deployed. The PCD 15 digitising table cluster PDP 11 computer was replaced by a multi-computer online to the ICL 2966 mainframe, and this development provided the capability to handle the output from 30 tables in all.

Further procurement of six digitising tables and five edit stations brought levels of digital production equipment in 1985–86 to 38 tables and 16 edit stations. Even at this stage there were quite serious delays in commissioning the new equipment. A Sigmex colour monitor was also purchased, such that an evaluation of the benefits of using colour during the edit and correction stages could be made. This additional facility soon proved its worth in terms of increased production rates, and additional colour screens were purchased and installed.

With the growing realisation that all production operations in Ordnance Survey should operate in a digital environment, priority for investment turned away from the initial digital data capture function of the cartographic factory. Instead, suitable digital equipment to capture data directly from photogrammetric machines and directly from field survey instruments via data recorders became the priority, and the full deployment of workstation equipment to digitise revision information in field offices became critical beyond completion of the task. It was already becoming clear and certain that the task of digitising revision information was best accomplished within field offices.

In reviewing the history of the equipment employed on the Ordnance Survey digitising task, much of the initial methodology for digitising and editing in fact persisted, materially unchanged, throughout the two decades or so that the task eventually took to be completed. This was in part due to the climate of inertia within by sticking with what existed and which had proved its worth; that was such a characteristic of the Department, particularly in the early years. Two decades saw an increasing amount of technical innovation by Ordnance Survey and its equipment suppliers. This was mostly achieved by a gradual process of refinement of methodology, but the discipline of cartography in its widest context was never sufficiently large to drive commercial innovation, which could be customised for the Ordnance Survey task.

So it was that Ordnance Survey, for instance, had to await the general development of screen technology to facilitate a move to interactive methods and away from the very labour-intensive 'blind' digitising. As plotter technology developed, Ordnance Survey did make successive purchases of technology to increase output and to remove bottlenecks in the production flowline. With the exception of the last few years of the programme, when colour interactive editing had clearly established its worth, the production process itself remained constant. The nature of the data itself did change during the life of the project, with additions and refinements dictated by customers, or the need for economy, or to take the opportunity provided by improved technology.

Chapter 18
The data: its specification and format

The concept of digital mapping arose originally as a possible alternative means of producing maps *abinitio* to assist and perhaps to hasten the post-World War Two programme initiated by the pre-war Davidson Committee's Review of the state of Great Britain's national mapping. From the outset there was a great deal of challenge to this initiative from more conservative elements within Ordnance Survey. In the 1970s Ordnance Survey was heavily engaged on the task of modernising: metrication based on the national projection and revision of the large-scale mapping of Great Britain. The target, imposed by Ordnance Survey soon after the start, for completion of this demanding programme was to have the task completed by the close of 1980. Each year, particularly throughout the late 1960s and the 1970s, a significant number of maps were planned for resurvey and publication, in a highly disciplined operation which consumed the lion's share of Ordnance Survey's considerable annual resources.

It was hoped that the digital techniques being developed in-house might both speed up and also reduce the cost of this considerable task, particularly in its later years. Each year, as this major mapping task moved ever nearer to completion, an increasing and commensurate number of maps reached the criteria established by Ordnance Survey for the publication of a new and revised edition. Increasingly, it was hoped that the digital techniques that had been developed and introduced could also be deployed on this burgeoning and enduring task. The data itself was therefore initially regarded by Ordnance Survey almost as a by-product of the map production task. There was considered to be little or no external requirement for the data, although visionaries such as Gardiner-Hill (Professional Paper No 23, 1972) and others did speculate on possible uses by customers for the data beyond the use Ordnance Survey itself made of it for map production.

The form and content of the data captured and stored over the years, with only a few minor variations, broadly remained the same right from the early days of experimentation and the launch of the pilot production project. Also in these early days, when the fundamental nature of the digital map data was decided, Ordnance Survey was itself very much a 'prisoner' of the technology that was available to it. The first major constraint on the digital mapping project was the very nature and the capacity of the mainframe computer itself, which Ordnance Survey had originally installed very much as a multipurpose machine. The ICL 1904 computer had been installed in 1967 to serve the department's emerging and very varied computing requirements.

With a steady growth in demand, particularly from digital mapping, a three-shift, seven-day week regime was no longer able to offer the levels of capacity demanded. This machine only permitted 32,000 words of memory to be accessed, and with disk storage still very expensive, the obvious solution of a magnetic tape-based digital mapping system was the inevitable choice from the outset. Thus, in the early 1970s the Digital Mapping System A, DMA as it became known, was launched. The digital map data captured on the digitising table was processed by sequential and multiple passes through a suite of program that ran on the mainframe computer.

The first pass of the raw data file through DMA labelled each map feature with its assigned feature code or descriptor (some 70 different feature codes were employed then), which had originally been established from a coordinate value selected from within the pre-programmed 'menu of feature codes', outside the area of the map itself on the digitising table's surface. Each feature was also assigned a unique, sequential feature serial number or FSN. Also at this time the coordinate values captured from the map on the digitising system were transformed to real-world National Grid 'Transverse Mercator Projection' values. The DMA data transformation also rectified for any distortions that might be present, either in the original map document or in the scales of the digitising table itself. The rectification assumed that any distortion was 'conformal' over the area of any one grid square on the map.

This rigorous rectification procedure was controlled by the operator digitising each grid intersection on the map at least three times as the basis of a 'set up'. Thus, the grid square in which any other data point or points denoting a feature on the map was determined and these points were transformed to National Grid values and rectified for any distortion. The method used for this stage of the processing operation was, from the outset, based upon the method of interpolation by complex divided differences after GB Lauf (see bibliography item 3 for references). The transformation required 12 sequential multiplications for each data point.

At quite an early stage of the digitising project, still very much during the period of experimental work, this procedure was reduced to eight sequential operations using a method to correct for film distortion described in *Photogrammetry after Harris, Tewinkel and Whitten* (see bibliography item 3 for references).

This change to the DMA programmes achieved a reduction in computer running times and made all data falling within one grid square on the map readily available. Also at this stage, the programme corrected the data to ensure that buildings 'denoted as square' by the surveyor on the map were in fact made mathematically rectilinear. Actually, in point of fact, the surveyor only indicated those buildings which were 'not square'. Also, in the case of curved line features, the programme used a published algorithm, after McConologue (see bibliography item 3 for references), which employed a mathematical spline to generate additional points along the curve, thus producing a continuous and smooth line through the 'control points' selected along the line by the operative, when digitising.

It was quite early in the experimental stage of digital mapping that this procedure was adopted. It served to do away with the need for a 'stream' digitising function on the digitising hardware and thereby limited the wasteful volume of data generated and stored that was needed to portray curvilinear lines. This new approach to digitising, however, placed a greater premium on the skill of the operator in selecting the 'control points' along the curvilinear feature on the map.

The storage system for the digitised data within DMA classified each cartographic feature as either 'point' or 'line'. There was no provision in the data system for the concept of an 'area' feature. There was, therefore, no facility for 'area' coding. A line was stored as a series of digitised points to be connected at the plotting stage and a point was represented by a single coordinate set. A line did not necessarily depict a real-world feature since it was determined subjectively by the digitising operative. Any line on the map depicting a boundary between two features (for example, between a house frontage and the edge of the pavement) was coded as either one or the other, and there was no mechanism within the data to associate the two phenomenon. Thus each point or line feature was assigned a feature code and a sequential and unique feature serial number. As there were many fewer feature codes in the early days of digitising than later on, it was not possible to disaggregate features without expensive and time-consuming reworking of the data.

This statement in point of fact illustrates clearly what was often to prove a major and debilitating constraint on Ordnance Survey's choices throughout the long life of the digitising project and one which was generally poorly understood by its many critics and commentators. With the digitising of the large-scale map archive proving to be such a prodigious task, spread almost inevitably over a great number of years, 'forward compatibility' of any data produced, was vital. Ordnance Survey was, by tradition and 'charter', fully committed to homogenous national map series. As the data was the 'fuel' for map production alone at the outset, there was always a reluctance initially to change the form of the data produced and, where changes to it became inevitable, there was a natural desire to re-engineer the data to the most recent system or specification.

Yet, at the outset, when the initial data 'design' was arrived at, following the lengthy period of experimentation and development, there were no users of the data to comment upon the choices made. Ordnance Survey really had, in isolation, to anticipate both its wider and longer-term domestic requirements from the data (for example, to produce derived mapping, at least, at scales of 1:10000 and 1:25000) and those of future possible customers, who the visionaries within Ordnance Survey predicted would emerge as data and suitable technology became more widely available. As the digital databank grew in volume and coverage, any new facilities that were demanded could, in general, only be achieved by re-engineering the data, either by software (cheapest to achieve) or by further digitising and edit stages (expensive and resource consuming).

Ordnance Survey struggled throughout the story of the digitising to produce and make available a consistent structure, form and content of data. This factor was to prove a determinant and a major deterrent to significant changes to or redesign of the data throughout the long period of the compilation of the national digital map archive through the 1970s, the 1980s and on to completion in 1996. It was to prove a frequent and often underestimated factor when, particularly, external pressure mounted from time to time to make other than minor changes to the nature and form of the map data. This was also the reason that most of the initial design features of the digital map data actually endured through to completion and still, to this day, characterise the data.

In the DMA system, which was created at the outset for the digitising project, the map data was held as a separate file for each individual map sheet. Data representing many sheets was stored on a magnetic tape, and together these tapes physically represented the 'databank'. These tapes could only be deployed and accessed on the mainframe computer. Each individual map file commenced with a 'header' record, which contained information keyed in offline, by the operative at the digitising table, with details of sheet number, map scale and the coordinates of the south-west (SW) corner of the map sheet. Other information held in the map 'header' element of the data included the date the map was surveyed, when it was last revised and the date of digitising. DMA records for each map sheet, were of variable length and the data was initially held in binary form rather than as characters.

It was also some years later in the life of the digitising project that features which crossed more than one grid square (100 m square at the 1:1250 map scale) were held as a number of distinct records, each of which had its points digitised in that particular grid square. To hold National Grid coordinate values of a digitised point to a 1-metre resolution required two six-digit numbers for each x and y ordinate. To achieve some degree of data compression, the DMA system broke down coordinates into three parts. The first was the SW corner of the map (origin), which was held at the beginning of each coordinate string. The sheet was then divided from the origin into basic grid square units (40 mm on the map). Each of these grid squares was identified from the origin by just two integers. Finally, each basic grid square unit was next divided into 1 024 units along both axes.

This particular arrangement meant that a digitised point could be stored as an x-y coordinate pair, represented in one word of 24 bits, on the ICL 1900 series of mainframe computers, which was the only realistic choice for Ordnance Survey throughout the 1970s and early 1980s under the strictures imposed by HM Government's 'buy British' purchase regulations. Thus there were 11 bits allocated for each element of the coordinate of a map feature, after the basic grid square indicator, each time a feature entered a basic grid square unit. Text was also held in feature records.

Each text record comprised a coordinate reference of the start position of the text string, the font and scale to be used and a code identifying the category of name (for example, a street name). Oriented text also had an identifier. This particular approach illustrates very clearly the strong map production orientation inherent in the design and operation of the DMA system. Four characters were stored per ICL word. The DMA format adopted by Ordnance Survey was almost entirely computer hardware-oriented. This arrangement undoubtedly served to reduce the flexibility of the data, but it did provide a fast, low-cost solution to Ordnance Survey's needs at the time. In reality, it was a very simple and pragmatic approach. DMA remained in use until 1977.

In April 1976 Ordnance Survey commissioned a new ICL 1906 S mainframe computer, which was, essentially, disk-based. The nine-year-old ICL 1904 machine, which it replaced, was decommissioned and some of its peripherals were moved to the new host to save expenditure. The basic structure of the digital map data remained largely as before, with data held in individual map files, in the sequence that the digitising operative had, at the outset, tackled the digitising of each map. Even by this time in respect of the digitising project, Ordnance Survey had very few realistic options for the future, because it had already become well and truly locked into its early practices and methodology. It most certainly was not, at this time, an organisation capable of critical self-review.

Indeed, at this particular point in time Ordnance Survey was still struggling with the pilot production digitising project and the last thing it could really contemplate was a radical change in approach to the task. It would eventually need the urgent stimulus of a strong and demanding external review to make it question its role and goals in connection with the digitising project. At this point in time, when the new mainframe computer was installed, this major external review was still a few years away. Oddly enough and in a peculiar sense, Ordnance Survey's strength as an organisation still relied very heavily on the discipline and unwavering ability to 'grind out' a lengthy and demanding programme or production task to completion, without any significant self-doubt or questioning.

Already by 1976 the digital mapping programme, albeit still in pilot production mode, was already showing the evidence and many of the same symptoms of lack of critical thought as that given to the post-war 1:2500 scale map overhaul programme. The overarching goal for

Ordnance Survey, at this time, with digital mapping was to press on to assist with the achievement and fulfilment of the 1980 plan to be followed by the endless task of revision, thereby to gradually and systematically increase the coverage of digital map data rather than to consider, only with relatively few tapes already in the databank, a somewhat different approach to the task. Those most closely involved with the digital mapping project, in the face of quite strong and persistent internal opposition to the project and its demands, were reluctant to publicise any possible alternative options to complete the task, with a different outcome in terms of the form and nature and organisation of the map data. Any such change would almost certainly have seen the closure of the digitising project in its formative years.

The largely external development project, which employed the software company PMA, on behalf of DOE, to make the basic map data more flexible in use eventually continued but was seen, by all parties, as an entirely consequential or 'bolt on' stage to the main digital data capture and storage procedures. This project was always seen, by all concerned, as one with the goal of 're-engineering' the map data. It didn't lead to any really serious questioning of what Ordnance Survey was producing in the first place. The struggle to make the digitising procedure a viable production system simply concentrated on achieving a cost-effective approach to map making and to the revision of existing maps, using digital techniques. Wider issues and considerations were, at the time, quite easily sacrificed to the successful fulfilment of this very demanding task.

The new disk-based digital mapping system, developed to run on the new mainframe computer, was successfully implemented in 1977 after a succession of implementation problems were solved. Not surprisingly perhaps, this new digital map data system was called 'DMB'. It was broadly similar to its predecessor, with a 24-bit word. It was different in that it afforded the capacity to produce a library of maps, but data was still held sequentially, as originally digitised by the draughtsman or draughtswoman. The problem this fundamental characteristic of the data created is perhaps best illustrated by considering a typical file of map data, which, when plotted, was in 'pen down' (that is drawing map data) mode for only some 35–40% of the distance the pen or the light head on the plotter carriage needed to travel.

No attempt to 'optimise' the data, either at capture stage or' by subsequent processing software, was ever seriously or realistically considered. The introduction of the DMB system inevitably gave rise to a growing realisation within Ordnance Survey that the organisation of the data needed significant improvement and the supply mechanism for data to customers, who were at long last beginning to appear, needed much further thought to make it as machine-independent as possible for the customer. By 1979 digital mapping activity on the mainframe computer consumed some 36% of its capacity. Faced with severe computer staff losses and a service-wide inability to attract such staff, Government's Central Computing Agency (CCA) advised Ordnance Survey, in its first review of the Department's activity, to introduce a moratorium on all fresh system development until the disk-based digital mapping system was fully commissioned.

As the extent of a line feature was decided by the operative at the time of initial digitising together with the assignment of the appropriate feature code, great inconsistency existed between the ideal structure for the graphical process of map making and the structure required subsequently for data manipulation, where 'clean links and nodes' were required, without over and undershoots. There was still no representation possible in the data of two-dimensional objects, for example, of built-up areas or for areas of vegetation. Three quite fundamental 'upgrades' to the nature of the map data were recognised as necessary and were soon scheduled for in-house development and evaluation. Given that the problems could be solved, the intention was to provide multiple feature coding for a particular feature (for example a line segment could necessarily represent the frontage of a house and the edge of a road), provision for two-dimensional or 'area' features and finally provision for the much-needed facility of edgematching map features that continued over the edges between adjoining map sheets.

With the rather random digitising of map sheets that the programme to date had dictated, particularly where change on the ground had occurred and reached established new edition criteria, Ordnance Survey had not been able to produce edgematched data in a routine manner. Increasingly, resulting inconsistencies between adjoining map sheets began to cause concern to customers and certainly served to reduce the 'credibility' of the data. However, these developments in data functionality brought additional complexity and made the overriding cost reduction goals of the pilot production project ever more difficult to achieve.

Ordnance Survey therefore faced a very difficult dilemma when pressure mounted for serial upgrades of the data with the reality that cost control on the project would likely be serially damaged.

Realistically restricted by the availability of technology to the medium of magnetic tape for customer supply of data, DMC (for customer supply) was introduced by Ordnance Survey as the proposed customer delivery format. DMC was conceived and designed to facilitate delivery to and use of the data by its customers. The DMC format carried the map data file in a 'loose, uncompacted' form. It was a Fortran readable format, which, by this time, had become an industry-wide standard by, for example, plotter manufacturers. When a tape with digital map data on it was purchased by a customer, an equipment-independent Fortran plotting programme known as D09 was also supplied on the magnetic tape by Ordnance Survey. This rather simplistic approach offered a relatively easy start for customers, but it was very limited in the functionality that it provided.

Again it worked on a large variety of plotting hardware. DMC was available in a number of character codings (EBCDIC, ASCII and ECMA). The data structure of DMC was very similar to that of DMA and DMB. It was held as characters in fixed logical records of eight-character length, in blocks of either 1 800 or 2048 characters. Map information in digital form continued to be restricted to line, point and text. However, by 1981 there were some 144 different feature codes deployed to meet emerging and increasing demands on the data. DMC certainly had the virtue of loading easily on most customer computer configurations and output systems, but it was clumsy of format, hungry of memory and inefficient for retrieval. With the eventual emergence of 'distributed' computing using the ever more powerful mini computers (for example, Digital Equipment Corporation's VAX range), Ordnance Survey developed a much more concise in-house transfer format for movement of digital map data between mini computers and, where required, the mainframe, called DMTXFER.

Each time that elaborations or improvements to the digital map data were sought and introduced, Ordnance Survey faced a major dilemma. Such changes were potentially numerous and with far-reaching consequences. It was, of course, in striving for the best, a great temptation to keep introducing changes that brought increased functionality in the data or improved its management and handling. Instead of holding the sheet's SW corner values with each coordinate set, this coordinate pair was only held once. Such changes meant that the databank inevitably contained data produced in different epochs with quite different characteristics. Either these differences had to be documented and retained until completion of the whole databank, when a further sweep could be made through the entire databank, or rework had to take place cyclically. Customers increasingly made clear that they wanted consistent and homogenous data, and so almost all of the map data captured within DMA eventually went back to the digitising sections at Ordnance Survey for re-digitising where necessary and for the required upgrade.

In 1985–86 all changes to digital mapping systems and the storage format DMB were frozen. A development project team within Ordnance Survey's R&D capacity was created to investigate the possibilities of a topographic database. Ordnance Survey remained committed to the concept of a National Transfer Format (NTF), which had developed from the cooperative efforts of a working party and a national steering group in which Ordnance Survey had played a prominent role since their inception. By 1988 the prototype Topographic Database System had quite rapidly proved its value, during experimental use. This conclusion coincided with the findings of the Chorley Enquiry, which professed to document the demand for digital map data that was organised in such a way ('structured') to allow much more intricate analysis and use of the data.

Ordnance Survey therefore took a decision to evaluate the concept further in a pilot area. Eventually, three areas were selected where there was felt to be a user demand for improved data. The structured map data for Milton Keynes; Tameside, Manchester; and Birmingham was created from the feature-coded vector data previously held in DMB. Software enhancement to achieve unique and 'clean junctions' between 'links' was carried out and 'real world' cartographic objects were created by software and considerable levels of interactive editing. Meanwhile, by 1989, all digital mapping systems on the mainframe computer had been converted to disc-based operations known as DMV, the third in the sequential series of data systems.

Consideration was also given to the need for a new map data system for the ever-growing digital map archive, at some time in the not-so-distant future. The goals set for DMV were soon met, with central storage of map data but with wider access to users inside Ordnance Survey and much more efficient customer supply. The next stage in the development of the digital mapping system was felt to be its ultimate removal from the ICL 3960 mainframe. This, it was felt, would offer further increased data traffic capacity, faster access and comprehensive and more helpful access control, with much less operator effort. In the meantime, the mainframe processing power was increased by 70% and further storage capacity was acquired. In 1988 the digital map data product for customers was packaged as 'Land-Line.88', and this became Ordnance Survey's base product. It simply provided a computerised image of a particular map file.

The year 1990 also witnessed a major validation exercise undertaken by Ordnance Survey to ensure that all data files on the databank were, in fact, error free. At this time Ordnance Survey adopted the finally agreed NTF as an option for supply of map data to customers. Soon after, NTF version 1.1 was implemented. Recognising the demands of other customers, supply was also made in DXF (Data Exchange Format) as an additional service. The Department's Annual Report for 1991–92 documents a major project to migrate digital mapping onto dedicated computer hardware off the mainframe. This involved the transfer of all processing software and all data captured to date and held on the databank to the new system, but without interruption to internal traffic and customer supply.

This large and demanding task was successfully completed by February 1992. The migration represented the latest development in Ordnance Survey's commitment to the UNIX® operating system and to open systems. The newly installed data management system incorporated four processors and some 63,000 million units of storage. In all, some 141,000 map units were moved over to the new system. This system move provided a tenfold increase in throughput compared to that provided by the vacated mainframe. In 1992–93 the digital map data was packaged by Ordnance Survey's marketing operation as 'Land-Line.93'. This became the 'family name' for the large-scale digital map data product. Increasingly, Ordnance Survey's more sophisticated customers were already seeking map data which was logically as well as visually coherent. This would increasingly replace the previous version of map data, which was simply a computer version of the map in question viewed as a picture.

From quite early days in the digitising project's history those most closely involved had harboured continuing doubt about the end product, its form and functionality. Overall, there was a rather naive view abroad in Ordnance Survey that could perhaps be called 'the alchemist's approach'. Complacently, there was the view that what had been produced so far could always be transmuted into other forms. Right from the start the view was heard that a suitable specification for 'structured' or 'object-based' data should be developed, but this was scarcely possible because of contemporary technology and the 'head down' mode and culture so characteristic of Ordnance Survey at the time.

The pilot database system mentioned above, so ably led by Peter Heywood, which reported to the senior management team at Ordnance Survey in 1987, suggested that object-based data was by then feasible. It was felt to be vital for better map image production for cartographic purposes and was the basis of many improved data products. Additional cost beyond routine digitising was assessed at a further £7 million pounds per annum. With consequential and significant improvement to data quality and integrity as a result, it was also calculated that longer-term annual digitising costs could reduce from £37 million pounds per annum to £25 million.

Unfortunately perhaps in retrospect, such development happened to coincide with ever more strident demands from the utility industries for the faster supply of ever-cheaper map data. The utility industry representatives were demanding a short-term solution that placed no value on structured data and were quite unwilling to fund, either directly or indirectly, more complex data capture. Ordnance Survey did not have access to the resources required for capturing more complex data, despite its stated benefits, and customers would not accept a slowing down of the capture programme that was implied as a consequence. The result of these deliberations was that the pilot project in the West Midlands was not to be built upon but the data there was simply to be kept under maintenance.

This significant compromise on the best way forward was not revisited until 1993–94. In truth, some six years were lost in achieving 'structured' data and the benefit denied to Ordnance Survey and customers alike in identifying shortcomings and failures in the data, which could have been eliminated by restructuring processes. The high levels of non-conformance of the data product that bedevilled Ordnance Survey and customers during the years since could perhaps have been avoided.

Chapter 19
The digitised data: its security, integrity and its accuracy

The first formal publication describing this major and defining project for Ordnance Survey was the Professional Paper No 23 entitled 'The Development of Digital Maps' authored by Col RC Gardiner-Hill OBE and his staff, which was published in 1972. It is interesting, so long afterwards, to note that this comprehensive account of the development up to that point in time carries no real reference to any of the issues covered by this chapter. The account by Gardiner-Hill simply refers to algorithms and programmes developed to capture and edit data. It was perhaps from this very early stage of developments that the dangerous assumption arose that data stored in a computer would be safe and secure.

There was, of course, an established discipline for computer and data management that controlled only authorised access and involved the disciplined storage of tape, with different 'generations' (a minimum of three) of the data held with geographic separation of different storage locations, that is disaster storage. Because of the remote nature of mainframe computer operations at this time, computer applications required by or devised by the 'sharp end' of production had to be communicated to system analysts and programmers, who were themselves often somewhat remote from the actual operation of the computer. Inevitably, there were frequent shortcomings in communication as very often neither side had a common language to summarise what was needed or what was possible.

The Professional Paper, however, did include the vision: 'The full potential of an automated system will not be realised unless and until all required topographic data is banked in digital form and continually updated, and is readily accessible for presentation in any required form of output'. Meeting the demands of data security and data integrity of any such system, if this vision were to come to pass, are only, at best, implied. In conclusion, the paper said: 'Finally we hope to make considerable savings on the storage of our master topographic records'. Because of the need for complete dimensional stability, the 1:1250 scale resurvey master negatives are now stored on glass plates at full scale. The paper went on to compare the 28 feet of magnetic tape (from a standard reel of 2,200 feet) required to store a recent 1:1250 scale map with the sheer volume and fragility of a glass plate to serve the same purpose under then current arrangements.

The next serious reference in documentation to issues concerning the storage of digital map data appeared in a paper prepared as a review of progress with the pilot production project by Ordnance Survey's Development Branch, dated as late as October 1979. The security of the very tight circuit between the small digital production unit and the mainframe computer had achieved its goal. This reference described the final stages of the pilot production system after data has been created as follows: 'The data is stored so that three copies of the latest version of databanked data is held together with one copy of each of the preceding databanked generations. Only when this record is completed, is the working map data file held on disc, finally erased'. Thus the end product of the digital mapping system was five copies of the digitised map held on magnetic tape in three different locations. One of these was at the OPCS at Titchfield, Hampshire. Because of the ever-present risk of 'a magnetic image writing through' to other parts of the tape itself if it was left unspooled for long periods, a rigorous discipline of running tapes through simply to 'refresh' the data on the tape was an integral aspect of the data housekeeping discipline in the days prior to disc storage.

In terms of the data volumes likely to be associated with the concept of a digital map databank, various estimates were attempted at different times. In 1981 Rhind and Adams estimated national coverage in DMC format would require storage on a total of 550 magnetic tapes containing thirty-one 250,000 blocks each of 512 bytes. Further work after this estimate was made suggested that it was, in fact, too conservative. Sara Finch, in her PhD thesis of 1987 entitled 'Toward a National Topographic Database', expressed the view that any such database of large-scale maps would be large and cumbersome and would demand careful management, even with improvements following gains still to come, from improved technology.

When steps were at last taken to convert DMA files to the new DMB system, there were some 5,000 map files already on the databank. It had always been accepted within Ordnance Survey that there were problems associated with data produced at different times with differing techniques and to varying specifications and standards. Many of these shortcomings would not be uncovered until they were exposed through actual usage of the map files. At this time there were very few customers and very few demanding applications that might cause embarrassment. In February 1981 Ordnance Survey set out to quantify this problem before deciding whether what was already old data was best captured afresh or was capable of being reprocessed for the new databank.

A random sample of 270 maps was extracted from the databank and examined. Of this sample 23% had no header information, an integral part of the data; 10% had incomplete header information; and 19% had no date of survey. This sample served to create considerable concern at Ordnance Survey over the integrity of file header information in general. During examination of this sample, 20 map files in all were found to lack 'feature terminators', which in fact served to corrupt related data. Also, because of weaknesses in validation procedures when data left the cartographic production area for the computer unit, occurrences of feature codes without coordinate information were also found. When some 1,722 map files were scrutinised later in 1981, a 4% fault rate was found. Rapid development with changes to the processing software and a series of innovations were said to be the main cause of the irregularities found.

In 1983, when the DMB tape archive was moved over to the disc-based DMV system, it was accepted that these quantified levels of cartographic and data errors in early work should be left for interactive correction, plan by plan, as they came up for revision operations or for some other procedure, before the files were moved across. The DMV concept was a response to increasing demands from within Ordnance Survey to access, to use or to modify the data files. It was probably at this time of this databank conversion, that the seeds of future problems were in fact sown. The DMV archive was not fully protected by a truly rigorous validation and a robust access control system because, of necessity, the system permitted 'owners', modifiers or producers of data within Ordnance Survey to 'overwrite' clean images in DMV.

As an example, the digital field update system (DFUS), then in the early stages of being deployed in some of the urban Ordnance Survey field offices, gave the necessary freedom to modify map data files with new revision information. Operatives, although trained, were inexperienced in the necessary rigours of data management and hence this sub-system was very prone, in these early stages, to overwriting good images with corrupted or inadequate data, which, following electronic transfer, became the master databank file for that particular map sheet. Validation, in any case, simply concentrated on the form and structure of the data and not the content.

However, these early occurrences and problems paled into insignificance when, toward the end of 1988, more and more defect occurrences on map files were reported, either by customers or were found when data was used increasingly in Ordnance Survey's domestic operations. At this time, many of these occurrences were regarded as unexplained mysteries. It is important to remember that by 1988, ever-increasing routine use of the digital map data itself was being made inside Ordnance Survey. This, in turn, meant that an ever-increasing number of staff, with little or no experience of managing data, became involved in all aspects of data management, including transmission, often for the first time.

For an organisation that in times past had always created and enforced absolutely prescriptive procedures for the performance of just about anything (in true military fashion), this was a serious lapse of concentration. From its inception, at the start of the pilot production project, the map data 'circuit' inside Ordnance Survey had been remarkably uncomplicated. A map was digitised in the production area and then databanked directly following processing, after transmission from the work area by magnetic tape – with rigorous validation at all stages. In the case of a new edition or update of an already banked map file, following extraction from the databank, the tape containing the map file had been physically delivered directly to the digital data production area demanding it.

When the revision was completed, the tape was again returned through validation, directly for processing before being returned to the databank. By 1988 the digital working environment at Ordnance Survey had already widened considerably and had quickly become much more complicated, with a number of differing access facilities created, possibly without sufficient concern over what could conceivably go wrong or with adequate precautions. Electronic data transfers between internal computers had been established successfully over a short timescale with an ever-growing number of Ordnance Survey field offices, with the work areas with responsibility for photogrammetric services and instrumental detail plotting; and with the ever-more important function of the supply of data to customers and between the mainframe computer holding the databank and the computer managing the clustered digitising tables in the digital production area.

Data could be moved between these units but only through the 'hub' of the mainframe. It was what could happen in these various production areas that was to create the largest peril for Ordnance Survey. In this flurry of activity the previous simplicity and rigorous control and validation had been let slip as an ever-greater number of managers and staff, without any great data handling experience, became involved. The ever-more complex business of data management within Ordnance Survey itself had effectively slipped somewhat out of overall control – and with very serious consequences indeed. Over and above an increasing series of domestic failures and shortcomings, intelligence gradually started to come in from customers. Fortunately, these reports of shortcomings in map data files delivered to utility companies, came in, most often, through the newly established key account executives, who had been placed with the utility industries by the management of Ordnance Survey's marketing operation.

Several of the areas new to managing digital map files created problems unique to their work areas. The digital field update operation was prone at one time to the hazard of sending the original file drawn from the databank back without the revision information but with the new date of survey in the header file. The newly revised version of the map was stored, in error, locally. Operations performed in the area responsible for instrumental detail survey corrupted a good number of map files by producing a quite common 'starburst' effect, where several blocks of data were pulled to the SW corner of the sheet. The situation seemed to deteriorate quite rapidly, and in August 1989 Ordnance Survey's senior management team decided to appoint a young IT professional, Andy Coote, with a small team, to stabilise and clear up what was viewed as a very dangerous situation indeed and which imperilled Ordnance Survey's operations.

The role of the new Manager of the Digital Archive in future would include quality assurance responsibilities for the complete system. It was also accepted finally that the past practice of quality control of the digital mapping system only on graphical outputs should cease and all aspects of digital operations should be quality assured. The call soon went out for any data failures or quirks to be notified and sent to this new unit at Ordnance Survey head office. All referrals were logged and each was investigated systematically. A regular situation report was given during this time of greatly heightened concern for the 'health' of the digital databank. Attempts were made to reassure customers who had already met these occurrences and, for a time, customer supply was actually suspended. A sample of 1,300 map files in total, drawn from the four main work areas concerned, were rigorously examined. Four error categories were devised as follows: 1, no error at all; 2, specification and other errors; 3, errors needing interactive correction; and 4, serious errors. The sample yielded the following results:

Error category	Found	Action required
1	3%	files validate
2	88%	need software correction
3	1%	minor text edit
4	8%	need interactive correction

Table of errors

These statistics covered a whole raft of problems. The main cause of failure had arisen from specification changes, which had not been applied retrospectively, and in a sense, this was the 'chickens coming home to roost'. Other failures and shortcomings included lost header information, missing map data, spurious straight-line joins, spurious or misplaced text, map data outside sheet margins, data on screen and plotted not compatible and so on. In the persisting domestic culture of blame, considerable friction and acrimony broke out amongst the various work areas concerned and, for a time at least, morale spiralled downward. At first, the problem had appeared to be confined mainly to the digital field update operation, but the file corruption problem was soon seen to have a much wider context. The conclusion reached was that, beside a very wide range of problems that had been stored up from the earliest days of digital data collection, more recent and serious problems had arisen, for example, from use of the ICL Solomon communications protocol.

The senior management team at Ordnance Survey accepted the seriousness of the situation and acted decisively to undertake a comprehensive examination or 'sweep' of the complete digital map archive. With the start of the sweep scheduled for February 1990, there followed a period of intense activity to write the test and quality assurance software. One major benefit anticipated from the action taken was that the sweep would lead to all of the format errors, which had been created over the past 15 years, would be found and ultimately eliminated. During the sweep and supporting corrective action, production areas were 'locked out' from the databank while rigorous validation procedures were created and implemented.

Two stages in the process were designed, of validate (VAL) and of validate and fix (VALFIX). Also, a comprehensive data integrity management system was devised for all digital data operations in the post-sweep era. This would ensure that all links to or from the databank and the customer supply suite with all domestic operations, whether in the main digital production area, photogrammetric services and survey computations, field update locations, head office or agents' Superplan (a graphic output product available through Ordnance Survey agents) outlets, would all have rigorous data integrity check or cyclic redundancy check. For all data transfers, these checks would ensure that no physical corruption (as opposed to logical corruption) had occurred.

As the sweep progressed, some worrying occurrences were noted. Files were found with large 'black holes', where all data in a patch had been lost. This was found to be caused by the duplication of FSNs between text and features. The conversion from IFF to OSTF deleted any duplicated numbers and hence data was lost. Some 17 map files were found to contain no data at all. The sweep proceeded as quickly as procedures permitted. By October 1990 some 54,090 map files had been 'swept' and completion by year end was achieved when a total of 70,158 had come under intense scrutiny and necessary remedial action. This was indeed a 'dark passage' for the digitising project and it served as a salutary lesson for corporate Ordnance Survey, which, hopefully, has been truly absorbed into the culture of the organisation for all time. It proved to be a period of great insecurity about the organisation's greatest asset (or at least that part of the archive that had already become digital). The harm, upon more distant reflection, was perhaps not too great. Prompt and very effective action taken by Ordnance Survey when the magnitude of the problem was understood served to limit any loss of confidence of customers in the digital product or indeed in Ordnance Survey itself.

Upon calmer reflection about this dramatic saga, in view of the many specification changes and system modifications that had occurred during 15 years of growing activity, the accompanying philosophy of only attending to them when needs must, together with the startling increase in the mobility of digital map files round the organisation, the overall damage was certainly not critical as it turned out. In the end no lasting harm was done and, indeed, the worrying and painful year of 1990 dramatised the situation with real fears of large-scale data loss and heightened awareness of the need for sustained vigilance and discipline in all matters pertaining to data management.

The occurrence overall forced the organisation to rethink matters of data security and integrity well ahead of the final push to complete the conversion process of all of Great Britain's basic-scale maps from analogue to digital form. The 'scare' ensured that all future operations and the links between them were conducted in a disciplined and secure manner and that the final form of the databank would be as homogenous as it ever could be in terms of specification, form and format.

Chapter 20
But how to establish the price of data?
The story of the pricing problem

Ordnance Survey, because of its unusual role as a department of government but with a product and service portfolio which had some sort of commercial value to its customers, had traditionally found the pricing of products a very difficult issue to manage. The modern era, post-1970, with increasingly demanding cost-recovery targets imposed by HM Government, proved particularly difficult for Ordnance Survey in striking a successful balance between commercial objectives and the need to encourage wider use of affordable Ordnance Survey products and services. The full benefits of a national and definitive map archive can only really be realised through universal utilisation of the information.

The pricing 'issue' has perhaps provided the topic of greatest sustained debate in connection with Ordnance Survey. Cost recovery and, consequently, the level of prices for products charged by Ordnance Survey have, for the last 30 or so years, been one of the most influential 'levers' in the hands of successive governments. Traditionally, the charges raised for Ordnance Survey's map products represented only a very small fraction of their total costs and the aggregate of all revenue was but a small percentage of the overall cost of Ordnance Survey's national mapping operation. The tradition that central government should bear almost all of the cost of the national survey as part of the infrastructure of the state had become firmly established and was widely accepted. Indeed, this well-established tradition effectively served to devalue the perception by many map users of the worth of Ordnance Survey's products and services.

Many other users simply came to take Ordnance Survey's output for granted. Against this established background, a charging formula had developed, which became widely accepted. This suggested that all the costs of the national survey itself would be borne by central government, but the costs of reproducing from it and the cost of distribution would be the basis of any charge to the actual consumer. Hence it was widely understood up to 1966 that the cost of map products would only be set at the level of the cost of 'ink and paper at the printing stage'. These low charges and the revenue earned from licensing under copyright provisions together had continued to make but a small contribution to Ordnance Survey's substantial costs.

In 1966 Government agreed to increase Ordnance Survey's resources to ensure that the post-war resurvey was in fact completed by 1980. As a quid pro quo, Ordnance Survey was directed to raise the price of all large-scale maps. In 1973 the Government appointed the Janes Committee, to review Ordnance Survey. In fact this Committee never rendered a report that was published, but the outcome of the review was that HM Government directed that revenue from all products should, in future, be 'maximised'. This conclusion was to have an ever-increasing impact on the Department's approach to pricing its products.

The first real distinction of digital mapping as a product in its own right, with a price of its own, was created following a brief internal debate that took place in 1973. This concerned the principles of pricing of digital map files, which were to be supplied to Bradford County Borough. The result of this brief initial internal debate was that the charge to be made would simply be set at the cost of copying the map file onto the customer's own magnetic tape. This initial price was clearly established as an incentive with a view to supporting Bradford's experimental use of digital map data. At the time of this initial pricing decision some thought was given to more realistic future pricing options, and eventually the price of a unit of digital map data was set 'at a premium' in relation to the cost of a copy of the map in its conventional 'chart paper' form.

The terms of purchase by the customer were thus established as 'purchase by a one-off payment' to Ordnance Survey in a manner identical to that already in place for the purchase of conventional printed maps. This adoption of simple outright purchase terms for digital map data, without much thought for its implications, was to have serious consequences in the future, when Ordnance Survey's objectives shifted and different terms for acquiring digital map data were required.

However, almost immediately after this initial premium pricing decision was taken, the charge for digital map data was reduced once more, again apparently to stimulate demand during a period of increasing user experimentation. Ordnance Survey remained torn between the objectives of encouraging wider use of a new product and of charging a more realistic proportion of the costs of its production. Because the number of customers remained so small, there was no significant loss of revenue in promoting the new product, but again the perception was bound to develop that digital map data had a low value placed upon it, not least by the producer. This could only serve to make the 'hill' that eventually Ordnance Survey had to 'climb' with users to establish the data's real worth even steeper. For the very few purchases made in the next few years, the emphasis on promotion, thereby encouraging greater use, persisted right up until the Ordnance Survey Review Committee sat during 1978–79.

The Ordnance Survey Review Committee heard a great deal of evidence relating to Government demands following the Janes Committee that Ordnance Survey should raise the level of its cost recovery and the impact of this on product pricing and consequent use of its products by customers. Most concern came from users of conventional large-scale products and services, who feared that they would, through increased prices for these products, be asked to subsidise the digitising programme, for which they had no foreseeable use. How often was heard the view 'that we have already paid for this or that with our taxes'. Eventually, the Review Committee reached some defining conclusions, which were destined to have a profound effect on future pricing of all products in the years ahead.

The Review Committee were asked by HM Government 'to devise a formula which struck a balance whereby the Exchequer should neither pay the full cost of the basic-scale survey nor, through Ordnance Survey, seek full cost recovery from users'. As the Review Committee prepared to seek a solution, by wide consultation, to this particular conundrum, interim financial guidelines for Ordnance Survey were imposed by Government. The level of cost recovery imposed was to serve as a stopgap measure until the Review Committee's recommendations could be implemented.

These interim guidelines demanded that small-scale products should achieve 100% cost recovery while the level of cost recovery for large-scale products, which included digital map data, should be increased from 20% to 25%. As a result, in 1978, Ordnance Survey imposed a price increase of 8% for all large-scale products, the first price increase for three years. Digital map data was not to be excepted from this increase. These particular years had, in fact, witnessed falling volumes of sales of large-scale map products, particularly of chart paper maps in favour of cheaper microfilm copies. Pricing of products soon and perhaps inevitably became enmeshed in Government's demands of Ordnance Survey for rising levels of cost recovery on all of its operations.

The Ordnance Survey Review Committee duly concluded that contemporary cost-recovery targets for the Department were generally 'too blunt an instrument', if Ordnance Survey was to meet all its objectives. Indeed, the all-too-easy mechanism of simply increasing existing cost-recovery targets was felt to hold certain real dangers, whereby, without clear policy objectives, the needs of users and the real benefit of expanding use of the national survey could actually be lost. The Review Committee recognised that previous cost-recovery targets had undoubtedly brought benefits to Ordnance Survey by giving a greater sense of commercial purpose, by stimulating the development of pricing policies, by making the Department more cost-conscious and by demanding greater attention to actual user needs.

However, these targets were considered to have a much too 'broad brush' effect on the wide and diverse nature of Ordnance Survey activities. The Review Committee eventually concluded in its Report that, for the longer term, Government should approach the question of financing Ordnance Survey on rather different lines, and should distinguish more sharply between activities in terms of their importance to the nation and, as a corollary, the financing arrangements appropriate to them. As a result the concept of 'core activities' and 'other or non-core activities' was introduced. 'Core activities' were deemed those which were considered so important that, to ensure their continued provision, the Exchequer should underwrite them. 'Core activities' were to include all aspects of the basic scale map archive which, in due course, would include the digitising project. For each 'core activity' a balance had to be struck between use and revenue.

'Other activities' were to be priced to achieve full cost recovery at least. The Review Committee proposed for 'core activities' that 'the level of service to be provided and the level of any charges imposed should be set to encourage efficient use of the map archive and services'. The Review Committee further recognised that 'while Ordnance Survey's call on the Exchequer has to be limited, any attempt to increase cost recovery that adversely affected use would run counter to such an objective'. The Review Committee recognised that the balance between Exchequer support and pricing and between activities that were liable to change had to be managed, in future years, by Ordnance Survey itself but within Government policies that were extant at the time.

Although these defining principles were ultimately accepted by Government some five years later, it was most certainly these particular aspects of the Report of the Review Committee which served to stall any reaction by the newly elected and reforming Conservative Government led by Mrs Thatcher. However, these principles were destined to have a sustained and significant impact on the future level of prices charged by Ordnance Survey for its products, not least for large-scale digital map data. The Review Committee had accepted that, if anything, levels of activity needed to increase if Ordnance Survey was to fulfil its proper future remit. They concluded finally that revenue levels for future years could not be increased significantly above the levels predicted by Ordnance Survey to them.

The Review had been unable to predict the scope for further price increases but concluded this was much more likely to be found amongst products from the 'non-core' rather than 'core' category where, most importantly, the aim should remain 'to encourage efficient use' by customers. The scope for further increases in cost recovery beyond those suggested in their proposals was felt to be very limited. The Review Committee warned that to go further would risk losing the many benefits anticipated from increased use of Ordnance Survey material, enhanced compatibility of data and better overall use of available resources on a national basis.

Still with no reaction at all from his Government to the Review Committee's Report, the Secretary of State for the Environment, in July 1981, increased the cost-recovery target for large-scale products from 25% to 30%. The story of the pricing of digital map data really begins here in 1982, when the price for a large-scale digital map data file was established at £21 per map unit. This charge was made up of £12 to write the tape for the customer on demand, £2.50 storage and distribution, £2.20 interest on capital, £2.20 as a contribution to the survey itself, with the balance as 'profit' on the transaction.

At this particular point in time and despite the pilot production project approaching its 10th birthday, with still only very limited coverage available, very few purchases of digital map files were in fact made by customers. The contribution of digital map data to any cost-recovery target at all for large-scales remained virtually nil. The purchase price of a map actually represented less than 2% of the cost of producing it in digital form, that is the conversion cost from analogue to digital. The very thorough *Study of User Needs*, which Ordnance Survey ran in 1983, suggested very forcibly that the price of digital map data was already considered by some respondents to be too expensive. What users of digital map data there were simply employed the map information in a similar manner to that which they had traditionally used paper maps for, with no significant increase in functionality available to them.

It was simply employed in early end-user systems as a positioning background or backdrop for other information. In 1984 the price for a digital map unit was increased to £32.50 per map and in 1985 a proposal by Ordnance Survey to raise the price to £50 was deferred until April 1986 following protests from certain customers, who were, by then, making some limited data acquisitions. Again in April 1987 the price was raised once more to £85 per map unit. Between 1984 and 1987 total revenues from digital mapping increased by 954% whilst the price increased by 230%. The actual level of revenue from this source, however, remained very modest indeed, certainly when set against the Department's budget. Ordnance Survey's pricing objectives still remained in serious conflict. Whilst seeking to assist with achieving cost-recovery targets, the price for digital map data needed to stimulate further demand and certainly not to inhibit its wider use.

The actual terms on which digital map data was supplied to customers was also soon destined to change. Since its first availability as a product, the digital map data could simply be purchased by customers for a one-off payment at the published rate. This transaction was eventually called 'single payment' terms. Even in 1990 the Ordnance Survey price list still referred to 'outright purchase'. An annual licence fee was also imposed by Ordnance Survey in respect of the use made of the map data under 'Crown copyright'. This was quickly seen by most early customers, on whom the subtle distinction was lost, as a 'double take' by Ordnance Survey for the same thing. For the duration of almost all of the remainder of the digitising project, this remained a serious bone of contention until 1993, when negotiated agreements with major groups of customers began to replace published prices and generalised copyright terms for most of the larger customers.

In 1987 several local authorities, which had already embarked on acquiring digital map data following trials, were finding it increasingly difficult to meet Ordnance Survey's one-off or 'single payment' charges. 'Single payment terms' represented a good deal for users who could capitalise the cost of map data. The local authorities, with their own funding characteristics, sought an alternative basis of supply and wished to acquire digital map data on 'spread terms'. The terms sought would permit the purchase of digital map data to be funded from running costs rather than from annual capital provisions. Ordnance Survey eventually introduced the concept of data acquisition by customers in return for annual payments at approximately one third of the 'one-off' charge. Initially, this was for an annual fee of £33 per annum, but with a maintenance commitment by Ordnance Survey to keep the map data files up to date.

Vitally for the long-term commercial future of Ordnance Survey, this innovation introduced for the first time the concept that the customer/user simply 'leased' the data and didn't 'own' it. This option for acquisition was called licensed access (annual charge). If the new form of contract was to be terminated by the customer, there was an obligation placed on them either to destroy the map data or to return it to Ordnance Survey. This and the accompanying annual copyright licence fee covering use of the data both served to emphasise and underpin the concept of 'leasing' rather than 'ownership' of the data.

Before the introduction of the 'licensed access terms' in 1990, it had become apparent to Ordnance Survey that the utility companies, particularly, would continue to demand 'single payment terms' using capital resources as they sought to make their ongoing operations lean and hungry for the looming stock market on privatisation. Serving this need came from the improved understanding of utility operations that Ordnance Survey key account executives provided. Any advance notice of the termination of 'single payment terms' would have brought a rush to purchase before the deadline. This would, in turn, have brought a one-off 'windfall' to Ordnance Survey with substantial overachievement of cost recovery targets within the year of sales, which could only have served to mislead Ministers of the Crown and wouldn't have helped Ordnance Survey, as the additional income would have passed straight to the Exchequer. The pragmatic decision was taken to continue with both purchase options.

It is almost certain that had Ordnance Survey been a commercial company it would have found this shift of its position much more difficult to introduce and manage than in fact it did as a government department. It wasn't until 1990, when major disputes began to surface with customers in connection with the terms of copyright licensing, that the whole gamut of issues in connection with the acquisition of data by customers was considered comprehensively and finally resolved, at least to Ordnance Survey's satisfaction. This was indeed a very difficult time for Ordnance Survey as it shifted its position for the future. Customers who had acquired data on 'single payment terms' were permitted to hold the data in perpetuity, although they were formally told they did not own it.

Timely and fortunately, as DFUS was deployed in Ordnance Survey field offices, the prospect of continuous revision in digital form became a reality. Reasonably priced as it was from its introduction, the digital revision service soon began to meet customer expectations. With suitable financial adjustment where necessary, most customers were eventually placed on the new annual payment terms for maintained map data. Ordnance Survey's future needs for a continuing and steady revenue stream were assured and what had seemed an intractable problem was managed pragmatically. The change also facilitated the development of the concept of SLAs with major customers that became a reality, for the first time, in the case of local authorities in 1993. These important agreements completed complex negotiations for both the acquisition and the licensed use of digital map data or 'Land-Line', as it was by then called. Customers who had already purchased data on 'single payment terms' were given a rebate on their subscription to the SLA.

Going back to the mid-1980s, the dilemma for Ordnance Survey, and particularly for its embryonic marketing function, was to maximise income from digital mapping in what was still a very immature market. It remained vital to avoid forcing potential customers into wasteful duplication of effort by digitising themselves or into seeking alternative sources of data, for example, by the use of raster data, which some, at least, saw as a realistic alternative to Ordnance Survey's vector data. In later years of the project the very real concern persisted within Ordnance Survey that setting the price of digital data too high might serve to encourage competitive digitising of urban areas where there were several customers for the map data.

These were sustained threats that marketing staff had to consider very real. However, throughout the following serial price increases, and despite a good deal of complaint and much criticism, Ordnance Survey retained one very strong 'card in its hand'. The price sought by Ordnance Survey for a digital map unit never ever got anywhere near the price that a digitising bureau might charge, even for a simplified output from an Ordnance Survey large-scale map. The actual value of the map data to emerging customers, at this particular time, still remained largely unknown to Ordnance Survey. In fact it soon became clear to all that the creation of digital map data was a classic example of the Ordnance Survey Review Committee's category of 'core activity'.

The very high cost of creating the map data, the relatively low price charged for it despite several price hikes and the overall paucity of customers meant that it very soon became starkly clear that the cost of creating the digital map data could not realistically be recovered from the marketplace. Nevertheless, the market needed to be expanded. Reliable intelligence about the longer-term value of the data to users simply wasn't available to guide Ordnance Survey with its approach to pricing the data. Fortuitously perhaps, in view of the urgent need to establish for its future the true value and worth of the map data, Ordnance Survey reacted by taking a very short-term and immediate view with respect to its more immediate financial objectives. With very few customers still for the map data, the cost of single payment terms to acquire the data was increased at the beginning of 1990 to £110 per map unit and to £120 later that year.

It wasn't really until marketing executives were placed with key customers and they, in turn, became fully operational that a view could be formed of the longer-term value these customers placed on the map data or how indeed the potential value of the market to Ordnance Survey could, more reliably, be assessed. As the number of customers increased and some began to acquire very large inventories of map data, pressure on Ordnance Survey to discount sales increased. Throughout, such demands were always resisted on the grounds that, by virtue of the net parliamentary vote, government was already actively supporting the manufacture and delivery of the product.

This series of increases in the price of digital map data was heavily criticised, often in public, by an increasingly coherent and organised customer community. Most certainly, the rapid and substantial price rises left committed customers vulnerable over project budgets and their cost/benefit analyses on which information system development projects were originally justified. Ordnance Survey persisted in the view that the price increases were supportable and sustainable because government, with cost recovery on the basic scales still well below 100%, was subsidising digital mapping operations' end product.

Through the 1990s the need became increasingly evident that Ordnance Survey should move from the mass marketing strategy of its traditional markets to 'target marketing' through segmentation, with more innovative marketing mixes, of which product price was but only one factor. Eventually this was achieved through the efforts of Ordnance Survey itself and by the opening up of opportunities for commercial private-sector partners. A whole range of map data products developed and produced on the back of the large-scale digitising project served to meet differing customer requirements at quite different price structures.

In a sense, between 1986 and 1991, with a still very immature market for the data product, it was fortunate and timely that Ordnance Survey managed to get the price of a unit of digital map data up substantially in price before resistance and effective customer pressure could be exerted, either economically or politically. At last, as customer numbers began to increase substantially, the basis of a successful business that Ordnance Survey enjoys as the twentieth century ends was built and generally secured for the future by innovative marketing and enforcement of its just reward under the Copyright, Designs and Patents Act.

In summary, the pricing of the large-scale digital mapping data product was never led by the cost of its creation. Initially, there was no market at all and customers were very slow to find uses for the data, hence for most of the life of the digitising project pricing was not customer-demand led. There was no realistic competition for the product. There was a possibility from time to time that someone else might provide quite different map data in customer 'hot spots of demand', but this never proved to be a serious threat. Ordnance Survey simply priced the product for most of the project's life on the basis of what they felt customers might tolerate without recourse to complaining to the several Ministers who serially held responsibility for Ordnance Survey. Ordnance Survey originally increased the price of the data in line with government's demands for increasing recovery of Ordnance Survey's costs. Only toward the end of the project – then well into the 1990s - did strategic considerations and pricing with a view to securing a stable and successful future business for Ordnance Survey on the back of rising demand, albeit within government, really enter into the pricing equation.

Chapter 21
The copyright issue

As the digitising project progressed and slowly gathered momentum, Ordnance Survey faced two main commercial and intellectual property issues. The first was the price that it should charge customers who wished to purchase files of digital map data and the second was the degree of copyright protection and further revenue that could lawfully be imposed and collected from its creative work. Ordnance Survey had sought to enforce protection for its intellectual property by means of copyright since 1816, but it was following the Davidson Committee of 1935 that Ordnance Survey came to regard 'copyright' as a means of defraying the cost of the survey.

The many aspects of copyright protection and the exploitation of its intellectual property were eventually to become an issue of supreme importance, both to Ordnance Survey and to its most significant customers for digital map data. Perhaps not surprisingly, the emergence of copyright as a critical issue very much mirrors in timing the actual evolution of the digitising project itself. The maps themselves, from which the data would be collected, as graphic images printed on chart paper for sale, already enjoyed a 50-year period of copyright protection as 'works of art'. It had become widely accepted, but without any significant test case, that these maps were to be regarded as 'works of art' performed by the Crown, under section 39 of the 1956 Copyright Act and therefore enjoyed the protection of Crown copyright.

This situation had remained largely unchallenged in times when the authority of government itself was seldom denied and when, in any case, the price charged for national mapping simply recovered the basic cost only of the printing ink and the paper stock on which the map was printed. This was the de facto charging formula for national mapping in Great Britain up to the start of the pilot production project for digital mapping. Copyright licensing for use of the basic-scale mapping, once acquired, was already well established for government departments, local government and the utility undertakings, but licence fees were still extremely modest. It was against this very stable background that the digital mapping pilot project slowly gathered momentum through the

1970s. Gardiner-Hill's professional paper of 1972, which did so much to set standards, did not cover any of the commercial aspects of digitised mapping, other than to recognise the obvious benefits to customers.

In terms of copyright on conventional mapping, it came to be accepted that fresh approaches were needed in any case, with the advent of the burgeoning use of photocopiers by conventional map customers. In December 1977 Ordnance Survey attempted to provide the same measure of protection for its computer-based mapping as that it had enjoyed for paper-based mapping. It published leaflet number eight in a new series of information leaflets for customers. Hardly surprisingly, this particular leaflet gave details of Crown copyright practice and provisions in the context of traditionally published maps, but the digitising of mapping was included for the first time in a list of prohibited acts, unless prior authority and due acknowledgement were agreed. The important issue of fees for use was not addressed at this time.

Financial pressures on Ordnance Survey in the late 1960s and early 1970s, culminating in the much more commercially oriented guidelines set for it in 1973 by the Janes Committee, encouraged Ordnance Survey to seek an increasing return on its intellectual property via copyright licensing. Up to the time of the Ordnance Survey Review Committee, which delivered its report in 1979, only very small volumes of data were available and most of the customers that had already surfaced were generally more preoccupied with technical issues rather than the rudimentary commercial arrangements that Ordnance Survey had put in place in connection with the acquisition of digital map data. This state of affairs was very much the basis of the narrative of the Serpell Report, which dwelt almost wholly but inconclusively for a complete chapter on the question of copyright.

Almost all of the evidence received by the Review Committee itself concerned the past. The evidence was generally critical of substantive arrangements for levying royalties on traditional paper-based mapping. Most of this 'hubbub' came from academics and small publishers. The Report of the Review Committee did document who the main large-scale map users were. With large-scale products responsible at that time for some 91% of copyright revenue received, 34% of this came from local authorities, 27% from the utilities, 5% from water boards and 9% from departments of central government. One statement made in the final Report of the Review Committee was to prove prophetic. The Report urged Ordnance Survey to devise a price structure for copyright 'which would reflect the value of map information to users and also the cost to Ordnance Survey of producing suitable data'.

Beyond this rather modest attempt to provide some protection within the provisions of an old copyright Act of Parliament that necessarily predated any concern at all for any of the consequences associated with modern computing, it was, in fact, an external proposal in 1979 that brought the problem of 'ownership' and exploitation of digitised data into sharper focus. Hunting Surveys Ltd, probably the most successful of Great Britain's private sector mapping companies at this particular point in time, had identified a business opportunity for themselves. This opportunity would be met by maintaining an inventory of their clients' map holdings and by customised plotting from their Ordnance Survey digital map data, using a modified version of Ordnance Survey's own D09 plot programme.

This approach to Ordnance Survey by Hunting Surveys Ltd has to be viewed in the context of Ordnance Survey's own minimalist marketing effort, which was witnessed by a real lack of information on data availability and about the longer-term plans of Ordnance Survey itself, with regard to digital mapping. It was this same paucity of information that the Ordnance Survey Review Committee, led by Sir David Serpell, was soon to highlight. The proposal from Hunting Surveys Ltd provoked a typical and initial defensive reaction from within Ordnance Survey. The response was based on concern for the protection of the services currently provided either by Ordnance Survey itself or by its official appointed map agents. Almost certainly assisted by the impetus provided by the Review Committee Report and following intensive internal debate at the highest levels within, Ordnance Survey eventually signed an agency agreement with Hunting Surveys Ltd in May 1980.

To sustain its 'neutral' public-sector position, the request for exclusivity was refused. Surprisingly perhaps at such an early stage of the development, Ordnance Survey recognised the strategic importance of retaining overall control of the exploitation of the digital map data. The initial two-year agreement with Hunting Surveys Ltd provided for the acquisition and storage of map data files on behalf of clients, the use of files already purchased by them, the plotting of maps from data and the maintenance of data availability records on behalf of their clients. Perhaps without realising all the implications, this initial commercial venture did cause deeper consideration by Ordnance Survey, than at any other time before, of the thorny issues of commercial exploitation and the protection of their intellectual property in digitised data.

In September 1981 and still without any response from HM Government to the Report of the Review Committee, Laser-Scan Laboratories of Cambridge, realising, a bit belatedly, that a precedent had already been created with the Hunting's deal, themselves approached Ordnance Survey for agency status within the digital mapping field. With still no greater clarity emerging concerning Ordnance Survey ambitions and plans for digital mapping, Laser-Scan's approach went much further. With still very low levels of production each year by Ordnance Survey itself, Laser-Scan's proposal sought permission to undertake digitising of Ordnance Survey maps on behalf of clients who wished to make progress with trials or the actual implementation of systems based on Ordnance Survey's large-scale digital map data.

The emerging fear of Ordnance Survey, in response to this new demand, focused on the concern whether their own 'standards' could be maintained, although such standards had never been codified and published. The then current copyright act singularly failed to cover the type of issue that such innovative deals raised. Laser-Scan Ltd, already in dialogue with its customers, continued to pressurise Ordnance Survey for a response. Ordnance Survey's natural instincts, despite the stimulus of the Review Committee's Report, was simply to retreat. However, the challenge would not go away. After a great deal of negotiation, an agreement offering digital mapping agency status to Laser-Scan Ltd was finally granted. Ordnance Survey was able only to impose terms within the broad guidance of the provisions of the 1956 Copyright Act and on which there had been no relevant case law in the intervening years.

Ordnance Survey 'retained the high ground' by simply continuing to regard digital maps as fully protected by Crown copyright under the 1956 Act. Meanwhile evidence was given formally by Ordnance Survey to the Whitford Committee, which had been established and which was tasked with a review of legislation in the field of copyright. Ordnance Survey set great store, in its evidence to Whitford, on the need for recognition of the impact of the computer in intellectual property matters. Specifically, protection was sought for computer programs and also for copyright provisions for the control and exploitation of mapping material in a computer-compatible form.

The Whitford Committee, however, did not recommend a separate section in the Bill it proposed for a modern Copyright Act, but it did recognise that existing legislation was inadequate and that copyright protection should indeed be given to modern forms of mapping. The Whitford Committee chose to regard a digitised map as a compilation of data similar to a computer programme and concluded that both should be afforded protection in a future Act of Parliament. The Whitford Committee, wisely in retrospect, recommended that both input and output from a computer be regarded as 'restricted' acts. The opinion of this learned Committee was that the input of copyright material into a computer generally constituted 'reproduction' in material form, with the consequence that digital mapping was lawfully included within Crown copyright and the protection it bestowed.

The eventual green paper, which sought to consult widely on the reform of the law relating to copyright, design and performer's protection, was eventually published in July 1981. This was to result in the modern Copyright, Designs and Patents Act, which eventually passed in to law in Parliament in 1988. In this lengthy interim period, Ordnance Survey faced mounting pressure to explain and clarify its rights to protection. Indeed, Ordnance Survey was the subject of considerable and mounting criticism for the stance that it took as it tried to address the very complex issues relating to the acquisition and utilisation of digital map data by an ever-increasing number of customers, many of whom were quite willing to challenge Ordnance Survey's intellectual property rights.

In 1982 Ordnance Survey had three main goals with regard to the management of its copyright interest in digital map data. Ordnance Survey, under mounting pressure from HM Government, needed to secure digital mapping as a growing source of income, particularly during the transition, for many customers, from traditional use of paper-based mapping to this modern use. At the same time, Ordnance Survey wished to extend this use but, at the same time, it also wished to guard against unauthorised use, a task, which everyone could foresee, would be much more difficult than in years gone by. At this time Ordnance Survey's copyright interest in the digitised map information really consisted of two elements. One was a royalty to be paid for the act of digitising itself by a third party and the other was a royalty payable when certain uses of the map data were made, for example, by the production of a graphic plot.

Worryingly for Ordnance Survey, there was an emerging counter view that computer systems would lead to users paying less in aggregate to Ordnance Survey. This opinion began to surface and harden as an element in the cost justification of some customer, information systems. Ordnance Survey responded to this growing trend with the publication, for the first time, of an information leaflet number 45 entitled 'Digital Mapping Copyright Arrangements' in June 1982. This particular, leaflet for customers represented a very forceful defence of Ordnance Survey's Crown copyright and of its main income stream from licensing, which, by 1983, represented one third (nearly £7 million) of Ordnance Survey's total earnings from the marketplace. This leaflet was indeed timely, as it was published just as plans by customers to use digital data were beginning to multiply significantly in Great Britain. The leaflet covered all aspects of copyright protection and reflected all of the experience and practice to date. However, it was seen by customers as lengthy and much too complicated; but at least it gave Ordnance Survey's position on such matters some contractual basis.

By this time, many local authorities and electricity boards (in particular) were licensed to digitise maps and also licensed to use digital map data obtained from Ordnance Survey mapping. Everyone else was expected to seek prior permission should they wish either to digitise Ordnance Survey's maps or to use data which they had acquired either directly or through one of the new data agents. As forecast and demanded in the Report of the Review Committee in 1979, pressure was mounting rapidly for data (truly compatible with that already produced) to be made available beyond the very limited areas that Ordnance Survey itself planned to tackle. This move raised several serious issues in connection with Ordnance Survey's copyright interests in digital map data.

Questions such as what rights should Ordnance Survey enjoy in data digitised by others from its maps, could it use such data itself, what royalties should be levied on contractors and under, what terms could such data be passed to a third party, were all raised. Current licensees were only permitted to make copies of maps they had actually purchased themselves. The utilities generally in their system development were already planning for 'plant information' exchange amongst themselves, but in every case, against a digitised Ordnance Survey map background. Thus data sharing and exchange were issues that Ordnance Survey simply had to resolve in dialogue with this important customer group. A formal review of all such copyright issues was made and taken to the highest level within Ordnance Survey.

This soon led to a growing realisation within that Ordnance Survey needed urgently to modernise its approach to copyright licensing and protection. Given mounting pressure from Government to recover an increasing percentage of its costs, any such shift in approach to raising revenue necessitated re-education of users. Ordnance Survey began to claim that if there was to be a viable national survey under the Government's sustained regime of ever-increasing cost recovery, licence fees should be paid for the beneficial use of survey information and should not be based simplistically on the number of copies taken from the map data. The use of ephemeral images derived from digital map data 'on screen' posed a major problem between Ordnance Survey and its customers.

It was at this time that the practice of seeking external expert legal opinion on difficult issues in connection with digital copyright was initiated. Ordnance Survey from this time forward developed a very effective relationship with Field, Fisher and Partners, a legal firm in London, particularly in connection with matters of copyright in the large-scale digital map data. A very wily partner of this legal practice, Mr R S Bagehot took the lead in all such matters on behalf of Ordnance Survey. This was indeed a sea change for Ordnance Survey, which, at last, was able to present a credible legal opinion in the face of several sustained challenges by those legal officers that were readily available to many of its customers.

Ordnance Survey's fundamental concern throughout this particular time was that any protracted transition in map use from paper copies to digital data by its principal customers, simply had to provide a steadily rising stream of revenue derived from copyright royalties, if Government-set cost recovery targets were, in fact, to be met. In 1984, from a total of £7.1 million earned from copyright royalties, some £6 million was derived from what was then still considered the public sector, which included principally the utilities, local authorities and other government departments. Almost all of that revenue was derived from use of the large-scale mapping in conventional forms. This necessitated a substantial Copyright Section at Ordnance Survey head office. In the same year Ordnance Survey prepared and published a consultative paper to raise this difficult issue of the transition from conventional to digital mapping with its customers.

Following the call in the Report of the Review Committee for closer cooperation between Ordnance Survey and its customers, a formal and more broadly based consultative mechanism had been created. To represent the utility sector, the Ordnance Survey NJUG was established. This consultative committee was populated and driven principally by representatives of utility bodies that were either experimenting with or, in some cases, were actually implementing computer-based information systems, the basic 'fuel' of which was the digital map data. The Utilities Consultative Committee established a Copyright Working Group to liaise and to work with Ordnance Survey. Together they developed a tariff for charging for copyright which was based on the concept of an annual charge per map unit held by the customer. Ordnance Survey tried to win over customers to the concept of an increased digital royalty. Undoubtedly, for many customers of Ordnance Survey the advent of corporate information systems typically offered easier and wider distributed access to the map data, whilst possibly still performing the same sort of level of business activity.

Further, Ordnance Survey, on behalf of HM Government, was by this time committed to embarking on a major investment programme when, at the same time, they might well miss out on sales because of 'licensed digitising', which was responsible for the existence and availability of an ever-increasing volume of digital mapping. The original 1982 leaflet, still as number 45 in the new leaflet series, was republished in January 1987 following this fundamental rethink about the copyright terms for digital mapping. What had developed into a very complex subject, without legal precedents, came out in the leaflet in a very lengthy and confusing form. Essentially, the charging mechanism for the future was set as an annual royalty charge of £10 per digital map unit held by the customer then to be multiplied or discounted for the particular, nature and intensity of use made by the customer of the map data.

One significant aspect in the administration of Ordnance Survey's copyright over the years was the agreement by the Controller of Her Majesty's Stationery Office (HMSO), in which the control of Crown copyright was traditionally vested, for the formal delegation of control of its own intellectual property to the Director General of Ordnance Survey. Traditionally, Ordnance Survey had always produced the most significant proportion of the revenues derived from the exploitation of' Crown copyright. This delegation, which Ordnance Survey always exercised with great care and always in close cooperation with HMSO officials, was to have a significant impact on the growth of Ordnance Survey's business, which increasingly became based on their substantial investment in digital mapping. A major relief for Ordnance Survey in the difficult task of getting its position on copyright in digital mapping across to customers, eventually came during 1988 with the passage into law of the Copyright, Designs and Patents Act 1988.

Ordnance Survey had gone to unprecedented levels to influence the form and provisions of this particular piece of legislation during the Bill's protracted consultation procedures. Suitable clauses were included in this Act that gave Ordnance Survey two levels of protection. The first was the recognition by the Act of the map itself as an 'artistic' work; and the second was the recognition of the contents of a database as a 'literary' work. Until 1988 all digital data 'sales' to customers by Ordnance Survey were simply regarded and described as 'outright purchases'. In point of fact, this was always a serious misnomer. However, its entrenched acceptance by Ordnance Survey and its customers alike contributed to a period of deep suspicion and challenge when Ordnance Survey, vitally, sought to adjust its position.

Toward the end of 1988, following receipt of Counsel's opinion and at last able to offer the prospect of a viable digital revision service for the large-scale map data, Ordnance Survey switched the basis of 'sales' from outright purchase by customers to one of 'licensed access to maintained digital map data'. In the meantime, before the new Copyright Act got on to the statute book, local authorities had already begun to mount a direct challenge over whether the use of ephemeral screen images constituted a restricted act under the terms of the awaited new copyright act. Prior to this particular challenge, Ordnance Survey had already sought and received supportive Counsel's opinion with regard to this particular issue. Ordnance Survey, in the face of widespread challenges to almost any reasonable form of copyright management, moved rapidly to the position whereby revenue streams for data utilisation were best secured by contractual terms within an SLA for a group of customers with common needs and map usage patterns.

Such SLAs would be designed to provide for distinct and homogenous use patterns such as those made by local authorities or utility undertakings which, in the latter case, were in the midst of becoming public companies, through privatisation. User groups within the newly formed Association for Geographic Information (AGI®), which had been established in the wake of Lord Chorley's Committee of Enquiry, demanded several key characteristics from any Ordnance Survey copyright charging mechanism. By this time there was widespread and profound suspicion of both Government's and Ordnance Survey's motives. The main characteristics demanded of any copyright licensing system included predictability of charges year on year, ease of understanding of Ordnance Survey's terms and conditions, obvious fairness between customer groups and with the ability to offer openings for licensed and lawful competition.

With negotiations already under way for an SLA with representatives of the Local Authorities Associations and armed with a plethora of suitable legal opinions, Ordnance Survey took part very patiently in a series of round-table meetings under the AGI banner, with intense correspondence in between. This dialogue did eventually serve to educate and inform customers about the realities of the Government's position with regard to Ordnance Survey recovering an ever-greater proportion of its costs. Ordnance Survey was able also, at long last, to get its own needs as a viable business, albeit within government, factored into this public debate.

At the commencement of the dialogue at the behest of AGI, Ordnance Survey froze the copyright charge per map sheet *pro tem* at £1.69 per annum. During the consultations under the AGI banner, customers voiced their concerns whilst Ordnance Survey held firmly to the status quo. In the debate that ensued, a conflict soon emerged between the AGI and users seeking simplicity and Ordnance Survey necessarily adhering to the principles of the Copyright, Designs and Patent Act. With no consensus reached by January 1994, the flat rate of £5.15 per map file per annum was set by Ordnance Survey. With rapidly increasing use this rate was moved to £10 in 1995.

The basis of charging for copyright in digital mapping had, in less than 10 years, therefore moved through two stages of evolution. Initially, the basis of such charges had mirrored those for traditional chart-paper mapping with a base charge and a sum levied per licensed use (traditionally by copying or tracing). Following the introduction of the modern Copyright Act in 1988 and armed with supportive legal opinions,

Ordnance Survey developed the concept of charging a fee for the use of a digital map per 'restricted' act. Five categories of use were described in the published terms and conditions and these ranged from 'low' to 'intensive' use. The annual fee for each category of use was then multiplied by an enhancement factor, based on the number of computer terminals deployed in the system of the host organisation.

These terms were carefully and specifically based on the provisions of' the new Copyright Act. They were certainly fair in terms of their legal basis and their applicability to all but they made for complication and some residual uncertainty. The concept of a charge to be levied per act of use, the fear of being moved arbitrarily by Ordnance Survey up the scale of use (hence unpredictability) and the system's complication all served to generate a considerable wave of concern and opposition amongst many leading customers. Opposition to Ordnance Survey's newly introduced terms soon intensified. Many potentially large customers were, at this very time, only at the stage of working up proposals and seeking to justify corporate information systems which would be based on Ordnance Survey's large-scale digital map data.

Most such projects were extremely sensitive to significant input cost variations. For most of them, an uncertain copyright royalty charging mechanism by Ordnance Survey posed a major threat to already fragile cost justifications. In the inevitable trade-off between fairness and simplicity in such matters, such a system favoured fairness under the law of copyright pertaining at the time. Almost inevitably in view of the stubborn opposition but with the real prospect, at last, of tackling the problem via the group contractual approach already mentioned, Ordnance Survey in 1993 agreed to modify this approach, *pro tem*, by assigning all digital customers to the lowest category of use at the royalty charge of £1.66 per map held, per year. Some of the opposition to these different approaches by Ordnance Survey arose from beliefs that with the taxpayer having already funded the survey and increasingly its conversion to a digital form, users should not be charged further for its use. This philosophy was consistently out of step with the Government's philosophy of 'let the user pay'.

The third successive approach that Ordnance Survey introduced for charging customers for licensed copyright use of digital map data again vitally preserved the proper legal basis under the 1988 Act of Parliament and also went some way toward achieving simplicity and ease of understanding. This approach was again based on an annual flat rate fee per map in use with a multiplier for the number of access points on the user's system. Both elements of this calculation could be assessed as matters of fact, by inspection, if necessary. At long last, the past practice, which had endured for so many years, of sample counts of user activity (for example, by copying) and the need for subjective assessments was removed from the process of extracting copyright royalties from customers. The new information leaflet published by Ordnance Survey, which described this new approach, duly received approval by the Plain English Campaign® and was formally published.

Ordnance Survey remained resolute throughout this period of challenge to their right to seek adequate return on their creative work. This period was, for them, a very uncertain and turbulent period. However, Ordnance Survey remained adamant that unless customers made a significant and continuing contribution to the costs associated with the creation and maintenance of the large-scale map database, the whole large-scale data operation would have to be seriously curtailed. The most significant benefit of the evolutionary approach described above was that it undoubtedly served to drive the Local Authority Ordnance Survey Committee into negotiations with Ordnance Survey to seek a customised SLA as initially proposed by Ordnance Survey. This agreement was eventually signed in March 1993 after very innovative approaches to the negotiations were adopted by both parties.

It was such a success in practice and effect that it was renewed following fresh negotiations for a further three years in March 1996. Without any doubt, the facilities that the initial SLA offered actually facilitated the ever-widening use of Ordnance Survey's maintained digital map data within the local authority community. The deal proved to be an excellent one for both parties. Details of the deal were successfully kept truly confidential but the obvious and clear success of the nature of the initial agreement with local authorities, together with sustained pressure from Ordnance Survey negotiators, soon brought about the start of negotiations with NJUG. By this time NJUG represented all the, by now, private-sector utility companies in the water, gas, telecommunications, cable, and electricity generation and supply industries.

The SLA with the very diverse utility group was almost certainly the greatest coup of all by Ordnance Survey in its urgent quest to sustain its vital copyright revenue stream in respect of its digital map database.

Ordnance Survey's negotiating team came up against very hard-nosed commercial negotiators and legal teams. In fact, during the lengthy negotiations, once the legal advisers were removed from the negotiations by mutual consent, steady progress was achieved to an ultimate and successful outcome. The reinstated lawyers on both sides eventually oversaw the final documentation of this landmark agreement. Ordnance Survey was aware during the negotiations that the utility representatives were working under the imperative of the long-promised Street Works Act. This Act demanded effective information exchange about buried plant amongst the various utility companies. Vital to this was the spatial framework of a common information system.

The SLA with NJUG representatives again led to rapid take-up of Ordnance Survey's revised digital map data. Having achieved this fundamental and successful breakthrough with its two most important customer groupings, Ordnance Survey had actually secured a very large proportion of its predominant source of revenue from copyright royalties on large-scale digital map data. Other customers, either individual or in generic groups, perhaps fearing the imposition of less favourable terms, very quickly sought customised agreements. The Scottish Office, British Waterways and many others followed in successive years up to the present time. As an illustration of the importance of these royalties to the well-being of the national mapping agency, in 1995–96 the income derived from copyright revenue on core activity was £20.8 million.

Almost all of this was derived either directly or indirectly from the successful compilation of the digital database of large-scale mapping of Great Britain. This turbulent period, both for the customers and for the administrators of Ordnance Survey's copyright and, indeed, for the organisation as a whole, saw the almost complete transition from a practice based on copying of 'hard copy' images of large-scale maps to the complex uses devised for the digital data products. Practice simply had to be developed as the situation evolved and, because of the law pertaining to such matters, it was not to be a simple transition.

As this very profound and sustained threat to Ordnance Survey's income from its intellectual property was at last cleared, other challenges appeared. Firstly, the 1988 Copyright Act started to come under challenge about its provisions for 'statutory usage' which, if successful, would have greatly diminished Ordnance Survey's right to levy charges in cases where the laws of the land necessitated the use of Ordnance

312

Survey's products. Secondly, and emanating from Europe, was the European directive providing access to Information on the environment. At the outset this appeared to offer the prospect of unfettered access to a wide diversity of information held on Ordnance Survey's mapping. Such challenges were negotiated successfully, but the most striking success in the 'copyright saga' was undoubtedly the concept and the successful development of user group SLAs that compounded copyright payments with acquisition and usage of the digital map data.

Chapter 22
Promotion and publicity

During the early years of the development of digital techniques for basic-scale and derived map production, Ordnance Survey, by custom and practice, relied on very limited and unambitious 'channels' to achieve publicity or to effect consultation about what it was attempting to do. Ordnance Survey, with its already long history, relied heavily upon its reputation and the enduring commitment of existing customers to its traditional product range. It is important to keep in mind that, although there were occasional statements from 'on high', which demonstrated enormous vision about the future potential of the digital techniques, the overwhelming justification for the experimentation and development was to effect cheaper or faster methods in the substantial production task that the organisation faced in the 1960s and early 1970s.

Interwoven with this was the ever-present fear, which was even 'seeded' from time to time into published annual reports, that the required levels of resources might be curtailed at any time by HM Government. The post-war mapping programme, if its completion schedule by 1980 was to be maintained, was indeed very hungry for resources. From personal witness and from contemporary documentation, it is clear that for most senior managers their attention was drawn most to the potential attraction of faster and cheaper production of mapping derived from the basic-scales data itself. Ordnance Survey had already long developed a reputation outside that bordered on arrogance, with a smug certainty about what it was attempting to achieve. This consistent denial of 'customers' tended to leave the highly planned organisation totally focused on production targets set in outline for them, pre-war, by an external committee of enquiry.

This 'certainty' about the future had the unfortunate side effect that not too much thought was applied to how the target might best be achieved or whether indeed the output was the best or correct one. This predominant task orientation was perhaps nowhere more clearly in evidence than in the sustained drive to fully complete the rural mapping of Great Britain using the uncertain and subjective techniques of 'overhauling', even when it became well understood that these techniques produced an unreliable and generally undesirable result. Throughout most of the 1960s and 1970s, Ordnance Survey really didn't accept external criticism very graciously; nor, indeed, react very positively to it. Ordnance Survey typically reacted by withdrawing from the debate or controversy. This was not wholly untypical of most of Government during this epoch.

In Ordnance Survey's case, this characteristic undoubtedly stemmed in good measure from its military style of management and operation. Initially, being a very closed type of organisation with a very clear, long-term mission and role established before World War Two, Ordnance Survey tended to communicate very infrequently with the 'outside world', and then usually on its own terms. What limited public 'engagement' there was, normally was achieved by publishing a very limited number of highly crafted and carefully worded papers, either in journals or at occasional professional or technical meetings and conferences, either at home or abroad. Any significant mention of Ordnance Survey by the press of the day almost always paralysed the organisation. Ordnance Survey in the 1960s had no semblance at all of a marketing or promotional operation within its ranks.

In terms of the still very embryonic digitising project, Professional Paper no 23: 'The Development of Digital Maps' written by Col RC Gardiner-Hill OBE, published in 1972, provided an important benchmark for Ordnance Survey in terms of information dissemination and publicity about its activity and achievements, albeit to a very limited audience. This publication was informative if slightly self-congratulatory in tone. It certainly and with novelty contained considerable vision about the longer-term potential of the production techniques, but its optimism and confidence in the approach made and the developments to date, which it described, at some length, were designed mainly to win support inside Ordnance Survey as much as to inform 'outsiders'.

The two or three members of staff involved internally with the digital mapping project continued to make important contacts outside the Department – but largely with their opposite numbers in sister organisations – through the meetings of the JASB Automated Cartography Committee and with representatives of emerging hardware suppliers. It should always be remembered that, in the very early days of the digital mapping project, digital data was not really seen as a 'product' in itself, other than by a few well-informed folk, who had the necessary belief in what they were trying to achieve. Generally, the digitising project was perceived as an eventual means, perhaps, to faster or cheaper map production, at basic and derived map scales.

Once the pilot production task got underway later, in 1972, the very first element of 'branding' of Ordnance Survey's digital map data, at least in tangible printed form, was devised and quickly implemented. This was the digital map symbol, which was retained throughout, whilst Ordnance Survey continued to publish printed, chart paper maps produced via the digital mapping flowlines. The original purpose of the symbol was to distinguish these maps from those produced by conventional scribing and lithographic technology. In a sense this early form of branding was almost unwitting. Amazingly, in an organisation that at the time employed a substantial and slow-moving committee to decide even the most trivial detail in connection with map design, content and so on, the digital symbol was designed and implemented very quickly within the Development team itself.

This very simple achievement probably had more to do with the general climate of scepticism and even derision in some of the more conservative quarters of Ordnance Survey, under the style of 'this new-fangled stuff will never catch on'. Such sentiment was heard frequently at the time from those not involved with the project. These opinions generally emanated largely from fears about 'deskilling' of previously much-admired craft skills. Reported failures and shortcomings in outputs were seized upon almost with delight in many parts of Ordnance Survey.

The shop-floor workforce at large in Ordnance Survey were not, of course, generally exposed to the vision of what the future might demand as perceived by the likes of Gardiner-Hill, who was most usually seen inside the Department as something of a maverick eccentric. The digital map symbol was soon described somewhat derisively inside Ordnance Survey as 'the digital snail'. Perhaps, charitably, this was because the symbol consisted quite simply of a stylised image of concentric rings of an unravelling spool of magnetic tape with the words 'digital map' imposed round the north-west quadrant of the spool. Nevertheless it was the first real attempt at 'branding' of the paper image derived from digital map data and its origins provide a very good insight into the contemporary 'house culture'.

Ordnance Survey by this time still had no separate marketing operation as such, but within the Directorate of Map Publication some appointments had been made earlier and post holders began to address the needs of the customer and the market with more focus. Following Gardiner-Hill's original published account of the digitising project in 1972, the next definitive attempt, other than by papers to meetings, conferences and so on, to formally publicise the digital mapping developments at Ordnance Survey, eventually got under way, in a commercial sense, in 1978. This effort culminated in a rather unprepossessing, rather downbeat, one-page leaflet, numbered 48 and published in May 1979, as one of Ordnance Survey's new green, house-styled leaflet series. The leaflet mostly dwelt, albeit quite tersely, on the equipment and techniques used by Ordnance Survey in its digital mapping procedures rather than on its outputs and their potential uses.

There was no attempt to sell the potential benefits of digital mapping to customers. The leaflet raised hopes about using the techniques internally to produce derived mapping and, for the first time formally, the leaflet contained details of the arrangements for customers who wished to purchase and to use digital map data to produce their own graphics. The leaflet concluded with a brief outline of the PMA project, which was seeking to restructure the digital data, to achieve wider acceptance and use of it in-house. The leaflet generally informed potential customers about the services of an embryonic marketing operation for digital map data that, in reality, was the capacity of one professional officer within Ordnance Survey's Development Branch. This singular post continued to provide a vital link with existing and future customers for digital map data.

This information (rather than promotion) leaflet was eventually revised quite substantially and was again republished in November 1980. Paragraphs outlining copyright conditions for use of the digital map data and on more recent developments with digital mapping generally were added to the leaflet. August 1982 saw this leaflet again republished but this time in four-page format in the new magenta coloured house style bearing the new corporate logo. Despite the 'opening up' of Ordnance Survey at the hands of the 1978–79 Review Committee and the subsequent development of the modern concept of customers, in a major sense, the leaflet regrettably became even more 'technology oriented'. Photographs of equipment and detailed descriptions of production techniques used by Ordnance Survey were included for the first time in the information leaflet.

This particular approach was perhaps not surprising, reflecting as it did the persistent 'corporate' bias – which was still very much alive and well at this time – toward methods and technology, rather than toward selling the benefits of products to existing or potential customers. The thrust behind a much more professional marketing operation, which the Review Committee particularly had sought with urgency, was still not adequately implemented and resourced. The new version of leaflet 48 included a rather regrettable 'hope' statement that one day edgematching of the data between neighbouring sheets would be possible. This in itself said much more about the protracted doubt within about the worth of the project. The leaflet also bore information on small-scales data, and a digital map data availability diagram also appeared in the published leaflet for the first time.

Further and regular revisions of this leaflet occurred in August 1983, November 1984, April 1986 and, finally, in April 1987. It was only at this point in time that modern product management and support with much improved customer orientation really began to develop as an approach toward the very successful modern marketing phenomenon at Ordnance Survey. It was in the 1983 version of leaflet 48 that a sample 1:1250 scale plot from digital data was included for the first time. The leaflet outlined the procedures for ordering digital map data and gave details of an informative audio-visual presentation, which Ordnance Survey had prepared, with details of its availability for customers and as a more general educative tool. This represented still more evidence of an increasing customer orientation, although much of the original text on production methods and equipment still persisted in the leaflet.

The revision of 1984 provided further evidence of this growing customer orientation. Other leaflets were produced at this time, with one setting out the prices of digital map data and the other attempting to establish the ground rules for the administration of copyright royalties. The main Ordnance Survey leaflet provided names and detail 'cameos' of some successful customers and their user applications based on digital mapping. The switch of emphasis from the digital techniques used for production of the map data to the use and benefits of a digital map data product had finally been completed.

The change certainly wasn't the result of a decision or decree, but it came about over several years, with growing external support as applications were initiated by its leading customers and from within as

Ordnance Survey developed self-confidence in what it was trying to achieve. At long last Ordnance Survey came to recognise large-scale digital map data as a core fuel to power its production and revision operations at the basic scales. The revisions of the publicity leaflet in 1986 and 1987 placed even greater emphasis on customers and their applications and at last began to promote the product rather than the domestic methods by which it was produced.

The long period during which this quite simple leaflet had been deployed saw a significant metamorphosis in Ordnance Survey's approach. The leaflet's evolution, in terms of content if not in terms of its appearance, represents an interesting documentation of an important cultural change to the national mapping organisation of Great Britain. This change had been stimulated from within by staff who anticipated a quite different style of operation for the future, as much as from pressure by central government, which had left the organisation in a vacuum for five years following the holistic external review which had published its findings in 1979. The role and influence of customers, who were emerging in ever larger numbers, also contributed greatly to this change in outlook and behaviour.

It was from this point onward that the concepts of product management and the management of key customers, which had been initiated earlier, really began to gather impetus toward the modern phenomenon. The system of consultation with focused groups of customers, which grew from the Review Committee recommendations, matured as a very strong customer determinant for Ordnance Survey, particularly to the path it took with the digitising project and the resulting digital map data products. From this point on, the power of branding and the identity of the Land-Line product family became central to Ordnance Survey's marketing of the large-scale digital map data. The rest is history!

Chapter 23
The major and parallel issue of revision and maintenance of the digital map data once created

Although this is primarily an account of a 30-year long project simply to digitise the basic large-scale mapping of Great Britain, it is impossible to do this without also taking into account Ordnance Survey's never-ending task of keeping the digital map data itself up to date. As change and development took place on the ground, which the mapping purported to document, it became vital that Ordnance Survey could merge the new data with the map file in question. At the very origins of the project the digitised data wasn't really even considered to be a product, but gradually the end result of the digitising project, after a decade or so of very limited progress, became the provision of up-to-date digital map data for those areas of Great Britain where it was available.

Hence the task of revising the data must be seen as an integral part of the story of the digitising project. Because the programmes for initial capture and revision soon, of vital necessity, ran in tandem, drawing on the same very limited production resources, it is impossible in practice to segregate them in this account of major developments at Ordnance Survey. All of the early experiments and subsequent development work associated with the digitising of maps was directed at the creation and publication of mapping, within the programme to modernise Great Britain's mapping. This programme had its origins with the major review of the national mapping in the late 1930s.

Even as late as 1970, with still much work remaining to be completed within this programme, the newly developed digital techniques were still seen within Ordnance Survey primarily and somewhat hopefully as a cheaper and faster production alternative to the production methodology of scribing, which itself had not long previously replaced drawing. However, it had still not proved possible to establish the economic advantage of using the digital production techniques against this very limited objective, during the 10-year life to date of the pilot project. As more and more mapping became available in digital form and as the national remapping project finally gained momentum toward completion soon after 1980, the workload arising from the need to revise already published mapping, by whatever means, continued to grow proportionately.

The limited digitising capacity that Ordnance Survey was able to deploy annually was either engaged on initial conversion of pre-existing National Grid mapping from its analogue form to digital map data or, increasingly, on producing revised new editions of mapping where significant levels of change on the ground had occurred. Digital conversion eventually ran for almost 30 years, but the burgeoning revision task of the digital map data later in the 1980s demanded an entirely different approach. Nevertheless, it must be regarded as an integral part of the compilation of the world first national digital map database at these national scales.

In the post-war years, as the basic-scale mapping of Great Britain was systematically produced and published by conventional drawing and scribing methods under the massive reconstruction programme, a judgement had to be exercised when these maps should again be republished because of the change taking place on the ground in the landscape of Great Britain. The pre-war Davidson Committee had placed great emphasis on the need to ensure that the national mapping of Great Britain should never again be allowed to fall out of date and into a similar state of disrepair that it had itself witnessed when the Committee considered the issue, just before the outbreak of the Second World War. This sentiment was soon taken very much to heart by successive management teams at Ordnance Survey, despite their itinerant senior personnel. By 1970 it had already become a fundamental element of deeply ingrained departmental culture. This fundamental belief was enshrined within a series of terse policy statements by which the operations of Ordnance Survey were managed by the military.

Successive redrawing of detail that remained unchanged on the ground when a map was to be revised and republished had contributed to the quite severe degradation in the integrity of the national survey that had occurred before the Davidson Committee sat to chart the way forward for national mapping in Great Britain. To deal with this problem Ordnance Survey had developed practices whereby unchanged map detail was taken forward by photo-mechanical processes to a new edition of the same map without redrawing it. By storing the final form of the published map on a stable glass (later, film) plate, Ordnance Survey sought to avoid redrawing any map detail that had remained unchanged when the time came for the revised map to be republished. This careful approach was seen as the means by which the integrity and accuracy of the national survey could be preserved. Any changes to the map detail or indeed new detail itself were recorded by the surveyor on a facsimile copy of the map image, which could be taken to the field and on which changes or fresh detail could be recorded.

This image was reproduced initially on a series of stable metal plates (butt-joint plates) and more recently on to a stable plastic film (MSD). Polyvinyl film (astrafoil) was used initially for this; but this tricky material, which called for mastery of 'treacly' etching ink, was soon replaced by polyester film, which was less prone to physical damage and much easier to draw upon in pencil and ink. These images, known as master survey drawings (MSDs), were produced for the field surveyor at the time when the map was printed and published. When the time came for a further new edition of the map to be produced, the MSD was called into head office from its host field office and the new revision information was carefully drawn and latterly scribed and was then incorporated into the new edition of the map, along with all the unchanged detail from the glass plate, by a series of reprographic processes.

All of the maps produced at 1:1250 scale were, by definition, declared by Ordnance Survey as 'active' and therefore became subject to a process of 'continuous' revision, as prescribed by the Davidson Committee. Maps at 1:2500 scale were individually declared either 'active' or 'inactive', depending on their location and the degree of change likely to take place on the ground. Those in the 'active' category were also all made subject to the processes of continuous revision. They were considered so if they covered minor towns, those areas where land registration had been declared compulsory or where concentrations of changed detail on them would, in practice, take more than one day's survey effort to revise it.

For 'inactive' areas a much-simplified system of 'intelligence' was maintained, such that if other than scattered minor changes took place, the map could be it classified as 'active'. These decisions, based on fairly rigid rules, were delegated to the field region that hosted the map. Beyond this and as a minimum, each National Grid basic-scale map, once completed, was to be republished at least once every 50 years with a view to re-initiating Ordnance Survey's copyright interest in the map. This elapsed time soon proved to provide the only certainty in the system. Eventually by empirical methods, Ordnance Survey had devised a system for deciding when a map should be revised and republished. This system took account both of the length of time since the map was previously published and also of the amount of change that had taken place to it on the ground (calculated by a scale of 'house unit' equivalents).

The house unit was a concerted attempt by Ordnance Survey to develop a system of common 'work units' by which effort and output could be judged. It was to become a major element within the management of map revision but, sadly, it remained poorly understood outside Ordnance Survey. The two-element revision convention became known as the 'age and change' criterion. Three hundred house units of change, rather than the previous fifty house units, without consideration of the passage of time, was quickly established in 1975 as the fundamental threshold for the publication of a full new edition of the map. By the time the Ordnance Survey Review Committee sat in 1978, the average new edition produced was actually found, during an audit, to contain some 370 house units of change. This audit served to illustrate further the overall lack of dynamism in the revision system that had been adopted and the fundamental instinct of Ordnance Survey to press on with the initial mapping programme, which had always been scheduled for completion soon after 1980.

With limited resources available, a continuing tug of war between publishing new mapping within the 1980 plan (with a public completion date set for it) and revising what had already been created (with no public targets for it) continued to exist and in fact worsened almost each year that passed. A certain degree of naivety persisted throughout Ordnance Survey and in its planning procedures that, once the initial programme was completed, the Department would embark on a 'catch up' programme of publishing revision information much more frequently.

The overall judgement about the need for a revised edition had not been operated with consistency by Ordnance Survey and variations to either or both of the component elements was capable of being used by Ordnance Survey as a regulator on activity, when the task loomed larger than anticipated or resources were constrained. The criterion was certainly degraded during 'lean' periods. 'Active' maps (the use of the term 'plan' was finally dropped in 1966) covering by definition urban and peri-urban areas, where the greatest amount of change took place on the ground, were, in fact, republished, in some cases, many times during the 1960s and 1970s. Each new edition saw the capital letter notation system, printed within the margin of the map, advanced to reflect the new publication.

To fully understand the evolution of Ordnance Survey's revision services, it is necessary to look back over procedures that were adopted serially in response to the Davidson Committee's exhortations never again to let the basic-scale national mapping become out of date. Published new editions of a particular map had traditionally been the only means of conveying revision information to the very limited number of Ordnance Survey's customers. Because of the inherent irregularity in development on the ground, it had always proved almost impossible to predict when a particular map would in fact come to be republished. On top of this uncertainty, even when the map was to be republished, production throughput times in the Ordnance Survey factory at Southampton were lengthy before a revised map became available once more.

Delay of the order of almost two years occurred following the decision to republish being made, and this on top of the 'built in' inertia in the 'age and change criteria' itself. At the outset of the modern remapping programme, certain privileged customers, most frequently the local authority in whose area the map fell, were permitted privileged access to Ordnance Survey field offices to trace, for themselves, information that they required urgently, ahead of republication, from the surveyor's field document. This limited service to a very limited number of favoured customers was fraught with difficulties of access and quality. However, this limited facility matured quite quickly in 1964 into the Advance Revision Information (ARI) service, which was eventually offered nationally following trials of suitable reproduction equipment in the London offices of Ordnance Survey.

The ARI map was simply a 'dyeline' copy of the surveyor's MSD with all its many shortcomings and imperfections. Most customers of Ordnance Survey seeking revision information overcame this problem of a generally poor-quality image by redrawing the revision information obtained, to very varying standards, onto their own library of chart paper published maps. Eventually, dependence on and the sheer size of these customer map libraries served to inhibit many customers' switching to the use of digital mapping. Despite its very varying quality, the major benefit of the ARI product was that it 'short-circuited' the protracted age and change

324

criterion and the lengthy new edition production timescale in the factory at Ordnance Survey's Southampton head office.

Faced with mounting criticism of this revision information service, the best bet for a more dynamic national revision service appeared to Ordnance Survey to rest with the emerging technology associated with microfilming. A high-quality microfilm copy of the new edition glass or film plate known as Survey Information on Microfilm (SIM) was made at the time of publication and in due course a further microfilm (SIM update), inevitably of much poorer quality, was made routinely from the surveyor's MSD, once a prescribed amount of change (latterly fifty house units) had been recorded upon it. This process required despatch of the field document to head office, but strict turnround times were enforced.

This SIM service, formalised and launched from 1977 onwards, offered an at-scale print from the aperture card containing the microfilm negative on demand by the customer. This service was actually offered by Ordnance Survey's commercial microfilm agents, who maintained a bank of microfilm aperture cards for their area of commercial interest. However, with its predetermined threshold and the randomness of change on the ground, the microfilm service still failed, in many cases, to meet the demands of some customers for a more responsive revision service and did nothing for the few customers who were already seeking revision for their digital map data.

The old ARI service from Ordnance Survey field offices eventually, in 1973, gave way to a new service whereby a facsimile copy made from the MSD itself became increasingly available nationwide. Diazo copiers were eventually located in each Ordnance Survey field office and the working copy of the map could be located and copied on demand for a customer. It was against this 'timeline' narrative of developing revision services for the basic-scale mapping of Great Britain that the consequences of the digitising project should be viewed.

When the digitising project was first initiated, the large-scale map revision policy adopted by Ordnance Survey was barely credible, as has been shown. Visions of a better world with digital map data were highly speculative and not at all based on any realistic plans or expectations. There was little thought about the secondary issue of performing revision employing the new computer-based digitising techniques. There had been the odd 'vision' of the future expressed by individuals within Ordnance Survey or in published papers for meetings and conferences, but no coherent effort had been made to harness the new techniques to the ever-larger revision task.

The passage of time and the consequences of other policies and approaches eventually brought digitising and revision into the same perspective. At the outset of the digital mapping pilot production project in 1973 and because of the limited capacity and the tediousness of the methodology adopted, only some of the maps coming to head office for their first 1980 plan publication were produced using the digital production flowline. As the dual task of producing *abinitio* mapping and publication of revised editions placed increasingly heavy demands on Ordnance Survey's production resources, it wasn't long at all before the digital production techniques were being used for the creation of new editions, usually at 1:1250 scale, of maps previously produced by conventional methods.

Further, it wasn't long at all before new editions of existing digital map files were also being made using the digital techniques, particularly in areas of very rapid change on the ground. The wider use of the digitising techniques for the production of new editions had not been thought through fully by Ordnance Survey and is rather symptomatic of the piecemeal approach adopted to the new technological developments. Each step was taken separately to address immediate and sometimes local issues most often without consideration of their overall consequences. It was to be a considerable number of years yet before a coherent strategy for digital mapping and its revision would be developed and pursued.

With new editions increasingly being produced by the very limited resources of the digital mapping flowlines, under the vagaries of the 'age and change' criterion, it very soon became apparent to Ordnance Survey and to customers alike that what became called a 'pepper pot' effect was occurring, with the creation of randomly scattered digital map files. This consequence ran almost completely counter to the requirements of what few customers existed who needed larger contiguous blocks of digital map data for their areas of interest or even for smaller areas, where they were conducting experiments, trials or pilot projects, using digital map data. This particular problem posed something of a dilemma for Ordnance Survey.

Clearly Ordnance Survey wished fundamentally to use its production resources, whether conventional or digital, as effectively as possible.

Thus digital flowlines were used increasingly for creating new editions and for those maps which helped to form contiguous blocks for customers and which had been drawn conventionally in earlier years of the re-mapping programme. In many cases these maps were not subject to the degree of change on the ground that would trigger a new edition. What eventually became simply called 'digital conversions' were seen increasingly, in the early years, as wasteful of precious digitising resources. However , without them, cohesive blocks of digital mapping simply couldn't be achieved.

Even by 1975, with the three hundred plus house unit threshold for a new edition firmly established, there was mounting concern amongst those involved with the digital mapping project that much of the digital data that had been captured would simply 'lie fallow'. Thus it was that many map files on the databank became increasingly out of date and indeed 'out of specification' as the form and content of the data inevitably changed as time passed. As a consequence of all this, when a customer seeking digital map data did come along, they were typically supplied with a file of 'fallow' map data and the D09 Ordnance Survey plot programme.

Increasingly, however, it became necessary for the 50 house unit 'packets' of change on maps, which increasingly were being made available to customers through the emerging graphic services, to be captured digitally, but there was still no realistic or coherent plan for revision and maintenance of the digital map data. However, the earlier but very broad strategic 'vision' voiced by Major General Dowson, Colonel Gardiner-Hill and Major General Irwin amongst others, with regard to the benefits to be gained from the use of the digital techniques in the mounting revision task of the Department, slowly and uncertainly became reality, but still without the benefit of a really strategic approach. The parallel implementation of the wholly graphic sale of the unpublished survey information (SUSI) service and the 50 house unit fixed update of digital data eventually commenced in 1977.

A special repayment service for update information below this threshold level was also advertised to known customers. With data produced over such an extended period of time, any revision also had implications for recoding to reflect the current specification of the digital map data at the time of capture. The thorny internal communication problem between the surveyor in the field and the digitising operative at head office was, of necessity, eased by the introduction and use of an 'additions and deletions trace' by the surveyor. The trace was maintained as a paper copy or 'pull' of the map when it was last published and was issued when the MSD was made and despatched to the field office that held responsibility for it. All changes recorded by the surveyor on the map itself were recorded on the trace.

The volume of digital map files completed and held on the databank increased slowly but steadily in the late 1970s. Ordnance Survey, overcome by inertia, had been very slow to consider the wider issues of the revision task (including the impact of digitising) once the 1980 plan was completed and what it intended to offer in future by way of a revision service for the basic-scale mapping. The Ordnance Survey Review Committee, sitting during 1978 and 1979, concluded that Ordnance Survey already faced major policy and investment decisions with regard to digital mapping. The Review Committee also concluded that the future cost of updating map sheets digitally could be reduced particularly if they were already held in digital format. As a consequence, the timescales required for production could also be greatly foreshortened. In connection with the many wider issues of revision, the external Review Committee had, during its deliberations, accepted that Ordnance Survey had, albeit rather belatedly, initiated a major review of the basic-scale revision task for the future and how it could best be tackled. Walter Smith, the Director General, had created a small team, working from within the Department, to consider the many issues in connection with future needs for and the techniques to be employed for revision and its dissemination. He arranged for Peter Wesley from the inter-departmental Joint Survey Service, who had himself been involved with early digital experiments, to return once more in early 1980 to Ordnance Survey to lead the 'Study of Revision', as it was to be called.

The Ordnance Survey Review Committee, in turn, demanded external input and wider public consultation but endorsed the Study team's broad terms of reference. The Study of Revision was duly completed to an agreed schedule, with a published final report in October 1981. Clearly, all aspects of revision fell within the remit given to the Study team. The needs of digital mapping and of future customers for up-to-date digital map information were duly addressed. Looking to the future, the team dwelt at length on all aspects of how digital map data could be maintained up to date and be made available to those customers who were already beginning to emerge from trial and experimental phases of its use. The Study of Revision provided the first really strategic insight into how the traditional map revision task could be converted into a wholly digital operation.

In the meantime, the Ordnance Survey Review Committee had been made well aware by a very large number of witnesses of the many shortcomings in the revision services offered to date, whether for digital data already captured and held or for the published paper mapping and the associated services for dissemination, which have already been described briefly. The Review Committee concluded in its report on revision that 'our discussions with Ordnance Survey and others over the past 18 months, for example, about the scope for economies and the introduction of more cost-effective methods, gave us the impression of a conservatively run organisation whose justifiable pride in its past achievements may have led to some complacency and to a defensive attitude toward outside comment. It is apparent, for instance, that Ordnance Survey's methods of revision had not been brought under critical review until recently.'

Somewhat prophetically, in view of what eventually came to pass, on the often-repeated theme of the need for urgent 'cultural change' at Ordnance Survey, the Review Committee Report noted 'there is scope for improvement in productivity through more flexible, imaginative and outward looking attitudes. In general, the Ordnance Survey staff would welcome such improvements and their introduction will constitute a major management task over the next few years, depending as it does on such issues as career structures, training, 'job satisfaction' and the opening up of creative thinking. They all require time to be implemented and close consultation with the staff concerned'.

The Ordnance Survey Review Committee recognised and supported in its report the key role of the basic-scale mapping in the affairs of the nation. Ordnance Survey was also found not to have, although it was felt very strongly that it should have, the capacity to predict, identify and to respond to changing emphases in the form and content of the large-scale map archive that customers actually required. It was clear that Ordnance Survey was facing a period of rapid technological innovation and change with rising software costs but falling hardware costs and a variety of opportunities that such innovation appeared to offer. The Review Committee, led by Sir David Serpell, noted the growing emphasis by customers on the provision of large-scale information rather than on the provision of conventional maps.

The Report of the Review Committee contained the opinion that 'in recent years Ordnance Survey has not given enough attention to assessing critically its approach to the maintenance of the basic-scale survey up to date and has not itself generated policy.' Whilst the Review Committee inclined to concentrate on a suitable programme to achieve rapid national cover of digital map data, the recommended two-stage approach clearly included plans and arrangements for the revision of the digital map data, once captured. Included in the major R&D effort that the Review Committee demanded of Ordnance Survey was the need for a cost-effective revision methodology for the digital map data. Its sustained importance was reflected in the 'core' status with which this particular task was designated. Thus the Review Committee Report was timely in that it recognised and recorded positive weaknesses in the procedures for customer supply, either by infrequent new editions or the poor-quality update services of SIM and SUSI. The Report arising from the Review identified the imperative for finding a solution to the revision and supply of digital map data. Precisely how and by what means a suitable digital revision service could be created was, however, left to Ordnance Survey's own Study of Revision.

In the intervening period, whilst these two major reviews took place, Ordnance Survey had already completed a very thorough and effective user needs study associated with the fast-approaching digital future that the external Review Committee Report had predicted so forcefully. The very complete response to Ordnance Survey by current and potential users of digital map data had indicated very clearly and unequivocally that the most recent approach to the revision of digital data – whereby, when MSDs with a further 50 house units of change came into head office to be microfilmed for the SIM update service, this change would also be digitised – was not really acceptable for the future at all.

Expectations, reasonable or otherwise, associated with the advent of a complete digital map data service, placed a much higher value on a fully digital revision service more closely aligned with the conventional SUSI service rather than with the periodic microfilmed SIM service. The user needs study found that the absence of a credible revision strategy for digital mapping represented the largest concern for users after that of the topic of initial data availability. Most users who responded were looking for a service at or about the level of 10 to 15 house units of change, with what came to be regarded as 'primary change' always made available to customers within six months after being built on the ground.

Responses clearly stated the expectation that when a user inspected either digitally produced mapping or digital map data of an area of particular interest, it must reliably represent what was in fact to be found on the ground. This expectation arose mainly from the potential for foreshortened timescales that digital methods appeared to offer. In a sense this expectation was quite illogical, but the perception was almost implicit that information stored and manipulated by computer needed to better reflect reality than had been demanded in the era of paper mapping. This may well have been due in part to the concept of 'the state of the art' and also the expected ease of recall and interrogation. Demand for faster response revision methods were widely considered almost certain to replace the tedious and labour-intensive procedures associated with mapping published and maintained by traditional graphic production methods.

Whether logical or not, this sort of demand from users, based on much heightened expectations was made clear once more to Ordnance Survey during its own Study of Revision. Such a user requirement from digital map data, once validated as representative of the wider user population and realistic, could really only be met by 'continuous digitising' on the back of continuous revision. Logistic problems associated with movement of the MSDs between the field offices and head office suggested that this could only be achieved realistically by a field office-based procedure with rapid data communications between the field office and the digital map data bank at Ordnance Survey head office in Southampton.

One of the most important outcomes from Ordnance Survey's Study of Revision was the call for prompt solutions aimed at providing for the revision of digital map data, preferably within the field survey office environment. The underlying concept developed by the study team was that a computer, system should be designed and developed for the field office that would permit 'at scale' digitising of any changed map detail on to the surveyor's MSD. A cost projection ceiling was also placed on the outcome to ensure that a cost-effective approach would be taken by the proposed development team. This was seen as a necessity in view of the large number of systems ultimately required to equip adequately the complete network of Ordnance Survey's field offices, once the initial digitising was completed.

This traditional network of offices itself also required radical rationalisation before the major investment could be justified. The solution to the problem was seen as the surveyor's revision work, still in pencil on the MSD, being digitised and drawn back in ink in its correct position on to the MSD, thus getting rid of the tedious and time-consuming procedure of manual 'inking up' by the surveyor.

Success with this approach would, it was felt, provide a significant cost reduction in the overall revision task. The map data file needing revision would be called up and downloaded from the databank at head office and sent initially via the physical form of a data cassette sent through the post or by courier. During the study, given further developments in telecommunications, it was projected that the map files would later be transmitted electronically in a data link via the telephone line between head office and the field office concerned.

Following the incorporation of change surveyed, either deletions or additions, the map file would then be returned to head office for the amended map data file containing the new survey work to be incorporated into the databank. This system concept was first tested with surveyors attempting to digitise their 'pencil work', at scale, on a Laser-Scan MADES workstation already in use on the digitising flowline at head office. Careful scrutiny and evaluation following the trial indicated a small but relatively insignificant degradation in accuracy when compared to the normally accepted procedure of using a five to three times enlargement of the MSD at head office.

Such an arrangement would simply not be possible in a field-based digital revision operation, when simply using the available MSD for digital capture. With existing techniques and methods by now deeply entrenched and the all-pervading climate of deep conservatism at large in the Department, any changes in approach simply had to be fought for, even when they were well justified. The all-pervading 'this is the way we always do that' internal culture stifled innovation and any creative thought associated with new approaches to an existing task. This defensive internal culture clearly also contained an element of job preservation for the future for head office-based digitising operatives when the initial capture task would be completed.

Driven by the urgency demanded by the external Review Committee and following the prompt and very broad acceptance by Ordnance Survey of the main thrust of the conclusions and recommendations of the Study of Revision, there had been considerable internal debate about how best to satisfy the need for a low-cost digital data revision system. There was a very strong demand, despite the very clear conclusion of the Study itself to the contrary, to retain all digitising in head office, even with all its attendant logistical problems. This sentiment had its origins in trade union-inspired job preservation.

It was perhaps inspired – or possibly fortunate – that upon completion of the Study of Revision Peter Wesley, upon promotion, was appointed to become Head of Topographic Surveys and thereby tasked with making a reality of the strategy and tactics of digital revision within the Ordnance Surveys field survey operations. Following the abandonment of the concept of revision being completed at head office, the second main cause of internal debate at this critical time concerned the method of procurement of a suitable system. In the world at large, this critical period in the account of developments at Ordnance Survey coincided with the era of the so called 'turnkey' systems, whereby an external supplier prima facie met a specification with a solution that the client didn't really need to understand when operating it. Ordnance Survey had, by this time, gathered little experience in developing computer' applications and generally lacked self-confidence in its abilities whilst it was, as usual, finding it difficult to recruit and retain talented information technology professionals, largely because of depressed Civil Service salaries in comparison with the private sector.

Initially and to get the digital revision project underway, Ordnance Survey's project team developed an operational requirement and an equipment specification for the proposed target system. This requirement was publicised by advertisement and was passed out to any known potential suppliers. Following a frisson of initial interest, a very small number of potential suppliers retained contact with the project team via briefings and demonstrations of what was actually required. Whilst Ordnance Survey was still rather weak at describing its role and its requirements, the commercial firms involved continued to demonstrate very poor comprehension of the client's rather novel requirement. Most naively persisted in trying to sell what they currently had to offer by way of existing systems or product lines, which generally were quite unsuited to the task proposed.

Possibly the main contenders developed a comprehension of the uniqueness of Ordnance Survey's needs, which arose because of its lengthy history and the sheer size of the actual task to be performed. Also, as suppliers came to realise the untypical and unusual nature of

Ordnance Survey's need and possibly the lack of any wider application of a solution, soon after an initial burst of enthusiasm, most of the commercial firms contacted all singularly failed to demonstrate how their equipment could fulfil Ordnance Survey's proposed task of digital revision in field offices. As time passed it became increasingly apparent that the solution to this development requirement lay in self-help with an in-house revision system development project.

The many recommendations of the Study of Revision were accepted by Ordnance Survey with untypical expedition. Seeking to achieve the development of a suitable low-cost system, a small development team was next assembled around the appointed leader Mr Bill Duckett, who had previously served as a surveyor before choosing fresh challenges in the world of computing at Ordnance Survey. With the identification of an ICL PERQ 16-bit microcomputer as the best available platform for the prototype development trial of the proposed update system within R&D, a contract programmer from ICL was also recruited and added to the team. The host computer selected was a derivative of the older 'Two Rivers Engine'. A GTCO digitising tablet with an accuracy of 0.003 inches was selected for digitising input and a Glaser 1603 A2 plotter, which interestingly had been developed for a data display application on board British nuclear submarines, was also added to the embryonic system for graphical output.

The experimental configuration for field update was completed with a Christie 656 cassette tape unit, which would serve initially as the communication interface requirement with the databank at head office. Experimental software for the system was developed entirely in-house. This was considered essential for eventual ownership and full familiarity with the system. This contrasted by design with the difficult situation and the risks associated with the use of proprietary software owned by suppliers in digitising operations within the cartographic 'factory' at Southampton. The prototype field update system was duly submitted to rigorous testing and evaluation by both digitising operatives from head office and by surveyors working in the field offices. These trials duly confirmed that the target accuracy requirement of 0.1 mm was capable of being met on a consistent basis, thus preserving the integrity of the survey. Trials also demonstrated that the accuracy required from manual penning could be met by the prototype, but to a much more consistent standard. The initial concept of the revision system was simply to replicate conventional techniques.

Perhaps the most difficult aspect of the entire system development concerned the unusual requirement in plotter technology to locate and eventually to plot a 'patch' of revision information back into its correct position on the MSD, the surfaces of which generally varied enormously. Almost all other computer-based plotting applications involved the sequential plotting of a map file with relation to one origin within the addressable format of the plot. The Digital Field Update System or DFUS development, as it soon became known, demanded that the surveyor/operative should carefully position or register the 'patch' of revision before plotting it back on to the MSD.

For this essential step a small optical telescope, interchangeable with the pen on the plotter's gantry, affording very high standards of precision was sought, procured and eventually utilised. Surveyors also soon successfully mastered the intricacies of assigning feature codes to all the elements of map data. By the time the system was actually created and evaluated the overall cost of the initial DFUS system was considerably above the target ceiling that the Study of Revision had initially established. However realistic expectations were that the costs of hardware would continue to fall by substantial amounts.

Little thought was given to the maintenance of the software that drove the system but there was great relief that it was part of Ordnance Survey's intellectual property. Vitally, all the concept requirements behind the operational requirement were met by the initial prototype of the target system. There were clearly many problems and frustrations to be overcome, but close cooperation by the development and trials team and equipment suppliers bore fruit and system feasibility was quite quickly established. Very strong objections to an in-house development, which had emerged at the outset of the project, were quietened and this project did much to help develop both a spirit of self-help and self-confidence within the several areas of Ordnance Survey that were involved. This rather speculative development project was one of the first to create a multi-discipline team spirit within Ordnance Survey. This undoubtedly contributed substantially to the ultimate success of the venture.

During this development phase new digital map data files were still being created in increasing volumes by the digitising capacity maintained at head office in Southampton. Very limited revision of existing map files also continued at either 300 or 50 house unit intervals. This activity still failed to provide a credible revision service for the very limited number of customers using digital map information. Following a full and systematic review of the development study and following extensive trials, some modifications to software and to operating procedures were introduced before the system was deployed for a pilot trial in the Birmingham office of Survey Group, WR1A, in late 1982.

An extended field trial confirmed both the suitability of the concept and of the prototype system itself. One surprising and quite serious outcome of this pilot project was that the field trial highlighted the very large number of serious shortcomings in the digital map data previously captured and held in the DMC map files that were extracted for DFUS from the databank in head office. This was a cause of much frustration for those concerned at the size of the 'repair and correction' task that had to be completed before update itself could really be commenced. This limited trial tended to suggest that despite claims about the high standards which were associated with initial digitising at head office, all in fact was not well.

The first phase of the field trial appeared to offer a reduction in production time for the surveyor of some 18%. The avoidance of 'penning' detail contributed a further saving of some 3%. The field update concept also avoided the loss of the MSD to head office for the typically lengthy periods previously encountered. On the basis of the clear success of this first field trial, the software for the DFUS was completely rewritten. The rewrite also took account of all the changes that had been introduced into the DMB system. The new version of the software was again completed by a team from Ordnance Survey itself by December 1984 and was tested in the early part of 1985. Computer Services at Ordnance Survey head office accomplished the rewrite in the language Pascal and thereby accepted responsibility for its ongoing maintenance and development as a soon-to-be routine production system. The cost estimate for the rewrite was agreed at £120,000.

It had become apparent that the communication requirement between the databank at head office and the field office was best accomplished by a telephone link, during the silent hours. This further development was taken up in April 1985. The first production system, still ICL PERQ computer based, went back to the Birmingham office. Actual operation in a truly realistic production environment highlighted the unacceptable burden of the undigitised backlog since the last SIM (update) at 50 house units, and frequently even beyond that, and also the considerable variation in specification of the map files for revision that had been extracted from the databank. Volunteer draughtsmen with experience of the head office initial digitising task were also sent out and tried in the field, and they quickly established a productive rapport with the surveyors whose work they digitised.

DFUS was duly declared a success generally and an investment business case for eventual full roll-out of the system, in a series of phases, was prepared and presented to Ordnance Survey's directors. A 'rapid response' digitising flowline was also created with a degree of urgency at Ordnance Survey head office. This flowline was designed and introduced to remove the very large backlogs of digitising and to effect the many specification changes on maps that were to feature within the scope of DFUS revision. DFUS had quite simply not been conceived and developed as a bulk digitising system and the more efficient head office interactive digitising and edit systems actually tackled this task with far greater ease than the field-based system, which itself was conceived and designed for the continuing purpose of digitising current revision, mostly in quite small 'packages'.

On the very long march to establishing a field-based revision digitising system working in parallel with the bulk head office-based digitising system to create and then maintain the digital map database of Great Britain, the next important step taken was in 1986, with the establishment within Topographic Surveys function of a DFUS implementation project team. Mr John Clift, an experienced Chief Surveyor, was selected and appointed to lead this team at head office. His sense of humour, his patience and his doggedness but easy rapport with field staff generally were to prove absolutely vital ingredients in a lengthy and often troublesome implementation programme, which eventually lasted for several years. He also developed good relations with head office-based software and system development staff.

His small head office-based team, suitably equipped, served as a test bed for new equipment and for rigorous testing of new versions of the DFUS software, before being released to the field offices. It also provided a consistent high-quality training facility for operatives who were brought in from the field, before taking up their new duties. Peter Wesley, following the completion of the Study of Revision, had by this time already been appointed as the Head of Topographic Surveys function. This appointment ensured that the project at least had a forceful 'champion' who was committed to the development. It certainly needed this, with scepticism still very much at large in the 'higher councils' of the Department, particularly with one set of DFUS equipment costing, at the outset, almost £42,000. There was, as usual, keen competition for departmental funds that were available for capital investment each year.

There was also at this time a very conservative and even cynical element to be overcome amongst the thousand or more field surveyors, most often those particularly in the more remote areas of Great Britain, where their working life, up to this point, had tended to continue largely unchanged. The project served to bring at least some aspects of the field operation, vitally, for the first time into the digital era. The DFUS implementation project – as it was rolled out – proved a very suitable vehicle for the message about the urgent need for the fundamental 'culture change' that senior management sought to deliver to the field survey operation of Ordnance Survey. It was, in fact, destined to be the first of a series of 'leading edge' technical development and implementation projects to bring modern digital techniques to the totality of the field survey data collection operation of the national survey.

These projects were together designed to convert Ordnance Survey's data-capture procedures into an efficient and cost-effective but wholly digital operation, which, at long last, finally removed the need for the dangerous and painful translations between digital and analogue forms and back again, as had previously been the case from the onset of digitising. Digital projects for DFUS, for MSD-less survey operations, for automated instrumental control and detail collection, and for collection of map detail by digital methods in photogrammetry had all been initiated and were moving forward to realisation at quite different speeds. This was an exciting period, particularly from a technical and development standpoint.

In 1986 an investment plan for the purchase of 11 field digitising systems was put forward to Ordnance Survey's directors. Marketing function became involved in the choice of locations for deployment with the need to meet committed customer demands for a more effective digital revision service. The 50 house unit digital update service, running in parallel with the microfilm graphic service, became increasingly discredited as Ordnance Survey continued to miss its own self-imposed targets. With the aim of making Ordnance Survey's DFUS software 'machine independent', the migration from the ICL PERQ to a Sun Microsystems®

platform began, using the by then almost universal UNIX operating system.

Also at this time the very innovative and supportive Director of Field Surveys, Mr Alastair Macdonald, took the case for a major and rapid expansion programme for the digital revision system to the Ordnance Survey Management Board. The response initially was one of rather cautious support. At this time the need for a further trial of more advanced concepts began to surface. With DFUS itself by this time already capable of routine deployment, given adequate support and funding, the need surfaced within Topographic Surveys to secure significant savings on equipment and a much-improved revision operation from the standpoint of the needs of customers and Ordnance Survey itself. Planning for a radical development project, called Project 88, was worked up and eventually received approval.

The concept behind this venture was that, in a chosen 'real-world' area, Ordnance Survey would create a 'test bed' for all new initiatives on the data capture side in one place such that their interaction could be evaluated and all consequences controlled and monitored. The Milton Keynes office, with a dynamic local authority and a good deal of development activity going on, was selected as the site for the development trial, which was to be led by a talented young professional surveyor: Mr Andy Coote. Essentially, the trial sought to evaluate the concept of removing the MSD totally from the digital revision operation. Instead, a plot drawn locally on the field update system – soon called the temporary survey document (TSD) – of the immediate area where revision detail had occurred would be prepared from the digital map file taken from the databank at head office via the overnight telephone service. Revision detail would then be surveyed and recorded on the TSD in pencil in the field and then once more back in the office would be digitised by the surveyor who had captured it. The updated map data file could then be returned to the databank overnight back to head office.

By this time in 1988 DFUS was already operating successfully in Birmingham, Dudley, Bristol, Stanmore, Stockton-on-Tees, Hedge End, Crawley, Oxford, Manchester, Glasgow, Central London and at head office in Southampton. The condition placed upon the agreement by Ordnance Survey's Board of Directors to proceed with the first significant expansion with more powerful workstations was the formal collection of reliable cost data and a realistic comparison with the widely condemned head office-based 50 house unit periodic update. This latter condition merely served to illustrate just how seriously some members of Ordnance Survey's leadership had misread the future requirement. The approval to expand further would be conditional upon a favourable review two years hence. The volumes of revision information to be digitised, which represented backlogs from the past and a sustained high level of specification changes and updates to be made during revision, continued to impose major burdens on the field update operation.

The next significant milestone in this account of revision digitising developments was the undisputed success of Project 88 at Milton Keynes, thanks particularly to the great energy, ingenuity and drive of the project manager, Andy Coote, and his staff. Not only could revision information be returned quickly to the databank but the revised digital map information could easily serve as the basis of a range of novel graphic products of superior quality that local and national customers commented very favourably upon when they examined them. This development was to become the basis of a very powerful future marketing operation selling up-to-date, large-scale digital and graphic products.

Up-to-date colour and customised graphic outputs from the Ordnance Survey field office were available to customers really for the first time, and the cost of the DFUS configuration, operating totally without MSDs, was appreciably cheaper and more user-friendly, once the tedious task of plotting back onto the MSD had been removed. In 1989 the Ordnance Survey Management Board was asked to approve a four-year programme for the full national roll-out of DFUS but without employing MSDs any longer than absolutely necessary. In the end an investment of some £330,000 per annum for each of the next four years was finally approved. The plan for each field office involved a two-stage approach. The first stage would see the continued use of MSDs for revision while undigitised backlogs, outstanding specification changes and bulk edgematching were accomplished on specially created head office flowlines.

The concept of edgematched digital map files had reverberated within Ordnance Survey almost from the outset of digitising. Edgematched data files now became an urgent requirement before the full benefits of seamless data and working across sheet edges could be realised and before customers for digital data or derived graphic products could be freed from the traditional constraints imposed by the arbitrary National Grid sheet lines. Early processing software constrained map features crossing map sheet edges together in certain circumstances and within tolerances. Various attempts were made to advance the cause of edgematched map data files. Eventually a head office-based flowline was created, which used a combination of software and interactive edit to harmonise all 'map sheet' edges before they were sent to the field for revision operations. Great care had to be taken in subsequent operations to preserve the 'harmonised' sheet edges.

There was, at this time, an interesting and praiseworthy outbreak of close and productive cooperation between the field operations and head office-based units, whereas before there had most often been rivalry and jealousy. John Clift and his now enlarged DFUS management team managed very complex relationships very successfully. The second stage in the implementation process at each office would see the progressive removal of MSDs from the revision operation until each office managed what was in effect a 'seamless' digital map for its complete area of their operations. In an attempt to reduce the problems associated with the ever-increasing communications 'bottleneck', the use of an optical disc for distributed bulk storage of map files was the subject of a trial, in the Crawley office.

By 1990 equipment had already been commissioned in 25 field offices round the country with some of these having multiple systems where the workload was heavy. Fourteen of these offices were scheduled to move quickly to MSD-less operation during a two- to three-year transition period. This intense programme was to be completed first in the area within the M25 motorway followed by the London to Birmingham 'corridor'. A further 12 new workstations were deployed in 1991, with two others moved to meet the strongest user demands for the modern style of revised map information. The major benefits from this initiative were the easing of sheet edge problems for customers, the much-improved quality of graphic outputs and quite significant economies and savings for Ordnance Survey in the update operation itself.

On the back of Project 88 and its successful MSD-less operations, the concept of a different approach to meeting customer needs for graphic products made from up-to-date digital map data began to surface within the Topographic Surveys management team. This led quite quickly to the development of the concept and rationale for what would soon become the Superplan graphic product. Initially offered as a trial product for customers from the seamless data on a DFUS from a field office in central London at Vauxhall, as it had been at Milton Keynes during Project 88, a prototype delivery system was specified by Marketing function and was developed with great innovation and skill by a small dedicated team at head office.

This system was installed in Ordnance Survey's London Agent's premises at the end of 1991 for an extended trial, and up-to-date, customised map graphics were soon made available to customers, on demand. The concept almost immediately became a success and plans were laid once more for a national roll-out at some 15 new style agents' premises across Great Britain. It was at this stage that Ordnance Survey field offices somewhat reluctantly, after so long, withdrew from formal contact for the supply of map products to customers. With the Superplan service well on the way toward successful deployment, Ordnance Survey stopped making even the small number of published new editions. By 1993 some 50,000 map files from the total archive were already available through this service. Full coverage would rest with the eventual completion of digitising of the basic-scale map archive and the full implementation of the field revision systems.

In 1991 the momentum of the national roll-out of the update system accelerated still further. In all, a further 46 workstations were purchased and 27 new locations were equipped and began the preparatory stages for the new-style revision operation. This latest configuration was built round a Sun Microsystems computer, a Calcomp 1042/3 pen plotter and Kontron® digitising tablet DK 2436, with improved communications systems with the head office database. After this further deployment only 15 out of the 102 existing field offices were left without computerised equipment. Many of those were already destined to close or co-locate during a wider drive for reduced overhead costs of the nationwide Topographic Surveys operation. All, however, did not proceed completely to plan. There were problems that arose from a variety of causes, some of which could have, perhaps with hindsight, been foreseen.

The revision operation without MSDs generally proved somewhat more difficult than the Project 88 trials had in fact suggested; the variations in the specification of the DMV data and errors within it accumulated over many years were much greater even than the most pessimistic observers had believed. The most worrying phenomenon was, perhaps, a major

DMV data file corruption for which, as a contributor, the DFUS operation was far from blameless. Generally, there was a very slow start with a low output of bulk edgematch from head office as previously unsuspected problems were uncovered and sequential releases of DFUS software versions never went anything like as smoothly as the developers promised or the field customer and user expected. One of the greatest successes within this great flurry of development activity was the performance of the communication links between the head office databank and the field offices. Even in 1992, some 800 map data files per night were being transmitted routinely and successfully.

Gradually, it became increasingly clear that there was a further stage still to come beyond the successful operation of digital field equipment in the evolution of a digital revision service for the large-scale mapping of Great Britain and before the national digitising project could really be described as completed. This involved the eventual development and deployment of small portable 'notebook' computers for each surveyor in the field. The survey task would be recorded and computed directly into the machine's memory. Data could be edited in real time and downloaded back at the office for transmission to head office in Southampton. This stage has in 1999 at last been successfully completed.

In summary review, the complete digital field update venture certainly helped to achieve a major and important transformation within Ordnance Survey during a relatively short period of time. In some six or seven years that the whole project really took, after trials and so on, some six or seven hundred staff had successfully adapted to entirely new and improved working practices. The initial DFUS operation and, eventually, revision without the MSD had been widely accepted, generally with enthusiasm. Ordnance Survey had also successfully managed a major capital investment programme approaching £2 million and had adopted and offered a radically different approach to its customers for both data and graphic products and services. Ordnance Survey was at long last able to offer a credible and soon-to-be much sought after update service for its large-scale digital map data. Not only that but on the back of this update service it was able to offer a range of customised graphic products as never before in its history. These were the main benefits of the digitising project that had started so many years before in the 1960s. With its ultimate political destiny and its commercial and social development decided, this project to achieve revision in a wholly digital environment was absolutely fundamental to Ordnance Survey's emergence as a truly successful customer-oriented business

Chapter 24
Tabulation of annual progress with digitising the large-scale maps

Year	1:1250 scale		1:2500 scale		1:10000 scale
	Digitised	Published	Digitised	Published	
1973–74	300	94	900	179	
1974–75	479	98	886	850	
1975–76	592	60	2006	1015	
1976–77	794	11	1880	1566	
1977–78	808	38	1920	1236	1
1978–79	579		708		10
1979–80	659		873		5
1980–81	438		416		17
1981–82	395		202		25
1982–83	428		96		28
1983–84	295		83		26
1984–85	1604		431		12
1985–86	2094		496		0

1986–87	4498	1302	0
1987–88	8013	2362	0
1988–89	10628	3924	0
1989–90	11363	10865	43
1990–91	6914	17782	44
1991–92	Total conversions: 32,834		
1992–93	Total conversions: 39,766		

Notes:

1   The table has been compiled from information in published annual reports for Ordnance Survey.

2   The tabulation shows in the early years the split between digitising and actual publication.

3   The programme was completed in 1993–94 when 40,610 conversions to digital were completed.

4   At the start of the pilot project, in 1973–74, the following numbers of maps in each scale bracket was as follows:

1:1250 scale: 51,962
1:2500 scale: 170,148
1:10000 scale: 3,704

5   1973–74 was the first complete year of the pilot production project.

6   1977–78 was the first year when revised new editions using the digital flowline were produced. In all the years after this time outputs are shown as both first and revised editions.

7   1981–82 saw the completion of the 1980 plan for the remapping of Great Britain. At this time the whole country was placed under revision and maintenance. The digitising programme therefore concentrated on revised editions or conversions from analogue to digital format.

8   1984–85 was the first year of the trials of digital revision in Birmingham. Also trials of contractor digitising commenced.

9   1990–91 was the first year for Ordnance Survey as a 'Next Steps Agency'. The number of maps digitised per year became an Agency target to be monitored annually.

10   The final completion of digitising, by the end of 1995–95, saw the completion of the 1:2500 scale series, the completion of the basic 1:10000 scale series and a major programme to tidy up the many anomalous situations of part sheets created as a result of past devices and conventions.

What is significant in this series is the very rapid completion of the task from 1989–90 onwards. With only a small but steady increase in the digitising capacity at Ordnance Survey, the increasing use of private-sector contractors was by far the most potent force in the later years. Sponsored digitising using these same contractors largely by utility organisations under the 'third-party digitising scheme' agreed between the utility companies and Ordnance Survey also helped to accelerate progress toward completion in 1995.

Over the period from 1973 onwards, when the pilot production project first got under way, the basis of reporting progress with the digitising task changed quite profoundly, both to meet changing circumstance in connection with the mapping itself and, perhaps more importantly, the changing nature and culture of Ordnance Survey as it began its transformation from a very staid and unresponsive government department to a customer-driven commercial organisation still within the realm of government.

When the pilot project commenced Ordnance Survey still had a long way to go to achieve its 1980 plan of reconstruction of the mapping. The resource of the embryonic production flowline was deployed on this task. This involved the production of a first edition for each map. Gradually as the size of this residual production task using both conventional and the new digital methods diminished, the need for new editions increased quite rapidly to reflect the change that had taken place on the ground. Thus increasingly and throughout until continuous digital update in the field offices became universal, revisions of the first editions were increasingly handled using the digital production capacity at Ordnance Survey. Finally and on top of all these it became necessary, if full digital cover was to be achieved, that all maps, whether undergoing revision or not, should be 'converted' from conventional into digital form. They were simply called 'conversions'.

During the later years Ordnance Survey went from deep pessimism that it would ever complete the digitising task (or need to) almost to 'oops' we have done it. It did convey to outsiders a lack of strategy and clarity of purpose.

Thus it was that in the series presented in the tabulation above changes in nomenclature inevitably occurred. It isn't therefore possible over such a long period of time to derive from Ordnance Survey Annual Reports a totally consistent picture of progress with the task. As Ordnance Survey, slowly and with a good deal of external leverage, transformed itself from a production-driven, method-oriented organisation to a product- and customer-oriented operation, reporting of necessity changed. The results tabulated overleaf, with that proviso, certainly illustrate the long, slow build-up of techniques and resources until the burgeoning in production, with the major increase in resources following the Review Committee Report and the use of private-sector contractors that had at long last developed a cost-effective response to the task.

Bibliography

Where references contain further bibliography, this listing has not been included here.

1   Official files. These have progressively been deposited with the Public Records Office (now The National Archives) at Kew. Files may well have been 'weeded', but are held under Ordnance Survey listings and may be accessed by the public.

2   Harley, J.B., 1975. Ordnance Survey Maps a descriptive manual. H.M.S.O.

3   Gardiner-Hill O.B.E., Colonel R.C., 1972. The Development of Digital Maps. Professional Papers – New Series No. 23: Ordnance Survey.

4   Finch, Sara, 1987. Towards a National Topographic Data Base. PhD thesis: Birkbeck College at the University of London.

5   Ordnance Survey Annual Reports, 1971-72 onwards. Director General's reports to the Secretary of State: H.M.S.O., 1971-72 to 197576; Ordnance Survey, 1976-77 onwards.

6   Keates, J.S., 1973. Cartographic Design and Production. J.S. Keates of Glasgow University. This text has photographs of early equipment and description of procedures. Longman® Group Ltd.

7   Thompson, Colonel C.N., 1978. Digital Mapping in Ordnance Survey. A paper presented to the International Society for Photogrammetry Congress, Ottowa.

8   Serpell K.C.B. C.M.G. O.B.E., Sir David (Chairman), July 1979. The Report of the Ordnance Survey Review Committee. H.M.S.O.

9   Rhind, D.W. and Whitfield, R.A.S., 1983. A Review of the Ordnance Survey Proposals for Digitising the Large Scale Maps of Great Britain. Report to the Director General.

10   House of Lords Science and Technology Select Committee Report, 1983. Remote Sensing and Digital Mapping. H.M.S.O.

11   The Department of Trade and Industry, 1984. Remote Sensing and Digital Mapping. Reply by H.M. Government to 10. H.M.S.O.

12   Chorley, Lord (Chairman), 1987. Handling Geographic Information. The Report of the Committee of Enquiry. H.M.S.O.

Glossary of abbreviations

AGI	Association for Geographic Information
AQL	Acceptable quality level
ARC	Applied Research of Cambridge
ARI	Advance Revision Information
BT	British Telecom (British Telecommunications)
CCA	Central Computing Agency
CCTA	Central Computer and Telecommunications Agency
DEC	Digital Equipment Corporation
DFUS	Digital Field Update System
DMA	Digital Mapping system A
Dmac	The company Dobbie McInnes Ltd, which became known as Dmac or Dmac Ltd
DMB	Digital Mapping system B
DMC	Digital Mapping system (for customer supply)
DMV	Digital mapping (vector form)
DOE	Department of the Environment
DRS	Digital Records System
DXF	Data Exchange Format
ECU	Experimental Cartography Unit
FSN(s)	Feature serial number(s)
GIS	Geographical information system
GISP	General Information System for Planning
HMSO	Her Majesty's Stationery Office
ICL	International Computers Limited
IFF	Internal free format
IPCS	Institution of Professional Civil Servants
ISDN	Integrated services digital network
JASB	Joint Advisory Survey Board
LAMIS	Local Authority Management Information System
LAMSAC	Local Authorities Management Services and Computing Committee
LITES	Laser-Scan interactive editing station
MADES	Map edit data system
MSD	Master survey document/drawing
NERC	National Environmental Research Council
NGD	National Geographic Database – formerly known as National Topographic Database
NJUG	National Joint Utilities Group

NTD	See NGD
NTF	National Transfer Format
OSTF	Ordnance Survey Transfer Format
PCD	Processor controlled digitiser
PCK	Process control disk
SIM	Survey Information on Microfilm
SLA(s)	Service level agreement(s)
SUSI	Supply of Unpublished Survey Information
TODDS	Topographic Database Development System
TSD	Temporary survey document
VALFIX	From validate and fix - part of the process

Glossary of abbreviations

AGI	Association for Geographic Information
AQL	Acceptable quality level
ARC	Applied Research of Cambridge
ARI	Advance Revision Information
BT	British Telecom (British Telecommunications)
CCA	Central Computing Agency
CCTA	Central Computer and Telecommunications Agency
DEC	Digital Equipment Corporation
DFUS	Digital Field Update System
DMA	Digital Mapping system A
Dmac	The company Dobbie McInnes Ltd, which became known as Dmac or Dmac Ltd
DMB	Digital Mapping system B
DMC	Digital Mapping system (for customer supply)
DMV	Digital mapping (vector form)
DOE	Department of the Environment
DRS	Digital Records System
DXF	Data Exchange Format
ECU	Experimental Cartography Unit
FSN(s)	Feature serial number(s)
GIS	Geographical information system
GISP	General Information System for Planning
HMSO	Her Majesty's Stationery Office
ICL	International Computers Limited
IFF	Internal free format
IPCS	Institution of Professional Civil Servants
ISDN	Integrated services digital network
JASB	Joint Advisory Survey Board
LAMIS	Local Authority Management Information System
LAMSAC	Local Authorities Management Services and Computing Committee
LITES	Laser-Scan interactive editing station
MADES	Map edit data system
MSD	Master survey document/drawing
NERC	National Environmental Research Council
NGD	National Geographic Database – formerly known as National Topographic Database
NJUG	National Joint Utilities Group

NTD   See NGD
NTF   National Transfer Format
OSTF   Ordnance Survey Transfer Format
PCD   Processor controlled digitiser
PCK   Process control disk
SIM   Survey Information on Microfilm
SLA(s)   Service level agreement(s)
SUSI   Supply of Unpublished Survey Information
TODDS   Topographic Database Development System
TSD   Temporary survey document
VALFIX   From validate and fix - part of the process

Trademark note

Ordnance Survey, the **OS Symbol, ADDRESS POINT, Land Line, Landplan, OSCAR, Superplan** and **Superplan Data** are registered trademarks of Ordnance Survey, the national mapping agency of Great Britain.

AEG is a registered trademark of AB ELECTROLUX.

AGI and **Association for Geographic Information** are registered trademarks of Association for Geographic Information.

Anglian Water is a registered trademark of Anglian Water Services Ltd.

Astrafoil is a registered trademark of South Wales Chemical Works Ltd.

Bendix is a registered trademark of Honeywell International Inc.

Birkbeck College is a registered trademark of Birkbeck College.

British Gas is a registered trademark of GB Gas Holdings Ltd.

BT is a registered trademark of BRITISH TELECOMMUNICATIONS PLC.

Computervision is a registered trademark of Computervision Corporation.

Contraves is a registered trademark of Oerlikon Contraves AG.

Daily Telegraph is a registered trademark of Telegraph Media Group Ltd.

Ferranti is a registered trademark of "Ferranti Computer Systems".

Fisher is a registered trademark of FISHER PEN COMPANY.

Glasgow University is a registered trademark of The University Court of the University of Glasgow.

Hewlett-Packard is a registered trademark of Hewlett-Packard Development Company LP.

ICL is a registered trademark of Fujitsu Services Ltd.

Intergraph is a registered trademark of Intergraph Corporation.

Kontron is a registered trademark of Kontron AG.

Land Registry is a registered trademark of HM Land Registry.

London Electricity is a registered trademark of EDF Energy plc.

Longman is a registered trademark of Pearson Education Ltd.

Marconi is a registered trademark of Telefonaktiebolaget LM Ericsson.

Mylar is a registered trademark of EI du Pont de Nemours and Company.

www.ingramcontent.com/pod-product-compliance
Lightning Source LLC
LaVergne TN
LVHW051221050326
832903LV00028B/2195